Short-Term Rental Platforms as Deemed Suppliers in the EU VAT System

EUCOTAX Series on European Taxation

VOLUME 74

Series Editors

Introduction

EUCOTAX (European Universities Cooperating on Taxes) is a network of tax institutes currently consisting of thirteen universities: WU (Vienna University of Economics and Business) in Austria, Katholieke Universiteit Leuven in Belgium, Université Paris-I Panthéon-Sorbonne in France, Universität Osnabrück in Germany, Libera, Eötvös Loránd University in Budapest in Hungary, Università Internazionale di Studi Sociali in Rome University of Lodz and University of Warsaw in Poland, in Italy, Fiscaal Instituut Tilburg at Tilburg University in the Netherlands, Universitat de València in Spain, Uppsala University in Sweden, Universität St. Gallen in Switzerland, and Georgetown University in Washington DC, United States of America. The network aims at initiating and coordinating both comparative education in taxation, through the organization of activities such as winter courses and guest lectures, and comparative research in the field, by means of joint research projects, international conferences and exchange of researchers between various countries.

Contents/Subjects

The EUCOTAX series covers a wide range of topics in European tax law. For example tax treaties, EC case law, tax planning, exchange of information and VAT. The series is well-known for its high-quality research and practical solutions.

Objective

The series aims to provide insights on new developments in European taxation.

Readership

Practitioners and academics dealing with European tax law.

Frequency of Publication

2-3 new volumes published each year.

The titles published in this series are listed at the end of this volume.

Short-Term Rental Platforms as Deemed Suppliers in the EU VAT System

Emilia Teresa Sroka

Wolters Kluwer

Published by:
Kluwer Law International B.V.
PO Box 316
2400 AH Alphen aan den Rijn
The Netherlands
E-mail: lrs-sales@wolterskluwer.com
Website: www.wolterskluwer.com/en/solutions/kluwerlawinternational

Sold and distributed by:
Wolters Kluwer Legal & Regulatory U.S.
920 Links Avenue
Landisville, PA 17538
United States of America
E-mail: customer.service@wolterskluwer.com

ISBN 978-94-035-4308-6

e-Book: ISBN 978-94-035-4318-5
web-PDF: ISBN 978-94-035-4328-4

Table of Contents

List of Abbreviations

API	Application Program Interface
B2B	Business-to-Business
B2C	Business-to-Consumer
C2B	Consumer-to-Business
C2C	Consumer-to-Consumer
CJEU	Court of Justice of the European Union
DSIG	Distance Sales of Imported Goods from Third Territories or Third Countries
DSM	Digital Single Market
DSR	Deemed Supplier Regime
EC	European Commission
ECOFIN	Economic and Financial Affairs Council
EP	European Parliament
EU	European Union
GST	Goods and Services Tax
ICDS	Intra-Community Distance Sales of Goods
IMF	International Monetary Fund
IOSS	Import One-Stop Shop
IR	Implementing Regulation 282/2011
ISP	Internet Service Provider
MOSS	Mini One-Stop Shop
OECD	Organisation for Economic Co-operation and Development
OSS	One-Stop Shop
OTA	Online Travel Agency
SME	Small- and Medium-Sized Enterprises
SMS	Single Market Strategy

STR	Short-Term Rental
TBE Services	Telecommunications, Broadcasting and Electronic Services
TOMS	Tour Operators Margin Scheme
VAT	Value Added Tax
ViDA	VAT in Digital Age
VoIP	Voice over Internet Protocol

List of Figures

List of Tables

Introduction

The digital realm stands out as one of the pivotal segments in the modern economy, with platforms at its core that mediate between their users for the supply of goods and provision of services. These platforms not only foster innovative business models but also wield a considerable impact across various sectors of the economy. A notable example is the accommodation sector.

This sector proves intriguing for research on multiple fronts. First, it holds significant economic and social importance, influencing the development of tourism, the housing market, and the hospitality industry. Second, it is a highly innovative and competitive sector. Third, the sector grapples with regulatory complexity, facing numerous challenges and problems related to ensuring compliance with existing regulations, including tax regulations.

VAT is one of the most important sources of public revenue in the EU and is key to ensuring competitive neutrality and economic efficiency. The development of the platform economy creates a lot of ambiguity regarding the VAT treatment of transactions provided via platforms. However, the intermediation of these platforms also provides greater transparency of transactions, which opens up new perspectives, particularly in the context of VAT collection. These new opportunities include, among others, the potential educational and communication role of platforms, formal cooperation agreements with platforms, reporting obligations of platforms, joint and several liability, their tax withholding function and the deemed supplier regime.

The primary objective of this book is to analyse the legal aspects of the EU VAT treatment of transactions conducted through platforms in the accommodation sector, with a particular focus on the potential role of these platforms in VAT collection as operators deemed to be suppliers (referred to as the deemed supplier regime). This regime is the most comprehensive solution, placing full liability on platforms for accounting for VAT on the transactions they intermediate.

The book is organized into an introduction, four chapters, and a conclusion.

The first chapter introduces the broader topic of the platform economy. It provides a definition of the platform economy and discusses the specific aspects of the accommodation sector. The analysis delves into the challenges faced by the sector's development, emphasizing potential perspectives on regulatory issues.

The second chapter outlines the legal basis for the VAT treatment of transactions conducted through platforms in the EU. It explores the existing VAT regulations relevant to the accommodation sector, with a specific focus on the status of the actors involved in the transactions, the nature of platform services, and the place of their supply. Moving forward, potential solutions to facilitate or enhance the collection of VAT on transactions involving platforms are explored. The potential qualification of platforms in the accommodation sector as so-called undisclosed agents is also discussed, as such qualification may result in the platforms' obligation to collect VAT on the transactions they mediate.

These chapters serve as an introduction to the focal point of the book, which meticulously examines the deemed supplier regime within the context of accommodation platforms.

The third chapter introduces the concept of the deemed supplier regime, wherein platforms bear full liability for VAT collection. Three models of the deemed supplier in the context of the European VAT regime are discussed and compared: (i) the digital model, applicable to platforms intermediating the supply of electronic services; (ii) the e-commerce model, applicable to platforms intermediating the supply of specific goods; and (iii) the planned service model, applicable to platforms intermediating the supply of accommodation services.

The fourth chapter evaluates these deemed supplier models. It considers the potential inclusion of accommodation sector platforms in the two of these models (digital and e-commerce) and analyses the advantages and disadvantages of the service model that applies to them. The final section of this chapter summarizes the analysis conclusions and presents recommendations for the EU legislator.

CHAPTER 1

Platform Economy in the STR Sector

1 BACKGROUND

Platforms have played a crucial role in the new technology industry from the outset. Initially, they primarily facilitated users' access to various digital content. However, as early as the 1990s, platforms such as eBay and Amazon also ventured into brokering the sale of 'tangible' goods in the 'real' world. Given that manufacturing and transporting physical goods are generally more expensive than disseminating digitized information, this model necessitated a heightened level of security and trust.[1] Consequently, platforms began implementing new solutions to ensure quality control, such as peer reviews of users, and collaborated with banks and payment service providers. This collaboration resulted in the creation of a specific infrastructure (the platform 'ecosystem') that significantly facilitates transactions between users.[2]

In the first decade of the twenty-first century, 'commodity' platforms were joined by platforms that facilitate services between their users. In 2015, in Europe, service platforms operating in five key sectors (accommodation, transport, household services, on-demand professional services, and crowdfunding) generated revenues of almost EUR 4 billion.[3]

These figures show the profound impact platforms have on the global economic landscape and its development. This phenomenon is sometimes referred to as the

---

1. Malgorzata Zieba and Susanne Durst, 'Knowledge Risks in the Sharing Economy' in Elena-Mădălina Vătămănescu and Florina Magdalena Pînzaru (eds), *Knowledge Management in the Sharing Economy*, vol 6 (Springer International Publishing 2018) 255–261.
2. Anssi Smedlund and others, 'Platform Ecosystem Orchestration for Efficiency, Development, and Innovation' in Anssi Smedlund, Arto Lindblom and Lasse Mitronen (eds), *Collaborative Value Co-creation in the Platform Economy*, vol 11 (Springer Singapore 2018) 29.
3. Robert Vaughan and Raphael Daverio, *Assessing the Size and Presence of the Collaborative Economy in Europe* (European Commission 2016) 30.

platformization of the economy[4] and its effect on the platform economy. In the opening chapter, the concept of the 'platform economy' will be defined, drawing comparisons with other terms prevalent in the literature, such as 'sharing economy' and 'collaborative economy'.

Within the platform economy, the accommodation sector assumes a particular role. EU market data[5] reveals that STR services are the most commonly accessed through platforms. The sector is highly cross-border;[6] approximately 80 % of small- and medium-sized STR platforms[7] facilitate transactions in all or nearly all Member States, with none operating in fewer than three countries.

The first chapter will discuss the fundamental business models prevalent in this market, exploring the associated challenges and opportunities. The chapter will focus on platforms that operate in the accommodation sector, i.e., facilitating STR transactions. Platforms that facilitate long-term property rental will remain outside the scope of the chapter.

It should be noted that, in economic practice, there are essentially two types of property rental: long-term and short-term. STR is sometimes referred to as accommodation or STR. Throughout the remainder of this book, these terms will be used interchangeably.

Whether a particular rental falls into one category or the other is closely related to the legal system of a particular country. Usually, rental of property is associated with meeting a person's longer-term housing needs and accommodation by providing only a temporary stay.[8]

There is some ambiguity regarding medium-term rentals in this context. It is increasingly common to utilize STR platforms for bookings that extend beyond short visits to a location, encompassing stays lasting several weeks or months.[9] This trend gained momentum during the COVID-19 pandemic, exemplified by rentals for self-isolation or the creation of temporary remote workplace that could not be provided in an office or home.[10]

It appears that the characteristics and objectives of medium-term rentals align more closely with STRs than long-term rentals. The purpose of such accommodation is

4. 'Digital Economy Report 2019. Value Creation and Capture: Implications for Developing Countries' (United Nations Conference on Trade and Development, UNCTAD 2019) 38.
5. European Commission, Directorate General for Internal Market, Industry, Entrepreneurship and SMEs and TNS Political & Social, *The Use of the Collaborative Economy* (Publications Office 2018) 4.
6. European Commission, Directorate General for Taxation and Customs Union and others, *VAT in the Digital Age: Final Report. Volume 2, The VAT Treatment of the Platform Economy* (Publications Office 2022) 32–33.
7. Platforms achieving a turnover below EUR 1 billion.
8. The CJEU stated that: 'one of the ways in which hotel accommodation specifically differs from the letting of dwelling accommodation is the duration of the stay. In general, a stay in a hotel tends to be rather short and that in a rented flat fairly long'. *Elisabeth Blasi v. Finanzamt München I* [1998] CJEU C-346/95 paragraph 23.
9. Laura Galluzzo and Giulia Gerosa, 'Shared Hospitality Platforms: Possible Design Repercussions, Introverted and Extroverted' in Maurizio Bruglieri (ed.), *Multidisciplinary Design of Sharing Services* (Springer International Publishing 2018) 58.
10. Nigel Lewis, 'Latest Trends: Covid Boosts Demand for Medium-Term Renting' (27 April 2021), https://www.landlordzone.co.uk/ accessed 17 September 2021.

not to fulfil normal, longer-term housing needs but rather ad hoc needs typically associated with a tourist stay. However, this classification may vary depending on the specific case. For instance, a three-week rental for self-isolation in a hotel upon arrival in a particular country might be categorized as an STR transaction. Conversely, renting a flat for three months to provide remote work from it appears closer to a long-term rental, as it addresses the longer-term housing needs. Given these considerations, medium-term rentals seem to encompass borderline cases that, depending on the specific context, can be classified as either long-term or STRs. Consequently, medium-term accommodation will not be singled out as a separate category in this chapter.

2 THE CONCEPT OF THE PLATFORM ECONOMY

The rise of innovative platform business models and their scale has attracted attention from the press, legislators, scholars, and the general public. This has resulted in the emergence of many new names to describe the phenomenon. These include 'platform economy', 'gig economy', 'peer economy', 'sharing economy'[11] and also 'collaborative economy', 'collaborative consumption', 'access economy', and 'on-demand economy'.[12] It is noteworthy that these terms are often used interchangeably.[13] In the following discussion, I will explore the two most commonly used terms to describe this phenomenon – the sharing economy and the platform economy.

'Sharing' can be defined as the act and process of giving away something we own for others to use and, conversely, receiving or accepting something from others for our own use.[14] The practice of sharing certain goods among individuals within the same social networks has existed 'since time immemorial'.[15] However, the advent of digital technologies has facilitated the sharing of assets with strangers worldwide.[16] Platforms have played a crucial role in expanding the scope and scale of sharing practices in an unprecedented manner.[17]

11. Seppo Poutanen and Anne Kovalainen, 'New Economy, Platform Economy and Gender' in Seppo Poutanen and Anne Kovalainen (eds), *Gender and Innovation in the New Economy: Women, Identity, and Creative Work* (Palgrave Macmillan US 2017) 76.
12. Andreia Gabriela Andrei and Adriana Zait, 'The Sharing Economy in Post-Communist Societies: Insights from Romania' in Elena-Mădălina Vătămănescu and Florina Magdalena Pînzaru (eds), *Knowledge Management in the Sharing Economy*, vol 6 (Springer International Publishing 2018) 42.
13. Patrizia Gazzola, 'Behind the Sharing Economy: Innovation and Dynamic Capability' in Elena-Mădălina Vătămănescu and Florina Magdalena Pînzaru (eds), *Knowledge Management in the Sharing Economy*, vol 6 (Springer International Publishing 2018) 78; similarly Oksana Gerwe and Rosario Silva, 'Clarifying the Sharing Economy: Conceptualization, Typology, Antecedents, and Effects' 34 Academy of Management Perspectives 65, 72 https://doi.org/10.5465/amp.2017.0010.
14. Russell Belk, 'Why Not Share Rather Than Own?' (2007) 611 The Annals of the American Academy of Political and Social Science 127 https://doi.org/10.1177/0002716206298483.
15. Russell Belk, 'You Are What You Can Access: Sharing and Collaborative Consumption Online' (2014) 67 Journal of Business Research 1595 https://doi.org/10.1016/j.jbusres.2013.10.001.
16. Gerwe and Silva (n. 13) 66.
17. Michèle Finck, 'The Sharing Economy and the EU' in Nestor M Davidson, Michèle Finck and John J Infranca (eds), *The Cambridge Handbook of the Law of the Sharing Economy* (Cambridge University Press 2018) 263.

As with many popular phrases, the origin of the term 'sharing economy' is unclear. Many authors[18] trace its origins to the appearance of the 2010 book *What's Mine Is Yours: The Rise of Collaborative Consumption* by Rachel Botsman and Roo Rogers,[19] which describes the phenomenon of sharing and collaborative consumption as an alternative to traditional economic models.

In the literature on the concept of the sharing economy, Russel Belk's article from 2014 'You are what you can access: Sharing and collaborative consumption online' is also considered groundbreaking.[20] Among the top 12 articles on the topic of the sharing economy, based on highly cited *Web of Science* records from 1978 to 2018, this publication ranked first.[21]

The popularity of the sharing economy topic has resulted in a surge of research and publications in recent years. This body of work spans various scientific disciplines.[22] The phenomenon has, therefore, been studied from various theoretical perspectives, resulting in a diverse range of definitions for the 'sharing economy' within the literature adopted to serve the specific needs of different disciplines. Consequently, there is no single, universally accepted definition of the concept.[23]

The concept of the sharing economy is highly controversial, and researchers often draw a distinction between 'pure' sharing and 'pseudo-sharing'. This classification is primarily based on whether the sharer anticipates some form of benefit in return for the shared asset.[24] In 'pure' sharing, there is an absence of any expectation of monetary return for the shared asset.[25] Platforms that facilitate free sharing between users, such as Couchsurfing, would be considered part of the sharing economy under this perspective. In contrast, platforms like Airbnb, where users receive payment for sharing their assets, might be categorized differently.[26]

It is essential to recognize that the potential for users to generate revenue directly impacts the growth potential of platforms and influences various aspects of their business models, including the evolution of payment systems. The expansion of 'revenue' platforms has been identified as a major driver of growth in the digital

18. For example, Davide Arcidiacono and Ivana Pais, 'Individual Rewarding and Social Outcomes in the Collaborative Economy' in Maurizio Bruglieri (ed.), *Multidisciplinary Design of Sharing Services* (Springer International Publishing 2018) 82; Scott Inara and Elizabeth Brown, 'Redefining and Regulating the New Sharing Economy' (2017) 19 University of Pennsylvania Journal of Business Law 6553, 558; Daniela Selloni, 'New Forms of Economies: Sharing Economy, Collaborative Consumption, Peer-to-Peer Economy' in Daniela Selloni, *CoDesign for Public-Interest Services* (Springer International Publishing 2017) 17.
19. Rachel Botsman and Roo Rogers, *What's Mine Is Yours: How Collaborative Consumption Is Changing the Way We Live* (Rev and updated edn, Collins 2011).
20. Belk (n. 15) 1595–1600.
21. Mokter Hossain, 'Sharing Economy: A Comprehensive Literature Review' (2020) 87 International Journal of Hospitality Management 2–3 https://doi.org/10.1016/j.ijhm.2020.102470.
22. *Ibid.*, 102470, 3–4.
23. For example, Marina Petruzzi, Catarina Marques and Valerie Sheppard, 'To Share or to Exchange: An Analysis of the Sharing Economy Characteristics of Airbnb and Fairbnb.Coop' (2021) 92 International Journal of Hospitality Management 2 https://doi.org/10.1016/j.ijhm.2020.102724.
24. Belk (n. 15) 1596–1597.
25. Petruzzi, Marques and Sheppard (n. 23) 3–4.
26. Gerwe and Silva (n. 13) 66–67.

economy. Currently, platforms facilitating transactions based on monetary consideration appear to be the dominant players – Airbnb has grown much more than Couchsurfing.[27]

Another characteristic often associated with the sharing economy is the reliance on untapped physical or human resources, such as empty rooms.[28] However, it is crucial to note that while a substantial portion of platform-facilitated transactions involves such assets, many providers now exclusively dedicate assets to operating through platforms as their primary source of income. For instance, a professional property manager transacting on Airbnb may not be considered part of the sharing economy. Instead, the sharing economy could encompass 'mission-driven platforms' whose intermediation aims, among other things, to support initiatives based on specific values, such as reducing waste through increased turnover of goods (reuse of used items).[29] However, the power of platforms grows with the increasing professionalization of the sharing economy as users dedicate more time or specialized resources to these platforms.[30]

Despite the outlined controversies, prevailing definitions of the sharing economy tend to be rather broad. The Joint Research Centre, for instance, notes that the term 'sharing economy' commonly encompasses a diverse range of business models of commercial or non-profit platforms. These platforms facilitate exchanges between different users, enabling them to consume or engage in activities using capital assets (e.g., money, property, equipment, cars), skills, or simply time.[31] A similar wide definition is also frequently employed by the OECD.[32]

EU institutions have also actively engaged in the debate surrounding the platformization of the economy. However, as rightly highlighted in the literature, their definitions exhibit inconsistency.[33] In 2015, the EC issued two communications related to the challenges of the digitalization of the economy: the first underscored the necessity to complete the DSM,[34] while the second emphasized the need to improve the

27. *Ibid.*, 73.
28. *Ibid.*, 70.
29. Aurélien Acquier and Valentina Carbone, 'Sharing Economy and Social Innovation' in Nestor M Davidson, Michèle Finck and John J Infranca (eds), *The Cambridge Handbook of the Law of the Sharing Economy* (Cambridge University Press 2018) 56.
30. Gerwe and Silva (n. 13) 73.
31. European Commission, Joint Research Center and Institute for Prospective Technological Studies, *The Passions and the Interests: Unpacking the 'Sharing Economy'* (Publications Office 2016) 22.
32. OECD, *Tax Challenges Arising from Digitalisation – Interim Report 2018: Inclusive Framework on BEPS* (OECD 2018) 208–209.
33. Catherine Easton, 'European Union Information Law and the Sharing Economy' in Tatiana-Eleni Synodinou and others (eds), *EU Internet Law: Regulation and Enforcement* (Springer International Publishing 2017) 165–166; Finck (n. 17) 262; Marco Inglese, *Regulating the Collaborative Economy in the European Union Digital Single Market* (Springer International Publishing 2019) 9–10.
34. European Commission, 'A Digital Single Market Strategy for Europe, COM(2015) 192 Final'; and European Commission, 'A Digital Single Market Strategy for Europe – Analysis and Evidence, SWD(2015) 100 Final'.

SMS.[35] In 2016, the Commission presented a European Agenda for the Collaborative Economy (Agenda).[36]

The DSM Communication used the term 'sharing economy'. In contrast, the SMS Communication and the Agenda saw the Commission adopting the expression 'collaborative economy'.

For its part, the Committee of the Regions, in its opinion on the local and regional dimension of the sharing economy,[37] utilized the term 'sharing economy'. It acknowledged that the EC's definition of the 'collaborative economy' focused on commercial and consumer aspects, neglecting the shared goods approach. The Committee urged the Commission to conduct a more detailed analysis and subsequently define the various forms of the sharing economy. However, in 2020, the Committee of the Regions, while referring to a European framework of regulatory solutions for the platformization of the economy, employed the term 'collaborative' rather than 'sharing' economy.[38]

Similarly, the EP, when addressing the platformization of the economy, used the term 'sharing economy'. This was evident, for example, in a study identifying the costs of not furthering European action in the field of the sharing economy.[39] The paper highlighted the lack of consensus among EU institutions regarding the definition of the platformization of the economy phenomenon. It is noteworthy that in 2017, the EP, in its resolution on the Agenda,[40] already employed the phrase 'collaborative economy' instead of 'sharing economy', aligning with the Commission's terminology.

In conclusion, there is no general consensus on the boundaries of the sharing economy, particularly which platforms and transactions fall within the term. One can agree that the term 'sharing economy' often carries an ideological connotation, with transactions involving the sharing of unused goods seen as fostering sustainability and thus considered morally 'superior' to an economy solely focused on profit maximization.[41]

It is crucial to note that platforms, as major players in the digital market, wield significant power and are primarily profit-driven. Yes, the origins of the platform economy often involved unpaid sharing, but the phenomenon has evolved over time. The literature indicates that the sharing economy has moved from non-profit platforms

35. European Commission, 'Upgrading the Single Market: More Opportunities for People and Business, COM(2015) 550 Final'.
36. European Commission, 'A European Agenda for the Collaborative Economy, COM(2016) 356 Final'.
37. The Committee of the Regions, 'The Local and Regional Dimension of the Sharing Economy, 2016/C 051/06'.
38. The Committee of the Regions, 'A European Framework for Regulatory Responses to the Collaborative Economy, 2020/C 79/08'.
39. Pierre Goudin, *The Cost of Non-Europe in the Sharing Economy Economic, Social and Legal Challenges and Opportunities* (European Parliament 2016) 9–11.
40. European Parliament, 'Resolution on a European Agenda for the Collaborative Economy, P8_TA (2017) 0271'.
41. Theresia Theurl and Eric Meyer, 'Cooperatives in the Age of Sharing' in Kai Riemer, Stefan Schellhammer and Michaela Meinert (eds), *Collaboration in the Digital Age: How Technology Enables Individuals, Teams and Businesses* (Springer International Publishing 2019) 188.

(such as Couchsurfing) to for-profit enterprises (such as Airbnb).[42] This leads one to argue that transactions through platforms do not always involve 'sharing' in the traditional sense. Consequently, using the term 'sharing economy' may be too narrow to describe the trend of the platformization of the economy. Therefore, in the remainder of this book, I will use the more neutral term 'platform economy'.[43]

In this context, it is important to observe the evolution of terms used in documents issued by European and international institutions. Initially, terms like collaborative economy and sharing economy were prevalent, but nowadays, the phrase platform economy is increasingly used. This term appears, for example, in documents of the Committee of the Regions,[44] the EC[45] or the EP.[46] Also, the OECD has recently indicated that the sharing economy is part of a wider phenomenon such as the platform economy.[47]

For the purposes of this book, 'platform economy' will be the term used to describe a model where the platform's role is to facilitate transactions between two or more users interacting via digital technology. In these transactions, one party offers the other a wide range of tangible and intangible resources, such as time, skills, goods, services, or access to them, in exchange for consideration (monetary or otherwise) or for free. A platform typically charges a fee for facilitating an interaction from one or all parties to the transaction or offers its services for free by funding itself through targeted advertising, among other means. This definition is very broad, as it is intended to encompass the complex nature of the platform economy and capture currently operating business models and potential models that may emerge in the future.

3 HISTORICAL BACKGROUND

STR existed before the advent of platforms. However, it is widely acknowledged that they have contributed to the rapid growth of the sector over the past decade.[48] Previously, transaction costs limited the possibilities for this type of business. Not only

42. Gerwe and Silva (n. 13) 65.
43. The more neutral nature of the term 'platform economy' is also indicated by Erez Aloni, 'Pluralism and Regulatory Responses' in Nestor M Davidson, Michèle Finck and John J Infranca (eds), *The Cambridge Handbook of the Law of the Sharing Economy* (Cambridge University Press 2018) 144.
44. The Committee of the Regions, 'Platform Work – Local and Regional Regulatory Challenges, 2020/C 79/07'.
45. European Commission, 'An Action Plan for Fair and Simple Taxation Supporting the Recovery Strategy, COM(2020) 312 Final'; Regulation (EU) 2019/1150 of the European Parliament and of the Council of 20 June 2019 on promoting fairness and transparency for business users of online intermediation services [OJ L 186, 11.7.2019, pp. 57–79].
46. H Hauben, K Lenaerts and W Waeyaert, *The Platform Economy and Precarious Work* (Publication for the Committee on Employment and Social Affairs, Policy Department for Economic, Scientific and Quality of Life Policies, European Parliament 2020) 13.
47. OECD, *The Impact of the Growth of the Sharing and Gig Economy on VAT/GST Policy and Administration* (OECD 2021) 21.
48. European Commission, Directorate General for Internal Market, Industry, Entrepreneurship and SMEs, VVA, and Spark Legal Network, *Study on the Assessment of the Regulatory Aspects Affecting the Collaborative Economy in the Tourism Accommodation Sector in the 28 Member States (580/PP/GRO/IMA/15/15111J): Final Report* (Publications Office 2018) 10–11.

was it difficult to find someone to contract accommodation at a specific date or location, but there were also many risks, from security concerns to the issue of ensuring payment.[49] The development of technology has transformed this situation. Expensive and inconvenient transactions have become relatively cheap and simple due to software provided by platforms, which has reduced the cost of finding, tracking, and verifying accommodation bookings.[50] Trust verification and payment processing mechanisms implemented by platforms have also increased transaction security. Consequently, the accommodation sector has undergone significant changes, attracting the attention of academic researchers across various disciplines, including tourism, hospitality, business, psychology, cultural studies, and law, resulting in an increase in publications on the subject.[51]

Platforms for the STR sector began to emerge as early as the 1990s. One of the pioneers was HomeExchange, founded in 1992 in Washington DC by Ed Kushins. This platform allowed members to swap homes, building on the existing practice of the Intervac International Group, which had been offering this opportunity to its members since 1953. Initially, HomeExchange operated more like an unconventional travel agency, but over time, the service grew. By 2021, it already had 470,000 homes available in 159 countries worldwide.[52]

HomeExchange's business model can be summarized as follows: after registering on the platform and creating an account and paying a one-off annual fee, each member gains access to the data necessary to contact the other party. Arrangements for exchanges (e.g., number of nights or guests) are made directly by the users via the messaging service provided by the platform. Users are solely responsible for providing the description, location and dates of availability and for setting the rules regarding the use of their property. Home exchanges are usually concluded free of charge; however, hosts may charge guests a cleaning fee. 'Consideration' for the host is the possibility to use their guest's home free of charge or so-called GuestPoints, which can be exchanged for an overnight stay in another user's home. Users enter into contracts directly with each other.[53]

There are currently many platforms offering similar services, for example, MindMyHouse, domzadom, LoveHomeSwap. In addition to the classic, temporary house swapping, house sharing or house exchange, housesitting is also popular, whereby guests take care of the host's home (and often left-over pets) while the host is

49. Kellen Zale, 'Scale and the Sharing Economy' in Nestor M Davidson, Michèle Finck and John J Infranca (eds), *The Cambridge Handbook of the Law of the Sharing Economy* (Cambridge University Press 2018) 39–40.
50. Martine Bakker, Elize Hendrica and Louise Twining-Ward, *Tourism and the Sharing Economy: Policy & Potential of Sustainable Peer-to-Peer Accommodation* (World Bank Group 2018) 15.
51. Amanda Belarmino and Yoon Koh, 'A Critical Review of Research Regarding Peer-to-Peer Accommodations' (2020) 84 International Journal of Hospitality Management 1 https://doi.org/10.1016/j.ijhm.2019.05.011.
52. 'HomeExchange – #1 Home Exchange Community' (*HomeExchange*), https://www.homeexchange.com/ accessed 6 September 2021.
53. 'Terms of Use – Home Exchange' (6 September 2021), https://www.homeexchange.com/p/general-terms-of-use accessed 6 September 2021.

away.[54] This type of care service provided by the guest is then regarded as 'consideration' in exchange for the use of the property for the host.

The data shows strong growth in the home exchange market over the last decade, and this trend is expected to continue in the coming years.[55]

One of the first platforms operating in the STR sector was also Booking.com, which started in 1996. Unlike HomeExchange or Airbnb, it is sometimes classified under the category of OTAs. These are online businesses that allow customers to book various travel-related services, such as transport or accommodation.[56] OTAs also include platforms such as Expedia or Tripadvisor, among others. Some authors are of the opinion that OTA platforms can be referred to as search engines[57] because unlike platforms such as HomeExchange or Airbnb, they do not have a major impact on the supply of places in the hotel sector (they do not generally enable the provision of accommodation which is the private property of the host). Booking.com is sometimes seen as the equivalent of Airbnb, however, with the difference that it offers traditional accommodation, such as hotels, from hosts who are entrepreneurs, and omits the need for social interaction between the two parties to the transaction.[58] It should be noted, however, that this division is becoming less and less valid.[59] For example, Airbnb now offers accommodation provided by professionals, while on Booking.com, visitors can find flats provided by private operators.

The OTA model seems to work very well in practice. As indicated by the World Bank's 2020 data,[60] Booking.com includes 29 million accommodation listings in 154,000 destinations worldwide and operates in 190 countries. In 2019, an average of 29.9% of hotel bookings in Europe were made via online platforms; among OTAs, Booking.com was the leader, with 67.7% of bookings made online.[61]

Many well-known STR platforms also emerged in the first decade of the twenty-first century. One example is Couchsurfing, created by US programmer Casey Fenton,

54. Doyinsola Oladipo, 'House Swaps and Dog Walks: Travelers Find Cheaper Alternatives to Lodging' *Reuters* (30 May 2023), https://www.reuters.com/business/retail-consumer/house-swaps-dog-walks-travelers-find-cheaper-alternatives-lodging-2023-05-22/ accessed 7 January 2024.
55. European Commission, Directorate General for Internal Market, Industry, Entrepreneurship and SMEs, VVA, and Spark Legal Network (n. 48) 39.
56. Bakker, Hendrica and Twining-Ward (n. 50) 11.
57. Francesco Scullica and Elena Elgani, 'Reinventing the Hospitality: Sharing Economy and New Hospitality Formats' in Maurizio Bruglieri (ed.), *Multidisciplinary Design of Sharing Services* (Springer International Publishing 2018) 66–67.
58. Kristóf Gyódi, 'Airbnb and Booking.Com: Sharing Economy. Competing Against Traditional Firms?' (2017) Working Paper DELab UW 3.
59. Bakker, Hendrica and Twining-Ward (n. 50) 15.
60. Ernesto Lopez-Cordova, *Digital Platforms and the Demand for International Tourism Services* (World Bank Group 2020) 7.
61. 'Economic Significance' (*Observatory on the Online Platform Economy*), https://platformobservatory.eu/state-of-play/economic-significance/ accessed 13 August 2021.

which started in 2003. The platform built a community of users who both hosted others and sought a 'couch' (*couchsurfing*), i.e., a place to sleep without paying.[62] For this reason, in the first phase of the platform's existence, its users were even expected to provide barter-back services such as cooking for hosts or helping with household chores.[63] The platform only provided an app and website to connect private accommodation providers and travellers, and the costs it incurred were covered primarily by advertising revenue.[64]

However, as the number of users grew (around 14 million members worldwide),[65] it became increasingly difficult for Couchsurfing to function as a platform based on volunteering and donations from users. In 2011, Couchsurfing lost its non-profit status and became a profit-driven enterprise,[66] adopting a freemium model from 2014 based on offering customers free access to basic services and introducing an annual fee for additional services.[67] Nevertheless, Couchsurfing continues to provide free accommodation to users, and the platform typically does not impose an intermediary fee between travellers and hosts.[68]

Despite Couchsurfing's undoubted success, however, it is not as famous as another platform that also entered the accommodation market in the first decade of the twenty-first century – Airbnb. Airbnb is often considered the 'most emblematic manifestation'[69] of the platform economy, hailed as 'the best-known online hospitality platform',[70] an exemplary case of 'winner-take-all competition',[71] and 'one of the major players on a global scale'.[72] The Airbnb business model is also the subject of much research relating to the accommodation sector.[73]

62. Constantin Bratianu, 'The Crazy New World of the Sharing Economy' in Elena-Mădălina Vătămănescu and Florina Magdalena Pînzaru (eds), *Knowledge Management in the Sharing Economy*, vol 6 (Springer International Publishing 2018) 9.
63. Adam Pawlicz, *Ekonomia współdzielenia na rynku usług hotelarskich: niedoskonałości, pośrednicy, regulacje* (Wydawnictwo Naukowe Uniwersytetu Szczecińskiego 2019) 93.
64. Claudia Vienken, Nizar Abdelkafi and Cyrine Tangour, 'Multi-Sided Platforms in the Sharing Economy – A Case Study Analysis for the Development of a Generic Platform' in Rim Jallouli and others (eds), *Digital Economy. Emerging Technologies and Business Innovation* (Springer International Publishing 2019) 378.
65. Beatrice Villari, 'A Service Design Approach to Analyse, Map and Design Sharing Services' in Maurizio Bruglieri (ed.), *Multidisciplinary Design of Sharing Services* (Springer International Publishing 2018) 16.
66. Galluzzo and Gerosa (n. 9) 58.
67. Pawlicz, (n. 63) 93.
68. Vienken, Abdelkafi and Tangour (n. 64) 378–379.
69. Jeroen A Oskam, *The Future of Airbnb and the 'Sharing Economy': The Collaborative Consumption of Our Cities* (Channel View Publications 2019) 7.
70. Scullica and Elgani (n. 57) 67.
71. Oskam (n. 69) 24.
72. Villari (n. 65) 17.
73. Hossain (n. 21) 8.

Airbnb was founded in San Francisco by Joe Gebbia, Brian Chesky and Nathan Blecharczyk. Either 2007 or 2008 is most often cited as the launch date,[74] depending on whether the author considers this to be the launch of the website (2007) or the placing of Airbnb within formal legal frameworks (2008). In the autumn of 2007, the founders of the platform were building a website in order to rent inflatable mattresses in their flat[75] to conference participants who could not find a place in the hotels.[76] In 2008, 'AirBed & Breakfast' began to formally operate as a company. In its inaugural year of operation, the platform provided accommodation for more than 600 people attending the Democratic National Convention when traditional Denver accommodations were overflowing.[77] In March 2009, the platform was renamed Airbnb.[78] Already after 2010, the platform grew rapidly: in February 2011, Airbnb announced its first million bookings; in January 2012 – 5 million; in June 2012 – 10 million; and in September 2017, it had already surpassed 200 million bookings.[79] In 2021, despite the COVID-19 pandemic, 4 million Airbnb hosts have already welcomed over 900 million arriving guests.[80]

The platform has also gradually expanded its geographical reach. In the EU, Airbnb was launched in mid-2011 in Germany and quickly spread across the continent.[81] Among European countries, the platform's most important markets are France, Italy, Spain, the UK and Germany.[82]

It is worth noting that globally only half of Airbnb listings are in urbanized areas (mainly in Eastern European and Asian countries), with the remainder located in smaller towns and rural areas (mainly in Southern European countries).[83] Interestingly, in recent years, the share of urban listings has fallen from 53.6% in 2018 to 49.1% in 2021, a trend that accelerated during the pandemic.[84]

---

74. For example, the year 2008 is cited by Hong Ngoc Nguyen, Timo Rintamäki and Hannu Saarijärvi, 'Customer Value in the Sharing Economy Platform: The Airbnb Case' in Anssi Smedlund, Arto Lindblom and Lasse Mitronen (eds), *Collaborative Value Co-creation in the Platform Economy*, vol 11 (Springer Singapore 2018) 233; Katarzyna Sledziewska-Kołodziejska and Renata Włoch, *Gospodarka cyfrowa: jak nowe technologie zmieniają świat* (Wydawnictwo Uniwersytetu Warszawskiego 2020) 267.
75. An inflatable mattress is called an *Airbed*. The name Airbnb alludes to it.
76. Sledziewska-Kołodziejska and Włoch (n. 74) 96.
77. Johanna Interian, 'Up in the Air: Harmonizing the Sharing Economy Through Airbnb Regulations' (2016) 39 Boston College International and Comparative Law Review 133.
78. Pawlicz, (n. 63) 91.
79. *Ibid.*
80. Airbnb, *Airbnb Report on Travel & Living* (2021) 7.
81. Tim Bradshaw, 'Airbnb Moves "Aggressively" into Europe' (*Financial Times*, 31 May 2011), https://www.ft.com/ accessed 12 March 2024.
82. Czesław Adamiak, 'Changes in the Global Airbnb Offer During the COVID-19 Pandemic' (2021) Oikonomics 5.
83. *Ibid.*, 6–7.
84. *Ibid.*

Airbnb primarily offers the possibility to rent accommodation through its platform. However, it is important to note that over the years the platform has significantly expanded the range of services offered to its users.[85] For example, the sub-platform has introduced the option to book local 'experiences' such as sightseeing tours, wine tasting, or cooking classes. It seems, therefore, that Airbnb's long-term strategy is to build a 'one-stop travel platform',[86] thus blurring the distinction between the activities of this platform and OTAs.

Airbnb's users are primarily hosts and guests. Both hosts and guests can act for business or private purposes (Airbnb allows bookings for business travellers; in 2018, 15% of bookings on the platform were for business trips).[87] Airbnb charges both parties. As with HomeExchange, Airbnb clearly defines its role in its Terms of Service, stipulating that it is not a party to contracts made directly between hosts and guests, is not a real estate agent, an insurer, or an arranger or seller of travel packages.[88]

Following the success of Airbnb, other platforms offering similar services to their users,[89] such as HomeAway, Homestay.com, Onefinestay, Xiaozhu, Tujia, and Wimdu, have also entered the accommodation market. Interestingly, 2019[90] also saw the launch of Fairbnb, which[91] aims to minimize the negative impact of platforms (mainly Airbnb, it seems – hence the name, presumably), promoting ideas such as using platform revenues to empower residents and fund community projects, supporting municipalities to better regulate STRs or retaining platform revenues in the local economy.

It is important to note that Fairbnb's objectives are part of a trend referred to in the Centre for Responsible Travel's 2020 Report.[92] This document identifies a continuously growing consumer demand for sustainable travel experiences. The emergence of platforms such as Fairbnb can be seen as a positive sign of the changes taking place in

85. *Airbnb Inc in Travel (World)* (Euromonitor International 2018) 7–8, https://www.euromonitor.com/airbnb-inc-in-travel/report accessed 12 February 2023.
86. Adamiak (n. 82) 9.
87. *Airbnb Inc in Travel (World)* (n. 85) 7.
88. 'Warunki Świadczenia Usług – Centrum Pomocy Airbnb' (*Airbnb*), https://www.airbnb.pl/help/article/2908 accessed 16 September 2021.
89. Laurenţiu-Mihai Treapăt, Anda Gheorghiu and Marina Ochkovskaya, 'A Synthesis of the Sharing Economy in Romania and Russia' in Elena-Mădălina Vătămănescu and Florina Magdalena Pînzaru (eds), *Knowledge Management in the Sharing Economy*, vol 6 (Springer International Publishing 2018) 60.
90. The project creation of this platform, however, was presented at the Platform Cooperativism Conference in New York as early as November 2016, *see*: Joël Foramitti, Angelos Varvarousis and Giorgos Kallis, 'Transition Within a Transition: How Cooperative Platforms Want to Change the Sharing Economy' (2020) 15 Sustainability Science 1189 https://doi.org/10.1007/s11625-020-00804-y.
91. Marina Petruzzi, Catarina Marques and Valerie Sheppard, 'To Share or to Exchange: An Analysis of the Sharing Economy Characteristics of Airbnb and Fairbnb.Coop' (2021) International Journal of Hospitality Management 2–3 https://doi.org/10.1016/j.ijhm.2020.102724.
92. Center for Responsible Travel, *The Case for Responsible Travel: Trends & Statistics 2020* (2020) 7, www.responsibletravel.org.

the accommodation sector, notably the promotion of more socially friendly business practices.[93]

Table 1.1 shows examples of STR sector platform business models.

Table 1.1 Examples of STR Sector Platform Business Models

Platform	*Dominant Transaction Subject*	*Dominant Transaction Type*	*Consideration*	*Platform Fee*
home exchange	Home exchange	C2C	Non-monetary consideration (barter)	One-time, annual fee
Booking.com	Hotel accommodation	B2C, B2B	Monetary consideration	Service fee charged to hosts
couchsurfing	Private accommodation rental	C2C	Free of charge	No consideration
airbnb	Private accommodation rental	C2C, B2C	Monetary consideration	Service fee charged to hosts and guests

Source: Own compilation.

Tourism is one of the largest service industries globally. Figures indicate that there were 1.2 billion international travellers in 2017, and it is estimated that by 2030, this number will reach 1.8 billion.[94] Consequently, there will be an increased demand for services to meet their needs, such as accommodation, among others. The World Economic Forum predicts that by 2025, 17% of the annual revenue of the global hospitality sector will come from STR services.[95] Therefore, the role of platforms operating in this sector is growing. In 2019, guests spent more than 554 million nights in properties booked through Airbnb, Booking, Expedia Group, or Tripadvisor in the EU. The number of nights spent in accommodation booked through these four platforms increased by 14% between 2018 and 2019.[96] Airbnb holds a clear lead in the EU market, accounting for approximately 62% of the estimated total revenue of the EU accommodation sector, according to a 2018 EC report.[97]

However, it is crucial to note that the outbreak of the COVID-19 pandemic and the social distancing measures implemented worldwide caused significant disruption to economic sectors involving the movement of people. Undoubtedly, one such economic sector is the STR sector.

93. Petruzzi, Marques and Sheppard (n. 91) 9.
94. Bakker, Hendrica and Twining-Ward (n. 50) 15.
95. *Ibid.*, 29.
96. 'Short-Stay Accommodation Booked via Collaborative Economy Platforms: First Data', https://ec.europa.eu/eurostat/web/products-eurostat-news/-/ddn-20210629-2 accessed 6 November 2021.
97. European Commission, Directorate General for Internal Market, Industry, Entrepreneurship and SMEs and others, *Study to Monitor the Economic Development of the Collaborative Economy at Sector Level in the 28 EU Member States: Final Report* (Publications Office 2018) 52.

Data from the Digital Platform Economy Observatory[98] reveals that the share of platform traffic on travel sites fell by almost 50% in June 2020.[99] For that year, Airbnb reported a USD 3.9 billion loss and a 22% drop in revenue. However, data from the first quarter of 2021 already indicated a clear rise in bookings made through this platform.[100] It therefore appears that the losses suffered by the industry were a one-off event rather than the beginning of a reversal of previous trends.

The COVID-19 pandemic has also influenced the development of new visitor habits. For instance, some accommodation services brokering platforms have introduced hourly rentals to cater to those forced to telework.[101] It is challenging to predict whether these trends will be sustainable or merely a response to changed consumer needs triggered by the pandemic. According to the OECD's assessment, many of the new habits developed during the pandemic can be expected to continue even after it has ended, potentially leading to a further increase in demand for STR accommodation.[102]

4 BASIC FEATURES

Within the platform economy, a distinction can be made between its subject and object aspects. The subject aspect refers to the role that the platform plays in the transaction, as well as the status of its users. The object aspect relates to the nature of transactions made through platforms and how they differ from traditional economic models.

4.1 The Subject Aspect

In principle, transactions in the platform economy involve two categories of entities: the platforms and their users. Among platform users, a distinction can be made between entities that provide goods or services (underlying suppliers) and entities that purchase goods or services (underlying buyers). Within the STR sector, these would be hosts and visitors, respectively. In the 'ecosystem' of the STR platform economy, there are also often other participants providing services to hosts or platforms.

98. The Observatory monitors and analyses the online platform economy, supporting the Commission in policy-making.
99. 'COVID-19 and Online Platform Economy' (*Observatory on the Online Platform Economy*), https://platformobservatory.eu/news/covid-19-and-online-platform-economy/ accessed 13 August 2021.
100. Urszula Lesman, 'Gigantyczna strata Airbnb. Firma wciąz wierzy w odbicie' *Rzeczpospolita e-wydanie* (26 February 2021), https://www.rp.pl/Biznes/302269921-Gigantyczna-strata-Airbnb-Firma-wciaz-wierzy-w-odbicie.html accessed 8 March 2021.
101. 'Platform Economy: Developments in the COVID-19 Crisis' (*Eurofound*, 7 August 2021), https://www.eurofound.europa.eu/data/platform-economy/dossiers/developments-in-the-covid-19-crisis accessed 7 August 2021.
102. OECD, *The Impact of the Growth of the Sharing and Gig Economy on VAT/GST Policy and Administration* (n. 47) 95–96.

4.1.1 STR Platforms

Platforms are considered to be the driving force behind the digital economy, occupying a central position in it.[103] However, answering the question of what they actually are is not easy. A platform is not an 'object' but rather a 'functionality', a shared space that facilitates exchange between parties.[104]

In this book, I will address platforms that facilitate interactions and transactions between users, i.e., platforms that can be described as 'transactional'[105] or 'matchmaker'[106] platforms. In this context, the term 'platform' is used to refer to a specific technology, often called a system or software.[107] As the literature points out, platforms are not the same as networks, nor are they simply infrastructure.[108] They are often referred to as network orchestrators,[109] using the organization of the platform to build infrastructure and develop interfaces to connect users in multilateral markets.[110]

Transactional platforms have diverse business models. In some cases, transactional platforms offer a truly open infrastructure that facilitates the matching of supply and demand among their users.[111] In other cases, platforms closely control the transaction, manage the quality of service, exercise strict oversight of information flows, and influence prices. Given this, it is challenging to develop a more general definition of these platforms. One has to agree with the conclusion of the OECD report that markets and businesses change, so any definition of platforms will have to evolve with them and therefore cannot be universal or permanent.[112]

At the same time, it seems that the most relevant features currently characterizing trading platforms are as follows:

- They facilitate transactions.

---

103. Inglese (n. 33) 19–20; Johanna Mair and Georg Reischauer, 'Capturing the Dynamics of the Sharing Economy: Institutional Research on the Plural Forms and Practices of Sharing Economy Organizations' (2017) 125 Technological Forecasting and Social Change 12 https://doi.org/10.1016/j.techfore.2017.05.023.
104. Marie Lamensch and others, 'New EU VAT-Related Obligations for E-Commerce Platforms Worldwide: A Qualitative Impact Assessment' (2021) 13 World Tax Journal 444–445 https://doi.org/10.59403/15yff24.
105. OECD, *An Introduction to Online Platforms and Their Role in the Digital Transformation* (OECD 2019) 62.
106. Acquier and Carbone (n. 29) 57–58; OECD, *An Introduction to Online Platforms and Their Role in the Digital Transformation* (n. 105) 62.
107. Xia Han, Veronica Martinez and Andy Neely, 'Service in the Platform Context: A Review of the State of the Art and Future Research' in Anssi Smedlund, Arto Lindblom and Lasse Mitronen (eds), *Collaborative Value Co-creation in the Platform Economy*, vol 11 (Springer Singapore 2018) 7–8.
108. Julie E Cohen, 'Law for the Platform Economy' (2017) 51 U.C. Davis Law Review 143–144.
109. Zale (n. 49) 39–40.
110. Sledziewska-Kołodziejska and Włoch (n. 74) 99. In this publication, it is posited that digital platforms create a new business model of virtual 'intermediation' between at least two distinct but interdependent (networked) user groups, forming market sides within multi-sided markets.
111. Guido Smorto, 'Regulating (and Self-Regulating) the Sharing Economy in Europe: An Overview' in Maurizio Bruglieri (ed.), *Multidisciplinary Design of Sharing Services* (Springer International Publishing 2018) 115.
112. OECD, *OECD Digital Economy Outlook 2020* (OECD 2020).

- A certain level of control is exercised over them.
- They use digital trust mechanisms (reputation systems).
- They use information obtained from users.
- They cooperate with other platforms.

So, in essence, platforms provide the infrastructure so that it only takes a few 'clicks' online to complete a transaction.

Also, STR sector platforms generally offer websites and applications to connect at least two sides of the market, as well as to develop business and provide STR services in different countries.[113] Most larger STR platforms provide hosts with limited hands-on or telephone support.[114] Platforms may also offer ancillary services, such as photographic services or the provision of instructional materials, as well as providing hosts with periodic transaction summaries to help them meet any tax obligations.[115]

Platforms reduce the fixed costs of entering new markets by diminishing the information asymmetry associated with matching buyers and sellers, which can be particularly beneficial for small businesses and the self-employed.[116] As the OECD points out, SME make disproportionate use of these services, especially in the area of cross-border trade.[117] At a time when business development requires considerable investment in logistics and marketing, platforms take on some of the costs in exchange for moderate user fees; in this way, small actors have easier access to the global market.[118]

This model of operation taps into a phenomenon known as network effects, which occurs when the value of a good or service increases as the number of people using it increases.[119] A platform attracts suppliers when there are many potential consumers on the platform, while consumers are interested in the platform when there are many suppliers on the platform.[120] Thus, the larger a platform is, the more users it has, making it more attractive to new members due to the greater benefits it can offer through its larger size.[121] Therefore, in essence, the aim of the platform is to shape its 'ecosystem' so favourably that it encourages more users to join and that they do not seek intermediary options elsewhere.[122] Interestingly, although the emergence of

113. Vienken, Abdelkafi and Tangour (n. 64) 381.
114. Bakker, Hendrica and Twining-Ward (n. 50) 18.
115. OECD, *The Impact of the Growth of the Sharing and Gig Economy on VAT/GST Policy and Administration* (n. 47) 105–106.
116. Mary Hallward-Driemeier and others, *Europe 4.0. Addressing the Digital Dilemma* (World Bank Group 2020) 49.
117. OECD, *OECD Digital Economy Outlook 2020* (n. 112).
118. Florina Magdalena Pînzaru, Andreea Mitan and Alina Daniela Mihalcea, 'Reshaping Competition in the Age of Platforms: The Winners of the Sharing Economy' in Elena-Mădălina Vătămănescu and Florina Magdalena Pînzaru (eds), *Knowledge Management in the Sharing Economy: Cross-Sectoral Insights into the Future of Competitive Advantage* (Springer International Publishing 2018) 31.
119. Christopher Yoo, 'Network Effect – Concurrences', https://www.concurrences.com/en/dictionary/Network-effect accessed 12 March 2024.
120. Koen Frenken and others, 'Safeguarding Public Interests in the Platform Economy' (2020) 12 Policy & Internet 403 https://doi.org/10.1002/poi3.217.
121. Theurl and Meyer (n. 41) 194.
122. Cohen (n. 108) 144–145.

platforms in a given sector initially encourages more competition, the presence of 'network effects' may eventually lead to market consolidation and the emergence of so-called super-platforms, which may impede market access for new players.[123]

In general, it is the actions of users that co-create the value of a platform,[124] as they generally do not own the assets on which transactions are based.[125] Platforms in the STR sector generally do not own the properties they broker.[126] Airbnb, for example, does not own hotels and does not employ hotel staff, but it does own the platform and employs people to run and improve it.[127] Thus, rather than building a competitive advantage on their own assets, platforms 'benefit' from users' assets. This means that the ability to generate profits is directly proportional to the value of the personal assets that users bring to it.[128] For this reason, platforms can grow much faster than their traditional competitors (e.g., Airbnb versus a traditional hotel chain) because they do not need to make any investment in the assets underlying the transaction (such as real estate) but only attract more suppliers to offer their resources.[129] As Tom Goodwin aptly summarized: 'Uber, the world's largest taxi company, does not own vehicles. Facebook, the world's most popular media owner, creates no content. Alibaba, the world's most valuable retailer, has no inventory. And Airbnb, the world's largest accommodation provider, has no real estate. Something interesting is happening.'[130]

In terms of consideration for facilitating transactions, platforms typically charge all or selected users, as well as advertisers.[131] In the EU, in the vast majority of cases, platforms only request a fee from suppliers. However, in this context, there are significant differences between sectors. For example, in transport, the share of fee revenue collected from buyers is relatively low (around 1.3 %), while in the accommodation sector, it is relatively high (around 18.8 %).[132] The consideration that a platform receives can also take a non-monetary form, often including, for example, access to

123. Bakker, Hendrica and Twining-Ward (n. 50) 18.
124. Antti Hautamäki and Kaisa Oksanen, 'Digital Platforms for Restructuring the Public Sector' in Anssi Smedlund, Arto Lindblom and Lasse Mitronen (eds), *Collaborative Value Co-creation in the Platform Economy*, vol 11 (Springer Singapore 2018) 94–95.
125. Gerwe and Silva (n. 13) 71.
126. However, they often impose qualitative and pricing requirements on users and have a significant impact on the services provided. Sofia Ranchordás, Zsuzsanna Gedeon and Karolina Zurek, *Home-Sharing in the Digital Economy: The Cases of Brussels, Stockholm, and Budapest* (European Commission 2016) 9.
127. Mair and Reischauer (n. 103) 13.
128. Aurélien Acquier, 'Uberization Meets Organizational Theory: Platform Capitalism and the Rebirth of the Putting-Out System' in Nestor M Davidson, Michèle Finck and John J Infranca (eds), *The Cambridge Handbook of the Law of the Sharing Economy* (Cambridge University Press 2018) 21.
129. Gerwe and Silva (n. 13) 71.
130. 'The Battle Is for the Customer Interface' (*TechCrunch*), https://techcrunch.com/2015/03/03/in-the-age-of-disintermediation-the-battle-is-all-for-the-customer-interface/?guccounter=1&guce_referrer=aHR0cHM6Ly93d3cuYmluZy5jb20v&guce_referrer_sig=AQAAAEhx9j_897RCDeIIUxR_o_o60hS8rYDK0QSWxQqJE8-T93uenyqQ5p_z3qb0xkEGVW0dz0Cg9Zp-05_q4hh99bN4pmRs3QQSgt6Z6IuAe-4-2kFagZCkHTGutHrH1xm1Z38pibJE_pXt3kGhBZX4E0-CnVn_ERuWgCj8JfPqQNbM accessed 13 August 2021.
131. Cohen (n. 108) 146–148.
132. European Commission, Directorate General for Taxation and Customs Union and others (n. 6) 36.

private data. Sometimes, too, platforms do not charge users for their services, sustaining their activities from advertising revenue and thanks to volunteers.

The pattern of transactions concluded through and by STR platforms is shown in Figure 1.1.

Figure 1.1 The Pattern of Transactions Concluded Through and by STR Platforms

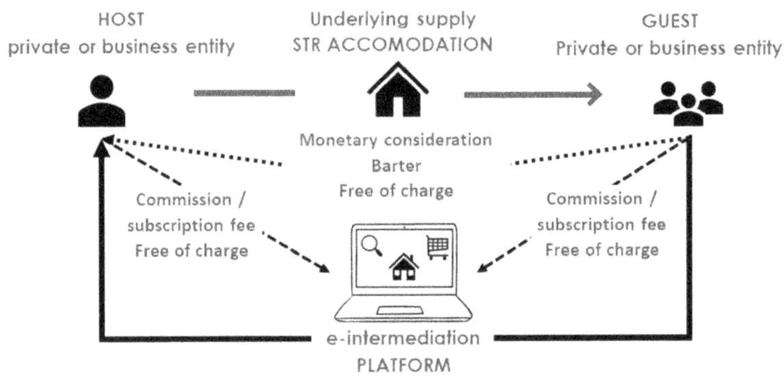

Source: Own compilation.

The prices of the accommodation itself are generally not set by the platforms but by the individual hosts.[133] However, STR platforms often offer the option of using a pricing algorithm. They can give hosts recommended prices that take into account many factors such as demand, season and local events.[134]

Platforms also often use rating and review mechanisms (reputation systems).

It is important to note that online marketplaces with geographically dispersed buyers and sellers who do not engage in repetitive transactions are not conducive to traditional trust-building mechanisms. To address this, almost all platforms employ some form of a feedback system, which is a record of qualitative and quantitative evaluations linked to the profile of a specific user, providing information about their trading behaviour.[135] These systems are particularly relevant for service intermediary platforms, as the deliveries of goods do not usually involve closer personal interactions,[136] although trust in the product and its provider is, of course, also important.[137] However, in terms of the quality of service, these systems are crucial for building and

133. Oskam (n. 69) 25–26.
134. OECD, *The Impact of the Growth of the Sharing and Gig Economy on VAT/GST Policy and Administration* (n. 47) 105–106.
135. Christoph Busch, 'Crowdsourcing Consumer Confidence: How to Regulate Online Rating and Review Systems in the Collaborative Economy' in Alberto De Franceschi (ed.), *European Contract Law and the Digital Single Market: The Implications of the Digital Revolution* (Intersentia 2016) 226.
136. Mareike Möhlmann and Andrea Geissinger, 'Trust in the Sharing Economy: Platform-Mediated Peer Trust' in Nestor M Davidson, Michèle Finck and John J Infranca (eds), *The Cambridge Handbook of the Law of the Sharing Economy* (Cambridge University Press 2018) 31.
137. Robin Teigland, Håkan Holmberg and Anna Felländer, 'The Importance of Trust in a Digital Europe: Reflections on the Sharing Economy and Blockchains' in Antonina Bakardjieva

maintaining trust between users, who are often complete strangers to each other.[138] For example, entering another person's home or spending a night in a flat with a host you have just met are risky transactions for both parties. How is the owner supposed to trust that the guest will not damage his property, and how is the guest supposed to trust that the description of the house corresponds to reality or even that the key fits the lock?[139] One of the innovations of the platforms is to develop mechanisms to mitigate these risks.[140] At the same time, by providing such mechanisms, the platform itself is seen as a trustworthy institution.[141]

The most popular tools supporting platforms' reputation systems include peer reviews by users, linking a user's profile to their social media networks.[142] Platforms can also provide dispute resolution and insurance protection, for example, by using deposits that users must pay to the platform to be held in escrow.[143] Additionally, the use of user identity verification technologies by platforms is becoming increasingly popular. The initial reliance of platforms on technology-assisted self-regulatory reputation systems is now giving way to an increasing number of centralized controls.[144]

Reputation systems are playing an increasingly important role in the decision-making of platform users when it comes to transacting through the platform. Because of this, there are instances where platforms encourage users to provide reviews by offering them products or discounts in return for giving a rating.[145] However, such incentives may result in biased reviews and thus mislead other users.[146]

It should be noted that both suppliers' and buyers' reputations can affect their access to platforms.[147] In situations where suppliers are unable to meet the expectations of their consumers, the platform may sanction them and even ban them from the platform.[148] The reverse is also possible, i.e., holding purchasers liable if they commit a particularly serious offence, such as damaging someone else's property.[149] This raises the issue of ensuring that users can be 'rehabilitated', i.e., that they can rebuild their reputation to a sufficient level to be able to re-enter the platforms again.[150]

Engelbrekt and others (eds), *Trust in the European Union in Challenging Times: Interdisciplinary European Studies* (Springer International Publishing 2019) 194.

138. Easton (n. 33) 174–175.
139. Teigland, Holmberg and Felländer (n. 137) 186.
140. Gerwe and Silva (n. 13) 67–68.
141. Möhlmann and Geissinger (n. 136) 31.
142. *Ibid.*, 34–35.
143. Marie Lamensch and others, 'Qualitative Assessment of Two Recent EU Commission Proposals to Impose (More) VAT Obligations on Platforms' (2024) 16 World Tax Journal, ibfd.org accessed 29 April 2024 https://doi.org/10.59403/x52sh9.
144. Easton (n. 33) 176–177.
145. *Ibid.*, 175.
146. Busch (n. 135) 237.
147. Vanessa Katz, 'Regulating the Sharing Economy' (2015) 30 (Annual Review 2015) Berkeley Technology Law Journal 1117.
148. Easton (n. 33) 175–176.
149. Inglese (n. 33) 13.
150. Easton (n. 33) 175–176.

The significance of reviews and reputation systems in influencing the decision to purchase goods or services has prompted the EC to introduce a directive[151] mandating platforms to report on how they verify the accuracy of reviews posted on their websites. Additionally, this directive prohibits sellers from posting or manipulating false consumer reviews and recommendations. These rules have been in effect in EU Member States since 28 May 2022.

It is crucial to acknowledge that, to facilitate transactions and ensure their security, platforms collect, use, and process substantial amounts of data. According to the OECD report,[152] as a general practice, STR platforms typically hold the following information: (i) user identification data (name and surname, email address, telephone number, residential address, tax identification number), (ii) transaction value, (iii) property address, (iv) payment data.

Advancements in data storage and analysis capabilities mean that the datasets held by platforms are continually expanding.[153] Leveraging new information processing and analysis technologies, platforms are increasingly personalizing products and services, enhancing the overall transaction experience for users.[154]

In practical terms, platforms frequently engage in collaborations with other platforms. Smaller and more specialized platforms may form agreements with dominant ones to provide specific services, such as payment processing. These arrangements prove beneficial for both specialized and dominant platforms, offering the former access to a larger user base and providing the latter with more information about users' online activities.[155]

As a final point, it should be noted that the term 'platforms' has started to appear in EU legislation. For example, in Directive 2016/1148/EU of the European Parliament and of the Council,[156] a platform means: 'a digital service that allows consumers and/or traders to conclude online sales or service contracts with traders either on the online marketplace's website or on a trader's website that uses computing services provided by the online marketplace'. In this case, the EU legislator, in defining the platform, refers more to the role it fulfils than to an indication of what it actually is. A similar definition is contained in Directive 2019/2161/EU of the European Parliament and of the Council.[157] However, this piece of legislation takes the view that the definition

151. Directive (EU) 2019/2161 of the European Parliament and of the Council of 27 November 2019 amending Council Directive 93/13/EEC and Directives 98/6/EC, 2005/29/EC and 2011/83/EU of the European Parliament and of the Council as regards the better enforcement and modernisation of Union consumer protection rules [OJ L 328, 18.12.2019, pp. 7–28].
152. OECD, *The Impact of the Growth of the Sharing and Gig Economy on VAT/GST Policy and Administration* (n. 47) 105–106.
153. Easton (n. 33) 171–174.
154. Śledziewska-Kołodziejska and Włoch (n. 74) 130.
155. Cohen (n. 108) 146–148.
156. Directive (EU) 2016/1148 of the European Parliament and of the Council of 6 July 2016 concerning measures for a high common level of security of network and information systems across the Union [OJ L 194, 19.7.2016, pp. 1–30].
157. Directive (EU) 2019/2161 of the European Parliament and of the Council of 27 November 2019 amending Council Directive 93/13/EEC and Directives 98/6/EC, 2005/29/EC and 2011/83/EU of the European Parliament and of the Council as regards the better enforcement and modernisation of Union consumer protection rules (n. 151).

should be more technology-neutral; therefore, it does not refer only to websites but also to newer technologies such as applications.

The definition of a platform is also included in Council Directive (EU) 2021/514[158] on administrative cooperation in the field of direct taxation. According to Annex 5, section 1(A)(1) of this legal act, a platform means: 'any software, including a website or a part thereof and applications, including mobile applications, accessible by users and allowing "sellers"[159] to be connected to other users for the purpose of carrying out a "relevant activity",[160] directly or indirectly, to such users. The term also includes any arrangement for the collection and payment of a consideration[161] in respect of the "relevant activity". The term "platform" does not include software that without any further intervention in carrying out the "relevant activity" exclusively allows any of the following: a) the processing of payments in relation to the "relevant activity"; b) users to list or advertise the "relevant activity"; c) redirecting or transferring of users to a "platform"'.

It should be noted that this definition only covers platforms that provide their services for consideration. In the context of direct taxation, this is of course understandable – in general, the absence of consideration means that there is no basis for direct taxation.

Importantly, the term 'interface' is increasingly being used in EU law instead of 'platform'. For example, in Regulation (EU) 2017/2394 of the European Parliament and of the Council,[162] 'online interface' means: 'software, including a website, part of a website or an application, that is operated by or on behalf of a trader, and which serves to give consumers access to the trader's goods or services'.

A similar term of 'electronic interface' is used by the VAT Directive.[163] However, the concept is not defined there. Article 14a(1) and (2) and Article 242a of the VAT Directive only give examples of what an electronic interface can be: 'Where a taxable person facilitates, through the use of an electronic interface such as a marketplace, platform, portal or similar means (...).' The concept is broad, and the use of the phrase

158. Council Directive (EU) 2021/514 of 22 March 2021 amending Directive 2011/16/EU on administrative cooperation in the field of taxation [OJ L 104, 25.3.2021, pp. 1-26].
159. In accordance with Annex V, s. I, letter B, point 1, 'Seller' means a platform user, either an individual or an entity, that is registered at any moment during the Reportable Period on the Platform and carries out a relevant activity.
160. In accordance with Annex V, s. I, letter A, point 8, 'Relevant Activity' means an activity carried out for consideration and being any of the following: (a) the rental of immovable property, including both residential and commercial property, as well as any other immovable property and parking spaces; (b) a personal service; (c) the sale of goods; (d) the rental of any mode of transport. The term 'Relevant Activity' does not include an activity carried out by a seller acting as an employee of the platform operator or a related entity of the platform operator.
161. In accordance with Annex V, s. I, letter A, point 10, 'Consideration' means compensation in any form, net of any fees, commissions or taxes withheld or charged by the reporting platform operator, that is paid or credited to a seller in connection with the Relevant Activity, the amount of which is known or reasonably knowable by the platform operator.
162. Regulation (EU) 2017/2394 of the European Parliament and of the Council of 12 December 2017 on cooperation between national authorities responsible for the enforcement of consumer protection laws and repealing Regulation (EC) No 2006/2004 [OJ L 345, 27.12.2017, pp. 1-26].
163. Council Directive 2006/112/EC of 28 November 2006 on the common system of value added tax [OJ L 347, 11.12.2006, pp. 1-118] 112.

'similar means' makes the catalogue of types of electronic interfaces open-ended. This position is confirmed by the EC's Explanatory Notes,[164] where it is indicated that the term 'electronic interface' is to be understood broadly and that 'similar means' has been used to also take into account other electronic forms that enable the conclusion of a sales contract and technological developments that may occur in the future. In the Commission's view, the concept of an electronic interface can therefore include, for example, a website, portal, web gateway, marketplace, API and other digital tools which allow two independent systems or a system and the end user to communicate with the help of a device or program.

It should be recognized that the concept of 'electronic interface' contained in the VAT Directive is constructed on the opposite principle to the definitions of 'platforms' contained in the various pieces of EU legislation cited above. Indeed, the definitions of 'platforms' under these acts mean various types of digital tools (such as websites and applications) through which transactions are facilitated. In the VAT Directive, it is 'electronic interfaces' that mean the various types of digital tools through which transactions are facilitated, and the platform is simply one such tool.

It is not entirely clear why the European legislator sometimes uses the term 'platform' and sometimes the term 'online interface' or 'electronic interface'. It should be noted that these definitions (leaving aside, of course, their nuances related to the purposes for which they appear in the acts in question) actually refer to the same thing – the digital tools by which transactions are facilitated.

4.1.2 STR Platform Users

4.1.2.1 Underlying Suppliers: Hosts

In scholarly literature, hosts operating through STR platforms are broadly categorized into two types: (i) non-professional hosts, referring to inexperienced individuals who rent out their spare rooms or apartments/houses and (ii) professional hosts, denoting experienced owners, usually managing more than one property.[165] Distinguishing the role in which a host operates poses numerous challenges.

The literature suggests that the conventional division between production and consumption is nowadays undergoing a transformation. With the advancement of new technologies, individuals can function as both producers and consumers of goods and services.[166] Such 'hybrid' entities are often referred to as prosumers. The name is a combination of two words – producer and consumer.[167] According to the literature, in certain instances, underlying suppliers may earn additional income without engaging

164. European Commission, *Explanatory Notes on VAT E-Commerce Rules. Council Directive (EU) 2017/2455. Council Directive (EU) 2019/1995. Council Implementing Regulation (EU) 2019/2026* (European Commission 2020) 11.
165. Jun Li, Antonio Moreno and Dennis J Zhang, 'Agent Pricing in the Sharing Economy: Evidence from Airbnb' in Ming Hu (ed.), *Sharing Economy: Making Supply Meet Demand* (Springer International Publishing 2019) 491.
166. Śledziewska-Kołodziejska and Włoch (n. 74) 81.
167. Arcidiacono and Pais (n. 18) 83.

in any form of stable activity, in their spare time, without subordination, and without a formal organization of anything.[168] They typically operate on a smaller scale compared to traditional service providers (e.g., renting a single bedroom/couch in someone else's house instead of a hotel room), utilize personal resources (like a house) rather than commercial assets (like a hotel building), and generally have less experience than professionals in traditional sectors.[169] Consequently, they can be identified as prosumers.[170]

It is important to highlight that, facilitated by new technologies and the platform's infrastructure, these actors can engage in transactions with relative ease, turning their activities into regular and profitable ventures. This occurs when underlying suppliers establish a permanent collaboration with the platform, acquire necessary equipment, establish lasting structures, and actively participate in the platform economy to generate regular income. As a consequence, transactions that initially had a C2C nature may evolve into B2C interactions. This transformation can have significant implications, as the law often imposes higher liability and specific obligations (including tax obligations) on professionals engaged in business activities.

Instances of professionalization are becoming increasingly prevalent. The scholarly literature highlights[171] that although platforms initially facilitated resource sharing, such as the founders of Airbnb offering an inflatable mattress in their guest room,[172] their evolution is now predominantly driven by collaborations with businesses or self-employed professionals.

In the context of this professionalization, it is noteworthy to mention hosts offering more than one property through platforms, often referred to as multilisters. This category includes hosts with multiple properties and professional investors who purchase or lease flats or entire buildings, typically situated in the most tourist-centric areas of cities, for STRs.[173] In contrast to hosts operating on an occasional basis, such as those renting out a single room or an entire house during their holiday, professional hosts exclusively allocate their flats and houses for rent,[174] commercializing their STR services. Professional hosts are inclined to achieve higher incomes through the platforms. A property managed by a professional host generates more than a 16.9% higher average daily income, and occupancy is 15.5% higher.[175] Moreover, professional hosts are more likely to receive special privileges, such as superhost status on Airbnb, granting them enhanced visibility.[176] Some authors argue that obtaining

168. Inglese (n. 33) 4.
169. Katz (n. 147) 1099–1100.
170. For example, Barbara Di Prete, 'Airbnb: A New Way of Housing Between Individual Experience and Collective Narration' in Maurizio Bruglieri (ed.), *Multidisciplinary Design of Sharing Services* (Springer International Publishing 2018) 220.
171. Sledziewska-Kołodziejska and Włoch (n. 74) 123.
172. Gerwe and Silva (n. 13) 90.
173. Such investors constitute over 70% of listings on major accommodation platforms in some of the most touristy cities, such as Barcelona and Lisbon. European Commission, Directorate General for Taxation and Customs Union and others (n. 6) 147–150.
174. Adamiak (n. 82) 7–8.
175. Li, Moreno and Zhang (n. 165) 485.
176. Oskam (n. 69) 59.

superhost status designates the host as a professional supplier.[177] The literature also underscores the platforms' dependence on such hosts due to their supply of a relatively reliable product that is regularly adapted to guests' preferences.[178]

Consequently, these types of hosts are beginning to compete with professionals in the accommodation industry, enjoying the advantage that they are not required to meet similar accreditation requirements as traditional hotels and face little or less restrictive taxation rules.[179] As indicated in the literature, the fact that the majority of Airbnb's supply (70.1%) comprises entire houses, especially those offered by multilister hosts,[180] intensifies product competition for hotel companies.[181]

It should also be noted that STR platforms' intermediation is increasingly utilized by hotels, hostels, and guesthouses, whose professional nature is unquestionable. This trend encourages other hosts to standardize and professionalize their offerings.[182]

However, it is essential to note that many small, 'semi-private' hosts still operate through platforms. According to the OECD, more than half of all STR properties are provided by individual hosts or small property managers.[183] In the EU, the vast majority of Airbnb hosts offer only one listing, earning approximately EUR 3,000 (data for 2021).[184] These small underlying suppliers may not be able to bear the same regulatory burdens that apply to traditional service suppliers[185] and cover the costs of operating in highly regulated economic sectors (e.g., the need for a supplier who occasionally rents out a vacant guest room to comply with hotel regulations).[186]

It is therefore crucial to distinguish between hosts operating on an occasional basis as private entities and those considered regular economic operators.[187] As highlighted by the EC, non-professional hosts should not automatically be treated as professionals, as this may discourage them from providing STR services.[188]

177. Inglese (n. 33) 128–129.
178. Stefan Brauckmann, 'City Tourism and the Sharing Economy: Potential Effects of Online Peer-to-Peer Marketplaces on Urban Property Markets' (2017) 3 Journal of Tourism Futures 120 https://doi.org/10.1108/jtf-05-2017-0027.
179. Marianna Sigala, 'Market Formation in the Sharing Economy: Findings and Implications from the Sub-Economies of Airbnb' in Sergio Barile, Marco Pellicano and Francesco Polese (eds), *Social Dynamics in a Systems Perspective* (Springer International Publishing 2018) 167.
180. As much as 59.8% of all listings are presented by hosts with multiple listings. This share has increased from 56.6% in 2018. 15.1% of the listings belong to hosts with more than 10 offerings, while 5.2% are attributed to hosts with over 50 listings. Adamiak (n. 82) 7–9.
181. Tarik Dogru and others, 'Airbnb 2.0: Is It a Sharing Economy Platform or a Lodging Corporation?' (2020) 78 Tourism Management 8–9 https://doi.org/10.1016/j.tourman.2019.104049.
182. Oskam (n. 69) 73.
183. OECD, *The Impact of the Growth of the Sharing and Gig Economy on VAT/GST Policy and Administration* (n. 47) 101.
184. Airbnb, 'Airbnb Welcomes EU Rules Proposals' (*Airbnb Newsroom*, 7 November 2022), https://news.airbnb.com/airbnb-welcomes-eu-rules-proposals/ accessed 20 July 2023.
185. Katz (n. 147) 1099.
186. Smorto (n. 111) 113.
187. It is also worth noting that for government authorities, determining whether a particular activity is of a professional or non-professional nature is significant in the context of fiscal regulations. Oskam (n. 69) 12–16.
188. European Commission, Directorate General for Internal Market, Industry, Entrepreneurship and SMEs, VVA, and Spark Legal Network (n. 48) 51–52.

The literature suggests using specific thresholds to distinguish in what capacity the host is acting.[189] The most popular thresholds are as follows:

- Limits on the number of nights a host can offer for an STR. For example, a threshold of 30, 60, or 90 days per year. This threshold is considered simple, neutral and easy to apply to all hosts equally.[190] However, the disadvantage of this solution is the need to check that a host renting a property through different platforms does not exceed the threshold and the need to rely on data provided by different platforms (which may not be entirely reliable).[191]
- The level of annual income of the host derived from renting a specific property. Such a threshold is also considered neutral and easy to administer, especially in cases where the tax return system is digitized.[192]
- The number (or percentage) of properties that a given host can rent out on a short-term basis. This type of system is based on the assumption that renting out, for example, one flat is unprofessional, whereas buying more properties for this purpose already shows that the host is acting as an entrepreneur.[193]

It is important to highlight that many limits typically do not apply to situations where the host stays with the guest in the rented property, a common scenario for single-room offers.[194] This criterion helps distinguish between hosts providing a property maintained for personal use and those maintaining it for investment purposes. To meet this distinction, hosts may need to remain the primary resident of the property.[195] However, enforcing this criterion poses challenges. It is difficult to verify whether the host has genuinely gone on holiday and rented out the entire empty flat; one has to rely on the guest's statement that the host stayed in the flat during his/her stay, etc. Despite these challenges, this approach benefits small, non-commercial hosts, allowing them to rent their properties without being subject to other limits, such as the 90-night threshold.[196]

In conclusion, the status of hosts operating in the STR sector remains unclear, especially regarding whether they function as professionals or private operators.[197] Thresholds can be instrumental in making this distinction by explicitly indicating when a host's activities become professional. One must agree with the EC's stance that the chosen threshold should not impede the provision of services within the STR platform

189. *Ibid.*
190. *Ibid.*
191. Pawlicz, (n. 63) 122–123.
192. European Commission, Directorate General for Internal Market, Industry, Entrepreneurship and SMEs, VVA, and Spark Legal Network (n. 48) 51–52.
193. Pawlicz, (n. 63) 122–123.
194. Peter Coles and others, 'Airbnb Usage Across New York City Neighborhoods: Geographic Patterns and Regulatory Implications' in Nestor M Davidson, Michèle Finck and John J Infranca (eds), *The Cambridge Handbook of the Law of the Sharing Economy* (Cambridge University Press 2018) 124–125.
195. European Commission, Directorate General for Internal Market, Industry, Entrepreneurship and SMEs, VVA, and Spark Legal Network (n. 48) 51–52.
196. Coles and others (n. 194) 124–125.
197. European Commission, Directorate General for Internal Market, Industry, Entrepreneurship and SMEs, VVA, and Spark Legal Network (n. 48) 12.

economy while allowing public authorities to apply policies that effectively protect the market in a proportionate manner.[198]

However, setting a threshold is not an easy task, as different EU countries, regions, and cities may have varying needs for regulating STRs. Therefore, it seems that it would be best to establish certain maximum criteria at the community level. For instance, by introducing a rule that defines a non-professional STR as one that lasts a maximum of X days per year and where the host earns a maximum of X income per year, provided they rent no more than a maximum of X properties. Each country, region, or city could, of course, set criteria that are more lenient than the maximum.

The main drawback of thresholds is the difficulty of monitoring cross-platform activity. Even when a single platform agrees to the monitoring and restriction of overnight stays at a specific property, a host using another platform could exceed the imposed limit. In such a case, the public authority should take responsibility for collecting information on overnight stays for a given property from multiple platforms and monitoring for exceeding the threshold. This requires the authority to use technically complex solutions (e.g., combining mandatory registration of hosts with a central database and a system in which platforms share information with public authorities),[199] which may prove costly. It is also worth noting that platforms choosing to cooperate with the authority and provide it with information on hosts' transactions will be at a potential disadvantage compared to those platforms that choose not to do so.[200] However, this risk, given the nature of the platform economy (the tendency for a few large platforms to form oligopolies in the market, benefiting from economies of scale), does not appear to be great. It is unlikely that users will abandon en masse the benefits afforded by the intermediation of well-known platforms and the security they guarantee in favour of smaller players in exchange for the promise of avoiding the reporting of their transaction data to public authorities.

Issues regarding the status of underlying suppliers are not limited to whether the host is acting as a professional or a private entity. If the underlying supplier is subject to the direction and control by the platform, it may also be considered an employee of the platform.[201]

Determining whether STR platforms should be considered hotel conglomerates, effectively 'employing' hosts around the world, is not easy. The answer to this question depends on the degree of control the platform exerts over the host and its transactions. It is widely agreed in the literature that platforms such as Airbnb currently do not 'employ' hosts because the degree of control they exercise is not sufficient.[202] However, as the business models of the STR platform economy evolve, this situation may one day

198. *Ibid.*, 51-52.
199. *Ibid.*
200. Coles and others (n. 194) 124-125.
201. In this context, attention should be drawn to the judgment of the British Supreme Court, which concluded that drivers employed by Uber are not its contractors but rather employees, entitling them to employment rights. *Uber BV and others v. Aslam and others* [2021] British Supreme Court UKSC 2019/0029.
202. Rashmi Dyal-Chand, 'Regulating Sharing: The Sharing Economy as an Alternative Capitalist System' (2015) 90 Tulane Law Review 297-301.

change. Platforms may seek to impose greater standardization of accommodation services provided through them and consequently limit the autonomy of hosts.[203] As it is challenging for small suppliers to operate with the same efficiency as professional hosts, they may begin to seek the security of a steady income, giving up their entrepreneurial independence and becoming employees, dependent on platforms.[204] Some authors argue that the status of hosts as sole proprietors is already a 'cover' for flexible wage labour. It is also pointed out that this type of work may be forced by rent increases (related to the development of the platform economy in cities) and is not an act of choice.[205]

Determining whether the underlying supplier is a professional, a private entity, or possibly an employee under the direction and control of the platform is extremely difficult, given the myriad possibilities for configuring transactions within the platform economy.[206] The EC is attempting to address this problem by proposing a directive to improve working conditions through platforms.[207] The purpose of this legislative proposal is to determine what kind of criteria should be decisive for a person to be considered a platform employee and to ensure that they are granted appropriate employment rights in the legal systems of EU Member States. On 11 March 2024, the Council confirmed an agreement on new rules aimed at enhancing the working conditions of platform workers.[208] The newly adopted directive introduces a rebuttable legal presumption that considers the relationship between a platform and a worker performing platform tasks as an employment relationship if certain control and direction factors are present. However, the platform can challenge this presumption by demonstrating that the contractual relationship is not one of employment. Member States will define the specifics of this presumption in their national laws, simplifying the process for platform workers to establish their employment status.

4.1.2.2 Underlying Buyers: Guests

Also involved in the platform economy, in addition to the platform and underlying suppliers, are those who use the goods or services offered to them (underlying buyers). It should be noted that some authors[209] use the term 'prosumer' also for these buyers, as they are producers of a valuable resource for the platform, such as data.

Within the STR sector of the platform economy, guests are mostly private individuals travelling for tourism. However, it should be noted that today, many of the guests using the intermediation of STR platforms are business travellers (business

203. Oskam (n. 69) 148–149.
204. *Ibid.*
205. *Ibid.*, 146–147.
206. Inglese (n. 33) 68.
207. Proposal for a directive of the European Parliament and of the Council on improving working conditions in platform work [COM/2021/762 final].
208. 'Platform Workers: Council Confirms Agreement on New Rules to Improve Their Working Conditions', https://www.consilium.europa.eu/en/press/press-releases/2024/03/11/platform-workers-council-confirms-agreement-on-new-rules-to-improve-their-working-conditions/ accessed 13 March 2024.
209. Sledziewska-Kołodziejska and Włoch (n. 74) 201.

customers). For example, in 2017, about 15% of all bookings on the Airbnb platform were made for business purposes.[210] The average length of stay for business travellers with Airbnb is 6.5 nights, three times longer than the average corporate traveller would stay in a hotel.[211]

4.1.3 Entities Partnering with STR Platforms

According to the OECD report,[212] meta-search engines play a significant role in the economy of STR platforms. These engines enable the comparison of prices and availability across different properties, redirecting customers to partner booking sites for finalizing transactions. Meta-search engines have been in existence since 2004, with the emergence of Kayak.com, followed shortly by Trivago (2005), Momondo (2006), and Skyscanner (2008).[213] It is noteworthy that initially, meta-search engines only provided users with information about potential transactions and directed them to the respective platform for completion. However, some contemporary meta-search engines allow direct bookings, earning commissions for these transactions.[214] The literature points out that such players blur the lines between platforms and traditional hotels and rental agencies.[215] Additionally, it is becoming more common for STR platforms to enable other platforms to offer their services (e.g., car reservations, insurance) on their sites to diversify their offerings.[216]

An integral part of the STR platforms' economy is occupied by the so-called super-listers, entities that manage bookings for individuals lacking the experience or time for such activities.[217] Super-listers professionally handle marketing, sales, and operational aspects of rentals for the hosts who engage them, optimizing rental prices and property occupancy in exchange for commissions.[218] Examples of super-listers include:[219] (i) host service providers offering specific services to property owners (e.g., bookings, key issuance, cleaning) for commissions and (ii) branded home managers providing full-service for owners of selected properties, often of higher standards (e.g., managers of buildings that have been specially built or converted for STRs).

---

210. Bakker, Hendrica and Twining-Ward (n. 50) 23.
211. Albert Boswijk, 'Transforming Business Value through Digitalized Networks: A Case Study on the Value Drivers of Airbnb' (2017) 3 Journal of Creating Value 104, 107–108 https://doi.org/10.1177/2394964317697736.
212. OECD, *The Impact of the Growth of the Sharing and Gig Economy on VAT/GST Policy and Administration* (n. 47) 101.
213. Pawlicz, (n. 63) 95–99.
214. *Ibid.*
215. Dyal-Chand (n. 202) 280.
216. OECD, *The Impact of the Growth of the Sharing and Gig Economy on VAT/GST Policy and Administration* (n. 47) 102–103.
217. Bakker, Hendrica and Twining-Ward (n. 50) 23.
218. Oskam (n. 69) 59–60.
219. Bakker, Hendrica and Twining-Ward (n. 50) 23.

Hosts using this type of intermediary often do not even know which platforms list their properties, receiving only rental fees less a management commission.[220] Super-listers may represent multiple owners by advertising their properties on one or more platforms. Because of this, the platforms do not always know the true identity of the host who rents properties through them.

In addition, as the OECD points out, there are also many other suppliers operating in the ecosystem of the STR platform economy acting on behalf of hosts or platforms, providing, for example, property management software, marketing solutions or developing websites or applications.

4.2 The Object Aspect

In the context of the object aspect of the STR platform economy, it is important to highlight the problem of the nature of the services provided by the platforms. A distinction should be made between the e-brokering service provided by the platforms and the underlying transactions, i.e., accommodation services provided by the hosts.

In practice, it is difficult to clearly decide the nature of STR platforms' services. It can be argued that the most popular platforms operating in this sector are not property owners and do not provide any direct accommodation services, and by matching supply and demand, they rather provide an electronic service.[221]

In this context, it is worth noting the CJEU ruling in the *Airbnb Ireland I*[222] case of 2019.[223] In that case, the Paris-based association of real estate agents argued that Airbnb was not only connecting two parties through its platform but also acting as a real estate agent without being properly licensed. Airbnb, however, claimed that the services it provided were not real estate brokering but fell into the category of information society services under the E-Commerce Directive, meeting the conditions of Directive 2015/1535.[224] The CJEU agreed with Airbnb in assessing that the platform's services cannot be considered merely ancillary to the general STR service. Indeed, the intermediation is in no way essential to the provision of STR services. Guests and hosts have many opportunities to make contact even without the platform's involvement, and Airbnb does not set or limit the amount of rental fees, offering only optional tools to estimate that price.

220. OECD, *The Impact of the Growth of the Sharing and Gig Economy on VAT/GST Policy and Administration* (n. 47) 102–103.
221. Ranchordás, Gedeon and Zurek (n. 126) 84–85.
222. Due to the recent rulings by the CJEU in several Airbnb-related cases, the case C-390/18 is referred to as *Airbnb Ireland I*, and the case C-674/20 is referred to as *Airbnb Ireland II*. Following this pattern, the case C-83/21 can be identified as *Airbnb Ireland III*. Vincent Delhomme and Augustine Chapuis-Doppler, 'Tax Legislation on Short-Term Rentals and Obligations of Intermediation Services Providers: Airbnb Ireland and Airbnb Payments UK' (2024) 61 Common Market Law Review https://doi.org/10.54648/cola2024007.
223. *Criminal proceedings against X, interveners: YA, Airbnb Ireland UC, Hôtelière Turenne SAS, Association pour un hébergement et un tourisme professionnels (AHTOP), Valhotel* [2019] CJEU C-390/18.
224. Directive (EU) 2015/1535 of the European Parliament and of the Council of 9 September 2015 laying down a procedure for the provision of information in the field of technical regulations and of rules on Information Society services [OJ L 241, 17.9.2015, pp. 1–15].

It is imperative to highlight that the CJEU arrived at a fundamentally divergent conclusion when scrutinizing the nature of the services furnished by the Uber platform. In its judgments in cases C-434/15[225] and C-320/16,[226] the Court determined that the intermediation services provided by Uber constitute an integral component of a comprehensive service, wherein the principal element is the provision of transportation services. In the Court's view, Uber's services are more than associative functions of putting a driver in contact with an individual via a digital application. Instead, the platform simultaneously organizes and offers urban transportation services. The Court emphasized the importance of a discernible degree of control exercised by Uber over the transactions (setting a maximum fare, the fact that the platform receives payment from the customer before paying part of it to the vehicle driver, checking the quality of vehicles, assessing the behaviour of drivers, which in certain circumstances can result in their exclusion from the platform).

The implications of the CJEU's rulings in the Uber cases are serious. They mean that the platform must comply with the rules of traditional taxi associations at a national level.[227] Furthermore, these judgments raise the question of whether the activities of the platforms can be separated from the material services on which they base their intermediation.[228]

The above CJEU rulings also raise the question of whether, in fact, the business models of Airbnb and Uber are so diametrically opposed that the service of one platform should be treated as an e-service and the other as a component of the underlying service.

The literature points out that Airbnb has functions comparable to Uber, namely price suggestions, tips for listing a flat, reputation systems, imposing cancellation fees or managing a complaints system.[229] At the same time, it is emphasized that the situation of hosts is different from that of Uber drivers, as their income is generated by available capital (real estate) and not by their labour.[230] In addition, compared to Airbnb, Uber appears to have more control over its users, as exemplified by the increased scrutiny that drivers must undergo to be accepted by the platform and the fact that it is the platform that sets the prices for rides.[231] It must be agreed that the factor that determines the nature of the platform service is the degree of control it

225. *Asociación Profesional Elite Taxi v. Uber Systems Spain, SL* [2017] CJEU C-434/15.
226. *Criminal proceedings against Uber France* [2018] CJEU C-320/16.
227. Antonio Aloisi, 'The Role of European Institutions in Promoting Decent Work in the "Collaborative Economy"' in Maurizio Bruglieri (ed.), *Multidisciplinary Design of Sharing Services* (Springer International Publishing 2018) 169–172.
228. Niamh Dunne, 'Competition Law (and Its Limits) in the Sharing Economy' in Nestor M Davidson, Michèle Finck and John J Infranca (eds), *The Cambridge Handbook of the Law of the Sharing Economy* (Cambridge University Press 2018) 94–95.
229. Inglese (n. 33) 128–129.
230. However, their earnings include a labour component, which can be divided into the following categories: initial setup efforts (preparing the apartment, setting up the platform account, and providing website details); ongoing sales activities (determining prices, managing reservations, and responding to clients); and variable activities per booking (welcoming guests and cleaning the apartment). Oskam (n. 69) 63–64.
231. Interian (n. 77) 151–154.

exercises over each transaction.[232] The more passive and automated the platform's role, the more the service it provides takes on the characteristics of an e-service.

It is worth noting, however, that if Airbnb's business model were to change (Airbnb begins to dictate, or is forced by legislation to begin to dictate, minimum terms and standards for rental properties), then the increased transactional influence of this platform could justify the view that it provides a hospitality service, just as Uber provides a transport service.

The discrepancy between the CJEU rulings in the Uber and Airbnb cases also raises certain concerns about the functioning and harmonization of the digital economy as a whole.[233] Some literature argues that such a piecemeal approach violates the principle of legal certainty within the platform economy, justifying the belief that no regulation is suitable to cover the sector in its entirety since its evaluation will depend on how platforms develop their own business models.[234] However, the mere fact that both transactions use a platform does not necessarily mean they require similar regulatory responses. As the literature points out, the accommodation sector faces issues such as compliance with zoning regulations, theft of property, and disruption of neighbourhood norms[235] – none of which apply to platforms that facilitate urban transit. Additionally, for decades, the accommodation and transportation sectors have had their own regulatory structures to address problems specific to them. Therefore, their counterparts in the platform economy also require differentiated regulatory responses. It is possible that developing a more uniform regulatory approach for the entire platform economy is impossible in practice.

5 EVALUATION

The relationship among the three main actors in the platform economy (platform, supplier, buyer) is considered a win-win-win situation.[236] Suppliers, often non-professionals, gain new profit opportunities and access to foreign markets when platforms operate internationally. Platforms facilitate transactions without full liability. Buyers can access goods and services they want faster, easier, and often cheaper.

Users and investors alike appreciate platforms' business models, leading to optimistic profit potential and high valuations, sometimes matching or exceeding those of much larger competitors. For instance, before the outbreak of the COVID-19 pandemic in early 2019, Airbnb was valued nearly as much (USD 31 billion) as the world's largest hotel chain, Marriott (USD 44 billion).[237]

232. Erwan Loquet and Dimitrios Karoutis, 'European Union – VAT Considerations on ECJ's Ruling That Airbnb Is Not a Real Estate Agent' (2020) 31 International VAT Monitor 1–5 https://doi.org/10.59403/17kmsv2.
233. Inglese (n. 33) 33–34.
234. *Ibid.*, 61–62.
235. Stephen R Miller, 'First Principles for Regulating the Sharing Economy' (2016) 53 Harvard Journal on Legislation 151–153 https://doi.org/10.2139/ssrn.2568016.
236. Inglese (n. 33) 19.
237. Jochen Wirtz and others, 'Platforms in the Peer-to-Peer Sharing Economy' (2019) 30 Journal of Service Management 453 https://doi.org/10.1108/josm-11-2018-0369.

The rapid growth of the platform economy significantly impacts the accommodation market, presenting both new opportunities and challenges. The growth of tourism and reduced entry barriers in the accommodation market are also considered opportunities. Additionally, the platform economy has contributed to making accommodations more affordable and accessible to a wider pool of customers, resulting in more and longer trips.[238]

Research conducted on behalf of the EC suggests that the STR platform economy contributes to the overall growth of tourism, although the impact varies across the cities researched.[239] STR platforms, while building the trust of their users, also encourage them to visit new places. This is particularly important for countries that are not popular tourist destinations (emerging markets).[240] Platforms enable the dispersal of tourists over a wider geographic area, attracting visitors to lesser-known areas, including rural areas,[241] complementing traditional accommodation facilities in areas where tourism services demand is lower and the supply of traditional accommodation is insufficient.[242] It is also worth noting that C2C residential rentals provide an opportunity to use existing homes instead of building new ones. This is important in naturally sensitive areas or areas with important cultural heritage.[243]

With platforms, individuals can offer rooms or entire houses as tourist accommodations directly to consumers without the need to create a website or handle payments directly.[244] Without platforms, the provision of accommodation such as single rooms by private individuals would be practically impossible (a significant marketing effort would be required to market their offering, which could not be offset by renting just one room), and thus their offer would remain outside the market.[245] The literature highlights that the almost seamless process of becoming a supplier on the platform is likely one of the main features attracting users. Without this competitive advantage, foundational to the success of the platform economy, its benefits could be lost.[246]

Despite the mentioned benefits, the expansion of the platform economy can also lead to various negative effects.

238. Orly Lobel, 'Coase and the Platform Economy' in Nestor M Davidson, Michèle Finck and John J Infranca (eds), *The Cambridge Handbook of the Law of the Sharing Economy* (Cambridge University Press 2018) 68.
239. European Commission, Directorate General for Internal Market, Industry, Entrepreneurship and SMEs, VVA, and Spark Legal Network (n. 48) 10–11.
240. Bakker, Hendrica and Twining-Ward (n. 50) 24–27.
241. According to the authors of a report commissioned by the EC and the World Bank, the platform economy contributes to the increase in the number of incoming tourists to peripheral areas of cities or rural regions: European Commission, Directorate General for Internal Market, Industry, Entrepreneurship and SMEs, VVA, and Spark Legal Network (n. 48) 10–11; Bakker, Hendrica and Twining-Ward (n. 50) 24–27.
242. European Commission, Directorate General for Internal Market, Industry, Entrepreneurship and SMEs, VVA, and Spark Legal Network (n. 48) 10–11.
243. Bakker, Hendrica and Twining-Ward (n. 50) 24–27.
244. *Ibid.*, 12.
245. Theurl and Meyer (n. 41) 195–196.
246. Ray Brescia, 'Finding the Right "Fit": Matching Regulations to the Shape of the Sharing Economy' in Nestor M Davidson, Michèle Finck and John J Infranca (eds), *The Cambridge Handbook of the Law of the Sharing Economy* (Cambridge University Press 2018) 166–167.

Platforms have a natural tendency to create monopolies.[247] Due to their rapid scalability, early players in a sector become strong market leaders.[248] New platforms entering the market lack the size necessary to become their potential competitor. This increases the risk of exploitation by the monopoly platform, e.g., by making it more difficult for new companies to enter the market.[249] Moreover, the transfer to another platform or to the traditional sector may be further hampered by investments that have been made by the user of a particular platform in the past. For example, the ratings that a member of a particular platform receives allow him or her to set higher prices only there. Such ratings are usually not transferable to a competing platform[250] or to a traditional business environment. The Digital Platform Economy Observatory report also points out that although most business users of platforms tend to use more than one platform to sell their goods and services (*multi-homing*), in practice, there are cases of platforms urging them to remain loyal to a single entity (*single-homing*).[251] In the hotel and tourism sector, for example, more than 15% of business users indicate that the platform they use makes it difficult to use other platforms.[252] This limits the growth opportunities for platforms just entering the market.

In this context, it is worth noting the conclusions of the Communication: Shaping Europe's Digital Future.[253] The paper acknowledges that some very large platforms are amassing such a huge amount of resources that they may threaten to limit the ability of subsequent innovators to successfully enter the market. There was support for EC work being carried out to ensure that markets - characterized by the presence of large platforms benefiting from significant network effects - remain fair and leave room for competition from new entrants.

The development of the platform economy may also have a negative impact on competition with traditional business models. In the context of the STR platform economy, it should be noted that the hospitality sector is subject to several specific rules,[254] which platforms are often not obliged to comply with, which can result in a lack of a level playing field and operating conditions.[255] Traditional suppliers may not be able to withstand this type of competition, with a consequent reduction in the availability of their services.[256] Traditional businesses are responding to these challenges in different ways. For example, business operators are modifying business models by specializing in segments where platforms are less competitive (e.g., offering

247. Sledziewska-Kołodziejska and Włoch (n. 74) 113–114.
248. Hossain (n. 21) 8.
249. *Ibid.*
250. Theurl and Meyer (n. 41) 195.
251. European Commission, Directorate General for Communications Networks, Content and Technology and others, *Study on 'Support to the Observatory for the Online Platform Economy': Final Report* (Publications Office 2021) 38–39.
252. 'Power over Users' (*Observatory on the Online Platform Economy*), https://platformobservatory.eu/state-of-play/power-over-users/ accessed 13 August 2021.
253. Council of the EU, 'Shaping Europe's Digital Future - Council Conclusions (9 June 2020), 8098/1/20'.
254. Pawlicz, (n. 63) 75.
255. Jeroen Oskam and Albert Boswijk, 'Airbnb: The Future of Networked Hospitality Businesses' (2016) 2 Journal of Tourism Futures 35–36 https://doi.org/10.1108/jtf-11-2015-0048.
256. Aloni (n. 43) 150–151.

professional services to business travellers), taking over the function of platforms (e.g., launching a booking application), or even setting up competing platforms.[257] Also of interest is the trend of merging platform economy companies with more traditional businesses, e.g., the acquisition of the Onefinestay platform by Accor Hotels.[258]

However, it should be noted that the study's results do not conclusively demonstrate the negative impact of the platform economy on the traditional hotel industry. On the one hand, it is pointed out that platforms have a negative impact on hotel performance,[259] long-term employment growth in the hotel industry,[260] that they are a viable alternative to some traditional types of accommodation (particularly mid- and lower-end hotels)[261] and that the industry should therefore view platform offerings as competitive.[262] But, on the other hand, platforms and hotels do not always offer exactly the same services. Evidence from some case studies suggests that C2C accommodation offers do not have a negative impact on traditional operators and do not discourage travellers from booking hotels, indicating that the two offers are complementary.[263] Perhaps the tourist maturity of destinations plays a role in this. In locations where tourism is still in a growth phase, platform offerings may be seen as complementary to the hotel sector. Conversely, in destinations with a more saturated tourism industry, they might be considered direct competitors.[264]

The development of STR platforms also raises concerns about the impact on the housing market.[265] According to the World Bank's assessment, C2C STRs may increase housing prices and rents[266] although this increase is also influenced by other factors.[267] The platform economy may also be contributing to a decline in the supply of long-term

257. Wirtz and others (n. 237) 465.
258. Mark Scott, 'AccorHotels of France Buys Onefinestay for $169 Million' *The New York Times* (5 April 2016), https://www.nytimes.com/2016/04/05/business/dealbook/accorhotels-of-france-buys-onefinestay-for-169-million.html#: ~ :text = April%205%2C%202016%20AccorHotels%2C%20one%20of%20Europe%E2%80%99s%20largest,company%2C%20for%20148%20million%20euros%2C%20or%20%24169%20million accessed 3 August 2021.
259. Dogru and others (n. 181) 2.
260. Bakker, Hendrica and Twining-Ward (n. 50) 29.
261. *Ibid.*; Georgios Zervas, Davide Proserpio and John W Byers, 'The Rise of the Sharing Economy: Estimating the Impact of Airbnb on the Hotel Industry' (2017) 54 Journal of Marketing Research 704 https://doi.org/10.1509/jmr.15.0204.
262. Karen L Xie and Linchi Kwok, 'The Effects of Airbnb's Price Positioning on Hotel Performance' (2017) 67 International Journal of Hospitality Management 182 https://doi.org/10.1016/j.ijhm.2017.08.011.
263. European Commission, Directorate General for Internal Market, Industry, Entrepreneurship and SMEs, VVA, and Spark Legal Network (n. 48) 41–43.
264. Shirley Nieuwland and Rianne van Melik, 'Regulating Airbnb: How Cities Deal with Perceived Negative Externalities of Short-Term Rentals' (2020) 23 Current Issues in Tourism 822–823 https://doi.org/10.1080/13683500.2018.1504899.
265. Nestor M Davidson and John J Infranca, 'The Place of the Sharing Economy' in Nestor M Davidson, Michèle Finck and John J Infranca (eds), *The Cambridge Handbook of the Law of the Sharing Economy* (Cambridge University Press 2018) 208–209.
266. Bakker, Hendrica and Twining-Ward (n. 50) 28–29.
267. European Commission, Directorate General for Internal Market, Industry, Entrepreneurship and SMEs, VVA, and Spark Legal Network (n. 48) 44–45.

rental housing. As indicated in the literature, in general, the provision of accommodation is more cost-effective than entering into traditional long-term contracts.[268] As a result, property owners may be encouraged to move out of the long-term rental market and into the more profitable STR market. The research commissioned by the EC in this regard is inconclusive. One study points out that the growth of the platform economy is contributing to a shortage of housing in the long-term rental market, with less housing available to local residents and higher prices. This is particularly evident in popular tourist destinations such as Paris and Barcelona.[269] However, another study suggests that there is no clear evidence that the growth of the STR platform economy affects the availability of housing for long-term rental. Local stakeholders tend to link these two factors, but it is not possible to establish such a correlation.[270]

The STR platform economy has also been criticized for contributing to the phenomenon called overtourism which in plain words means overcrowding of popular tourist destinations.[271] To date, the problem has been addressed by limiting the number of permits for STR services, but the increase in C2C accommodation via platforms has stripped the authorities of this control mechanism.[272]

As a result, the STR platform economy has become the subject of considerable attention in the regulatory area.

There was a need to clarify whether and how current law applies to transactions within the platform economy and to develop appropriate regulatory policies. It should be noted that the business models of the STR platform economy are not compatible with traditional accommodation regulations, and most EU Member States do not have specifically designed regulations for them.[273] However, it appears that the current law - supplemented by traditional rules of interpretation and developments in case law - does not cease to have effect simply because new technologies were not foreseen by their authors.[274] Also, in the EC Agenda, it was pointed out that platforms are already subject to existing EU legislation, but new business models pose problems in applying the existing legal framework in a uniform manner.

Thus, just as important as clarifying how current law applies to platform economy transactions is the development of additional solutions dedicated to the platform economy. This is not an easy task.

The difficulty may be the potentially expansive geographical market in which platforms operate. The nature of their business is largely borderless.[275] Platforms often

268. Leopoldo Sdino and Sara Magoni, 'The Sharing Economy and Real Estate Market: The Phenomenon of Shared Houses' in Adriano Bisello and others (eds), *Smart and Sustainable Planning for Cities and Regions* (Springer International Publishing 2018) 247–249.
269. European Commission, Directorate General for Taxation and Customs Union and others (n. 6) 147–150.
270. European Commission, Directorate General for Internal Market, Industry, Entrepreneurship and SMEs, VVA, and Spark Legal Network (n. 48) 10–11.
271. Bakker, Hendrica and Twining-Ward (n. 50) 31.
272. *Ibid.*, 12.
273. European Commission, Directorate General for Internal Market, Industry, Entrepreneurship and SMEs, VVA, and Spark Legal Network (n. 48) 16–17.
274. Brescia (n. 246) 159–160.
275. However, platforms often take regional differences into account. Dunne (n. 228) 93.

do not have a physical presence in the jurisdiction where the transactions they facilitate are carried out[276] (e.g., a platform based in one country facilitates the rental of a house located in another country), with the result that regulatory issues often require operating across jurisdictions.

It is also important to share the view presented in the literature that the challenge of regulating the platform economy is its scale.[277] Because of its dichotomy,[278] on one end of the spectrum, there exist massive platforms like Airbnb, while, on the other end, the individual transactions they facilitate are often small in scale. Although small-scale activities are typically subject to more lenient regulations, their potential cumulative impact transcends their individual nature, collectively giving rise to a myriad of negative consequences. Traditional models used to delineate between activities requiring strict regulation and those considered exempt from such treatment due to their private nature may prove inadequate when confronted with the platform economy.[279] Existing regulatory regimes inadequately capture the scale configurations inherent in the platform economy, where the cumulative effects of individual, small-scale actions can culminate in global issues.

In the context of potential regulations, three main strategies for action can be identified: inaction, prohibition or restriction of platforms' activities, and legislative changes (amendment of existing legislation or introduction of new legislation).

The former approach may result from a conscious decision to allow the development of STR services facilitated by platforms or involuntary inaction, for example, due to political inertia.[280] This strategy may result in unequal treatment between traditional suppliers and new players, inviting criticism.[281]

The latter approach is to ban or restrict STR platforms. According to the literature, some groups affected by the development of the platform economy can exert disproportionate pressure on the relevant regulators to push them to pursue their interests.[282] In this context, it is worth noting that initially traditional hotel companies had legal battles with STR platforms,[283] and regulators often imposed restrictions on their activities.[284] For example, in 2016, 47 platforms in an open letter asked the EU institutions to intervene, indicating that many national and local governments were

276. OECD, *The Impact of the Growth of the Sharing and Gig Economy on VAT/GST Policy and Administration* (n. 47) 22.
277. Kellen Zale, 'When Everything Is Small: The Regulatory Challenge of Scale in the Sharing Economy' (2016) 53 San Diego Law Review 1016 https://doi.org/10.1017/9781108255882.004.
278. Zale (n. 49) 38.
279. *Ibid.*, 43.
280. Oskam (n. 69) 96–99.
281. Pawlicz, (n. 63) 118.
282. Gabriel Doménech-Pascual, 'Sharing Economy and Regulatory Strategies Towards Legal Change' (2016) 7 European Journal of Risk Regulation 720–721 https://doi.org/10.1017/s1867299x0001014x.
283. Oskam (n. 69) 70–71.
284. Koen Frenken and Juliet Schor, 'Putting the Sharing Economy into Perspective' (2017) 23 Environmental Innovation and Societal Transitions 8–9 https://doi.org/10.1016/j.eist.2017.01.003.

trying to restrict their service provision.[285] Rarely, but there have also been decisions to completely ban STR of housing in cities through platforms (e.g., in New York or San Francisco).[286]

The strategy of restricting or banning platforms is not considered very effective. As the literature points out, where authorities have been persuaded to impose stricter rules, difficulties in controlling them and new consumer habits have often caused enforcement problems.[287]

For this reason, a more moderate approach of introducing new regulations that respond to the specifics of the STR platform economy should be adopted.[288] This strategy might involve revising existing regulations or implementing entirely new solutions. It is important to acknowledge the perspective that the challenges in the platform economy do not necessarily call for the rejection of existing rules.[289] Instead, in areas where the economy has evolved significantly, these rules should be redrafted to achieve the same goals as the traditional economy. This approach ensures that the interests of various market actors, both traditional and digital, are duly considered.

According to the World Bank, the introduction of new regulations for the STR platform economy should be done in three steps: the first to assess the scale of the problem, the second to intervene, and the third to provide additional support.[290]

Step one requires the development of independent information systems to provide correct data on the STR sector of the platform economy so as not to rely solely on studies produced by platforms or hotel companies.[291] The analysis carried out should be aggregate, considering technology-induced changes in the STR sector as a whole (working only with the dominant players in the market may be useful, but the entire legislative strategy should not be based on it).[292] When considering a legislative response, the legislator must first understand what segment of the market is subject to disruption. In this context, it is worth noting the initiative of Eurostat's agreement with Airbnb, Booking.com, Expedia and Tripadvisor, whereby these platforms made available data on rental properties in EU and EFTA countries.[293]

Step two is regulatory intervention, carried out according to specific standards. The level of intervention required depends on several factors, such as the importance of the accommodation sector to the overall economy.[294] New regulations should be non-discriminatory, necessary and proportionate.[295] In this context, it is worth noting

285. 'Uber and AirBnB Call on EU to Support "Collaborative Economy"' (*the Guardian*, 11 February 2016), http://www.theguardian.com/technology/2016/feb/11/uber-airbnb-eu-support-collaborative-economy accessed 31 August 2021.
286. Oskam (n. 69) 96–99.
287. *Ibid.*, 70–71.
288. Pawlicz, (n. 63) 118.
289. Miller (n. 235) 153–154.
290. Bakker, Hendrica and Twining-Ward (n. 50) 42–45.
291. *Ibid.*, 42–25.
292. Miller (n. 235) 151–153.
293. 'Airbnb, Booking, Expedia and Tripadvisor to Share Data with Eurostat', https://ec.europa.eu/eurostat/web/products-eurostat-news/-/cn-20200305-1 accessed 13 March 2024.
294. Bakker, Hendrica and Twining-Ward (n. 50) 42–45.
295. European Commission, Directorate General for Internal Market, Industry, Entrepreneurship and SMEs, VVA, and Spark Legal Network (n. 48) 11–13.

the CJEU ruling in the *Cali Apartments* case of 2020.[296] The case concerned the permissibility of French solutions whereby, in some municipalities, a permit is needed to change the function of a dwelling on pain of financial penalties. The Court found this type of regulation to be: (i) justified by an overriding reason relating to the public interest consisting in combating the rental housing shortage and (ii) proportionate to the objective pursued, which cannot be achieved by less restrictive measures. It can therefore be concluded that the right of the state to create housing policy is no less important than the general principle of establishing the freedom to pursue economic activity. Nevertheless, it is also worth mentioning that the CJEU's ruling is being criticized because it deals a very serious blow to the activities of STR platforms by allowing local authorities to impose extremely restrictive measures on hosts wishing to make use of spare housing capacity.[297]

Step three is to further support the economy of STR platforms by issuing subsequent guidance on the application of the relevant legislation, including the rights and obligations of all actors involved.[298]

When new regulations are introduced, the main challenge is their subsequent enforcement.[299] As suggested in the literature, one of the solutions to ensure the effectiveness of implementing new rules is cooperation with platforms.[300] This might involve entering into agreements where platforms voluntarily block a property after being informed by the competent authority that the maximum number of days allowed by law for STR of that facility has been reached.[301] However, there is uncertainty about whether authorities can consistently rely on platforms, particularly if enforcement actions conflict with their commercial interests. A platform strictly enforcing the rules may be at a disadvantage compared to competing platforms that apply the regulations less rigorously.[302]

In summary, it is difficult to develop adequate solutions for the STR platform economy. On the one hand, the introduction of restrictive regulations may discourage innovation. It should be noted that there are relatively few world-leading transactional and globally competitive technology companies in the EU.[303] Europe lags behind North America and Asia in terms of platform penetration. In 2015, 82 platform companies

296. *Cali Apartments SCI and HX v. Procureur général près la cour d'appel de Paris and Ville de Paris* [2020] CJEU C-724/18.
297. Vassilis Hatzopoulos, 'Disarming Airbnb – Dismantling the Services Directive? Cali Apartments' (2021) 58 Common Market Law Review 917 https://doi.org/10.54648/cola2021054.
298. European Commission, Directorate General for Internal Market, Industry, Entrepreneurship and SMEs, VVA, and Spark Legal Network (n. 48) 36.
299. For instance, in Paris, the enforcement capabilities of regulations are limited. In 2018, 118 unregistered owners received fines totalling almost EUR 2 million; however, it is highly likely that the number of non-compliant individuals is higher. Furthermore, monitoring the 120-night limit is challenging (e.g., the limit can be bypassed through direct contact with potential tenants and/or multiple registrations under different names on various platforms). European Commission and Joint Research Centre, *Who Owns the City? Exploratory Research Activity on the Financialisation of Housing in EU Cities* (Publications Office 2020) 52.
300. Bakker, Hendrica and Twining-Ward (n. 50) 42–45.
301. European Commission, Directorate General for Internal Market, Industry, Entrepreneurship and SMEs, VVA, and Spark Legal Network (n. 48) 52–53.
302. Frenken and others (n. 120) 415–416.
303. Hallward-Driemeier and others (n. 116) 6.

were from Asia, 64 from North America and only 27 from Europe.[304] In 2018, there were only 51 EU transaction facilitation platforms operating in more than one country (10 in the accommodation sector) – less than 1 % of all transaction platforms.[305] Almost 40% of revenues within the EU platform economy are generated by platforms originating outside the EU (i.e., dominant market players such as Airbnb).[306] There is therefore a concern that the EU will be left behind and less able to reap the benefits of these developments.[307]

On the other hand, the introduction of very liberal rules or the lack of them can contribute to problems in the hotel industry, housing or overtourism.

However, it seems that it is primarily the lack of legal clarity that hinders economic growth in the STR sector of the platform economy. The EC's initiative to adopt new legislation in this area should therefore be welcomed.[308] In response to these expectations, in 2022, the EC prepared a proposal for a regulation on data collection and sharing relating to STR services.[309] This regulation aims to promote a transparent and responsible platform economy in the EU while protecting consumers from fraudulent STR offers. The new proposal mandates simplified registration procedures and data sharing for STR platforms. It emphasizes the need for reliable host information and visible registration numbers on listings to enhance traveller safety. Additionally, EU Member States are obliged to establish a centralized digital entry point for platforms to submit monthly data, aiding authorities in monitoring compliance and implementing effective policies in the STR sector. On 29 February 2024, the EU Parliament adopted this proposal,[310] which representatives of the European Cities Alliance on Short-Term Holiday Rentals welcomed.[311]

304. Peter Evans and Annabelle Gawer, *The Rise of the Platform Enterprise: A Global Survey* (The Center for Global Enterprise 2016) 10.
305. European Commission, Directorate General for Internal Market, Industry, Entrepreneurship and SMEs and others (n. 97) 31.
306. European Commission, Directorate General for Internal Market, Industry, Entrepreneurship and SMEs. and others, *Study to Monitor the Economic Development of the Collaborative Economy at Sector Level in the 28 EU Member States: Final Report* (Publications Office 2018) 162, https://data.europa.eu/doi/10.2873/83555 accessed 26 August 2021.
307. The risk was already pointed out in 2016. Goudin (n. 39) 6.
308. 'Tourist Services - Short-Term Rental Initiative' (*Tourist services – short-term rental initiative*, 14 October 2021), https://ec.europa.eu/info/law/better-regulation/have-your-say/initiatives/13108-Tourist-services-short-term-rental-initiative_en accessed 13 March 2024.
309. Proposal for a regulation of the European Parliament and of the Council on data collection and sharing relating to short-term accommodation rental services and amending Regulation (EU) 2018/1724 [COM(2022) 571 final].
310. Jasmina Yakimowa, 'New Rules for a Responsible and Transparent Short-Term Rental Sector | Aktuelles | Europäisches Parlament' (29 February 2024), https://www.europarl.europa.eu/news/de/press-room/20240223IPR18094/new-rules-for-a-responsible-and-transparent-short-term-rental-sector accessed 4 March 2024.
311. Femke Halsema, 'New EU Rules to Stop Illegal Short-Term Rentals are a Welcome Change' (*euronews*, 1 March 2024), https://www.euronews.com/my-europe/2024/03/01/new-eu-rules-to-stop-illegal-short-term-rentals-are-a-welcome-change accessed 2 March 2024.

6 SUMMARY

Over the past few years, the platform economy has evolved from a community practice based largely on sharing unused private resources into profitable business models as participants have become more professionalized. Consequently, a more fitting term for this trend is the platform economy rather than the sharing economy.

Transactions in the platform economy involve two primary categories of actors: platforms and their users, underlying suppliers and underlying buyers. In the case of the STR sector, these users will be hosts and guests, respectively. The platform economy also creates additional opportunities to operate for other entities such as payment operators and property managers.

It should be noted that despite the key role platforms play in transactions, defining what they actually are is not easy. It is also not entirely clear why the EU lawmakers sometimes use the term 'platform' and sometimes the term 'online interface' or 'electronic interface'. However, one has to agree with the conclusion that the dynamic nature of technological progress makes it difficult to establish a universal or permanent definition for platforms.

Much ambiguity surrounds the status of the underlying suppliers (hosts) in terms of whether and when they can be considered private entities, businesses or platform employees. A distinguishing feature of the platform economy is the active role of hosts, who, thanks to the infrastructure provided by the platform, can transact with relative ease, and their activities take on a regular and for-profit character. This is important because for-profit hosts are beginning to compete with traditional hospitality operators, with the advantage that they are not subject to the same requirements as professionals. Although platforms generally treat underlying suppliers as independent contractors, the level of control they exercise over a transaction may justify the view that these suppliers are employees of the platform.

Because of this ambiguity, legislative changes have been called for, such as the introduction of specific thresholds that would unambiguously establish the status of hosts. The problem remains the ability to monitor them.

Many business models can be distinguished within the STR platform economy. The problem of the nature of platform services, in particular, distinguishing whether they are electronic services or accommodation services, is questionable. Currently, the factor that determines this is the degree of control the platform has over each transaction. The more passive and automated the platform's role, the more the service it provides takes on the characteristics of an e-service.

The rapid development of the STR platform economy presents both opportunities and challenges. First and foremost, the growth of tourism, the lowering of barriers for hosts to enter the STR market, or cheaper and more accessible accommodations for guests should be considered opportunities.

At the same time, this growth raises several concerns. These can include, first and foremost, the problem of the emergence of monopolies in the platform economy or the adverse impact of the STR sector on the hotel industry, the housing market and overtourism.

For this reason, the STR platform economy has become the subject of considerable attention in the regulatory area. There has been a need to clarify how current law applies to platform economy transactions and to develop appropriate legislative policies. In this context, three main strategies for action can be distinguished: inaction, banning or restricting platform activities, and making legislative changes. Given that overly restrictive regulations can discourage innovation and their absence can distort competition in the STR market, the third approach seems to make the most sense, provided it remains consistent with the principle of proportionality.

CHAPTER 2

VAT Treatment of STR Platforms

1 BACKGROUND

One of the main issues related to the platform economy is that of its proper taxation. The 2016 EC Agenda already pointed out the importance of this issue: 'Like all economic operators, those in the collaborative economy are also subject to taxation rules. These include personal income, corporate income and value added tax rules. However, issues have emerged in relation to tax compliance and enforcement: difficulties in identifying the taxpayers and the taxable income, lack of information on service providers, aggressive corporate tax planning exacerbated in the digital sector, differences in tax practices across the EU and insufficient exchange of information.'[312]

These observations are also relevant to the STR sector of the platform economy. The report commissioned by the EC points out that, as STRs provided through platforms are a relatively new phenomenon, most Member States do not have any specific tax rules for this activity.[313] However, this situation is rapidly developing and changing, leading to an increasingly fragmented and diverse EU legal framework for the STR platform economy.

It is worth noting that the EC has taken numerous legislative initiatives in recent years to regulate also the taxation of the platform economy. These issues have become the subject of intense discussion in the context of possible changes related to direct taxation[314] and VAT taxation.

312. European Commission, 'A European Agenda for the Collaborative Economy, COM(2016) 356 Final' (n. 36).
313. European Commission, Directorate General for Internal Market, Industry, Entrepreneurship and SMEs, VVA, and Spark Legal Network (n. 48) 53-55.
314. For example, in 2018, the EC proposed the adoption of two legal acts: Proposal for a Council directive laying down rules relating to the corporate taxation of a significant digital presence [COM/2018/0147 final]; Proposal for a Council directive on the common system of a digital services tax on revenues resulting from the provision of certain digital services [COM/2018/0148 final].

From a VAT perspective, the development of the platform economy poses a particular challenge. The OECD has pointed out that this development may create regulatory pressures related to VAT treatment, particularly in the accommodation and transport sectors, which together represent around 90% of the total market value of the platform economy worldwide and are expected to have high growth rates in the coming years.[315] In the EU alone, the largest share of VAT receipts – around EUR 3.6 billion in 2019 – came from the STR sector.[316] The VAT treatment of the EU STR platform economy therefore requires special attention.

The second chapter will outline the most significant problems faced by the STR platform economy under the EU VAT system. These problems primarily revolve around the tax status of entities involved in providing services through platforms and the nature of platform services. Additionally, the chapter will explore possibilities for the involvement of accommodation sector platforms in the VAT accounting process, without however discussing their full liability for VAT collection (the deemed supplier regime), as this role of platforms will be presented in detail in the third chapter which specifically addresses the models of the deemed supplier regime dedicated to platforms under the EU VAT system. However, there is already some uncertainty regarding whether platforms in the accommodation sector can be classified as so-called undisclosed agents under Article 28 of the VAT Directive, as this classification might require these platforms to collect VAT on the transactions they intermediate. As a result of that, platforms would have a liability similar to that envisaged under the deemed supplier regime. This issue will also be thoroughly analysed in this chapter.

2 THE EU VAT SYSTEM

VAT plays a key role in the functioning of the internal market and is one of the main sources of revenue for EU Member States.[317] Since its introduction, VAT has become an integral element of the EU tax system. Many VAT systems around the world are also based on the European model (nearly 170 countries use this form of VAT).[318]

The history of turnover tax harmonization in the EU dates back to 1967, when the Member States of the then European Economic Community decided to implement a common turnover tax system in the form of VAT.[319] The First,[320] Second[321] and then

315. OECD, *The Impact of the Growth of the Sharing and Gig Economy on VAT/GST Policy and Administration* (n. 47) 14–15.
316. European Commission, Directorate General for Taxation and Customs Union and others (n. 6) 54.
317. Ad van Doesum and others, *Fundamentals of EU VAT Law* (Second edition, Kluwer Law International BV 2020) 3.
318. Robert F van Brederode, 'Introduction: VAT Does Well, but Does It Do Well Enough?', *Virtues and Fallacies of VAT* (Wolters Kluwer Law International 2021) 1–3.
319. Doesum and others (n. 317) 3.
320. First Council Directive 67/227/EEC of 11 April 1967 on the harmonisation of legislation of Member States concerning turnover taxes [OJ 71, 14.4.1967, pp. 1301–1303].
321. Second Council Directive 67/228/EEC of 11 April 1967 on the harmonisation of legislation of Member States concerning turnover taxes – Structure and procedures for application of the common system of value added tax [OJ 71, 14.4.1967, pp. 1303–1312].

Sixth[322] VAT Directives were adopted. The Sixth VAT Directive was amended several times, with the result that it became increasingly unclear, leading to the decision to recast it as Directive 2006/112/EC, commonly referred to as the VAT Directive.[323] This directive entered into force on 1 January 2007, becoming the main piece of VAT legislation in the EU. Although the existing rules were amended and reordered, the recast VAT Directive contained few fundamental changes. This means that CJEU judgments that refer to articles of the Sixth VAT Directive generally remain relevant for the interpretation of the corresponding articles of the current Directive.[324] The Regulation laying down implementing measures for the VAT Directive (Implementing Regulation 282/2011, hereinafter 'IR') is also an important piece of legislation regulating VAT taxation in the EU.[325] According to the recitals of this legislation, the common implementing rules deal with certain issues related to the application of the VAT Directive and are designed to ensure uniform treatment throughout the Union only for these specific cases. Their scope of application should therefore be interpreted restrictively.

VAT is now harmonized across the EU. This harmonization is essential for the functioning of the single market which entails the free movement of goods, services, persons, and capital between Member States.[326] However, under Article 395 of the VAT Directive, Member States may be authorized to introduce special measures for derogation from the provisions of this directive, simplify the procedure for collecting VAT or prevent certain forms of tax evasion or tax avoidance. To adopt such special rules, a Member State must submit an appropriate request to the EC and secure the consent of other Member States.[327]

Key features of EU VAT law include: (i) it is a general consumption tax, (ii) it is proportional to the price of goods and services, (iii) it is levied at all stages of the production and distribution process up to and including the retail stage, (iv) taxable persons have the right to a deduction.[328]

As literature indicates, levying consumption tax at all stages of the supply chain could result in the same good or service being taxed multiple times, depending on the chain's length.[329]

This issue is mitigated by allowing taxable persons to deduct VAT[330] and by applying the tax rate to each supply.[331] Ultimately, VAT is borne by the final consumer

322. Sixth Council Directive 77/388/EEC of 17 May 1977 on the harmonization of the laws of the Member States relating to turnover taxes – Common system of value added tax: uniform basis of assessment [OJ L 145, 13.6.1977, pp. 1-40].
323. Doesum and others (n. 317) 17-18.
324. *Ibid.*
325. Council Implementing Regulation (EU) No 282/2011 of 15 March 2011 laying down implementing measures for Directive 2006/112/EC on the common system of value added tax [OJ L 77, 23.3.2011, pp. 1-22].
326. Jasmin Kollmann, *Taxable Supplies and Their Consideration in European VAT: With Selected Examples of the Digital Economy* (IBFD 2019) 13-17.
327. Doesum and others (n. 317) 19.
328. *Ibid.*, 36.
329. *Ibid.*, 38.
330. From the VAT that the taxable person is liable to pay can be deducted the VAT that is charged to him by other taxpayers. If the input VAT exceeds the amount of output VAT, the taxable

who cannot pass on the amount of tax to himself, ensuring that businesses remain neutral to the tax and private consumption is taxed only once.[332]

EU VAT is applicable when the person carrying out a certain transaction is a 'taxable person'. Article 9 of the VAT Directive defines a 'taxable person' as any person who, independently, carries out in any place any economic activity, whatever the purpose or results of that activity. However, the VAT Directive outlines a special procedure for small enterprises, permitting Member States to grant VAT exemptions to taxable persons whose annual turnover falls below a specific threshold (Articles 281–294 of the VAT Directive). The rationale for the exemption for small enterprises is that the administrative costs of compliance of such taxable persons are high in relation to the potential benefits.[333] As a result, small businesses are regarded as non-taxable or non-registered entities. As rightly emphasized in doctrine, the term 'registration threshold' does not necessarily mean that businesses whose turnover remains below the threshold do not have to be registered in some form. For example, small businesses must be registered under a special procedure in Belgium, France, Greece, and Malta.[334]

Transactions subject to VAT typically involve the supply of goods or services for consideration within the territory of an EU Member State. The VAT Directive contains a list of transactions that can be regarded as a supply of goods (Articles 14–19 of the VAT Directive), while 'services' are all supplies that do not constitute a supply of goods (Article 24 of the VAT Directive). In addition to these transactions, the Directive identifies two more taxable events: (i) intra-Community acquisition of goods (Articles 20–23 of the VAT Directive) and (ii) importation of goods from third countries (Article 30 of the VAT Directive). Generally, transactions deemed to take place within a single Member State (domestic transactions) are subject to the VAT rules of that Member State. In the case of cross-border transactions, the place of taxation for VAT purposes needs to be determined based on the criteria outlined in the VAT Directive.[335]

A crucial source for interpreting EU VAT law is the case law of the CJEU which holds a monopoly on deciding questions of interpretation of the VAT Directive. When national courts of the Member States have doubts about the interpretation of the

person is entitled to reclaim this surplus from the tax authorities (the Member States may, however, carry forward the excess to the following period). Not all supplies give rise to a deduction of input VAT. If the taxpayer uses goods and services for both taxed and non-taxed supplies, he must calculate his deductible proportion. *Ibid.*, 55.

331. Member States must apply a standard rate of VAT, which is fixed by each Member State as a percentage of the taxable amount and which is the same for the supply of goods and for the supply of services. Member States may apply either one or two reduced rates. *Ibid.*

332. *Ibid.*, 38.

333. Liam Ebril, Michael Keen and Victoria Perry, *The Modern VAT* (International Monetary Fund 2001) 90; it is also pointed out that the primary purpose of a registration threshold is to reduce administrative and compliance costs; study after study shows that the administrative costs incurred by tax authorities to apply the VAT to small businesses and the compliance costs incurred by small businesses are disproportionate to the revenue that these enterprises generate: Yige Zu, 'VAT/GST Thresholds and Small Businesses: Where To Draw the Line?' (2018) 66 Canadian Tax Journal 311.

334. Fabiola Annacondia, 'VAT Registration Thresholds in Europe' (2023) 34 International VAT Monitor 251 https://doi.org/10.59403/9cwepp.

335. Doesum and others (n. 317) 50.

provisions of the VAT Directive, they can turn to the CJEU for guidance on the correct interpretation.[336] This solution ensures that VAT issues are clarified in a harmonized manner across the EU.

In this context, the EC's explanatory notes and the VAT Committee's guidelines should also be noted. The explanatory notes provide informal guidance on the application of VAT, and their purpose is to provide a better understanding of EU legislation. The VAT Committee[337] also provides guidance on the application of VAT-related legislation by adopting guidelines after examining issues raised by the EC or a Member State. Although not legally binding, both explanatory notes and guidelines serve as valuable resources for interpreting VAT law.

Regarding legislative matters, OECD VAT reports serve as valuable sources of information. While lacking binding force, these reports seem to form a solid basis for EU legislative work in the area of platform economy since a coordinated approach based on international consensus is very important in this respect.[338] Their success is a demonstration of political unity on platform economy issues.[339]

3 CHALLENGES RELATED TO THE VAT TREATMENT OF THE STR PLATFORM ECONOMY

The VAT treatment of STR platforms presents considerable ambiguity, leading to divergent approaches by the tax administrations of Member States.[340] This legal uncertainty is rooted in the fact that the European VAT system was designed for the traditional economy, and only partial reforms have been implemented since its introduction to address the legal uncertainties arising from the rapid evolution of the digital economy.[341]

As highlighted in the literature, the most prominent challenges faced by the STR platform economy within the EU VAT system primarily revolve around the status of entities engaged in providing services through platforms and the nature of these platform services.[342]

---

336. Kollmann (n. 326) 13–17.
337. The VAT Committee was set up under Article 398 of the VAT Directive to promote the uniform application of the provisions of the VAT Directive. Because it is an advisory committee only and has not been attributed any legislative powers, the VAT Committee cannot take legally binding decisions. It can however give some guidance on the application of the Directive. 'VAT Committee – European Commission', https://taxation-customs.ec.europa.eu/vat-committee_en accessed 15 March 2024.
338. European Commission, 'VAT Expert Group No 095: VAT Treatment of the Sharing Economy, Taxud.c.1(2020)5816454'.
339. Christina Pollak, *Platforms in EU VAT Law: A Legal Analysis of the Supply of Goods* (Kluwer Law International, BV 2022) 116.
340. Loquet and Karoutis (n. 232) 221.
341. Fabiola Annacondia, 'Cross-Border B2C Digital Services: A New Way to Collect VAT?' (2018) 29 International VAT Monitor 177 https://doi.org/10.59403/3hx6et2; Pollak (n. 339) 313–314.
342. For example: Giorgio Beretta, 'VAT and the Sharing Economy' (2018) 10 World Tax Journal https://doi.org/10.59403/1ptvcv0; Fernando Matesanz, 'VAT Treatment of the Sharing Economy' (2021) 32 International VAT Monitor https://doi.org/10.59403/37eh3fd; Marcos Álvarez Suso, 'E-Platforms Providing Services in the Short-Term Rental Accommodation

3.1 Hosts as VAT Taxable Persons

As mentioned in the first chapter, determining the status of underlying suppliers (hosts) as professionals, private entities, or potentially employees under the direction and control of the platform poses significant challenges. These difficulties are also problematic on EU VAT grounds. A particularly contentious issue is the assessment of whether underlying suppliers, operating through platforms, qualify as VAT taxable persons.[343]

According to Article 2(1)(a) and (c) of the VAT Directive, the supply of goods or services for consideration within the territory of a Member State by a taxable person acting as such is subject to VAT. Article 9 of the VAT Directive defines a 'taxable person' as any person who, independently, carries out in any place any economic activity, whatever the purpose or results of that activity. 'Economic activity' encompasses activities of producers, traders or persons supplying services, including mining and agricultural activities and activities of the professions or recognized as such. Notably, the exploitation of tangible or intangible property for the purposes of obtaining income therefrom on a continuing basis is considered an economic activity.

As indicated in the literature, of the elements outlined in Article 9 of the VAT Directive, two in particular deserve closer attention in the context of the platform economy. The first element is the assessment of whether the activity conducted by the individual supplier can genuinely be considered an 'economic activity'. The second element is whether the activity is carried out independently by that entity.[344]

According to some legal scholars, the mere fact that a person decides to join a platform to offer goods or services to other users in exchange, in principle, for monetary consideration implies a certain intention to generate income on a continuing basis, which leads to the conclusion that it is an economic activity.[345] A similar perspective is endorsed by the EC which notes that while the continuity of the activity of each host receiving consideration from a traveller for renting accommodation must be assessed individually, joining a platform may suggest an intention of the host to

Market: The Challenges for Taxation of These Services under the EU VAT' (2020) 31 International VAT Monitor https://doi.org/10.59403/1wpx3e1.

343. Carrie Brandon Elliot, 'Taxation of the Sharing Economy: Recurring Issues' (2018) 72 Bulletin for International Taxation, ibfd.org accessed 22 November 2022 https://doi.org/10.59403/2qs2nh; Christina Maria Pollak, *How Should Peer-to-Peer Housing and Transportation Services Provided via Sharing Economy Platforms Be Treated under the VAT Directive?* (Lund University 2018).

344. Giorgio Beretta, *European VAT and the Sharing Economy* (Kluwer Law International, BV 2019) 75–78.

345. Becoming part of a platform signifies a commitment akin to that of a producer, trader, or service provider. This engagement in activities inherently constitutes economic involvement, thus classifying the participant as a taxable entity. In essence, evading the classification of a 'taxable person' for sharing economy providers becomes nearly unfeasible. Elliot (n. 343); a similar view is also presented by: Matesanz, 'VAT Treatment of the Sharing Economy' (n. 342) 104–105.

provide accommodation based on a certain continuity (it is not a one-off transaction).[346] In addition, the EC, citing the CJEU judgment in the *Słaby* case,[347] suggested that when a host takes steps and efforts to use a platform to market accommodation, he is behaving very similarly to a manufacturer or trader.[348]

However, although suppliers register on platforms, it is not obvious that they do so to continuously receive income, as their motivation may be, for example, simply to see how the platform works.[349] The determination of the host's tax status can also be called into question if he only exploits the property occasionally and without a staff or property organization.[350] As pointed out in the literature, the 'continuity' requirement appears to be rebuttable in the case of Airbnb rentals if it is shown that the purpose of renting the property for a very short period was not to generate income on a continuing basis.[351] There is therefore no consensus among legal scholars as to whether mere registration on a platform is sufficient to qualify a given supplier as a taxable person – the actual activities of the supplier, particularly their frequency and professionalism, are considered decisive.[352]

Nevertheless, it can be generally assumed that if a host operating through a platform exploits the property to generate income, the host will be considered a taxable person in most cases. Consequently, the host's economic activity will be subject to VAT.[353]

It should also be noted that for an economic activity to be subject to VAT, it must be carried out independently. According to Article 10 of the VAT Directive, the condition that the economic activity is carried out independently excludes VAT taxation of employees and other persons in so far as they are bound to an employer by a contract of employment or by any other legal ties creating a legal relationship of employer and employee as regards working conditions, remuneration and the employer's liability.

346. European Commission, 'Group on the Future of VAT No 086: VAT Treatment of the Sharing Economy, Taxud.c.1(2019)1950741'.
347. According to this judgment, the mere exercise of property rights and management of private assets do not constitute economic activity. However, if an individual actively engages in actions aimed at selling property, utilizing resources comparable to those of a producer, trader, or service provider as defined in the VAT Directive, then that individual must be considered as conducting an 'economic activity' within the scope of the Directive. Consequently, they should be classified as a taxable person for VAT purposes. *Jarosław Słaby v. Minister Finansów and Emilian Kuć and Halina Jeziorska-Kuć v. Dyrektor Izby Skarbowej w Warszawie* [2011] CJEU C-180/10 and C-181/10.
348. European Commission, 'Group on the Future of VAT No 086: VAT Treatment of the Sharing Economy, Taxud.c.1(2019)1950741' (n. 346).
349. Pollak (n. 343).
350. Suso (n. 342) 15.
351. It remains unclear how, for example, someone who has rented out his apartment every August for the past five years should be assessed. Katerina Pantazatou, 'Taxation of the Sharing Economy in the European Union' in Nestor M Davidson, Michèle Finck and John J Infranca (eds), *The Cambridge Handbook of the Law of the Sharing Economy* (1st edn, Cambridge University Press 2018) 373.
352. Katharina Artinger, *Taxing Consumption in the Digital Age: Challenges for European VAT* (1st edn, Nomos 2020) 196–197.
353. Pantazatou (n. 351) 372–373.

As indicated in the first chapter, within the platform economy, particularly in the STR sector, an employer-employee relationship binding the supplier and the platform does not usually exist. Furthermore, it is pointed out that within the platform economy, individual suppliers: (i) are not organically integrated into the platform on which they operate, nor are they obliged to operate only through one platform; (ii) have sufficient organizational autonomy in terms of human and material resources to conduct business; and (iii) generally bear the associated economic risk entailed in the supply of the underlying service (e.g., in the case of damages to property).[354] However, if, in a specific situation, the actual relationship between the platform and the supplier resembles an employer-employee relationship, then the supplier will not be considered a VAT taxable person.[355]

It should also be noted that for a business activity carried out by a taxable person to be subject to VAT, it must be carried out for a consideration. Barter transactions such as house swaps, where the 'consideration' is in kind, pose some problems in this context. In the CJEU's view, barter agreements are economically and commercially identical to transactions where the consideration is monetary.[356] However, given the specificity of the house swap, there are some doubts as to whether the persons involved in the transaction can be classified as taxable persons and whether in such a case there is a direct link between the service provided and the consideration.[357] In the EC's view, the qualification of users swapping accommodation as VAT taxable persons can easily be questioned, as the main purpose of offering a house on the platform is to gain access to another house. If the main purpose of the user was to obtain income, the user would probably not use this scheme but would simply rent the house. However, this issue needs to be considered on a case-by-case basis, taking into account factors such as the purpose of income generation, continuity and frequency of accommodation swapping.[358] The literature suggests that the overriding objective in determining whether a supply of services is subject to VAT is to avoid giving platform users an advantage over competitors who do not use the platforms. Thus, if the exchange of services without VAT via a platform harms his competitor, it is more likely that the transaction will be subject to VAT.[359]

The VAT Committee has provided guidance on the issue of the tax status of underlying suppliers. According to the Committee, the supply of services by individuals to other users through platforms, involving monetary consideration or exchange for

354. However, the regulatory autonomy enjoyed by individual providers varies significantly. While HomeExchange hosts are bound by a limited number of rules set by the platform, the operations of Airbnb hosts appear to be subject to a greater number of constraints (e.g., deactivation or suspension of accounts due to multiple poor ratings): Beretta (n. 344) 99–100.
355. Elliot (n. 343).
356. *Serebryannay vek EOOD v. Direktor na Direktsia 'Obzhalvane i upravlenie na izpalnenieto' – Varna pri Tsentralno upravlenie na Natsionalna agentsia za prihodite* [2013] CJEU C-283/12, paragraph 39; *Direktor na Direktsia 'Obzhalvane i upravlenie na izpalnenieto' – grad Burgas pri Tsentralno upravlenie na Natsionalnata agentsia za prihodite v. Orfey Balgaria EOOD* [2012] CJEU C-549/11, paragraph 35.
357. European Commission, 'Group on the Future of VAT No 086: VAT Treatment of the Sharing Economy, Taxud.c.1(2019)1950741' (n. 346).
358. *Ibid.*
359. Elliot (n. 343).

other goods or services (provided a direct link between the transaction and the consideration in kind is demonstrated), qualifies as transactions subject to VAT under Article 2 of the VAT Directive, if the person supplying the services conducts an economic activity as a taxable person within the meaning of Article 9 of the Directive.[360] The Committee emphasizes also that the assessment of whether there is a direct link between the transaction and the consideration should be conducted on a case-by-case basis.

These guidelines are therefore very general and do not clarify the key issue of whether suppliers offering services via platforms actually qualify as VAT taxable persons. The Committee's guidelines have also come under criticism for indicating that transactions should be assessed on a case-by-case basis without providing any specific guidance as to what circumstances should be specifically considered in this context.[361]

3.2 Qualification of Services Provided by Platforms

The qualification of platform services is also highly questionable under the EU VAT framework. In some Member States, they are regarded as electronically supplied services, while in others as intermediation services.[362] According to some legal literature, STR platform services could also be considered as services connected with immovable properties.[363]

According to Article 7(1) of the IR, the electronically supplied services referred to in the VAT Directive include services which are delivered over the internet or an electronic network and the nature of which renders their supply essentially automated and involving minimal human intervention, and impossible to ensure in the absence of information technology. Electronic services include, in particular, the transfer for consideration of the right to put goods or services up for sale on an internet site operating as an online market on which potential buyers make their bids by automated procedures and on which the parties are notified of a sale by electronic mail automatically generated from a computer (Article 7(2)(d) of the IR).

The VAT Committee was almost unanimous in pointing out that if platforms enable two parties to come into contact for the purpose of supplying goods or services, providing only passive automated services requiring minimal human intervention, then they do not meet the conditions for their services to be considered intermediation services and therefore do not fall under Article 46 of the VAT Directive.[364]

360. European Commission, 'VAT Committee Guidelines Resulting from the 105th Meeting of 26 October 2015: VAT Treatment of Sharing Economy, Taxud.c.1(2016)1162824 - 889'.
361. Ivo Grlica, 'How the Sharing Economy Is Challenging the EU VAT System' (2017) 28 International VAT Monitor 130–131 https://doi.org/10.59403/rx256.
362. European Commission, 'Impact Assessment Report, SWD(2022) 393 Final'.
363. Suso (n. 342).
364. European Commission, 'VAT Committee Guidelines Resulting from the 107th Meeting of 8 July 2016: Interaction between Electronically Supplied Services and Intermediation Services and Initial Discussion on the Scope of the Concept of Intermediation Services When Taken in a Broader Context, Taxud.c.1(2017)1402399 - 914'.

However, certain features of the platforms suggest that the services provided are tailored to the individual needs of their users. It is pointed out that when the services provided by STR platforms include several additional functionalities (e.g., the possibility for hosts and guests to write reviews, customer support in case of booking problems), this means that they should not be qualified as electronically supplied services.[365] Such supply can be considered to require more than minimal human intervention and therefore does not meet the definition of electronic services.[366]

However, the opposite position is also presented in the literature, according to which the platform operator does not act as a true intermediary since the supply of the booking service is usually fully automatic.[367] Furthermore, it is pointed out that the extent of the platform operator's influence on the vendor's service should not be taken as an indicator of exceeding 'minimal human intervention'. The fact that the platform operator can bring suppliers and customers together without human intervention, while exercising a high level of authority over their contractual relationships, should not lead to the non-application of the rules relating to electronically supplied services or to their replacement by the rules relating to intermediation.[368]

According to the EC, the diverse array of business models employed by accommodation sector platforms makes it impossible to make a general conclusion about whether the services they offer necessitate more than minimal human intervention, which could potentially preclude their classification as electronic services.[369] Assessing the level of human intervention ultimately depends on the platform's business model.[370]

This means that an abstract qualification of the services provided through the platforms is impossible, compounding the legal uncertainty.[371] This raises the issue of which Member State will be the place of supply of services when the transaction is B2C.[372] It should be noted that the general rule, as set out in Article 45 of the VAT Directive, is that the place of supply of services to a non-taxable person is the place

365. European Commission, 'VAT Committee Working Paper No 990: Services Supplied by Digital Platforms Intervening in Short-Term Leasing or Renting of Immovable Property, Taxud.c.1(2020)1181920'.
366. Loquet and Karoutis (n. 232) 220; A similar position, which suggests that the influence exerted by the platform on the underlying accommodation service typically extends far beyond mere automated intervention, is presented by: Suso (n. 342) 10.
367. Hans-Martin Grambeck, 'Online Intermediation Services – The Italian Case of Booking.Com' (2022) 33 International VAT Monitor 132 https://doi.org/10.59403/30jj7rp.
368. Lily Zechner, 'Understanding VAT in Three-Party, Platform-Based Business Models: Which Party Is Supplying Which Service?' (2022) 31 EC Tax Review 180 https://doi.org/10.54648/ecta2022018.
369. European Commission, 'VAT Committee Working Paper No 990: Services Supplied by Digital Platforms Intervening in Short-Term Leasing or Renting of Immovable Property, Taxud.c.1(2020)1181920' (n. 365).
370. *Ibid.*
371. Pollak (n. 339) 85.
372. This issue does not apply when the service recipient is a taxable person (B2B transactions) because both intermediary services and electronic services are covered by Article 44 of the VAT Directive. According to this provision, the place of supply of services to a taxable person acting as such is the place where that taxable person has established their business. Therefore, regardless of the classification adopted for the service provided by the platform, the place of supply is where the service recipient has established their business.

where the supplier has established his business. However, there are exceptions to this rule. Under Article 46 of the VAT Directive, the place of supply of services to non-taxable persons by an intermediary acting in the name and on behalf of third parties is the place where the underlying transaction is carried out. Article 58 of the VAT Directive, however, provides that the place of supply of electronic services to non-taxable persons is the place where such person is established, has his permanent address or usually resides. Both Articles 46 and 58 of the VAT Directive constitute *lex specialis* to the general rule of the place of supply of services set out in Article 45 of the VAT Directive, so it is questionable whether Article 46 of the VAT Directive can be regarded as *lex specialis* to Article 58 of the VAT Directive or vice versa.[373]

In the STR sector of the platform economy, the question of the place of taxation holds particular relevance. If the platform service is categorized as an electronic service, VAT is levied at the place of residence of the consumer. Conversely, if the service is deemed intermediation, VAT is charged in the Member State where the property is situated.[374] Moreover, when the property owner is not a taxable person and resides in a Member State different than the Member State where the property he rents is located, VAT will be charged either in the Member State of the owner's residence or at the property's location, depending on whether the platform service is classified as electronic service or intermediation service.[375] A divergent classification of platform services between Member States may therefore lead to double taxation or non-taxation.[376]

A report commissioned by the EC revealed that most surveyed platforms, approximately 80%, considered their services as electronic, while only about 20% classified them as intermediation services.[377] Legal scholars underline that applying the place of supply principle outlined in Article 58 of the VAT Directive provides a more legally certain approach.[378] In addition, this qualification implements the principle of taxation at the place of consumption since, according to Article 58 of the VAT Directive, the place of supply for electronically supplied services is the consumer's location.[379] However, Member States with relatively developed tourism industries tend to treat STR platform services as intermediation services, making them taxable at the location of the property.[380] Also, some legal commentators argue that the fact that the main purpose of the platform is to connect supplier and customer, which is the core of the

373. Pollak (n. 339) 81.
374. This would also apply in the case where the services provided by the platform were considered an integral part of a general service, i.e., if they were deemed to be services related to immovable property.
375. European Commission, Directorate General for Taxation and Customs Union and others (n. 6) 124–125.
376. European Commission, 'Group on the Future of VAT No 086: VAT Treatment of the Sharing Economy, Taxud.c.1(2019)1950741' (n. 346); European Commission, 'Impact Assessment Report, SWD(2022) 393 Final' (n. 362).
377. European Commission, Directorate General for Taxation and Customs Union and others (n. 6) 36–37.
378. Pollak (n. 339) 84.
379. *Ibid.*, 85.
380. European Commission, Directorate General for Taxation and Customs Union and others (n. 6) 70.

intermediary's activity, should lead to the recognition of the services provided by platforms as intermediation services.[381]

It should be noted that the Commission plans to clarify that a service provided by a platform to non-taxable persons should be considered as an intermediation service (planned Article 46a of the VAT Directive).[382] This regulation seems to be welcomed as it will allow a uniform application of the rules on the place of supply of platform services. However, it should be noted that reaching a consensus on this issue may be difficult. Depending on whether the platform service is classified as an electronic service or intermediation service, VAT will be charged in the Member State of residence of the owner or in the place where the property is located. This classification therefore affects the shifting of income between Member States. If the platform services are treated as intermediation, a certain proportion of the revenue would be shifted to the countries where the property is located rather than where the owners or consumers reside. The choice of an intermediation services approach would therefore benefit the Member States with developed tourism, while an e-services approach would benefit the Member States where the tourist originates.[383] However, it is important to bear in mind that these factors may change over time – countries with less developed tourism may become more popular, tourists may start to prefer domestic tourism, etc. For this reason, the uniform approach adopted by the Commission seems a good solution, regardless of whether platforms are ultimately accepted as providing an electronic service or intermediation service.

4 THE ROLE OF STR PLATFORMS IN VAT COLLECTION

The platformization of the economy undoubtedly presents challenges for the EU VAT system, introducing uncertainty about the correct application of the rules of this tax, which amplifies the risk of non-compliance. The question arises whether any action is needed to improve the collection of VAT in the context of the digital economy and, in particular, to prevent double taxation and/or non-taxation. According to doctrine, the most obvious response must surely be 'yes'.[384] Nevertheless, it should be acknowledged that it is rather unlikely to involve a fundamental re-think of the jurisdictional basis upon which decisions are made about which country has the right to tax

381. Madeleine Merkx and others, 'VAT in the Digital Age Package: Viva La ViDA or Livin' La ViDA Loca?' (2023) EC Tax Review 138–139 https://doi.org/10.2139/ssrn.4437300.
382. Proposal for a Council Directive amending Directive 2006/112/EC as regards VAT rules for the digital age [COM/2022/701 final]; This approach has been maintained in the compromise text: Draft Council Directive amending Directive 2006/112/EC as regards VAT rules for the digital age – compromise text 8 May 2024 [2022/0407(CNS)].
383. In absolute terms, the revenue shifting would not be significant: EUR 209 million in the case of adopting the intermediary services approach and EUR 50 million under the electronic services approach, which corresponds respectively to 2.9% and 0.7% of the VAT revenue from platform-based STR economy: European Commission, Directorate General for Taxation and Customs Union and others (n. 6) 126.
384. Rebecca Millar, 'VAT/GST in a Global Digital Economy – Looking Ahead: Potential Solutions and the Framework to Make Them Work' (2016) Sydney Law School Research Paper 1.

consumption.[385] It is rather an opportunity to enhance the effectiveness of tax collection methods. Digital technologies offer novel tools for enforcing tax obligations,[386] and the advent of the platform economy has been swiftly recognized as an opportunity to enhance VAT collection.[387]

4.1 Collection of VAT by Third Parties

The collection and remittance of tax dues to the competent authorities is fundamental to the smooth functioning of any tax system. The literature on this subject suggests that this process requires striking a balance between the intentions of decision-makers and the capacities provided by available information and administrative tools. The efficiency of tax collection relies on the ability to accurately measure the tax base, which requires significant investment in developing the administrative competencies of the tax system and enforcing compliance with existing rules.[388] For the effectiveness of tax collection, administrability is also crucial, which has two major components: the ease of government enforcement and the ease of taxpayer compliance. Administrability may seem relatively superficial or more concerned with form than efficiency, but it is key to the effectiveness of tax collection.[389]

A common feature of tax systems is the imposition of various obligations on third parties to ensure tax collection.[390] Currently, there is a noticeable trend towards an increased burden of tax collection being shifted from states to private entities.[391]

The literature acknowledges the possibility of a certain 'privatisation' of the tax system, wherein specific administrative tasks can be outsourced to the private sector if such delegation enhances efficiency or effectiveness of such tasks.[392] However, the state does not lose its autonomy when delegating certain administrative activities, as a private entity does not have the freedom to set a tax that results from a law or government decision.[393]

There is also a trend known as 'responsibilization'. As indicated in the literature, this phenomenon involves private parties not part of the criminal justice system being

385. *Ibid.*, 2.
386. Thomas Fetzer and Bianka Dinger, 'The Digital Platform Economy and Its Challenges to Taxation' (2019) 12 Tsinghua China Law Review 56.
387. Lamensch and others (n. 104) 477–479.
388. James A Mirrlees, 'The Economic Approach to Tax Design' in James A Mirrlees, Stuart Adam and Institute for Fiscal Studies (Great Britain) (eds), *Tax by Design: The Mirrlees Review* (Oxford University Press 2011) 43.
389. Leandra Lederman, 'Statutory Speed Bumps: The Roles Third Parties Play in Tax Compliance' (2007) 60 Stanford Law Review 709.
390. Philip Baker, Pasquale Pistone and Katerina Perroun, 'Third-Party Liability for the Payment of Taxes and Their Fundamental Rights' (2023) World Tax Journal 86 https://doi.org/10.59403/1h2sm78.
391. *Ibid.*, 111; Luisa Scarcella, 'E-Commerce and Effective VAT/GST Enforcement: Can Online Platforms Play a Valuable Role?' (2020) 36 Computer Law & Security Review 5 https://doi.org/10.1016/j.clsr.2019.105371.
392. Luis Fernando and Ramirez Acuna, 'Privatization of Tax Administration' in Richard M Bird, Milka Casanegra de Jantscher and International Monetary Fund (eds), *Improving tax administration in developing countries* (International Monetary Fund 1992) 377.
393. *Ibid.*

legally or administratively held responsible for crime prevention. The concept of responsibilization emerged as a new method of governing crime, challenging the idea that the state alone should bear the responsibility for crime control. Instead, a new strategy was devised, which involved identifying private organizations and individuals who should share the responsibility for effectively reducing opportunities for crime.[394]

Responsibilization can also be observed in the realm of VAT. As the literature suggests, there is a trend of imposing responsibility on third parties with certain business connections to VAT fraudsters (such as the seller of the goods to the alleged fraudster, the purchaser of those goods, an intermediary, or even a warehouse keeper) in this regard.[395]

It is worth emphasizing that in the *Italmoda* case,[396] the CJEU ruled that imposing certain responsibility on third parties in the fight against VAT fraud is permissible. The Court found that liability for VAT fraud may arise in the absence of national provisions foreseeing it, which essentially transformed third-party liability for VAT fraud from a rule into a principle. As rightly pointed out in doctrine, this has significant theoretical and practical implications: the scope of the new principle of third-party liability for tax fraud, as developed by the Court, appears to apply to any type of fraud and to extend to the potential creation of VAT obligations to any party within the production chain, including intermediaries such as warehouse owners or online retail platforms.[397]

According to the legal literature, measures establishing the liability of a third party fall into two broad categories. The first group places the burden of tax collection on the person who already has (physically or legally) the funds from which the tax due from another person will be paid. The second group includes measures introducing joint and several liability of the third party for the tax liability of the taxable person. In this situation, the third party may or may not have the funds from which the tax is to be paid. If such third party does not have the funds and is required to pay the tax, it will have to seek a refund from the taxable person.[398]

In doctrine, it is also pointed out that the person or organization legally liable for the tax (*legal incidence*) is not necessarily the same as the entity bearing its economic burden (*economic incidence*).[399] It should be noted that the basic structure of VAT itself is structured in such a way that, although the consumer is the entity that ultimately pays the VAT, VAT is accounted for and paid by the entrepreneur who is the third party between the consumer and the state. In VAT law, the trader (the taxable person) is merely the tax collector acting in the interest of the state.[400] Thus, in the case of VAT, the law imposes an obligation on entrepreneurs (taxable persons) to remit the tax that

394. Rita de la Feria, 'Tax Fraud and Selective Law Enforcement' (2020) 47 Journal of Law and Society 261 https://doi.org/10.1111/jols.12221.
395. *Ibid.*, 258.
396. *Staatssecretaris van Financiën v. Schoenimport 'Italmoda' Mariano Previti vof and Turbu.com BV and Turbu.com Mobile Phone's BV v. Staatssecretaris van Financiën* [2014] CJEU C-131/13.
397. de la Feria (n. 394) 261.
398. Baker, Pistone and Perroun (n. 390) 87.
399. Mirrlees (n. 388) 27.
400. *See*, for example: 'Opinion of Advocate General Kokott Delivered on 16 November 2023 in Case C-606/22 Dyrektor Izby Administracji Skarbowej w Bydgoszczy v B. Sp. z o.o.', paragraph 48 and the case law of the CJEU cited therein.

is ultimately paid by other parties, namely consumers of goods or services. Only entrepreneurs are liable for the output tax, are obliged to collect it from the consumer, and, after deducting the input VAT, pay it to the state.[401] As indicated in the literature, this collection model was designed in an era when the vast majority of transactions were domestic and when collecting taxes and remitting them to the home tax administration resulted in acceptable compliance costs for businesses.[402] However, with the growth of cross-border transactions, there was a need to change the VAT system to avoid non-compliance.[403]

While the ideal scenario is for VAT to be collected and remitted by the taxable person, certain situations warrant the involvement of third parties, such as intermediaries.

The imposition of an obligation to pay the tax on an entity other than the taxable person aims to increase the likelihood that the tax will actually be collected.[404] In doctrine, it is emphasized that imposing liability on third parties can also serve to generate additional revenue from businesses that do not engage in fraud in order to compensate for losses incurred as a result of fraud; in this scenario, reducing the VAT gap may be partially attributed not to the reduction of fraud itself but to the implementation of measures that simply maximize revenue collection.[405]

Moreover, legal literature highlights that the main advantage of such a third-party liability regime is that intermediaries tend to be fewer in number and thus easier to monitor than their clients, especially if the latter are end consumers.[406] Targeting legal enforcement efforts towards a concentrated group of larger and wealthier actors is a much simpler task than monitoring a dispersed group of low-income individuals.[407] The intermediaries generally possess the information and resources required to fulfil the obligations stemming from being assigned liability for VAT collection and refund.[408] According to legal commentators, digital platforms are among the categories of intermediaries that can be held liable for the collection of VAT.[409] The suppliers using internet platforms to reach customers for their supplies may be found in a multitude of jurisdictions and are more difficult to locate than the platform operator. Thus, from a

401. However, there are many exceptions to this general rule. One example is the mechanism of reverse charge specified in Articles 194 and 196 of the VAT Directive, whereby the responsibility for VAT collection and refund shifts from the supplier to the purchaser. Other situations include, among others, the responsibility of tax representatives under Article 204 of the VAT Directive and joint liability under Article 205 of the VAT Directive.
402. Marie Lamensch, 'Is There Any Future for the Vendor Collection Model in the 21st Century Economy?' (2016) 27 International VAT Monitor 182–183 https://doi.org/10.59403/1eeejg0.
403. *Ibid.*
404. Baker, Pistone and Perroun (n. 390) 87; in doctrine, it is indicated, for example, that structural systems which involve third parties to assist in ensuring compliance with federal income tax are highly successful. Lederman (n. 389) 698.
405. de la Feria (n. 394) 242.
406. Beretta (n. 344) 273–275.
407. Manoj Viswanathan, 'Tax Compliance and the Sharing Economy' in Nestor M Davidson, Michèle Finck and John J Infranca (eds), *The Cambridge Handbook of the Law of the Sharing Economy* (1st edn, Cambridge University Press 2018) 362.
408. Beretta (n. 344) 273–275.
409. *Ibid.*, 311.

revenue collection perspective, it is easier if the liability to account for VAT on supplies via platforms lies with the platform operator.[410]

Although the involvement of third parties does not constitute a penalty or any form of sanction (it is a normal means of collection integrated into the tax system), it often entails the liability of these persons for the breach of an increasing number of formal obligations, including the filing of returns and the reporting of data.[411] For this reason, a mechanism involving third-party liability should be proportionate to the purpose it serves.[412] The literature highlights the necessity to consider whether the collective interest of ensuring effective payment of taxes justifies the involvement of third parties in the collection process.[413] In this context, it is worth noting the CJEU judgment, according to which it is, in principle, for the tax authorities to carry out the necessary inspections of taxable persons to detect VAT irregularities and fraud.[414]

Furthermore, as indicated in doctrine, it appears that tax enforcement actions focus on revenue maximization by gravitating towards tackling the 'low-hanging fruit': tax authorities are likely to prioritize cases that increase their revenue but involve low administrative costs.[415] The primary focus of anti-fraud policy now seems to be on managing the revenue costs of tax fraud rather than suppressing it.[416] In the context of the responsibilization phenomenon, under the principle of third-party liability, this is associated with the privatization of some of the costs of crime. Under the principle of third-party liability, businesses are required to conduct due diligence to ensure that their business partners are not involved in fraud. Because when tax authorities present objective evidence that businesses should have known that fraud was being committed, those businesses may be held liable for the unpaid tax.[417] As a result, it is third parties, not those who commit fraud, who may feel any potential financial, stigmatizing, reputational, or personal negative effects resulting from the targeting of their property by tax authorities.[418] These remarks can be analogously applied to situations where third parties are held liable for the tax liabilities of other entities.

It would therefore seem that Member States should not shift excessive liability for overseeing the VAT system to private parties, as, for example, digital platforms.

410. Oskar Henkow, 'Acting in One's Own Name on Someone Else's Behalf: A Changing Concept?' in Karina Kim Egholm Elgaard (ed.), *Momsloven 50 år* (Første udgave, første oplag, Ex Tuto Publishing 2017) 243.
411. Baker, Pistone and Perroun (n. 390) 86.
412. *Ibid.*, 87.
413. *Ibid.*, 93.
414. *Mahagében Kft v. Nemzeti Adó- és Vámhivatal Dél-dunántúli Regionális Adó Főigazgatósága and Péter Dávid v. Nemzeti Adó- és Vámhivatal Észak-alföldi Regionális Adó Főigazgatósága* [2012] CJEU C-80/11 and C-142/11, paragraph 62.
415. de la Feria (n. 394) 266.
416. *Ibid.*, 265.
417. *Ibid.*, 262.
418. *Ibid.*, 264.

4.2 The Potential Role of Platforms in VAT Collection

At the national, European, and international levels, discussions on the enforcement of existing tax laws have begun to focus on platforms facilitating transactions. The platform economy, indeed, introduces new avenues for settling tax liabilities. This is notably due to the increased traceability facilitated by platform intermediation. Undoubtedly, platform operators possess accurate information about transactions conducted through them, and leveraging this advantage by the tax authorities aligns perfectly with the trend towards a modern tax system relying increasingly on third parties.[419] Furthermore, concentrating regulatory efforts on a singular entity (the platform) has paved the way for designing solutions that reduce legal enforcement costs.[420] Collecting VAT through several platforms, as opposed to from numerous individual suppliers, proves to be more efficient.[421] These considerations make platforms seem well placed to play a role in VAT collection[422] or in facilitating compliance for their underlying suppliers.[423]

In the 2016 Agenda, the EC encourages Member States to improve tax collection by taking advantage of these opportunities, also highlighting the importance of tax authorities and platforms working together, in particular, to share information.[424] Opportunities for the involvement of STR platforms in the tax collection process include their entering into voluntary cooperation agreements for the collection and remittance of hotel and tourism taxes,[425] possibly with an accompanying provision that they are then jointly and severally liable for this.[426] Platforms may also assist hosts[427] in meeting their tax obligations[428] or may be required to collect and remit taxes due on hosts' rental income.[429]

419. Scarcella (n. 391) 15.
420. Bianca Kuijper, Todd Cameron and Zsolt Szatmari, 'Technology-Enabled Tax Compliance' (2020) 74 Bulletin for International Taxation 589 https://doi.org/10.59403/2v58pym; Zale (n. 49).
421. Scarcella (n. 391) 15.
422. Simon Thang and Nicolas Shatalow, 'Digital Cross-Border Supplies' in Robert F van Brederode, *Virtues and Fallacies of VAT* (Wolters Kluwer Law International 2021) 433.
423. Elliot (n. 343).
424. European Commission, 'A European Agenda for the Collaborative Economy, COM(2016) 356 Final' (n. 36).
425. For example, in the EU, Airbnb has entered into such agreements with cities like Amsterdam, Paris, and Lisbon. The taxes collected are then transferred to the cities in quarterly or annual lump sums (which is considered a drawback of this solution because aggregating payments allows platforms to conceal the identity of hosts, making it impossible for authorities to verify declared payments): Oskam (n. 69) 94.
426. European Commission, Directorate General for Internal Market, Industry, Entrepreneurship and SMEs, VVA, and Spark Legal Network (n. 48) 12–13.
427. For example, in Estonia, Airbnb hosts have the option, on a voluntary basis, to report their earnings through the platform to tax authorities: Beretta (n. 344) 33–34.
428. Marcos Álvarez Suso, 'European Union – E-Platforms Providing Services in the Short-Term Rental Accommodation Market: The Challenges for Taxation of These Services under the EU VAT' (2020) 31 International VAT Monitor 8–9 https://doi.org/10.59403/1wpx3e1.
429. For example, in Italy, since mid-2017, Airbnb is required to collect and remit taxes owed on the income earned by hosts from renting out their own residential properties and to provide rental data to tax authorities: Beretta (n. 344) 33–34.

Regarding VAT, the OECD in turn distinguishes the following roles of platforms: (i) educational and communication role, (ii) formal cooperation agreements, (iii) information sharing role, (iv) joint and several liability, (v) collection/withholding role, and (vi) full liability role (the deemed supplier regime).[430] These roles will be discussed below, excluding the deemed supplier regime which will be analysed in detail in the next chapter.

4.2.1 The Education and Communication Role of Platforms

The literature notes that a lack of awareness among small underlying suppliers is one of the contributing factors to the low level of compliance within the platform economy - such entities may not, for example, consider their participation in the STR market as doing business.[431] By playing an education and communication role, platforms can change this situation by providing accurate information to their suppliers about their VAT obligations.[432] For example, a platform operator can send each vendor a general statement on their tax obligations when they first register on the platform and in periodic emails, text messages or alternative means of communication.[433]

The literature points out that while platforms can help hosts understand local regulations, the duty to ensure actual compliance with these regulations lies with the hosts.[434] This means that the discussed role of platforms is intended to complement, not replace, the existing communication strategies deployed by tax authorities to inform (potential) taxable persons of their obligations.[435] The key objective of this policy is therefore to promote and facilitate legal compliance.

4.2.2 Formal Cooperation Agreements with Platforms

Formal cooperation agreements are concluded with platforms on a voluntary basis to engage them in increasing the level of compliance regarding the collection of taxes, including VAT.[436] Typically, such agreements require platforms to provide information (on request or periodically) to carry out education activities through platforms or to

430. OECD, *The Impact of the Growth of the Sharing and Gig Economy on VAT/GST Policy and Administration* (n. 47) 59–61.
431. Anna Cameron, Mukesh Khanal and Lindsay M Tedds, 'Managing Airbnb: A Cross-Jurisdictional Review of Approaches for Regulating the Short-Term Rental Market' (2022) MPRA Paper 34 https://doi.org/10.2139/ssrn.4009268.
432. OECD, *The Impact of the Growth of the Sharing and Gig Economy on VAT/GST Policy and Administration* (n. 47) 65.
433. OECD, 'Code of Conduct: Co-Operation between Tax Administrations and Sharing and Gig Economy Platforms', www.oecd.org accessed 5 April 2021.
434. European Commission, 'Developing a Responsible, Fair and Trusted Single Market for Short-Term Rental Services. Workshop 1: Enhancing Transparency on Short-Term Accommodation Rentals in the EU. 22 October 2021 – Conclusions, GROW.G.3/CD'; Viswanathan (n. 407) 364–366.
435. OECD, *The Impact of the Growth of the Sharing and Gig Economy on VAT/GST Policy and Administration* (n. 47) 65.
436. *Ibid.*, 66–67.

alert tax authorities of suspected fraud.[437] Cooperation agreements may also assign certain enforcement obligations to the platform, which may include, for example, the blocking and removal of non-compliant users.[438]

One existing example of such cooperation is the tax collection agreements between Airbnb and local tax authorities around the world. Under these agreements, Airbnb collects tourism or accommodation taxes in the name of the host and remits them directly to the relevant tax authority.[439] Airbnb has entered into several agreements in jurisdictions that impose sales tax on hotels and home rentals, such as France, Bermuda, Brazil and Canada.[440] Data suggests that Airbnb's tax collection agreements can significantly increase tax compliance.[441]

Indications are that this type of formal cooperation can be useful, particularly in cases where the platform has no liability or role in collecting taxes on the underlying supply.[442] According to the academic opinion, in addition to ensuring mutually beneficial cooperation between platforms and tax authorities, the agreements may also be the first step towards introducing a full liability regime into the EU VAT system.[443]

4.2.3 The Information Sharing Role of Platforms

As part of its information sharing role, the platform is legally obliged to provide relevant data to the tax authority, upon request, spontaneously or periodically.[444] An interesting solution could also be the introduction of a real-time reporting obligation by platforms or the option for platform users to consent (through it) for their payment data to be sent directly to tax authorities immediately. The imposition of a reporting obligation on the platform can be introduced as a stand-alone measure or as a complement to its other roles.[445] The literature points out that the use of third parties to collect and verify information - in this case from platform operators vis-à-vis its vendors - makes the information obtained from the suppliers more reliable, as it will be comparable with the information obtained from those third parties.[446]

According to CJEU case law, the imposition of reporting obligations on platforms, in principle, is not contrary to EU law. In the case of *Airbnb Ireland II*, the CJEU confirmed the compatibility with EU law of the imposition of an obligation on providers

437. *Ibid.*
438. Beretta (n. 344) 308–311.
439. Fetzer and Dinger (n. 386) 50.
440. Richard Asquith, 'Co-Opting Gig & Sharing Platforms as Tax Collectors' (25 October 2021), https://www.vatcalc.com/global/co-opting-gig-sharing-platforms-as-tax-collectors/ accessed 28 November 2022.
441. Andrew J Bibler, Keith F Teltser and Mark J Tremblay, 'Inferring Tax Compliance from Pass-Through: Evidence from Airbnb Tax Enforcement Agreements' (2021) The Review of Economics and Statistics 650 https://doi.org/10.1162/rest_a_00910.
442. Scarcella (n. 391) 9.
443. Beretta (n. 344) 308–311; Scarcella (n. 391) 9.
444. OECD, *The Impact of the Growth of the Sharing and Gig Economy on VAT/GST Policy and Administration* (n. 47) 67.
445. *Ibid.*, 69–70.
446. Filip Majdowski, 'Obowiązki Sprawozdawcze Operatorów Platform Cyfrowych w Unii Europejskiej – Kolejny Przykład "Wielkiego Brata" w Podatkach?' (2022) Przegląd Podatkowy 39.

of property intermediation services to provide the tax authority with the data of the operator of an accommodation establishment, as well as information on the number of nights and the number of accommodation units operated during the previous year.[447] Similarly, in the case of *Airbnb Ireland III*, the CJEU found compatible with EU law the imposition of an obligation on platforms, providing property intermediation services, regardless of where they are established and how they intermediate, to collect and then transfer to the national tax authorities data on the rental contracts concluded as a result of their intermediation.[448] The Court noted that while the obligation to provide tax authorities with rental contract data may incur extra costs for intermediaries, especially regarding data search and storage, it is important to highlight that digital intermediaries, like platforms, already store and digitize such data. Therefore, the additional costs for these intermediaries appear to be relatively lower.[449]

The judgment in the case of *Airbnb Ireland III* is generally considered balanced, and its outcome is deemed satisfactory.[450]

Nonetheless, as the legal scholars rightly point out, the CJEU's conclusions on the lawfulness of platform obligations should not be detached from the specific circumstances of these cases – these judgments should not lead one to think that the imposition of reporting requirements on intermediaries is always compatible with EU law, as these measures should not constitute a restriction of the EU's fundamental freedoms or be unjustified or disproportionate.[451] The need for proportionality in imposing reporting obligations on platforms is also emphasized by the OECD. The OECD indicates that this obligation should only cover information that can reasonably be expected to be available to platforms in the ordinary course of their business and that consideration could be given to limiting the applicability of this obligation to platforms that operate above a certain materiality threshold.[452] It is also worth emphasizing that, in order for this measure to be effective, the tax administration must have adequate technological capabilities and human resources to process the information received.[453] In this context, attention should be paid to the opportunities offered by the implementation of technology for compliance audit automation and data mining solutions based on artificial intelligence. As pointed out in the legal literature, an automated audit starts with the use of data mining techniques to gather publicly available information from STR sector platforms to create a standardized list of active properties in a given jurisdiction. Such list is then automatically compared with information held by tax authorities to catch potential anomalies. This requires little or

447. *Airbnb Ireland UC v. Région de Bruxelles-Capitale* [2022] CJEU C-674/20.
448. *Airbnb Ireland and Airbnb Payments UK* [2022] CJEU C-83/21.
449. *Ibid.*, paragraph 50.
450. Delhomme and Chapuis-Doppler (n. 222) 220.
451. Juan Manuel Vázquez, 'Airbnb (C-83/21). Compatibility of the Italian Tax Regime for Short-Term Property Rentals with EU Law' (*Kluwer International Tax Blog*, 3 May 2023) 21, www.kluwertaxblog.com accessed 7 August 2023.
452. OECD, *The Impact of the Growth of the Sharing and Gig Economy on VAT/GST Policy and Administration* (n. 47) 69–70.
453. *Ibid.*; Pollak (n. 339) 299.

no human involvement, allowing it to move more quickly to the tax enforcement stage.[454]

Various reporting obligations are currently imposed on platforms operating in the EU in the areas of both direct taxation and VAT. One of the most significant initiatives in this respect is the adoption of the revision of the Directive on administrative cooperation in the field of taxation (the so-called DAC7 Directive).[455] The purpose of this directive is to obtain information on sellers operating via platforms and then verify that they comply with their tax obligations in Member States. Therefore, the DAC7 Directive introduces the obligation for operators of platforms facilitating, *inter alia*, the rental of real properties to report certain data in annual reporting periods[456] and the automatic exchange of this data between Member States.

Importantly, the information transferred under the DAC7 Directive between Member States may be used for the purposes of VAT and other indirect taxes (Article 16(1) of the Directive on administrative cooperation in the field of taxation,[457] as amended by the DAC7 Directive). The DAC7 Directive may therefore prove to be an important source of information not only for income tax accounting but also for VAT purposes.

Nevertheless, it is pointed out that the usefulness of the DAC7 Directive from a VAT perspective may be limited for, *inter alia*, the following reasons: (i) the DAC7 Directive assumes the reporting of information on an annual basis, which does not coincide with the deadlines for submitting VAT returns (quarterly or monthly); (ii) the DAC7 Directive contains certain thresholds,[458] which may prevent Member States from obtaining a proper picture of the whole transaction chain; (iii) the data collected for the purposes of the DAC7 Directive are global, whereas the data required for VAT purposes are more detailed and relate to individual transactions (a tax administration cannot make a meaningful assessment of the correct accounting for VAT without a description of the goods or services).[459]

In addition to the reporting obligations set out in the DAC7 Directive, platforms are also required to keep records of the transactions they facilitate for the purposes of the VAT Directive. Under Article 242a of the VAT Directive, where a platform facilitates the supply of goods or services (including accommodation services) to a non-taxable person within the EU, it is required to keep records of those transactions and make

454. Michelle Havich, 'Are Short-Term Rental Hosts Ready for a Technologically Powered Compliance Crackdown in 2023?' (*American City and County*, 13 February 2023), www.americancityandcounty.com accessed 1 March 2023.
455. Council Directive (EU) 2021/514 of 22 March 2021 amending Directive 2011/16/EU on administrative cooperation in the field of taxation (n. 158).
456. The first report from platforms for the year 2023 should be submitted no later than 31 January 2024.
457. Council Directive 2011/16/EU of 15 February 2011 on administrative cooperation in the field of taxation and repealing Directive 77/799/EEC [OJ L 64, 11.3.2011, pp. 1–12].
458. Directive DAC7 provides exemptions from reporting for sellers for whom the platform operator facilitated fewer than 30 relevant transactions and for whom the total compensation for such transactions did not exceed EUR 2,000 during the reporting period.
459. European Commission, 'Group on the Future of VAT No 116: VAT and the Platform Economy – Focus on Specific Issues – Follow up, Taxud.c.1(2022)669826'.

them available electronically to the Member States concerned upon their request.[460] The records must be kept for a period of 10 years from the end of the year in which the transaction took place and must be sufficiently detailed[461] to allow the tax authorities to verify that VAT has been correctly accounted for.

The wording of Article 242a of the VAT Directive may soon change. The EC plans to add paragraph 1a, which states that where a platform facilitates the supply of STR services and is not considered a deemed supplier, then this platform shall be obliged to keep records of those supplies.[462] While this provision may seem somewhat complicated,[463] its general aim is to impose reporting obligations on STR platforms for B2B transactions. This provision has undergone some modifications in the compromise text, which now clarifies that it concerns services supplied within the Union and adds that the records shall be sufficiently detailed to enable the tax authorities of the Member States where those supplies are taxable to verify that VAT has been accounted for correctly.[464] However, this does not appear to change its overall objective.

As pointed out in the literature, there are many similarities between the DAC7 Directive and the record-keeping obligation set out in Article 242a of the VAT Directive - in particular, the information that platforms must keep and provide is very similar and there is some overlap.[465] There are also noticeable differences. For example, under the DAC7 Directive, a platform only reports once a year in one Member State, which then automatically exchanges the data indicated there with other Member States. Under the VAT Directive, the platform must make the records available whenever requested by an authority. Such a formulation of the rules means that the platform can receive up to 27 requests for information from 27 EU Member States. This solution is criticized in the literature, where it is recommended to introduce a provision allowing

460. It is worth noting that in the compromise text, an option was introduced for Member States to impose a more regular and automated obligation on platforms to provide records. Article 242a, paragraph 2 of the VAT Directive specifies that Member States may continue to request the records to be provided regularly and systematically until automated access to these records is available. Draft Council Directive amending Directive 2006/112/EC as regards VAT rules for the digital age - compromise text 8 May 2024 (n. 382).
461. In Article 54c(2) IR, it is stipulated that the platform should keep the following information: (a) the name, postal address and electronic address or website of the supplier whose supplies are facilitated through the use of the electronic interface and, if available: (i) the VAT identification number or national tax number of the supplier; (ii) the bank account number or number of virtual account of the supplier; (b) a description of the goods, their value, the place where the dispatch or transport of the goods ends, together with the time of supply and, if available, the order number or unique transaction number; (c) a description of the services, their value, information in order to establish the place of supply and time of supply and, if available, the order number or unique transaction number.
462. Proposal for a Council Directive amending Directive 2006/112/EC as regards VAT rules for the digital age (n. 382).
463. As ironically (but rightly) pointed out in the doctrine: 'Finally, the spelling out and deciphering of the record-keeping obligations imposed on all platforms convince us that only the strongest will survive in the market.' Lamensch and others (n. 143).
464. Draft Council Directive amending Directive 2006/112/EC as regards VAT rules for the digital age - compromise text 8 May 2024 (n. 382).
465. Madeleine Merkx, Anne Janssen and Maxime Leenders, 'Platforms, a Convenient Source of Information under DAC7 and the VAT Directive: A Proposal for More Alignment and Efficiency' (2022) 31 EC Tax Review 215 https://doi.org/10.54648/ecta2022020.

the platform to report in only one Member State, which would then automatically exchange data with the country where the supply is subject to VAT.[466] Furthermore, according to Article 242a of the VAT Directive, the buyer of goods or services via the platforms must be a non-taxable person for VAT purposes, which excludes the reporting of B2B and C2B transactions by the platform. The DAC7 Directive does not contain such a restriction.[467] However, it should be noted that the Commission plans to clarify the wording of Article 242a of the VAT Directive so that the platform in some cases is also obliged to keep records of B2B transactions.[468] If the planned amendment enters into force, this will make the scope of application of the DAC7 Directive and the VAT Directive even more similar.

The overlap of data reporting obligations set out in the DAC7 Directive and the VAT Directive is viewed negatively by the legal scholars. It is emphasized that the cumulative effect of the various reporting obligations that platforms must comply with in the field of direct and indirect taxation should not be underestimated - such inconsistent and sometimes overlapping obligations can, as a whole, significantly affect the resources of platform operators and therefore place a disproportionate burden on them.[469] Also, the OECD encourages countries to implement a coordinated approach to ensure that data received from platforms can be used for different types of taxes, both direct and indirect, to minimize the risk of duplicate reporting systems.[470]

However, it must be accepted that a complete harmonization of information obligations under EU law may not be possible, as income tax and VAT differ significantly - while income tax aims to tax the seller's income and is usually collected after the calendar year based on an annual return, VAT taxes the consumption of the seller's customer and is collected on each transaction based on periodically submitted VAT returns.[471]

4.2.4 *Joint and Several Liability of Platforms*

As a general rule, only one entity is liable for accounting for VAT on a given transaction. However, under joint and several liability, this obligation can be assigned to more than one person. Joint and several liability is a type of 'secondary' liability, i.e., a liability that is attributed to a person for an infringement committed by another person due to the special relationship that exists between the two entities and is intended to ensure that the amount due is ultimately remitted to the competent tax authorities.[472]

466. Merkx and others (n. 381) 140–141.
467. Merkx, Janssen and Leenders (n. 465) 212.
468. Proposal for a Council Directive amending Directive 2006/112/EC as regards VAT rules for the digital age (n. 382); Draft Council Directive amending Directive 2006/112/EC as regards VAT rules for the digital age - compromise text 8 May 2024 (n. 382).
469. Vázquez (n. 451) 21.
470. OECD, *The Impact of the Growth of the Sharing and Gig Economy on VAT/GST Policy and Administration* (n. 47) 71.
471. Merkx, Janssen and Leenders (n. 465) 215.
472. Beretta (n. 344) 306–308.

Under joint and several liability of platforms, if the underlying supplier does not correctly account for VAT, the tax authorities have the possibility to hold the platform facilitating the transaction jointly liable for the unpaid VAT.[473]

In the OECD's view, the solution in question can operate under two main options, which are not mutually exclusive. The first option is that the platform is jointly and severally liable for future undeclared VAT - when the tax authority detects a case of irregularity on the part of the underlying supplier, it reports it to the platform, and when the platform fails to take appropriate action within a set period of time (e.g., by failing to remove the underlying supplier from the platform), it becomes jointly and severally liable. Under the second option, the platform may be held jointly and severally liable for the past undeclared VAT of the underlying supplier when it could reasonably have been expected to know, based on that supplier's actions (e.g., because the supplier's turnover exceeded a certain threshold), that it should have registered for VAT but failed to do so.[474] In this case, there may be uncertainty as to whether the platform actually had sufficient knowledge, or at least should have known, of the existence of the breach committed by the individual supplier, but nevertheless failed to take any appropriate action against such supplier.[475]

The VAT Directive provides an option for Member States to introduce joint and several liability. Under Article 205 of that directive, Member States may decide that a person other than the person liable for payment of VAT is to be held jointly and severally liable for payment of that tax. This provision does not, in principle, impose any limitation as to the person who is to be held jointly and severally liable for the payment of VAT or the type of transactions to be taken into account.[476] Nevertheless, the literature indicates that the imposition of such liability should be fully in line with the principles of legal certainty and proportionality underpinning EU VAT.[477] A similar position has also been expressed in CJEU case law.[478]

This means that Member States can adopt their own rules to ensure more efficient collection of VAT and introduce joint and several liability for platforms. Several Member States (including the UK, before its exit from the EU) have chosen to adopt such a solution.[479]

Academic legal writers also stress that the imposition of joint and several liability on platforms does not guarantee fully effective and efficient collection of VAT.[480] Placing full liability on the platforms to account for the VAT on the underlying

473. OECD, *The Impact of the Growth of the Sharing and Gig Economy on VAT/GST Policy and Administration* (n. 47) 73–74.
474. *Ibid.*
475. Beretta (n. 344) 306–308.
476. *Ibid.*, 280–282.
477. *Ibid.*, 306–308.
478. For example: *Vlaamse Oliemaatschappij NV v. FOD Financiën* [2011] CJEU Case C-499/10.
479. In the literature, it is indicated that national systems of liability can generally be divided into three models: the Austrian model, the British model, and the German model: Anne Janssen, 'The Problematic Combination of EU Harmonized and Domestic Legislation Regarding VAT Platform Liability' (2021) 32 International VAT Monitor 234–236 https://doi.org/10.59403/1he7gqc.
480. Pollak (n. 339) 300.

transactions they facilitate appears to be more effective. It should be noted that harmonized solutions of this type are currently being introduced at EU level (e.g., the deemed supplier regime for e-commerce platforms). This raises the question of how to treat the coexistence of the harmonized deemed supplier regimes and joint and several liability imposed on platforms by individual Member States. It seems that once full liability of platforms for the underlying transactions is introduced, the application of local joint and several liability rules in individual Member States may unduly burden platforms and is therefore not justified.

4.2.5 *Platforms as VAT Withholding Agents*

In its collection/withholding role, the platform is liable for collecting the VAT due on the underlying supply and remitting it to the tax authorities 'in the name' of the underlying supplier. The underlying supplier still must fulfil the remaining VAT accounting obligations - the platform merely acts as an intermediary for the payment of this tax.[481] The solution in question entails the need to inform underlying suppliers of the amounts of VAT paid by the platform to the tax authorities in their name so that they can fulfil their own reporting obligations.[482]

As the OECD points out, the withholding role of platforms is regarded as a 'lighter' version of the deemed supplier regime in the sense that the platform merely collects or withholds the VAT due on the underlying supplies facilitated and is not fully liable for their accounting. In contrast to the role of full liability of the platforms, it is the underlying supplier that ultimately remains liable to the tax authorities to account for the VAT on its supplies.[483]

The possibility of imposing an obligation on platforms to collect taxes where they have received or participated in the collection of the relevant rents or consideration has been confirmed by CJEU case law. In the case of *Airbnb Ireland III*, the CJEU stated that it is compatible with EU law to impose an obligation on providers of property intermediation services to withhold the amount of tax due on the amounts paid to hosts by tenants and to remit it to the State Treasury of that Member State.[484] The CJEU acknowledged that this may lead to a 'much greater burden' for platforms, but considering the overall operations of the operators involved, these costs can be regarded as low or limited.[485]

Thus, the accommodation sector platforms may participate in the remittance of taxes as withholding agents. For example, some such platforms remit the tourism tax, but this does not exempt STR service providers or tourists from their other tax

481. OECD, *The Impact of the Growth of the Sharing and Gig Economy on VAT/GST Policy and Administration* (n. 47) 81.
482. *Ibid.*, 83–84.
483. *Ibid.*
484. *Airbnb Ireland and Airbnb Payments UK* (n. 448).
485. Delhomme and Chapuis-Doppler (n. 222) 218.

obligations under the relevant legislation.[486] The EU legislator, however, has not chosen to introduce similar arrangements into the VAT system.

Nonetheless, it is worth noting that in November 2023, the Booking.com platform agreed to pay approximately EUR 94 million to settle a tax dispute in Italy related to its withholding obligations. Prosecutors in Genoa launched an investigation into Booking.com's, alleging that the company evaded EUR 153 million of VAT related to holiday rentals from 2013 to 2019. The Guardia di Finanza checked 896,500 property owners affiliated with Booking.com and concluded that VAT owed to Italy had not been paid, often due to the property owners' lack of VAT registration. According to Italian tax authorities, OTAs should act as withholding agents in such cases, responsible for collecting tax. Booking.com stated that the responsibility lies with the property owners and that the company acts solely as an intermediary. Finally, as part of the settlement, Booking.com filed its VAT return in Italy for the year 2022, amounting to more than EUR 19 million in taxes, and agreed to act as a tax substitute for all transactions involving private individuals not registered for VAT. It is noteworthy that Booking.com issued a statement affirming the company's continuous compliance with applicable Italian VAT law and clarified that the payment resulted from a mutual agreement with the Italian Revenue Agency covering the period from 2013 to 2021.[487]

4.3 Accommodation Sector Platforms as Undisclosed Agents

As indicated by the OECD, platforms can be held fully liable for the collection of VAT on the underlying transactions they facilitate.[488] It is possible that this type of solution will soon apply in the EU, as the Commission is planning to introduce the deemed supplier regime for, *inter alia*, accommodation sector platforms (this reform is discussed in detail in the third chapter). However, there is some doubt as to whether STR platforms can already, under Article 28 of the VAT Directive, qualify as so-called undisclosed agents and therefore be obliged to collect and account for VAT on the transactions they facilitate.

Under Article 28 of the VAT Directive, where a taxable person, acting in his own name but on behalf of a third party, takes part in the supply of services, that taxable person is deemed to have received and supplied those services himself. This provision dates back to 1977. It appeared in the original version of the Sixth Directive and then, when that directive was repealed, was moved unchanged to Article 28 of the VAT

486. European Commission, Directorate General for Internal Market, Industry, Entrepreneurship and SMEs, VVA, and Spark Legal Network (n. 48) 53–55.
487. A description of the *Booking.com* case based on the following press information: 'Booking.Com Betaalt € 94 Miljoen Bij Schikking Belastingzaak Italië', https://www.taxlive.nl/nl/documenten/nieuws/bookingcom-betaalt-94-miljoen-bij-schikking-belastingzaak-itali%C3%AB/ accessed 4 March 2024; Emilio Parodi, 'Booking.Com Settles Italian Tax Dispute with 94-Million Euro Payment' *Reuters* (10 November 2023), https://nieuws.nl/economie/20231110/booking-com-betaalt-94-miljoen-bij-schikking-belastingzaak-italie/ accessed 4 March 2024.
488. OECD, *The Impact of the Growth of the Sharing and Gig Economy on VAT/GST Policy and Administration* (n. 47) 61.

Directive. The reason for the introduction of this provision is not clear[489] although some authors point in this regard to the reasoning for the proposal for the Second Directive: '(...) whenever a sale or purchase transaction is effected through an agent or other intermediary acting in their own name or in the name of their companies, the supplies are always taxable, even if the object of the transaction is transferred directly from the first seller to the last buyer. Thus, in the case of a commission sale, the principal makes a taxable supply to the agent and the agent in turn makes a taxable supply to a third party (the buyer). In the case of a commission purchase, the third party (the seller) makes a taxable supply to the agent and the latter makes a taxable supply. When the intermediary does not act in his own name (e.g. a broker), he does not make the supply but performs a taxable service on the amount of the intermediation fee received'.[490]

As indicated in doctrine, the concept of a commissionaire is an old concept in civil law that has been well understood, if not always easy to apply, in a national setting. In light of this, it is not surprising that the VAT Directive contains rules regulating intermediaries acting in their own name on behalf of another.[491]

However, Article 28 of the VAT Directive (the wording of which has not changed since the 1970s) was not certainly intended to cover intermediaries such as platforms, as such entities did not exist in the market at the time. However, the provision is worded so broadly and generally that in practice there are doubts as to whether it does not cover platforms of the accommodation sector in certain cases.[492] In the following, the subject and object aspect of Article 28 of the VAT Directive and its mechanism of operation will be discussed. It will also be considered whether it could potentially apply to platforms intermediating STR services.

4.3.1 The Subject Aspect

The VAT Directive distinguishes between the situation of intermediaries acting both in the name of and on behalf of others and that of intermediaries acting in their own name but on behalf of third parties.

In the former case, intermediaries are referred to as 'disclosed agents'.[493] These are entities that simply facilitate contact between two parties. Such 'mere' intermediaries are outside the scope of Article 28 of the VAT Directive.

489. Christian Amand, 'Disclosed/Undisclosed Agent in EU VAT: When Is an Intermediary Acting in Its Own Name?' (2021) 32 International VAT Monitor 243-244 https://doi.org/10.59403/fs8dn9.
490. Ben Terra, Julie Kajus and Zsolt Szatmari, 'Chapter 4 - Taxable Transactions', *Commentary on European VAT* (IBFD online 2022).
491. Henkow (n. 410) 253.
492. For example: Beretta (n. 344); European Commission, 'VAT Expert Group No 095: VAT Treatment of the Sharing Economy, Taxud.c.1(2020)5816454' (n. 338); Matesanz, 'VAT Treatment of the Sharing Economy' (n. 342); Suso (n. 342).
493. Amand (n. 489); Beretta (n. 344) 284-285.

The provision of Article 28 of the VAT Directive deals with the second case and refers to an intermediary defined in legal writings as an 'undisclosed agent'[494] or more precisely as an 'agent of an undisclosed principal'.[495] These entities, acting in their own name, are not seen as intermediaries but as entities directly supplying goods or services to the customer.[496]

The provision of Article 28 of the VAT Directive sets out the conditions under which an undisclosed agent is considered to be a supplier under the EU VAT system. For this provision to apply, the intermediary must first meet three requirements: (i) take part in the supply of services, (ii) act in his own name, but (iii) on behalf of a third party. If even one of these three requirements is not met, the provision of Article 28 of the VAT Directive will not apply.

The first requirement means that the intermediary must be involved in the same supply chain which includes both the supplier and the final consumer of the service.[497] Reconstructing such a chain can be a difficult task, as they are often long, can cross national borders, and it is difficult to determine who is to be considered as the supplier of a given service to the final consumer.[498] Also, it is not easy to define the nature of taking part in the supply of services. It is fair to share the view that the more an intermediary is involved in the supply of a given service, the more likely it is to be classified as an undisclosed agent.[499] According to the academic opinion,[500] several criteria set out by the UK Supreme Court in the case *Secret Hotels2*[501] may be helpful in this regard. In that case, the company Secret Hotels2 operated a website through which it marketed accommodation in hotels, villas and flats in the Mediterranean and the Caribbean. The UK tax authorities concluded that Secret Hotels2 was providing accommodation services and therefore had to account for VAT in the UK. However, in the entrepreneur's view, he was acting as a disclosed agent of the actual supplier (the hotel operator), and therefore VAT on the supply of STR services should be payable in the country where the hotel was located rather than in the UK. In assessing Secret Hotels2's involvement in the supply of accommodation services, the Court specifically considered the following factors: (i) dealing with customers in its own name through its own website, (ii) dealing with customers in its own name where the hotel operator is unable to provide accommodation as booked, (iii) dealing with matters of complaint and compensation in its own name and without reference to the hotel operator, (iv) using the services of other taxable persons to provide travel facilitation services

494. This term is used, for example, by Amand (n. 489); Matesanz, 'VAT Treatment of the Sharing Economy' (n. 342).
495. 'Opinion of Advocate General Kokott Delivered on 24 February 2005 in Case C-305/03 Commission of the European Communities v United Kingdom of Great Britain and Northern Ireland', paragraph 41.
496. Beretta (n. 344) 284-285.
497. *Ibid.*, 311-312.
498. European Commission, *Explanatory Notes on the EU VAT Changes to the Place of Supply of Telecommunications, Broadcasting and Electronic Services That Enter into Force in 2015* (European Commission 2014) 22.
499. Amand (n. 489) 245-246.
500. Beretta (n. 344) 286-290.
501. *The Commissioners for Her Majesty's Revenue and Customs v. Secret Hotels2 Limited (formerly Med Hotels Limited)* [2014] British Supreme Court [2014] UKSC 16.

through the website, (v) treating deposits and other monies received from customers as its own monies, (vi) booking a number of rooms in advance at a number of hotels through an intermediary. Ultimately, the UK Supreme Court found that an intermediary such as Secret Hotels2, despite playing a fairly active role in the supply chain, is nevertheless a disclosed agent for EU VAT purposes.

The second requirement of Article 28 of the VAT Directive requires the intermediary to act in his own name. According to CJEU case law, intermediation in one's own name means that a legal relationship is brought about not directly between the ultimate purchaser of the service and the undertaking on whose behalf the intermediary operator acts, but between that operator and the purchaser of the services, on the one hand, and between that operator and the said undertaking, on the other.[502]

In turn, the academic literature notes that the following factors may be taken into account in this context: (i) the awareness of the parties' involvement in the supply of the services, primarily the awareness of the consumer about who is providing the service and what service is provided; (ii) the issue of building the brand of the services provided, who makes himself appear to be a supplier in the chain; and (iii) the possible added value to the supply, whether the intermediary changes in any way the service provided.[503]

It is worth noting, however, that in certain circumstances the mere fact that the final customer knows the identity of the actual supplier may not be sufficient to reject the application of Article 28 of the VAT Directive. Indeed, the CJEU has noted that: '(...) the argument put forward by Fenix that it would be contrary to Article 28 of the VAT Directive to treat the taxable person referred to in that article as the supplier of services when the final customer is aware of the existence of the agreement between the principal and the agent and the identity of that principal cannot be accepted either. (...) even if, despite the complexity of the chains of transactions which may characterise the supply of electronically supplied services, the final customer is, in certain cases, in a position to know the existence of the agency and the identity of the principal, those circumstances are not sufficient in themselves to exclude that the taxable person, taking part in the supply of services, acts in his or her own name but on behalf of another person, within the meaning of Article 28 of the VAT Directive (...). It is above all the powers enjoyed by that taxable person in the context of the supply of services in which he or she takes part which matter'.[504] The CJEU's opinion is, moreover, shared by the academic writers who recognize that the view that an intermediary would be a disclosed agent simply because the final buyers of services know who the actual supplier is could have a disruptive effect on the rules of the EU VAT system.[505]

It also appears that the internal relationship between the intermediary and the supplier (principal) should not affect the criterion of acting in one's own name, as the client usually has no insight into the internal relationship between these entities.[506] It

502. *Belgian State v. Pierre Henfling and Others* [2011] CJEU C-464/10, paragraph 33.
503. Jordan Goring, 'VAT: Agent vs Principal', https://www.crowe.com/uk/insights/avp-vat accessed 25 November 2022.
504. *Fenix International* [2023] CJEU C-695/20, paragraphs 87–88.
505. Amand (n. 489) 245–246.
506. Pollak (n. 339) 43.

is the external relationship (i.e., between the intermediary and the client) that determines whether the supplier is acting in his own name or in the name of a third party.[507]

The third requirement that the intermediary should act on behalf of a third party does not seem to raise any major doubts over its interpretation. It is worth noting that this provision only requires the intermediary to be a VAT taxable person,[508] meaning that the person on whose behalf he acts does not need to have this status. Moreover, it does not follow from Article 28 of the VAT Directive that it is a condition for its application that the taxable person acts in the name of the supplier of the underlying service – the provision should therefore be interpreted as meaning that an undisclosed agent may act either in the name of the supplier or in the name of the recipient of the service.[509]

The differences between a disclosed agent, an undisclosed agent and a supplier are illustrated in Figure 2.1. When an intermediary does not act in his own name but in the name of another party, then he should be considered a 'regular' disclosed agent. When he acts in his own name and on behalf of a third party, then he acquires the status of an undisclosed agent. When the intermediary acts only in his own name but not on behalf of a third party, then he is neither a disclosed agent nor an undisclosed agent but an entity providing his own service.

Figure 2.1 Differences Between a Disclosed Agent, an Undisclosed Agent and a Supplier

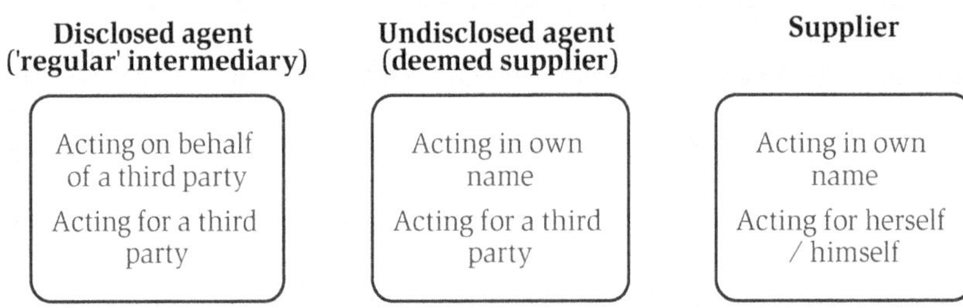

Source: Own compilation.

These conditions must be interpreted based on the contractual relationships. Although the VAT Directive does not stipulate in what form (oral or written) an order should be transmitted, it should be assumed that there must be an agreement between the intermediary and the supplier, the object of which is the award of the order in question.[510] As the legal literature rightly points out, contrary to what one might think,

507. Zechner (n. 368) 174.
508. BJM Terra and J Kajus, 'Chapter 10 – Taxable Transactions', *Introduction to European VAT* (IBFD online 2022).
509. Marta Papis-Almansa, *Insurance in the European VAT: On the Current and Preferred Treatment in the Light of the New Zealand and Australian GST Systems* (Lund University 2016) 269.
510. *ITH Comercial Timişoara SRL v. Agenţia Naţională de Administrare Fiscală – Direcţia Generală*

the examination of contractual documentation in practice may not be at all easy, as it must be assessed solely in the light of EU VAT, which means that the qualification may not match the interpretation of rights and obligations under contract law.[511]

In addition, in the event of discrepancies between contractual obligations and economic reality, the latter should be given priority.[512] Thus, when examining the fulfilment of the conditions of Article 28 of the VAT Directive, all the factual circumstances must be considered. As the CJEU points out: '(...) although it is for the referring court to inquire inter alia as to the nature of the contractual obligations of the trader concerned towards its customers, the proper working of the common VAT system nonetheless requires that court to check specifically so as to establish whether, in the light of all the facts of the case, that trader was in fact acting in its own name when supplying its services (...)'.[513]

4.3.2 The Object Aspect

It should be noted that Article 28 of the VAT Directive is worded in general terms and contains no limitations on its scope of application. Therefore, it covers all categories of services.[514]

As pointed out in the case law of the CJEU, for the application of the provision of Article 28 of the VAT Directive, it is also irrelevant whether the participation in the supply of services is for consideration.[515] Furthermore, it follows that if the services in the supply of which a trader acts as an intermediary are subject to VAT, the legal relationship between that trader and the entity on whose behalf he acts is also subject to VAT.[516] Similarly, if the supply of services in which an agent acts as an intermediary is exempt from VAT, the exemption also applies to the legal relationship between the principal and the agent, insofar as the exemption does not have special features in relation to the other exemptions.[517] According to the academic writings, the position of the CJEU is rather ambiguous; nevertheless, it seems that in the case of certain specific

Regională a Finanţelor Publice Bucureşti and Agenţia Naţională de Administrare Fiscală – Direcţia Generală Regională a Finanţelor [2020] CJEU C-734/19, paragraph 52.

511. Beretta (n. 344) 286–290.
512. Similarly: *Ibid.*, 311–312; Joe Dalton, 'Court of Appeal Ruling in Secret Hotels Confirms Economic over Contractual VAT Approach' (*ITR*, 13 December 2012), www.internationaltaxreview.com accessed 22 February 2023.
513. 'Opinion of Advocate General Richard de La Tour Delivered on 1 October 2020 in Case C-501/19 UCMR – ADA Asociaţia Pentru Drepturi de Autor a Compozitorilor v Pro Management Insolv IPURL, Acting as Liquidator of Asociaţia Culturală "Suflet de Român"'; in the opinion, the Advocate General referred to the judgment: *Belgian State v. Pierre Henfling and Others* (n. 502), paragraphs 38, 40 and 42.
514. *Fenix International* (n. 504), paragraph 54.
515. *Amărăşti Land Investment SRL v. Direcţia Generală Regională a Finanţelor Publice Timişoara and Administraţia Judeţeană a Finanţelor Publice Timiş* [2019] CJEU C-707/18, paragraph 42.
516. *European Commission v. Grand Duchy of Luxembourg* [2017] CJEU C-274/15, paragraph 87; *Amărăşti Land Investment SRL v. Direcţia Generală Regională a Finanţelor Publice Timişoara and Administraţia Judeţeană a Finanţelor Publice Timiş* (n. 515), paragraph 38; *UCMR – ADA Asociaţia pentru Drepturi de Autor a Compozitorilor v. Asociatia culturala 'Suflet de Român'* [2021] CJEU C-501/19, paragraph 49.
517. *Belgian State v. Pierre Henfling and Others* (n. 502), paragraphs 36–37.

exemptions, which are subject to strict requirements, the exemption should not apply to both supplies because they do not meet these specific conditions.[518] For example, where a platform intermediates an exempt educational service, the first transaction (from the supplier to the platform) will meet the subjective condition for exemption (the supplier meets the specific requirements for exemption), and the second transaction (from the platform to the consumer) should ultimately be exempt from VAT, even though it is highly unlikely that the platform will meet the objective and subjective requirements for that exemption.[519]

4.3.3 Mode of Operation

The CJEU explicitly indicates that Article 28 of the VAT Directive establishes that a taxable person who, in the context of a supply of services, acts as an intermediary in their own name but on behalf of another person is presumed to be the supplier of those services.[520]

Although not explicitly regulated in Article 28 of the VAT Directive, it is considered that an undisclosed agent, first, receives services from the entity in whose name he acts and then provides these services to the final customer.[521] It follows from the above that, as far as the legal relationship between principal and intermediary is concerned, the corresponding roles of payer and supplier are fictitiously reversed for VAT purposes.[522] According to well-established CJEU case law,[523] this provision therefore creates a legal fiction of two identical services provided in succession.[524] This means that a trader who intermediates in the supply of services, and who is an undisclosed agent, first receives the services in question from the entity on whose behalf he is acting (the principal) and second provides the same services to the customer. The intermediary is therefore considered, for EU VAT purposes, to be

518. Fernando Matesanz, 'The Increasing Liability of Digital Platforms in the Collection of EU VAT' (2023) 34 International VAT Monitor (online) https://doi.org/10.59403/qepx18.
519. *Ibid.*
520. *Fenix International* (n. 504), paragraph 55.
521. Terra and Kajus (n. 508).
522. *Belgian State v. Pierre Henfling and Others* (n. 502), paragraph 35.
523. *Amărăşti Land Investment SRL v. Direcţia Generală Regională a Finanţelor Publice Timişoara and Administraţia Judeţeană a Finanţelor Publice Timiş* (n. 515), paragraph 37; *Belgian State v. Pierre Henfling and Others* (n. 502), paragraph 35; *European Commission v. Grand Duchy of Luxembourg* (n. 516), paragraph 86; *UCMR – ADA Asociaţia pentru Drepturi de Autor a Compozitorilor v. Asociatia culturala 'Suflet de Român'* (n. 516), paragraph 43; *ITH Comercial Timişoara SRL v. Agenţia Naţională de Administrare Fiscală – Direcţia Generală Regională a Finanţelor Publice Bucureşti and Agenţia Naţională de Administrare Fiscală – Direcţia Generală Regională a Finanţelor* (n. 510), paragraph 49.
524. It is worth noting that, according to some authors, the existence of identical supplies should not be a condition for the application of the undisclosed agent fiction, as identical supplies are merely a consequence of applying this fiction. Considering the literal wording of Article 28 of the VAT Directive, which only requires that the agent acts in their own name, this view can be seen as justified: Ad van Doesum, 'Revisiting the Commissionaire Fiction in EU VAT Law: Cause, Effect and the Role of Identical Supplies' (2024) 35 International VAT Monitor, ibfd.org accessed 25 July 2024.

making a supply to the customer. In reality, therefore, he is a deemed supplier, which means that liability for collecting and accounting for VAT is imposed on him.[525]

Figure 2.2 illustrates the mechanism of Article 28 of the VAT Directive.

Figure 2.2 Mode of Operation of Article 28 of the VAT Directive: Fiction of Two Identical Services Provided in Succession

Source: Own compilation.

Consequently, because of the application of Article 28 of the VAT Directive, intermediaries are liable for the collection and payment of VAT. As pointed out in the literature, the service provided by an undisclosed agent does not constitute a stand-alone service (it is integrated into the commissioned service).[526] Under Article 28 of the VAT Directive, the activities of an intermediary are not distinguished from the tangible services upon which it bases its intermediation. This means that the intermediary charges VAT on the total price of the service, not just on the agreed fee or commission for the intermediary services.[527]

4.3.4 Application of Article 28 of the VAT Directive to STR Platforms

In practice, it seems quite difficult to distinguish when an intermediary acts as a disclosed agent and when as an undisclosed agent. To do so requires analysing each case individually, based on rather vague and broadly formulated considerations, which may lead to divergent interpretations. At the same time, the distinction is extremely important, as qualification into one or the other category of intermediaries entails completely different consequences under the VAT Directive.

Drawing inspiration from case law and academic literature, it is possible to identify several considerations that may help in assessing whether the selected business models of platforms in the accommodation sector, represented by platforms such as Airbnb, Booking.com, Couchsurfing and HomeExchange, could potentially meet the criteria set out in Article 28 of the VAT Directive.

525. Beretta (n. 344) 286–290.
526. Zechner (n. 368) 181.
527. It is worth noting that, according to some authors, the undisclosed agent fiction should not be applied to, or extended to, elements that the agents add in their own name and on their own behalf when these are not merely ancillary: Doesum (n. 524).

It is also worth noting the VAT Committee's guidance on the liability of platforms mediating the supply of transport services.[528] Of course, these guidelines should not be directly applied to platforms in the accommodation sector, but they do provide some guidance as to when platforms may be considered a supplier under Article 28 of the VAT Directive. In the guidelines, the VAT Committee almost unanimously concluded that when a platform participates in the supply of a service, acting in its own name but on behalf of another person materially performing that service, the platform is deemed, under Article 28 of the VAT Directive, to be the entity that has itself received and performed the service in question. However, this applies when the electronic platform assumes legal liability for the proper functioning and supply of the service materially provided by another person, and when the following conditions are met: (i) the platform has control over all material aspects necessary to provide the service in question; (ii) the average customer perceives the platform (and not the person actually performing the service) as the provider of the service; (iii) the service cannot be provided under the same conditions without the platform's involvement. The selected considerations are set out in Table 2.1.

528. European Commission, 'VAT Committee Guidelines Resulting from the 111th Meeting of 30 November 2018: Services Provided by an Electronic Platform Connecting for Remuneration, by Means of a Smartphone Application, a Driver Using His Own Vehicle with Persons Who Wish to Make Urban Journeys, Taxud.c.1(2019)4045223 – 964'.

Table 2.1 A List of Example Criteria That Can Be Considered to Determine Whether STR Platforms Participate in the Provision of Services, in Accordance with Article 28 of the VAT Directive

	Criteria	*Airbnb*	*Booking.com*	*Couchsurfing*	*HomeExchange*
1	The platform provides users with access to its own website/application	V	V	V	V
2	The platform establishes general terms of service provision	V	V	V	V
3	The platform provides contact details of each party to the underlying transaction to the other party	X	V	X	V
4	The platform controls or sets the price of accommodation	X	X	X	V
5	The platform mainly uses its own properties to provide accommodation services	X	X	X	X
6	The platform is involved in a complaints and compensation system	V	V	X	V
7	The platform prepares VAT settlements for hosts	V	V	X	X
8	The platform acts as an intermediary in payment matters between the host and the guest	V	V	V	V
9	The platform has the right to remove its user under certain circumstances	V	V	V	V
10	By using the platform, the user is aware that the accommodation service will be provided by a specific host	V	V	V	V
11	Value added to the delivery (platform provides, for example, payment system or reviews)	V	V	V	V

Source: Criteria (from 1 to 9) and analysis for Airbnb and HomeExchange platforms developed by G. Beretta.[529] Criteria 2, 4, 5, 8, and 10 are also referenced by L. Zechner in assessing whether the platform can be considered a undisclosed agent.[530] Criteria (from 10 to 11) and their analysis for Airbnb and HomeExchange platforms as well as the analysis of all criteria for Booking.com and Couchsurfing platforms – own compilation. It should be emphasized that the indicated list of criteria is neither final nor do the conditions presented have to be met collectively for the STR platform to be considered participating in supply services, in accordance with Article 28 of the VAT Directive.

The table illustrates certain commonalities among the analysed business models of platforms in the accommodation sector. Specifically, all the assessed platforms meet certain conditions listed in the table. For instance, each platform provides its users with

529. Beretta (n. 344) 294–295.
530. Zechner (n. 368) 178.

access to its website or application, establishes general terms and conditions of service, sets standards of interaction between users, generally does not utilize its own properties for the supply of accommodation services, mediates payment matters, and retains the right to deactivate a user's account under specific circumstances. Users using these platforms also seem to be aware that accommodation services will be provided by specific hosts of their choice. Moreover, the analysed platforms, through payment and review systems, appear to add some value to the accommodation services provided.

Despite these commonalities, there are notable differences. Both Airbnb and Booking.com are platforms that do not control or directly influence the consideration for the underlying service, as this is determined by the hosts. In the case of Couchsurfing, accommodation use is free, making it challenging to discuss consideration for accommodation. While HomeExchange is essentially free (the host's consideration is the opportunity to use their guest's home at no cost), the platform grants GuestPoints which can be exchanged for a night's accommodation in another user's home. GuestPoints can be considered a form of consideration for accommodation, with the amount set by the platform.

Airbnb and Couchsurfing also do not – other than in a limited way – share the contact details of each party to the underlying transaction with the other party, unlike HomeExchange and Booking.com which share such data. All platforms, except for Couchsurfing, participate in the complaints and compensation system. Airbnb and Booking.com help hosts account for VAT, unlike Couchsurfing and HomeExchange.

Referring generally to the way and conditions in which the platforms identified above do business, it appears that individual hosts remain the dominant party to these transactions. Furthermore, the underlying (accommodation) services as such could potentially be provided under similar conditions without the involvement of the platforms. Yes, until guests choose a specific accommodation, the platforms deal with them in their own name, but once the booking is made, the platforms start acting in the name of the hosts. It is also essential to note that in platform-created business models, the end consumer is typically fully aware of both the suppliers (the hosts) and the intermediary (the platform). In situations where the power of attorney is evident, and the identity of the supplier is known, the intermediary, as a general rule, should not be treated as if it is providing or receiving a supply of services. Indeed, in order to apply Article 28 of the VAT Directive, the platform should fulfil the requirements of acting in its own name and in the name of the supplier.[531] However, it should be emphasized that this circumstance alone is not sufficient to reject the application of Article 28 of the VAT Directive.[532]

In terms of the transactions concluded, the analysed platforms seem to offer services separate from those provided by hosts (the underlying services and the final services provided by the platforms are not identical). All the platforms examined offered payment and review systems, and Booking.com, Airbnb, and HomeExchange also provided complaints and compensation systems. Therefore, it can be argued that while the host provides a service consisting simply of accommodation, the platforms

531. Pollak (n. 339) 308.
532. *Fenix International* (n. 504), paragraphs 87–88.

also provide ancillary services aimed at enhancing the use of the underlying service. It is difficult to argue for the idea that the principal (the host) provides a service to the intermediary, and the intermediary provides an identical service to the guest.[533] This perspective is supported by the fact that various transactions can now be concluded through a single platform[534] (some STR platforms, such as Booking.com or Airbnb, enable booking not only accommodation but also car rentals, trips to cultural events, etc.). It should be emphasized, however, that according to some legal doctrines, the undisclosed agent fiction can apply even if the agent adds elements; it should not matter whether the supply by the agent remains identical to the supply from the principal.[535] Thus, if this view is accepted, whether the STR platform provides identical services or adds additional elements would be irrelevant for the application of Article 28 of the VAT Directive.

It is also worth noting that, according to some authors, STR platforms might fall under Article 28 of the VAT Directive if the services they provide are classified as intermediation.[536] Thus, if it is considered that the platforms provide an electronic service, the problem will not arise. This view is debatable because such a requirement does not directly follow from the wording of Article 28 of the VAT Directive, which only refers to acting for a third party, and the concept of 'intermediation' as such is not defined under EU VAT rules.

Although the qualification of the services provided by the platform remains contentious, the prevailing view at present is that they are electronic services.[537] Assuming that Article 28 of the VAT Directive only applies to platforms providing intermediation services, a platform is currently unlikely to be considered a deemed supplier under this provision. However, it should be noted that the Commission plans to clarify that a service provided by a platform to non-taxable persons should be considered an intermediation service (planned Article 46a of the VAT Directive).[538] Such a change may increase the likelihood of STR platforms potentially being covered by Article 28 of the VAT Directive.

It should be noted that part of the doubt as to whether certain platforms are intermediaries covered by Article 28 of the VAT Directive has been eliminated by the clarification contained in Article 9a of the IR. According to this provision, platforms intermediating in the supply of electronic services and internet telephone services, in the circumstances set out in this regulation, are covered by Article 28 of the VAT Directive. However, the provision of Article 9a of the IR only applies to platforms facilitating the supply of electronic services or telephone services provided through the internet. It does not therefore apply to STR platforms, as these intermediate in the

533. Matesanz, 'VAT Treatment of the Sharing Economy' (n. 342) 105–107.
534. *Ibid.*
535. Doesum (n. 524).
536. Suso (n. 342) 11.
537. European Commission, Directorate General for Taxation and Customs Union and others (n. 6) 36–37.
538. Proposal for a Council Directive amending Directive 2006/112/EC as regards VAT rules for the digital age (n. 382).

supply of accommodation services, and these services are explicitly excluded from the definition of electronically supplied services (Article 7(3)(u) IR).

It therefore seems that if Article 28 of the VAT Directive were to cover other platforms, for example, those intermediating in the supply of accommodation services, a corresponding clarification should also be included in the IR, as was the case for platforms facilitating the supply of electronic services and telephone services provided through the internet. Since there is no such supply, it can be concluded *a contrario* that Article 28 of the VAT Directive does not apply to platforms other than those covered by the clarification in Article 9a of the IR.[539] Furthermore, Article 9a IR was implemented because 'it is necessary to specify who is the supplier for VAT purposes where electronically supplied services, or telephone services provided through the internet, are supplied to a customer through telecommunications networks or via an interface or a portal'.[540] Since such clarification was not necessary for platforms providing other services, such as accommodation platforms, it can be assumed that there is no doubt that they were not subject to Article 28 of the VAT Directive.

However, a different interpretation is also possible. It is worth noting that Article 9a IR explicitly indicates that if a platform fulfils at least one of the following conditions: (i) approves the charging of payment to the customer, (ii) approves the supply of the facilitated services, or (iii) establishes general terms and conditions for the supply of the facilitated services, it will be treated as a deemed supplier. At the same time, in the *Fenix* case, the CJEU found that Article 9a IR does not change the normative content established by Article 28 of the VAT Directive, but, on the contrary, it limits itself to specifying its application.[541] Therefore, the conditions for the participation of platforms in the supply of services indicated in Article 9a IR should be considered in the interpretation and application of Article 28 of the VAT Directive. Since these three characteristics are present in all the business models of accommodation sector platforms discussed (especially given the broad interpretation of these concepts in the EC Explanatory Notes),[542] this would mean that they could be treated as deemed suppliers for the purposes of Article 28 of the VAT Directive.[543]

However, it is worth bearing in mind that the judgment in question was delivered in specific factual circumstances and that it primarily concerned the conditions for the

539. This conclusion seems to be confirmed by the fact that even before the introduction of Article 9a IR, there were guidelines from the VAT Committee, according to which intermediaries participating in the provision of electronic services to final consumers were presumed to act on their own name but on behalf of the electronic service provider, as provided for in Article 28 of the VAT Directive (unless another entity is expressly indicated as the electronic service provider): European Commission, 'VAT Committee Guidelines Resulting from the 93rd Meeting of 1 July 2011: Electronic Services Supplied by Service Providers Using the Network of Telecommunications Provider, Taxud.c.1(2012)1410604 – 709'.

540. Council Implementing Regulation (EU) No 1042/2013 of 7 October 2013 amending Implementing Regulation (EU) No 282/2011 as regards the place of supply of services [OJ L 284, 26.10.2013, pp. 1-9], recital 4.

541. *Fenix International* (n. 504), paragraph 86.

542. European Commission, *Explanatory Notes on the EU VAT Changes to the Place of Supply of Telecommunications, Broadcasting and Electronic Services That Enter into Force in 2015* (n. 498).

543. Further discussion on this topic can be found in Ch. 3.

application of Article 9a IR and their compatibility with Article 28 of the VAT Directive. It would therefore appear that Article 9a IR is *lex specialis* to Article 28 of the VAT Directive, and the specific conditions contained therein are laid down for the specific entities defined therein. They should therefore not be extended too broadly to other platforms not directly affected by Article 9a IR.

It is worth noting that a different interpretation is also possible. It can be argued that presumptions defined in Article 9a IR, which is only there to explain the VAT Directive, should also apply to other than the two services specifically addressed in that provision. As pointed out in doctrine, 'Actually, it would seem strange that Article 9a was irrelevant as an explanation of Article 28 of the VAT Directive with regard to other services (...). Article 9a of the Implementing regulation is important for the interpretation of art 28. The presumptions are applicable mutatis mutandis to other services.'[544]

Furthermore, it seems that to apply the discussed criteria from Article 9a IR, one must first meet the more general criteria set out in Article 28 of the VAT Directive. To apply this provision, the supplies of services transferred to the principal should be identical.[545] It is rather indisputable that this criterion is met in the case of electronic services - the service provided by the supplier and intermediated by the platform will be the same service received by the recipient. As mentioned above, in the case of STR platforms, it is not entirely clear whether it can be argued that the service provided by the host to the platform would be identical to the service subsequently provided by the platform to the guest and therefore whether this criterion would be met.

In conclusion, it appears that the analysed business models of accommodation sector platforms do not currently meet the conditions of Article 28 of the VAT Directive.[546] However, it is worth emphasizing that the factors indicated above are not in themselves sufficient to exclude a priori the applicability of this provision. The analysis made referred primarily to publicly available contractual documentation and the terms and conditions of service of the platforms, and it is equally important to consider the economic reality of each case. Furthermore, Article 28 of the VAT Directive is so broadly worded that it does not seem possible to unambiguously decide from it whether a given STR platform is an undisclosed agent.

Due to the ambiguities related to the status of platforms under Article 28 of the VAT Directive, the legal literature has advocated the introduction of a new liability regime dedicated to service platforms in the EU VAT system.[547] To meet these expectations, the Commission has drafted a legislative proposal[548] which aims, *inter alia*, to update the VAT rules for STR platforms. Under the planned Article 28a of the

544. Henkow (n. 410) 249–250.
545. 'Opinion of Advocate General Rantos Delivered on 15 September 2022 in Case C-695/20 Fenix International Limited v Commissioners for Her Majesty's Revenue and Customs', paragraph 52.
546. Similarly: Pollak (n. 339) 308. Literal and systemic interpretation seems to argue against the application of Article 28 of the VAT Directive to services facilitated by platforms.
547. Beretta (n. 344) 293–297.
548. Proposal for a Council Directive amending Directive 2006/112/EC as regards VAT rules for the digital age (n. 382).

VAT Directive, when the underlying supplier (the host) does not charge VAT because he is, for example, a natural person or benefits from the special scheme applicable to SMEs, the platform will account for VAT on the underlying supply (the accommodation).

However, it appears that the introduction of a new liability regime dedicated to STR platforms in the EU VAT system as proposed will not resolve definitively the issue of whether Article 28 of the VAT Directive applies to them. It should be noted that if Article 28a of the VAT Directive comes into force, it will only cover C2C and C2B transactions, but not B2B and B2C.[549] Accordingly, in theory, it will still be possible for accommodation sector platforms facilitating B2B and B2C transactions to be deemed a supplier under Article 28 of the VAT Directive. Therefore, it seems that the EC should further clarify this issue.

5 SUMMARY

The development of the STR platform economy is a relatively recent phenomenon and therefore faces problems and challenges in relation to the correct VAT taxation. This tax was introduced in the EU before the rise of the digital economy, and the solutions contained in this tax are therefore proving to be inadequate for new models of doing business. The most significant problems experienced by the platform economy under the EU VAT system are mainly related to divergent interpretations regarding the status of entities involved in the supply of services through platforms and the nature of the platform services.

A particularly controversial issue revolves around determining whether hosts operating through STR platforms can be considered VAT taxable persons. The literature lacks unanimity on whether joining a platform to offer accommodation services implies an intention to earn a recurring income, which may potentially qualify this activity as a business activity. Establishing a direct link between the supply of the service and the host's receipt of consideration in barter transactions, such as house swaps, also poses challenges. Currently, each case needs to be analysed on a case-by-case basis, resulting in legal uncertainty in this area.

Member States and the academic community interpret differently also the nature of platform services. The classification of STR platform services as electronic, intermediation, or services connected with immovable properties is a subject of dispute. These differing interpretations not only contribute to legal uncertainty but also lead to double taxation or non-taxation issues. Although the Commission plans to clarify regulations in this area, it may be difficult to reach a consensus on this issue, given the impact the qualification of platform services has on income distribution among Member States.

While the dynamic growth of the platform economy presents challenges to the EU VAT system, it also offers new opportunities for the enforcement of tax obligations. With access to relevant transaction information, platforms have the potential to play an important role in VAT collection. For example, platforms can educate underlying

549. Further discussion on this topic can be found in Ch. 3.

suppliers on their tax obligations, enter into formal cooperation agreements with tax authorities, provide information and data to these authorities, be jointly and severally liable with underlying suppliers, or act as VAT collectors.

Platform liability may also extend beyond the roles indicated above. For example, platforms can also be held fully liable for the collection of VAT on the underlying transactions they facilitate (the deemed supplier regime). It is possible that this type of solution will soon apply in the EU, as the Commission is planning to introduce the deemed supplier regime for, *inter alia*, accommodation sector platforms. However, there is already some doubt as to whether platforms in the accommodation sector can qualify as so-called undisclosed agents (Article 28 of the VAT Directive) and therefore be obliged to collect VAT on the transactions they facilitate. As a result of that, platforms would have a liability similar to that envisaged under the deemed supplier regime. The case law and views of the legal academia analysed lead to the conclusion that the accommodation sector platforms do not appear to meet the conditions of Article 28 of the VAT Directive and therefore should not be treated as undisclosed agents. However, Article 28 of the VAT Directive is so broadly worded that this cannot be conclusively determined based on it, and therefore each case currently requires a case-by-case analysis.

CHAPTER 3
The EU Models of the Deemed Supplier Regime

1 BACKGROUND

Platforms are increasingly involved in the collection of taxes, including VAT. Legislators are also increasingly coming to the conclusion that platforms could directly collect VAT on the transactions they facilitate as taxable persons.

Assuming that Article 28 of the VAT Directive does not apply to STR platforms, these entities are currently only liable to account for VAT on the consideration they receive intermediating in the supply of accommodation services. They are not liable for accounting for VAT on the STR services. In this case, the hosts are liable for VAT collection. It is likely that this situation will change over the next few years, and arrangements will be put in place that will put these platforms in the position of deemed suppliers.[550] Under this concept, in certain situations, platforms would be liable for assessing and collecting VAT also on the underlying transactions they facilitate. The platforms, deemed to be the supplier, would therefore have the same rights and obligations for VAT purposes as currently their users have, who actually supply the services in question (the underlying suppliers). Consequently, in the case of STR platforms, they would also be treated as VAT taxable persons for accommodation services supplied by hosts.

Figure 3.1 shows how the liability for the accounting for VAT on accommodation transactions concluded via platforms in the EU is currently structured.

550. Proposal for a Council Directive amending Directive 2006/112/EC as regards VAT rules for the digital age (n. 382).

Figure 3.1 Liability for the Accounting for VAT on STR Transactions Concluded via Platforms

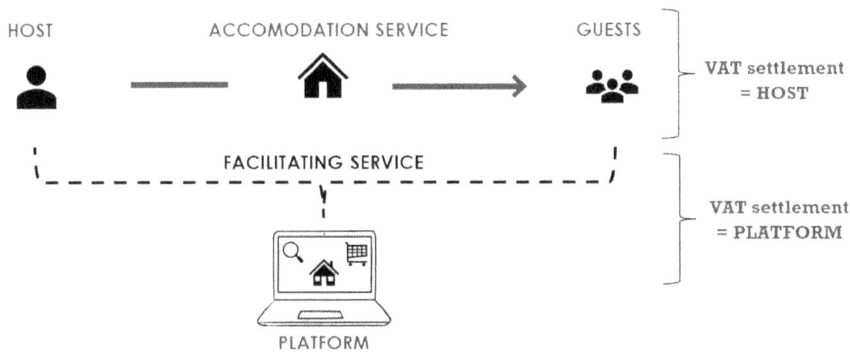

Source: Own compilation.

This chapter will present the concept of the deemed supplier as the most far-reaching legislative solution imposing liability on the platform for the collection of VAT. Three models of the deemed supplier relating to platforms under the European VAT system will be discussed: the model governed by Article 9a of the IR, the model governed by Article 14a of the VAT Directive and the model to be governed by Article 28a of the VAT Directive assuming the amendments proposed by the EC come into force.

The first model refers to platforms intermediating the supply of intangible digital services. This model will hereinafter be referred to as the digital model. The second model refers to platforms facilitating certain supplies of goods. This model will be referred to as the e-commerce model. The third model refers to platforms facilitating the supply of tangible services (including STR services). This model will be referred to as the service model in the remainder of the book.

For each model, the historical background will be presented, followed by a discussion of the basic principles underlying its operation under EU law, including the rationale for its application (the subject and object aspects), as well as its method of operation. The evaluation of each model, however, will be presented in the fourth chapter.

2 THE CONCEPT OF THE DEEMED SUPPLIER

There are several names to describe the idea that transaction intermediaries (such as platforms) become directly liable for collecting and accounting for VAT on the underlying transactions they facilitate.

For example, the OECD in 2015 used the name 'intermediary collection model' which it defines as follows: a model where VAT on imports of low-value goods would be collected and remitted by intermediaries[551] on behalf of non-resident vendors, assuming that such intermediaries would have the required information to assess and remit the right amount of taxes in the country of importation.[552] In another 2017 study, the OECD uses the term 'deemed supplier approach', noting that it introduces presumptions under which an intermediary is deemed to be the statutory designated supplier for VAT compliance purposes.[553] In the 2019 paper, the OECD also uses the term 'full liability regime', explaining that this regime makes the platform fully and solely liable for assessing, collecting and remitting the VAT/GST due on the online sales it facilitates.[554] The same wording is also used by the OECD in its 2021 report, where it is written that under this regime, the platform is designated by law as the supplier, making it solely and fully liable for assessing, collecting and remitting the VAT on the activity that goes through the platform.[555]

In the context of the European VAT system, the EU institutions seem to use the phrase 'deemed supplier' most frequently. This is the term used, for example, by the EC in its explanatory notes to the VAT e-commerce package,[556] or in the latest legislative proposal concerning, *inter alia*, the VAT treatment of STR platforms[557] and in its impact assessment.[558] Also, in European VAT scholarly literature, authors often use the phrase 'deemed supplier'[559] in the context of solutions relating to making platforms fully liable for the VAT obligations of their underlying suppliers.

Given the above, in the remainder of this book, the term 'the deemed supplier regime' will be used. This concept will mean introducing a mechanism into the VAT system whereby an intermediary, such as a platform, will, in certain circumstances, be deemed fully liable for accounting for VAT on the underlying transaction, as if it were the underlying supplier itself. The platform will, as it were, step into the tax role of the underlying supplier.

By introducing the deemed supplier regime, the assumption is made that platforms have sufficient control over the transactions they facilitate and have the necessary data to account for VAT on transactions carried out by their underlying suppliers. As has been rightly emphasized by the OECD, the imposition of the deemed

551. The OECD has identified four main types of intermediaries in the context of electronic commerce: (i) postal operators, (ii) express carriers, (iii) e-commerce platforms, and (iv) financial intermediaries. OECD (ed.), *Addressing the Tax Challenges of the Digital Economy: Action 1: 2015 Final Report* (OECD 2015) 125.
552. *Ibid.*
553. OECD (ed.), *Mechanisms for the Effective Collection of VAT/GST* (OECD 2017) 26.
554. OECD, *The Role of Digital Platforms in the Collection of VAT/GST on Online Sales* (OECD 2019) 22.
555. OECD, *The Impact of the Growth of the Sharing and Gig Economy on VAT/GST Policy and Administration* (n. 47) 76.
556. European Commission, *Explanatory Notes on VAT E-Commerce Rules. Council Directive (EU) 2017/2455. Council Directive (EU) 2019/1995. Council Implementing Regulation (EU) 2019/2026* (n. 164) 8.
557. Proposal for a Council Directive amending Directive 2006/112/EC as regards VAT rules for the digital age (n. 382).
558. European Commission, 'Impact Assessment Report, SWD(2022) 393 Final' (n. 362).
559. For example: Lamensch and others (n. 104); Sergio Messina, 'VAT E-Commerce Package: Customs Bugs in the System?' (2021) 13 World Tax Journal https://doi.org/10.59403/1p1nknf; Janssen (n. 479).

supplier regime should be limited to intermediaries who control key aspects of a digital supply.[560] Intermediaries who do not play a direct role in the transaction, such as payment processors or technical intermediaries who provide internet access, should generally not be considered capable of acquiring the status of the deemed supplier for VAT purposes.[561]

In general, the deemed supplier regime does not cover all, but only a selection of, underlying transactions supplied through the platform. The distinction may arise, for example, from: (i) the nature of the transaction (the deemed supplier model may be limited to only certain electronic transactions, the supply of goods or services), (ii) the type of transaction (B2B, B2C, C2C, C2B) or (iii) the location of the underlying suppliers (some jurisdictions have decided to limit the deemed supplier model to platforms that facilitate the supply of services to foreign suppliers).[562]

It seems that over the next few years, legislators will increasingly introduce solutions that will position platforms as deemed suppliers.[563] In this context, it is worth noting the 2018 US Supreme Court decision in *South Dakota v. Wayfair*.[564] The US court ruled that businesses can be subject to sales tax in a state even if they do not have a physical presence in the taxing state. Previously, sellers were only required to collect this tax if they had a physical presence in the state. The Court held that such rules were removed from economic reality, especially considering the increasing number of transactions conducted exclusively online. As a result of this decision, state authorities were able to start requiring the collection and remittance of tax by sellers who met the state's income or number of transactions threshold (even if they did not have a physical presence there). In practice, therefore, the ability of individual states to impose sales taxes was expanded.[565] While the decision applied to all sellers, not just those using the intermediation of platforms, it also significantly affected the platforms' sales tax obligations. As indicated in the literature, following the *Wayfair* decision, it was recognized that platforms as marketplace facilitators sometimes own the transaction process on behalf of their sellers and may therefore be required to meet the tax obligations of those sellers.[566] Currently, all US states that collect sales tax have enacted legislation requiring platform operators that qualify as marketplace intermediaries and have a physical presence in the state to collect and remit tax on behalf of retailers selling through the platform.[567] It is worth noting, however, that even before the *Wayfair* decision, platforms in some states were voluntarily collecting and remitting

560. OECD, *Mechanisms for the Effective Collection of VAT/GST* (n. 550) 26.
561. *Ibid.*
562. Scarcella (n. 391) 6–7.
563. Asquith, 'Co-Opting Gig & Sharing Platforms as Tax Collectors' (n. 440).
564. *South Dakota v. Wayfair, Inc, et al* [2018] Supreme Court of the United States Nos 17–494.
565. Viswanathan (n. 407) 364–366.
566. Kuijper, Cameron and Szatmari (n. 420) 589–590.
567. However, these provisions differ from each other. Two states in the USA issued private rulings examining nearly identical scenarios but reached divergent conclusions as to whether the platform operator was obligated to collect tax. Aleksandra Bal, 'Platform Economy: Will The Real Tax Collector Please Stand Up?' (*Forbes*), https://www.forbes.com/sites/aleksandrabal/2023/03/15/platform-economy-will-the-real-tax-collector-please-stand-up/ accessed 4 April 2023.

sales taxes, presumably considering such an arrangement preferable to waiting for future, more onerous regulations.[568]

Of course, the decision in question had no direct impact on the EU VAT system. However, because the problems concerning the platform economy, also in the area of accommodation, are of a global nature, solutions relating to indirect taxation introduced by some jurisdictions may provide inspiration for others. For example, the platform liability solutions presented by the EC in the VAT e-commerce package are considered to be very similar to those introduced in Australia,[569] and the planned solutions for accommodation sector platforms to those of Canada.[570] However, it is worth noting that there is no uniform international approach in this respect – a platform operator carrying out the same activity may be a deemed supplier in one country but no longer in another. It is fair to say that this patchwork of inconsistent and ambiguous rules makes it difficult for global platform operators to manage tax compliance.[571]

The growing popularity of the deemed supplier regime appears to be driven by several factors. First and foremost, this arrangement shifts the liability for tax accounting and collection from many, usually small entities (the underlying suppliers) to entities that are smaller in number but generally much larger (the platforms mediating transactions). This makes it easier for tax authorities to monitor and enforce whether underlying transactions are accounted for correctly. It seems less burdensome to investigate fewer but larger platforms than to audit many small underlying suppliers. As pointed out in the literature, by placing the burden of tax accounting on platforms that have 'more to lose' than individual hosts, tax administrations increase the likelihood of tax compliance of these transactions.[572] It also seems safer to collect tax from a platform in situations where its underlying suppliers are not established or registered as taxable persons in a particular jurisdiction.[573] Furthermore, it is accepted that platforms have a greater ability to make appropriate tax decisions and correctly

568. Viswanathan (n. 407) 364–366.
569. Aleksandra Bal, 'Managing EU VAT Risks for Platform Business Models' (2018) 72 Bulletin for International Taxation, ibfd.org accessed 4 February 2021 https://doi.org/10.59403/2xs72f7.
570. European Commission, Directorate General for Taxation and Customs Union and others (n. 6) 108–109; however, it should be noted that referring to 'Canadian solutions' involves some generalization, as they are not uniform. In Canadian jurisdictions, sales taxes (e.g., GST/HST, PST, QST) are levied on STR transactions. For instance, in Saskatchewan, accommodation platforms are now mandated to register as vendors to collect and remit the 6% PST on all transactions conducted through their platforms. Moreover, in 2021, Québec implemented changes that necessitated the collection of QST on all STR bookings, regardless of whether the owner is registered for QST. Consequently, individuals renting an STR in Québec through platforms such as Airbnb will be automatically charged QST, irrespective of the host's status as a small supplier. More recently, in 2022, amendments to the Provincial Sales Tax Act were enacted, compelling online accommodation platforms to register for collecting and remitting the 8% PST on the booking services they offer, as well as on the sale of accommodation (on behalf of hosts): Anna Cameron and Lindsay M Tedds, *Managing the Short-Term Rental Market in Canada: A Comparative Analysis of Policy, Planning, and Regulatory Strategies in 25 Municipalities* (City of Calgary 2023) 32–33.
571. Bal (n. 564).
572. Viswanathan (n. 407) 363–364.
573. European Commission, 'Impact Assessment Report, SWD(2022) 393 Final' (n. 362).

account for transactions than a wide range of, usually small, traders.[574] It can also be argued that shifting the burden to platforms is fair, as they are the beneficiaries of the development of the digital economy.[575] Shifting the liability for tax accounting to platforms thus also reduces the tax compliance burden on the underlying suppliers. This is because suppliers do not have to deal with charging the correct amount of VAT to the customer and remitting it to the tax office.[576]

For these reasons, tax administrations may see the deemed supplier regime as an effective way to enforce obligations on smaller vendors who are unwilling or unable to increase their tax collection and reporting efforts.[577] The reduction in compliance obligations also increases opportunities for expansion of the underlying suppliers in foreign markets.[578]

3 THE DIGITAL MODEL

3.1 Historical Background

Until a few years ago, buying items like music, software, and films in physical formats was the norm; however, the rise of downloads has now made them the prevailing method. This shift has resulted in VAT complications - while software stored on physical mediums is typically classified as a good, its electronic download is treated as a service. Such differentiation necessitates alterations in determining tax jurisdictions, applicable VAT rates, and other administrative requirements.[579]

As outlined in the first chapter, initially platforms mainly enabled their users to circulate all types of digital content.[580] When there was a strong increase in this type of supply, especially cross-border, this led to problems with VAT, notably no tax collection or an inappropriately low amount of tax collection.

As an example, the OECD cites the situation where digital content is supplied to consumers via mobile devices by suppliers who are not established in the same jurisdiction as its customers. If the right to levy VAT is assigned to the jurisdiction in which the supplier is established and that jurisdiction does not levy VAT, then a situation can easily arise where VAT will not be collected anywhere. Therefore, domestic suppliers required to remit VAT on digital services provided to their domestic consumers may be at a disadvantage compared to foreign suppliers based in jurisdictions where no or an inappropriately low amount of VAT would be collected on such

574. OECD, *Mechanisms for the Effective Collection of VAT/GST* (n. 550) 26–27.
575. *Ibid.*
576. Madeleine Merkx, 'Platform Liability: An Efficient and Fair Collection Model for VAT?' in Christian Amand and others, *VAT Challenges and Opportunities in the New Digital Economy* (Madrid VAT Forum Foundation 2022) 15.
577. Kuijper, Cameron and Szatmari (n. 420) 589–590.
578. OECD, *Mechanisms for the Effective Collection of VAT/GST* (n. 550) 26–27.
579. Maruša Pozvek, 'VAT in Digital Electronic Commerce' (2017) 4 Journal for the International and European Law, Economics and Market Integrations 38 https://doi.org/10.22598/iele.2017.4.1.3.
580. Zieba and Durst (n. 1) 255.

supply. This may also encourage domestic suppliers to restructure their affairs so that digital services are supplied by them from offshore locations.[581]

With this in mind, the OECD recommends that the supply of intangible services in B2C transactions should be subject to VAT in line with the destination principle (the jurisdiction of residence of the consumer). This ensures an even playing field between domestic and offshore suppliers, as this solution ensures there is no tax advantage for companies based in low- or no-tax jurisdictions.[582]

Assuming that the VAT taxing right is allocated to the jurisdiction in which the consumer is resident, it proves to be a challenge to ensure the effective collection of VAT. This is particularly the case when digital services are purchased by the consumer from foreign suppliers. In such a case, the collection of VAT from many small consumers can be very burdensome for tax administrations. For this reason, some jurisdictions have not introduced any mechanism for collecting VAT on digital services imported by private consumers. However, as the OECD points out, the development of the digital economy, and particularly the increasing scale of trade in B2C digital products, may make this approach increasingly difficult to maintain.[583]

For this reason, jurisdictions are increasingly looking for ways to ensure the effective collection of VAT on digital services. One option is to require private consumers to self-assess VAT in their jurisdiction of residence. However, engaging consumers to act as tax remitters is not a viable option as it imposes a disproportionate burden on them, and tax compliance is extremely difficult to monitor in such a scenario, at least using conventional tax tools.[584] As this mechanism rarely proves effective in practice, the OECD recommends this solution only for B2B transactions.[585]

Another approach is to introduce regulations that require the non-resident supplier to register, collect and remit VAT according to the rules of the jurisdiction in which the consumer is resident.[586] This mechanism is sometimes referred to as the vendor collection regime.[587] In the OECD's view, this solution is effective – the experience of countries that have implemented this approach shows that a significant number of foreign suppliers (despite the limited ability of national jurisdictions to enforce these requirements on them) comply with these rules, particularly high-profile operators that occupy a significant share of the market.[588]

Under this model, intermediaries involved in the supply of digital services between foreign suppliers and domestic consumers can play a particularly important

581. OECD, *Addressing the Tax Challenges of the Digital Economy* (n. 548) 121–122.
582. *Ibid.*, 126–127.
583. *Ibid.*, 121–122.
584. Cristian Oliver Lucas-Mas and Raul Felix Junquera-Varela, *Tax Theory Applied to the Digital Economy: A Proposal for a Digital Data Tax and a Global Internet Tax Agency* (The World Bank 2021) 80–81.
585. OECD, *Mechanisms for the Effective Collection of VAT/GST* (n. 550) 23–24; it is worth noting that OECD guidelines present separate solutions for B2B and B2C trade, acknowledging that VAT systems often use different mechanisms to collect tax for these transaction categories. OECD, *Addressing the Tax Challenges of the Digital Economy* (n. 548) 126.
586. OECD, *Addressing the Tax Challenges of the Digital Economy* (n. 548) 121–122.
587. John Brondolo, *Administering the Value-Added Tax on Imported Digital Services and Low-Value Imported Goods* (International Monetary Fund 2021) 9.
588. OECD, *Addressing the Tax Challenges of the Digital Economy* (n. 548) 121–122.

role (an example of such an intermediary would of course be a platform). In the IMF's view, the inclusion of platforms in the vendor collection regime significantly increases the efficiency and effectiveness of the system, as it significantly reduces the number of entities required to register for VAT purposes and eliminates the rationale for suppliers to split their businesses to stay under the country's registration threshold.[589]

In the OECD's view, there are essentially two possible approaches involving intermediaries in VAT collection: the contractual approach and the deemed supplier mechanism. Under a contractual approach, the intermediary and the supplier can establish an arrangement whereby the intermediary fulfils the supplier's obligations to the taxing authorities. This arrangement may produce greater consistency in determining the liability to collect and account for VAT. However, this approach can cause practical problems in cases where the contractual arrangements are unclear. The deemed supplier mechanism, however, introduces presumptions under which an intermediary is deemed to be the statutory designated supplier for the purpose of accounting for VAT. With this approach, the VAT due is collected by fewer parties that can be monitored more easily and who may have better access to the information required to make the appropriate taxing decision.[590]

In the OECD's view, individual countries in practice have little ability to enforce the requirement to register and collect VAT from non-residents. Therefore, imposing such requirements on foreign suppliers also requires the development of a mechanism to simplify their VAT compliance. Otherwise, it is likely that many foreign suppliers will fail to register and remit VAT in the consumer's jurisdiction.[591] The highest feasible levels of compliance by non-resident suppliers are likely to be achieved if their requirements are limited to what is strictly necessary for the effective collection of the tax.[592]

For this reason, as the IMF points out, some jurisdictions will only require foreign suppliers to register for VAT when the supplies of taxable digital services to consumers have exceeded or are expected to exceed a prescribed amount in a 12-month period.[593] The purpose of this threshold is to limit registration to entities that are making sufficient sales in the country and are presumed to have the capacity to cope with the obligations of the VAT on imported digital services.[594] Like the OECD, the IMF stressed that VAT accounting procedures for non-resident suppliers of services should be simplified to minimize compliance costs.[595] However, as the literature rightly points out, if all countries having a VAT system were to eventually adopt a simplified registration system, the mere coexistence of the numerous systems could not, by definition, offer simplicity to businesses.[596]

589. Brondolo (n. 584) 9.
590. OECD, *Mechanisms for the Effective Collection of VAT/GST* (n. 550) 25–27.
591. OECD, *Addressing the Tax Challenges of the Digital Economy* (n. 548) 121–122.
592. *Ibid.*, 126–127.
593. Brondolo (n. 584) 9.
594. *Ibid.*
595. *Ibid.*, 10.
596. Lamensch (n. 402) 183–184.

The approach proposed by the OECD and IMF is consistent with the arrangements currently in place in the EU. Starting from 1 January 2015, in accordance with Article 58 of the VAT Directive, all telecommunications, broadcasting and electronic services (TBE services) are taxable at the place of residence of the consumer, which is a derogation from the general rule applicable to B2C supplies of services set out in Article 45 of the VAT Directive.[597] The EU legislator has also recognized the important role played by intermediaries (*inter alia*, platforms) in the supply of telecommunications and electronic services and, in Article 9a IR, has introduced a rebuttable presumption that they will be liable for collecting VAT 'on behalf of' their actual suppliers in certain circumstances. Article 9a IR is the first deemed supplier regime introduced at EU level that explicitly applies to platforms.

Although the EU does not provide for a registration threshold for non-EU suppliers, the new legislations were also accompanied by the introduction of a mechanism to simplify VAT accounting. The optional MOSS[598] special scheme came into force which allows suppliers (including foreign suppliers)[599] to fulfil their EU VAT obligations for TBE services in one Member State of their choice. This allows suppliers to avoid having to account for VAT separately in each country where they supply the aforementioned services. It should be emphasized that the platform, as a deemed supplier, will be able to benefit from the simplification under the MOSS procedure on the same terms as other taxable persons carrying out this type of transaction.

3.2 Legal Basis

The main principles behind the digital model in EU law are regulated in Article 9a IR.[600] According to this provision, where electronically supplied services or internet telephone services (telephone services provided over the internet) are supplied through a

597. If the services provided are actually consumed outside the EU, Member States may choose to apply the 'use and enjoyment' principle, as referred to in Article 59a(a) of the VAT Directive, and refrain from taxing such supply. Member States may also tax services actually consumed within their territory if these services are provided to customers from third countries, in accordance with Article 59a(b) of the VAT Directive.
598. On 1 July 2021, the special MOSS procedure underwent a significant expansion, reflected in its name change from 'mini' to the comprehensive OSS. This does not imply major changes to MOSS operation rules; the mechanism remains the same, but the number of transactions eligible for settlement through it has increased.
599. It is worth noting that the simplified registration system for non-EU entities providing electronic services has been in place since 2003. MOSS expanded this system to include EU suppliers as well as telecommunications and broadcasting services. Lamensch (n. 402) 183–184.
600. It is worth noting that even before the implementation of Article 9a IR, the VAT Committee almost unanimously agreed that the service shall be deemed to have been supplied to the final consumer by: (a) the intermediary where, in supplying the electronic service, he acts in his own name but on behalf of the electronic service provider, as provided for under Article 28 of the VAT Directive; (b) the electronic service provider where, in supplying the electronic service, the intermediary acts in the name and on behalf of the electronic service provider; (c) the third party intervening in the supply where, in supplying the electronic service, the third party acts in his own name and on his own behalf. The Committee also indicated that in providing the electronic service to the final consumer the intermediary or the third party intervening in the supply shall be presumed to have acted in their own name unless, in relation to the final

telecommunications network, interface or portal, e.g., an app shop, it is presumed for the purposes of applying Article 28 of the VAT Directive that the taxable person involved in the supply of those services is acting in his own name but on behalf of the supplier of those services, unless the taxable person explicitly designates that supplier as the person supplying the service and this is reflected in the contractual arrangements between the parties. The provision of Article 9a IR therefore introduces a rebuttable presumption[601] that in certain situations the tax liability will rest with the intermediary.

This provision was introduced by Implementing Regulation 1042/2013[602] and entered into force on 1 January 2015. According to recital 4 of this regulation, it was necessary to specify who is the supplier for VAT purposes where electronically supplied services, or telephone services provided through the internet, are supplied to a customer through telecommunications networks or via an interface or a portal. Following the adoption of the legislative changes on 3 April 2014, the Commission also published non-legally binding explanatory notes on this provision[603] ('Explanatory Notes 2014') and subsequently, as businesses continued to point out difficulties with the application of Article 9a IR due to different interpretations by Member States,[604] the VAT Committee issued additional guidance ('Guidelines 2016').[605]

Article 9a IR refers directly to Article 28 of the VAT Directive, discussed in detail in the second chapter: 'For the application of Article 28 of the VAT Directive'. In this context, it is therefore worth noting the relationship of these provisions. Article 9a R contains three, practically the same conditions for application as Article 28 of the VAT Directive: 'the taxable person taking part in the supply of those services acts in his own name but on behalf of the supplier of those services' and Article 28 states that: 'where a taxable person acting in his own name but on behalf of another person takes part in a supply of services'.

Given the literal wording of Article 9a IR, the relationship between this provision and Article 28 of the VAT Directive appears to be as follows:

consumer, the electronic service provider is explicitly indicated as the supplier of the electronic service. European Commission, 'VAT Committee Guidelines Resulting from the 93rd Meeting of 1 July 2011: Electronic Services Supplied by Service Providers Using the Network of Telecommunications Provider, Taxud.c.1(2012)1410604 – 709' (n. 536).

601. According to some authors, Article 9a IR does not shift the burden of the proof but rather clarifies which specific proof must be provided in order to make a distinction between a disclosed and an undisclosed agent, therefore the use of the word 'presumption' is probably confusing. Amand (n. 489) 244.

602. Council Implementing Regulation (EU) No 1042/2013 of 7 October 2013 amending Implementing Regulation (EU) No 282/2011 as regards the place of supply of services (n. 537).

603. European Commission, *Explanatory Notes on the EU VAT Changes to the Place of Supply of Telecommunications, Broadcasting and Electronic Services That Enter into Force in 2015* (n. 498).

604. European Commission, Directorate General for Taxation and Customs Union and Deloitte, *VAT Aspects of Cross-Border e-Commerce: Options for Modernisation: Final Report. Lot 3, Assessment of the Implementation of the 2015 Place of Supply Rules and the Mini-One Stop Shop* (Publications Office 2016) 72–73.

605. European Commission, 'VAT Committee Guidelines Resulting from the 106th Meeting of 14 March 2016: VAT 2015 Harmonised Application of the Presumption, Taxud.c.1(2016)3604550 – 904'.

- In terms of the subject aspect, Article 9a IR explicitly indicates whom it applies to. These include operators of telecommunications networks, interfaces and portals, such as app shops. The provision then goes on to indicate under what circumstances these entities are excluded from the scope of application of Article 9a IR. It can be assumed that in this part of the provision, the rule *lex specialis derogat legi generali* will apply, according to which the more specific law must be applied before the more general law,[606] in this case Article 28 of the VAT Directive.
  There will be only three exceptions, common to both Article 28 of the VAT Directive and Article 9a IR, under which the intermediary must meet the following requirements for these provisions to apply: (i) take part in the supply of services, (ii) act in his own name, but (iii) on behalf of a third party and/or service supplier. Due to the similarity of these regulations, their interpretation under Article 9a IR should take due account of existing scholarly views and case law developed based on Article 28 of the VAT Directive.
- Regarding the object aspect, it should be pointed out that Article 9a IR explicitly indicates which services it covers. The provision of Article 28 of the VAT Directive does not contain any restrictions in this respect. Therefore, bearing in mind the *lex specialis derogat legi generali* rule cited above, there will be no need to refer to Article 28 of the VAT Directive when analysing the object aspect of the digital model.
- With regard to the modus operandi of Article 9a IR, it should be noted that this regulation refers explicitly to Article 28 of the VAT Directive. The comments on how this provision works discussed in the second chapter will therefore remain valid.

In addition, it is worth bearing in mind that the relationship between Article 28 of the VAT Directive and Article 9a IR is so unclear that it has been the subject of proceedings before the CJEU.[607] The Court ruled whether Article 9a IR should apply, bearing in mind that its purpose is merely to clarify Article 28 of the VAT Directive and not to supplement or amend it.

The facts in these proceedings were as follows: the UK company Fenix operated on the internet a platform known as Only Fans. On the platform, some users had the status of creators who published content such as photos, videos and messages, which could be accessed, for a fee, by other users, known as fans. The platform operator set the general terms and conditions for the use of the interface, provided a system to enable financial transactions and, through a deduction, took 20% of any amount paid by fans to the creators. The company paid VAT only on the remuneration it collected, which was challenged by the UK tax authorities. In their view, the company, as a deemed supplier under Article 9a IR, should have paid VAT on all of the sum received from fans. The platform disagreed with the authorities' position, questioning the

606. Rafał Michalczak and Maciej Pach, 'Lex Specialis Derogat Legi Generali' in Monika Florczak-Wątor (ed.), Andrzej Grabowski, *Argumenty i rozumowania prawnicze w konstytucyjnym państwie prawa: Komentarz* (Ksiegarnia Akademicka Publishing 2021) 719.
607. *Fenix International* (n. 504).

validity of Article 9a IR, on the basis of which the disputed decision was issued. The company argued, *inter alia*, that the wording of this provision goes beyond the scope of Article 28 of the VAT Directive. The tax authorities disagreed with this view, and the case went to court which referred the following question to the CJEU for a preliminary ruling: 'Is Article 9a of [Implementing Regulation No 282/2011] invalid on the basis that it goes beyond the implementing power or duty on the Council established by Article 397 of [the VAT Directive] in so far as it supplements and/or amends Article 28 of [that directive]?'

The referring court pointed out that the implementing provisions contained in the IR should only serve to implement the main legislative act which is the VAT Directive. The Court harboured doubts as to whether Article 9a of this regulation is a mere technical measure, as it appears to constitute a change in the existing situation of certain taxable persons more than a clarification.

This interpretation was disagreed with by the Advocate General.[608] He pointed out that the Council may be required to provide further detail regarding the content of a legislative act, especially when new technologies, such as e-commerce, need to be considered in order to implement existing legislative acts.[609] In his view, Article 9a IR has a technical nature and provides further detail in the area of e-commerce in relation to the application of Article 28 of the VAT Directive, without supplementing or amending it, even as to its non-essential elements.[610] In particular, the Advocate General pointed out that the specific situation referred to in Article 9a IR falls within the scope of Article 28 of the VAT Directive. Thus, Article 9a IR complies with the essential general aims pursued by Article 28 of the VAT Directive.[611]

The Advocate General's view was shared by the CJEU. This Court examined whether Article 9a IR: (i) complies with the essential general aims pursued by the VAT Directive and, in particular, with Article 28 thereof; (ii) is necessary or appropriate for facilitating the uniform implementation of Article 28; and (iii) does not in any way supplement or amend Article 28 of the VAT Directive.

On the compatibility of Article 9a IR with the essential general aims pursued by the VAT Directive, the Court noted that this provision ensures - from 1 January 2015 - the uniform application of the presumption established in Article 28 of the VAT Directive regarding taxable persons supplying services electronically via a telecommunications network, interface or portal, such as an app shop. Therefore, the provisions of Article 9a IR are in line with the essential general objectives of the VAT Directive and, in particular, with those of its Article 28.[612]

On the question of the necessity or appropriateness of Article 9a IR, the Court stated, *inter alia*, that the rationale behind the introduction of this regulation was the need to ensure legal certainty for suppliers and to avoid divergent implementations related to the introduction of the amendments to the VAT Directive regarding the place

608. 'Opinion of Advocate General Rantos Delivered on 15 September 2022 in Case C-695/20 Fenix International Limited v Commissioners for Her Majesty's Revenue and Customs' (n. 542).
609. *Ibid.*, paragraph 39.
610. *Ibid.*, paragraph 93.
611. *Ibid.*, paragraph 59.
612. *Fenix International* (n. 504), paragraphs 59–60.

of taxation for telecommunications and electronic services from 1 January 2015. Therefore, the amendments made to IR were appropriate, or even necessary, for the uniform implementation of Article 28 of the VAT Directive.[613]

When examining the question of whether Article 9a IR supplements or amends Article 28 of the VAT Directive, the CJEU noted that the presumption in the first paragraph of Article 9a(1) IR does not alter the nature of Article 28 of the VAT Directive, but is limited, by fully integrating it, to giving concrete expression to it in the specific context of the supply of electronically supplied services through a telecommunications network, an interface or a portal, e.g., an app shop.[614] The Court also pointed out that the remaining paragraphs of Article 9a(1) IR are closely related to the wording of the first paragraph of the provision, giving more detail to the conditions contained therein.[615]

In conclusion, the CJEU clarified that the presumption in Article 9a IR is valid. However, it should be stressed that this ruling is controversial. It can be argued convincingly that Article 9a IR exceeds the scope of the VAT Directive by introducing irrebuttable presumptions, which essentially constitute new rules, and that Article 9a IR diverges from the traditional concept of a commissionaire as understood in international law and the civil law traditions of the Member States.[616]

3.3 Rationale for Using the Digital Model

3.3.1 The Subject Aspect

The provision of Article 9a IR covers operators of telecommunications networks, interfaces and portals, such as app shops. These terms are not defined in the EU VAT legislation,[617] but some guidance in this respect is provided by the non-legally binding Explanatory Notes 2014. According to the document, 'telecommunications networks' are networks that can be used to transfer voice and data. They include but are not necessarily limited to cable networks, telecom networks and ISP networks. They should cover any facility and technical solutions which allow access to, among other things, telecommunications and electronic services. For VAT purposes, the terms 'telecommunication networks' and 'communication networks' are interchangeable.[618]

A 'portal', however, is any type of online shop, website or similar environment that offers electronic services directly to the consumer without diverting them to another supplier's website, portal, etc., to conclude the transaction. Common examples are app stores, electronic marketplaces and websites offering e-services for sale. 'Interface' includes a portal, but it is a wider concept. In computing, it should be

613. *Ibid.*, paragraphs 61-62.
614. *Ibid.*, paragraph 70.
615. *Ibid.*, paragraphs 76, 86.
616. Henkow (n. 410) 251-254.
617. Merkx (n. 573) 18.
618. European Commission, *Explanatory Notes on the EU VAT Changes to the Place of Supply of Telecommunications, Broadcasting and Electronic Services That Enter into Force in 2015* (n. 498) 14-15.

understood as a device or a program which allows two independent systems or the system or the end user to communicate.[619]

Undoubtedly, platforms are also included in the definition of 'interfaces'. As was explained in the first chapter, it is not entirely clear why the European legislator sometimes uses the term 'platform' and sometimes the term 'interface'. It should be noted that these terms actually refer to the same thing – the digital tools by which transactions are facilitated.

Article 9a IR will therefore apply when electronic services and internet telephone services are supplied via the electronic interface operators indicated above. However, in the remainder of this book, the term 'platform operators' or 'platforms' will be used for consistency in terminology with the rest of the book.

The first paragraph of Article 9a IR introduces a rebuttable presumption that the platform is acting in its own name but on behalf of the supplier of electronic or internet telephone services in the supply of which it takes part. This provision mirrors the legal situation set out in Article 28 of the VAT Directive which requires analogous conditions to be met, namely: (i) taking part in the supply of services, (ii) acting in one's own name, but (iii) on behalf of a third party. In this respect, Article 9a IR does not supplement or amend the content of Article 28 of the VAT Directive and is fully in line with its logic.[620] Therefore, the interpretation of Article 9a IR should in this regard take due account of the existing scholarly views and case law developed based on Article 28 of the VAT Directive, as discussed in the second chapter.

Nevertheless, the application of the presumption in question in practice needs to be clarified in more detail, in particular regarding the condition of 'taking part in the supply of services'. For this reason, the Explanatory Notes 2014 provide examples of such activities. These include: (i) owning or managing the technical platform over which the services are delivered; (ii) being responsible for the actual delivery; (iii) being responsible for collecting payments unless the only involvement of the taxable person is the processing of payments; (iv) controlling or exerting influence over the pricing; (v) being the one legally required to issue a VAT invoice, receipt or bill to the end user in respect of the service supplied; (vi) providing customer care or support in relation to queries about or problems with the service itself; (vii) exerting control or influence over the presentation and format of the virtual marketplace (such as app stores or websites) such that the brand and identity of the taxable person are significantly more prominent than those of other persons involved in the supply; (viii) having legal obligations or liabilities in relation to the service provided; (ix) owning the customer data related to the supply in question; (x) being in a position to credit a sale without the supplier's permission or prior approval in cases where the supply was not properly received.[621]

619. *Ibid.*, 15.
620. *Fenix International* (n. 504), paragraphs 68–69.
621. European Commission, *Explanatory Notes on the EU VAT Changes to the Place of Supply of Telecommunications, Broadcasting and Electronic Services That Enter into Force in 2015* (n. 498) 29–30.

In contrast to Article 28 of the VAT Directive, Article 9a IR also explicitly singles out situations where the platform is not taking part in the supply of electronic and internet telephone services. This is the case when the platform only processes payments for these services and does not otherwise take part in their supply (Article 9a(3) IR). Therefore, the presumption in question will not apply to this type of platform (e.g., a credit card operator). Consequently, it will not be treated as supplying a service to the end user unless it takes part in the supply of the service in another way.[622] According to the Explanatory Notes 2014, one of the tests that should help to identify whether a platform operator takes part in the supply of a service is to verify whether the payment collection covers only a simple charge to a bill.[623]

In addition, the Explanatory Notes 2014 provide an illustrative catalogue of cases where platforms are not seen as taking part in the supply of a service within the meaning of Article 9a IR. Such entities are not, for example, providers who only make the internet network available or operators who only perform the functions of carrying the content.[624] Indeed, their participation in the supply of services is not sufficient for them to be considered as deemed suppliers. It is also worth noting that initially the Explanatory Notes 2014 also indicated that actions such as accepting bad debt risk or providing first-line customer care (redirecting to the supplier) are not sufficient to consider platforms as deemed suppliers.[625] However, in 2016, the Commission concluded that any other involvement of the platform in the supply chain (other than processing of payments) should suffice for it to be seen as an entity taking part in the supply within the meaning of Article 9a IR.[626] Ultimately, the VAT Committee in the Guidelines 2016 almost unanimously acknowledged that when a taxable person provides services, other than processing of payments, that taxable person is subject to the presumption under Article 9a IR, unless he is only making the platform available for carrying the content.[627]

It seems, therefore, that content-carrying platforms (of which advertising platforms may be an example) can be considered a borderline case. If they are limited to displaying and carrying content only, they should not be considered a supplier under Article 9a IR. However, when an advertising platform actively mediates in the supply of service, for example, when such active meditation takes the form of providing channels for a direct communication between users or a provision of detailed information requested by them, such 'advertising' may be regarded as transactions facilitation,[628] and consequently be covered by the presumption in question.

622. *Ibid.*, 27.
623. *Ibid.*, 31–32.
624. *Ibid.*, 30.
625. *Ibid.*, 33–34.
626. European Commission, 'VAT Committee Working Paper No 895: Harmonised Application of the Presumption (Follow-up) from the 106th Meeting, Taxud.c.1(2016)921938'.
627. European Commission, 'VAT Committee Guidelines Resulting from the 106th Meeting of 14 March 2016: VAT 2015 Harmonised Application of the Presumption, Taxud.c.1(2016)3604550 – 904' (n. 602).
628. European Commission, Directorate General for Taxation and Customs Union and others (n. 6) 26.

The provision of Article 9a IR also contains a catalogue of specific conditions when the presumption contained therein may be rebutted. In such a case, the underlying supplier of the electronic service or internet telephone service will again be deemed to be supplying the service to the end customer and will consequently have to account for VAT in the Member State of the customer.[629]

The conditions required to rebut the presumption in question are listed at the end of the first paragraph of Article 9a(1) IR and further developed in the second and third paragraphs of the provision in question. According to them, the actual supplier should be explicitly indicated by the platform as the supplier of service, and that should be reflected in the contractual arrangements between the parties (the first condition). For this to occur, two conditions must be met cumulatively: (i) the invoice issued or made available by each taxable person taking part in the supply of services must identify such service facilitation and the supplier thereof; (ii) the bill or receipt issued or made available to the customer must identify the service facilitation and the supplier thereof (the second condition). In addition, a platform that, with regard to electronically supplied services, authorizes the charge to the customer or the delivery of the services, or sets the general terms and conditions of the supply, must not be permitted to explicitly indicate another person as the supplier of those services (the third condition). These conditions must be met cumulatively.

According to the first condition, the platform should explicitly indicate the actual supplier as the supplier of the service in the contractual arrangements. Material contractual provisions are therefore the first indicator to be taken into account when it comes to determining who are the supplier and customer in a transaction. This condition takes into account the contractual and commercial reality of the relationships between the persons involved in the chain of transactions.[630]

However, it is worth noting that the Guidelines 2016 indicate that a supplier in the chain cannot, contrary to the facts and legal requirements, be entitled to decide that it is not involved in the supply and therefore not covered by Article 9a IR. The VAT Committee in these Guidelines also unanimously agreed that a clause in a contract excluding a taxable person from a chain of transactions, where this does not reflect economic reality, is not sufficient for that taxable person to be regarded as not having taken part in the supply as referred to in Article 9a IR.

The second condition requires that, first, the invoice issued or made available by each taxable person taking part in the supply of the service identifies the service in question and its actual supplier. Throughout the supply chain, this condition applies to B2B transactions.[631] Second, the second condition requires that the receipt or bill (or VAT invoice if required for B2C transactions in the Member State) also specifies the

629. European Commission, Directorate General for Taxation and Customs Union and Deloitte (n. 601) 72–73.
630. *Fenix International* (n. 504), paragraph 71; 'Opinion of Advocate General Rantos Delivered on 15 September 2022 in Case C-695/20 Fenix International Limited v Commissioners for Her Majesty's Revenue and Customs' (n. 542), paragraph 74.
631. European Commission, *Explanatory Notes on the EU VAT Changes to the Place of Supply of Telecommunications, Broadcasting and Electronic Services That Enter into Force in 2015* (n. 498) 34–35.

service in question and its actual supplier. Throughout the supply chain, this condition applies to final B2C transactions in the supply chain.[632]

According to the Explanatory Notes 2014, different identification methods can be used to explicitly identify the actual supplier and the service. Accordingly, reference can be made either in full or by using a specific and unique reference, code or similar identifier provided that the reference used is clear enough for all parties concerned. The description of the provider should be unambiguous enough to allow any recipient of the service to identify the provider.[633]

As the documents in question are among the elements that fall within the scope of commercial and contractual relations, and which are supposed to reflect the economic and commercial reality of the transactions in question, they are treated as evidence to rebut the presumption referred to in Article 9a IR.[634] The specific assessment of this evidence is a matter for the tax authorities and the courts of the Member States.[635]

The third condition consists of three elements, the fulfilment of which renders the presumption in question unrebuttable and therefore irrebuttable.[636] It is sufficient that the platform meets at least one[637] of the following conditions: (i) authorizes the charge to the customer, (ii) authorizes the supply of the services, or (iii) sets general terms and conditions for the supply of the services. In such a situation, the platform will not be able to designate another person as the actual provider, which means that the platform will always take part in the supply of services. In other words, in the case of services provided through a platform, the platform is always presumed to be a deemed provider if it authorizes the charge to the customer, authorizes the supply of these services or sets the general terms and conditions for their supply.

The Explanatory Notes 2014 clarify how these three conditions are to be understood. The phrase 'authorises the charge to the customer' refers to a situation where the taxable person can influence whether, at what time, or under which preconditions the customer pays. This means, for example, that the app shop is not responsible for payment between the end consumer and the app content owner.[638] 'Authorisation of the supply (provision) of services' refers to a situation where the taxable person can influence whether, at what time, or under which preconditions the delivery is made, and where the taxable person authorizes the delivery or either sends approval to commence the delivery of the service, delivers the service himself or

632. *Ibid.*
633. *Ibid.*
634. *Fenix International* (n. 504), paragraphs 78–79; 'Opinion of Advocate General Rantos Delivered on 15 September 2022 in Case C-695/20 Fenix International Limited v Commissioners for Her Majesty's Revenue and Customs' (n. 542), paragraph 76.
635. *Fenix International* (n. 504), paragraph 79.
636. *Ibid.*, paragraph 81; 'Opinion of Advocate General Rantos Delivered on 15 September 2022 in Case C-695/20 Fenix International Limited v Commissioners for Her Majesty's Revenue and Customs' (n. 542), paragraph 77.
637. European Commission, *Explanatory Notes on the EU VAT Changes to the Place of Supply of Telecommunications, Broadcasting and Electronic Services That Enter into Force in 2015* (n. 498) 34–35.
638. *Ibid.*, 25–26.

instructs a third party to make the delivery. This implies that the delivery, for example, of an app, from the content owner via the app shop is not authorized by the app shop.[639] By contrast, 'setting the general terms and conditions of the supply of services' refers to a situation where the platform takes the decision on the general terms and specific conditions (e.g., rights and obligations such as price, payment terms, delivery conditions, and warranty rules) and can impose them on other participants in a transaction. These may be terms and conditions in relation to user account maintenance or licence agreements which the final customer has to agree to before receiving any access to an app or content.[640] This means, for example, that the terms and conditions for the sale of an app via the app shop are not set by the app shop.[641] In addition, all these elements should be reflected in contractual arrangements, for example, between the app store and the app content owner. If this is not the case, the rebuttal of the presumption cannot take place.[642]

It is worth noting that, in particular, the interpretation of the condition of 'setting the general terms and conditions of the supply of services' made in the Explanatory Notes 2014 is regarded as highly controversial. Fenix argued in the proceedings before the CJEU that, contrary to what was indicated in the Explanatory Notes 2014, the general terms and conditions of use of an online platform should not be treated as general terms and conditions of the supply of services within the meaning of Article 9a IR. If that were the case, all platforms would fall within the scope of Article 28 of the VAT Directive, regardless of the contractual terms and conditions related to the agency and of the economic and commercial realities. In contrast, it would be commercially imprudent for the platform to establish no general terms and conditions of use.[643]

The Advocate General disagreed with this view, pointing out that it is the choice made by the platforms to either set or not to set general terms and conditions of use of platforms. This may be commercially essential, but which has tax consequences, even if those tax consequences are not desired by the platforms.[644] In the Advocate General's view, the general terms and conditions for the provision of services within the meaning of Article 9a IR include the general terms and conditions of use of online platforms, which simply means that the legislator has taken into account the economic and commercial realities, rather than just the contractual relationships.[645]

Finally, the CJEU did not directly address this issue. The Court pointed out that: 'taxable person, who takes part in the supply of a service by electronic means, by operating, for example, an online social network platform, has the power to authorise the supply of that service, or to charge for it, or to lay down the general terms and conditions of such a supply, that taxable person may unilaterally define essential

639. *Ibid.*
640. *Ibid.*, 36.
641. *Ibid.*, 25–26.
642. *Ibid.*
643. 'Opinion of Advocate General Rantos Delivered on 15 September 2022 in Case C-695/20 Fenix International Limited v Commissioners for Her Majesty's Revenue and Customs' (n. 542), paragraph 79.
644. *Ibid.*, paragraph 82.
645. *Ibid.*, paragraphs 86–87.

elements relating to the supply, namely the provision of that service and the time at which it will take place, or the conditions under which the consideration will be payable, or the rules forming the general framework of that service'.[646]

Since the ETS employs the phrase 'general terms and conditions of such a supply' and lists examples such as 'the rules forming the general framework of that service' and 'essential elements relating to the supply of electronic service', it can be understood that, in its assessment, the general terms of using the platforms, as not directly linked to those services, would not fall within the scope of Article 9a IR. It therefore seems that the 'general terms and conditions' specified in Article 9a IR are closely linked to the supply of electronic services and should not be interpreted more broadly.

Nonetheless, as platforms generally authorize charges to the customer and set the terms and conditions under which the supply is made, they will practically always be obliged to collect VAT on both their own transactions and those who sell services via them.

With this in mind, one has to agree with the widely held view that it is not easy, if not impossible, for intermediaries to rebut the presumption of Article 9a IR. It is therefore hardly surprising that this presumption is very rarely rebutted in practice by platforms.[647] This broad construction of the provision in question means that the platform taking part in the supply chain will normally be a deemed supplier.[648] The practical steadfastness of this presumption may suggest that Article 9a IR does indeed not clarify the existing rule in Article 28 of the VAT Directive but creates a new one.

However, this is in line with the objectives of the reform carried out. As the EC points out, during the discussions in the Council, there was a general consensus that the presumption of Article 9a IR should be applied as widely as possible in the interest of simplicity.[649] This approach also ensures that businesses that are in a stronger market position do not force taxable persons placed earlier in the supply chain to take over responsibility for B2C supplies. Therefore, the presumption in Article 9a IR should apply almost automatically and, in practice, only payment service providers should be exempted from its application[650] (given the content of the Guidelines 2016, operators who provide the platform for the sole purpose of carrying content will also be exempted). Moreover, legal literature highlights that, perhaps rather than looking to avoid this presumption, it would be wiser to accept that the role of platforms in VAT collection is becoming increasingly important and that this responsibility will be extended to more and more activities.[651]

646. *Fenix International* (n. 504), paragraphs 83-84.
647. European Commission, Directorate General for Taxation and Customs Union and Deloitte (n. 601) 131.
648. Beretta (n. 344) 291-293.
649. European Commission, 'VAT Committee Working Paper No 895: Harmonised Application of the Presumption (Follow-up) from the 106th Meeting, Taxud.c.1(2016)921938' (n. 623).
650. *Ibid.*
651. Fernando Matesanz, 'What Does the Fenix Case Mean for VAT Management?' (*ITR*, 14 March 2023), www.internationaltaxreview.com accessed 23 March 2023.

3.3.2 *The Object Aspect*

Article 9a(1) and (2) IR explicitly indicates that this provision applies to electronically supplied services and internet telephone services (telephone services provided through the internet, including VoIP).

The concept of electronic services is defined in Article 7 IR which also includes examples of services that count and do not count as electronic services. Importantly, from the point of view of the platform economy, the concept of 'electronically supplied services' does not include services of a tangible nature, for example, accommodation, car-hire, restaurant services, passenger transport or similar services booked online (from Article 7(3)(u) IR).

As emphasized in the literature on the subject, this means that Article 9a IR will not apply to the service sectors of the platform economy.[652] For Article 9a IR to apply, the underlying services must be either electronic services or internet telephone services. Thus, where the underlying transactions are tangible rather than digital in nature (involving the exploitation of a tangible asset such as a dwelling accommodation),[653] Article 9a IR will not apply. This means that this provision does not apply to STR platforms, as these intermediate in the supply of accommodation services, and these services are explicitly excluded from the definition of electronically supplied services (Article 7(3)(u) IR).

Article 9a IR also applies to internet telephone services. As pointed out in the Explanatory Notes 2014, since this type of service can be provided through intermediaries, in this case too there is a need to introduce a presumption as to who is actually providing the service to the final consumer. Therefore, for the purposes of the application of Article 9a IR, the telephone services delivered through the internet are to be treated in the same way as electronic services.[654]

It is notable that the wording of neither Article 9a IR nor Article 28 of the VAT Directive makes it explicitly clear as to what the nature (B2B, B2C, C2B, C2C) of the underlying transaction in which the platform is involved must be. It is not clear from these provisions whether the underlying supplier must have taxable or non-taxable status. In particular, the provision of Article 9a IR only refers to a 'supplier of services', and Article 28 of the VAT Directive refers to a 'third party' without indicating its status. However, according to Article 28 of the VAT Directive, there is no separate service supplied by the intermediary (the service supplied by the undisclosed agent is integrated into the commissioned service). This means that when Article 28 of the VAT Directive applies, the underlying service and the service supplied by the intermediary are combined in a way. As the intermediary (platform) must have VAT status,

652. Beretta (n. 344) 312–313; Suso (n. 342) 11.
653. Beretta (n. 344) 312–313.
654. European Commission, *Explanatory Notes on the EU VAT Changes to the Place of Supply of Telecommunications, Broadcasting and Electronic Services That Enter into Force in 2015* (n. 498) 44.

consequently the transaction in which it participates will be B2C or B2B.[655] It is worth noting that some legal systems are significantly more precise in this regard, which should be positively assessed due to the legal certainty it provides for entities involved in transactions. For example, in Japan, the Platform Taxation Regime applies only to foreign businesses supplying electronic services to Japanese consumers via digital platforms, thereby excluding domestic businesses from this regime.[656]

Regarding the status of the customer of the services, it should be emphasized that if electronic services and telephone services delivered through the internet are provided to a consumer (a B2C transaction), then the entity liable to account for and pay VAT to the tax authorities is the supplier (or the platform deemed to be the supplier). If the service is to be provided to a customer who is a taxable person established in a Member State other than that of the supplier (a B2B transaction), the latter should not assess VAT as the customer will be liable to pay the tax under the reverse-charge mechanism.

The IR provides some guidance to allow taxable persons (including platforms that are deemed suppliers) to determine the status of customers. According to the second paragraph of Article 18(2) IR, irrespective of information to the contrary, the supplier of TBE services may regard any customer as a non-taxable person as long as that customer has not communicated his individual VAT identification number to him. As indicated in the Explanatory Notes 2014, the main purpose of this provision is to provide more legal certainty for the suppliers as to the status of their customers by disregarding information other than the VAT identification number. This allows the supplier to determine immediately and with certainty whether the obligation to pay VAT falls to him or whether the customer needs to account for the tax (because the supply is to a taxable person in another Member State). It is optional for the supplier to make use of this provision because where the supplier knows that his customer is indeed a taxable person (despite his failure to provide a VAT number), this wording of the regulation allows him to not treat such a customer as a non-taxable person.[657]

In this context, it is worth noting the 2018 guidelines of the VAT Committee, which unanimously held that the supplier of telecommunications, broadcasting or electronically supplied services can treat the customer as a non-taxable person when that customer does not provide his VAT identification number and can do so without any additional checks. However, in the reverse situation (when the supplier believes that the consumer is a VAT taxable person), the VAT Committee almost unanimously

655. In the literature, it is emphasized that the wording of Article 9a IR does not contain any limitation regarding the status of the service recipient. Rosamund Barr and others, *E-Commerce and EU VAT: Theory and Practice* (Wolters Kluwer 2021) 43.
656. This is because the Japanese Platform Taxation regime is primarily designed to target non-compliant foreign suppliers. Takato Masuda, 'Japan Introduced Full VAT Liability Regime to Digital Platforms' (2024) 35 International VAT Monitor 105–106 https://doi.org/10.59403/1a5eezn.
657. European Commission, *Explanatory Notes on the EU VAT Changes to the Place of Supply of Telecommunications, Broadcasting and Electronic Services That Enter into Force in 2015* (n. 498) 50–51.

agreed that the burden of proof is on the supplier and he must hold sufficient information to substantiate the status of his customer being a taxable person.[658]

Finally, it is worth noting that doubts have recently arisen regarding the scope of VAT obligations of digital platforms prior to the introduction of the VAT rules for electronic services and digital platforms from 1 January 2015. The German Federal Tax Court has posed the following prejudicial question in this regard: under circumstances such as those in the main proceedings, in which a German taxpayer (developer) provided a supply of services, before 1 January 2015, electronically to a non-taxpayer resident elsewhere in the EU (end user) via an app store of an Irish taxpayer, is Article 28 of the VAT Directive to be applied with the result that the Irish taxpayer is treated as if they had received this supply of service from the developer and provided it to the end user because the app store first named the developer as the supplier and showed German VAT in the order confirmation provided to the end user?[659]

Scholars point out that this case could shed some light on the liability of platforms for sales of non-digital services, which currently are not in the scope of the explicit deeming provision for digital services facilitated by intermediaries.[660]

3.4 Mode of Operation

The OECD proposes the following mechanism for the operation of the deemed supplier model for platforms intermediating the supply of digital content:

(1) the platform as an intermediary is interposed into the digital supply chain;
(2) assuming that the intermediary meets the conditions to be considered as the supplier, then the transaction made by the supplier of the digital service to the consumer is considered to be a supply by the intermediary to the consumer, and therefore the platform must calculate and remit the VAT due to the tax authorities in the jurisdiction of consumption.[661]

The EU digital model is based on this solution. It should be noted that, as Article 9a IR refers explicitly to Article 28 of the VAT Directive in terms of the mechanism of operation, the comments on the operation of this provision discussed in the second chapter remain valid. This means that if the conditions for the application of Article 9a IR are met, there will be a legal fiction of two identical services provided consecutively. In the first instance, the platform must be considered to have received an electronic service or a telephone service provided through the internet from the actual supplier.

---

658. European Commission, 'VAT Committee Guidelines Resulting from the 110th Meeting of 13 April 2018: The Significance of the VAT Identification Number, Taxud.c.1(2018)7386249 – 956'.
659. *Finanzamt Hamburg-Altona* CJEU C-101/24.
660. 'EU: VAT Obligations of Digital Platforms Pre-2015 (CJEU Referral)' (*KPMG*, 12 March 2024), https://kpmg.com/us/en/home/insights/2024/03/tnf-eu-vat-obligations-digital-platforms-pre-2015-cjeu-referral.html accessed 17 March 2024.
661. OECD, *Mechanisms for the Effective Collection of VAT/GST* (n. 550) 26–27.

This type of transaction will generally be considered a B2B transaction.[662] In the second step, the platform should be considered to have provided an 'acquired' service to the final customer. Since the service provided by the platform, acting as an undisclosed agent, should be treated as integrated with the commissioned service, the platform will charge VAT on the total price of the service, not just on the agreed fee or commission for the intermediary service.

The mechanism of Article 9a IR, using the OnlyFans platform as an example, is illustrated in Figure 3.2.

Figure 3.2 Mode of Operation of Article 9a IR, Using the OnlyFans Platform as an Example

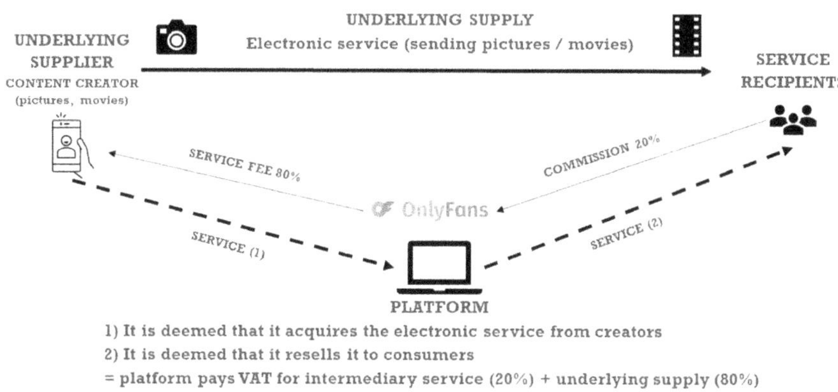

Source: Own compilation, based on the factual situation presented in the CJEU judgment in the *Fenix* case.[663]

The presumption in question should be applied to any transaction in the supply chain between an e-service provider and the final consumer.[664] The assessment of a given service should start at the level of the final consumer (as it is usually the supplier placed in the supply chain just before the final consumer who will be seen to be supplying the electronic service or telephone services provided through the internet to the latter) and continue up the chain.[665]

662. European Commission, Directorate General for Taxation and Customs Union and Deloitte (n. 601) 72–73.
663. *Fenix International* (n. 504).
664. European Commission, *Explanatory Notes on the EU VAT Changes to the Place of Supply of Telecommunications, Broadcasting and Electronic Services That Enter into Force in 2015* (n. 498) 24–25.
665. *Ibid.*, 37.

4 THE E-COMMERCE MODEL

4.1 Historical Background

As mentioned in the first chapter, the internet has made it possible to purchase goods and services without the geographical and time constraints characteristic of traditional commerce. Consequently, the existing EU VAT rules for e-commerce have proved insufficient.

One of the main problems is the development of platforms, used by tens of thousands of small goods suppliers to reach customers around the world. Importations of goods of negligible value were either exempt from VAT or taxed at a very low rate in many countries. Such an arrangement was introduced at a time when online shopping did not exist, and the level of imports benefiting from tax breaks was relatively low.[666] At the time, the administrative costs of collecting VAT on goods seemed to exceed the amount of VAT that would have been paid on those goods. In implementing VAT exemption thresholds for low-value imports, jurisdictions have generally sought to strike an appropriate balance between administrative costs, compliance costs and the loss of revenue and potential distortions of competition that these exemptions could cause.[667]

In recent years, however, there has been a significant and rapid increase in the volume of low-value imports of physical goods.[668] This resulted not only in decreased VAT revenues but also in increasing unfair competitive pressure on domestic retailers.[669] Indeed, the exemption puts them at a disadvantage compared to non-resident suppliers who are exempt from assessing VAT on the same low-value goods.[670] Within the EU, for example, many third-country suppliers supplying their goods via platforms did not comply with EU VAT rules – these suppliers did not fulfil their registration obligations in the country of destination and did not pay VAT, resulting in distortions of competition as EU suppliers charged this tax.[671] In addition, there were also concerns that this state of affairs could encourage domestic suppliers to relocate to a foreign jurisdiction in order to sell low-value goods free of VAT.[672] Consequently, the idea arose that the exemption for low-value imports should be abandoned.[673]

666. Marta Papis-Almansa, 'VAT and Electronic Commerce: The New Rules as a Means for Simplification, Combatting Fraud and Creating a More Level Playing Field?' (2019) 20 ERA Forum 216–217 https://doi.org/10.1007/s12027-019-00575-9.
667. OECD, *Addressing the Tax Challenges of the Digital Economy* (n. 548) 120–121.
668. The data suggests that the majority of packages entering borders from online trade consist of low-value goods, posing significant logistical challenges for customs authorities. Parcel volume surged from 44 billion in 2014 to 65 billion in 2016 across 13 major markets and is projected to continue growing at a rate of 17–28% annually between 2017 and 2021. OECD, *The Role of Digital Platforms in the Collection of VAT/GST on Online Sales* (n. 551) 31–32.
669. OECD, *Addressing the Tax Challenges of the Digital Economy* (n. 548) 120–121.
670. Brondolo (n. 584) 15.
671. Pollak (n. 339) 294.
672. OECD, *Addressing the Tax Challenges of the Digital Economy* (n. 548) 120–121; Millar (n. 384) 5.
673. It is worth noting that consumers may oppose the abolition of this exemption, fearing that, in addition to the tax, the collection costs would be passed on to them. Millar (n. 384) 5.

Leaving aside the traditional model of collecting VAT on low-value imports, the OECD distinguishes three possible approaches to this issue: (i) the purchaser collection model, (ii) the vendor collection model, and (iii) the intermediary collection model.[674] The distinction between these collection models is essentially based on the person liable to account for VAT. In the OECD's view, the first collection model, whereby the purchaser himself pays VAT on low-value imports, does not appear to be a sufficiently efficient solution and would be highly complex and costly for customs and tax administrations to implement and operate. As for the second model, the OECD pointed out that its implementation could improve the efficiency of VAT collection on low-value imported goods, especially if complemented by a simplified VAT registration system for foreign suppliers (a similar solution has, incidentally, been suggested in the context of the supply of digital services). The OECD also considered the intermediary collection model to be effective, but with the assumption that the intermediary has the required information to assess and remit the right amount of VAT in the country of importation. This model would involve minimal compliance burdens on vendors.[675] In this context, the OECD distinguishes four main types of intermediaries: (i) postal operators, (ii) express carriers, (iii) payment operators, and (iv) e-commerce platforms.[676]

An approach whereby the VAT on imports of low-value goods from online sales would be collected and remitted by platforms was identified as presenting great potential (around 67% of e-commerce goods deliveries are made via platforms).[677] Platforms generally have access to the key information that is needed for assessing the VAT due in the country of importation, and some of them already provide tax compliance services to their vendors.[678] In addition, platforms are highly automated, and it is therefore indicated that they could easily cope with accounting for VAT.[679]

Also, in doctrine, recommendations have emerged that in cases where goods or services are sold/delivered through online marketplaces (or through intermediaries), consideration should be given to imposing the obligation to pay VAT on the marketplace operator (or intermediary). Where appropriate, a rebuttable or irrebuttable presumption that the marketplace operator is the supplier, rather than an intermediary, could be employed.[680]

For this reason, an increasing number of jurisdictions have implemented or are considering implementing a system that places full liability for the collection and payment of VAT on platforms. Such a system has, for example, been implemented in Chile,[681] New Zealand, Norway and the UK.[682] Australia has also been at the forefront

674. OECD, *Addressing the Tax Challenges of the Digital Economy* (n. 548) 123.
675. *Ibid.*, 123–125.
676. *Ibid.*
677. OECD, *The Role of Digital Platforms in the Collection of VAT/GST on Online Sales* (n. 551) 30–31.
678. *Ibid.*
679. Chris Evans and Richard Krever, 'Counting the Costs of VAT Compliance' in Robert F van Brederode, *Virtues and Fallacies of VAT* (Wolters Kluwer Law International 2021) 147.
680. Millar (n. 384) 22.
681. Ignacio Gepp, 'Chile Taking Baby Steps: VAT on Digital Services' (2020) 31 International VAT Monitor 185, ibfd.org accessed 5 February 2021 https://doi.org/10.59403/27w8btq.

of trying to overcome the legal and practical difficulties associated with the platform phenomenon,[683] and is a pioneer in abolishing the threshold for low-value imported goods and introducing new mechanisms for clearing cross-border e-commerce.[684] For this reason, the Australian experience has proved relevant to other countries.

As early as 1998, the EC stated that if online deliveries become faster and more reliable, this could generate problems with VAT taxation of imports of goods, in particular, by private individuals. The Commission therefore considered that the development of e-commerce should be monitored in this respect and potential new tax mechanisms should be designed to be fully compatible with new commercial practices and proportionate, given the transnational, diverse and decentralized nature of this market.[685]

As expected, the e-commerce market in Europe developed rapidly, with a significant increase in cross-border transactions. Already in 2015, nearly 150 million VAT-free small consignments were imported.[686] It is essential to recognize that even despite the UK's exit from the EU single market, e-commerce turnover grew at a rate of 16% in 2021.[687] Between 2014 and 2029, the number of consumers shopping cross-border is forecast to increase from 30 million in 2014 to 160 million in 2029 and the volume of consignments worth less than EUR 22 from 40 million in 2014 to around 460 million[688] (the total value of consignments from third countries is expected to increase from EUR 14 billion in 2014 to EUR 37 billion in 2029).[689]

For this reason, the EC has decided to take legislative action in the area of e-commerce. Already in 2015, the EC stated that: (i) it aims to reduce VAT-related burdens and obstacles when selling across border, (ii) the MOSS procedure should also cover supplies of tangible goods ordered online both within and outside the EU, (iii) market distortions should be eliminated, to ensure a level playing field for EU businesses and to ensure that VAT revenues accrue to the Member State of the consumer (VAT exemption for small consignments to private individuals in the EU gives third-country suppliers a competitive advantage over EU suppliers, reducing their turnover by up to EUR 4.5 billion annually).[690]

682. Messina (n. 556) 120–121.
683. Michael Walpole, 'The Australian GST Cross-Border Rules in a Global Context' (2020) 18 eJournal of Tax Research 311–313.
684. Evgeny Guglyuvatyy and Nikolai Milogolov, 'GST Treatment of Electronic Commerce: Comparing the Singaporean and Australian Approaches' (2021) 19 eJournal of Tax Research 33–36.
685. European Commission, 'Communication from the Commission to the Council, the European Parliament and the Economic and Social Committee – Electronic Commerce and Indirect Taxation, COM(1998) 374 Final'.
686. European Commission, 'Communication from the Commission to the European Parliament, the Council, and the European Economic and Social Committee on an Action Plan on VAT towards a Single EU VAT Area – Time to Decide, COM(2016) 148 Final'.
687. S Lone and JWJ Weltevreden, '2022 European E-Commerce Report' (Amsterdam University of Applied Sciences & Ecommerce Europe 2022).
688. European Commission, 'Impact Assessment Report, SWD(2022) 393 Final' (n. 362).
689. *Ibid.*
690. European Commission, 'A Digital Single Market Strategy for Europe, COM(2015) 192 Final' (n. 34).

Accordingly, it was announced that in 2016, the EC would present the relevant legislative proposals in this area,[691] which finally happened on 1 December 2016,[692] and they were adopted by the EU Council on 5 December 2017: (i) Council Directive (EU) 2017/2455,[693] (ii) Council Regulation (EU) 2017/2454[694] and (iii) Council Implementing Regulation (EU) 2017/2459.[695] These were the first legislative drafts belonging to the so-called VAT e-commerce package, a comprehensive tax reform aiming to modernize European VAT while simplifying the system and making it fraud-proof. On 21 November 2019, the following legislative acts were additionally included in the package: the Council Directive (EU) 2019/1995[696] and the Council Implementing Regulation (EU) 2019/2026,[697] as well as on 12 February 2020 the Implementing Regulation (EU) 2020/194.[698] In addition, on 9 June 2021, the package was completed by Commission Implementing Regulation (EU) 2021/965,[699] on 10 June 2021 by

691. European Commission, 'Communication from the Commission to the European Parliament, the Council, and the European Economic and Social Committee on an Action Plan on VAT towards a Single EU VAT Area – Time to Decide, COM(2016) 148 Final' (n. 682).
692. Proposal for a Council Directive amending Directive 2006/112/EC and Directive 2009/132/EC as regards certain value added tax obligations for supplies of services and distance sales of goods [COM/2016/0757 final].
693. Council Directive (EU) 2017/2455 of 5 December 2017 amending Directive 2006/112/EC and Directive 2009/132/EC as regards certain value added tax obligations for supplies of services and distance sales of goods [OJ L 348, 29.12.2017, pp. 7–22].
694. Council Regulation (EU) 2017/2454 of 5 December 2017 amending Regulation (EU) No 904/2010 on administrative cooperation and combating fraud in the field of value added tax [OJ L 348, 29.12.2017, pp. 1–6].
695. Council Implementing Regulation (EU) 2017/2459 of 5 December 2017 amending Implementing Regulation (EU) No 282/2011 laying down implementing measures for Directive 2006/112/EC on the common system of value added tax [OJ L 348, 29.12.2017, pp. 32–33].
696. Council Directive (EU) 2019/1995 of 21 November 2019 amending Directive 2006/112/EC as regards provisions relating to distance sales of goods and certain domestic supplies of goods [OJ L 310, 2.12.2019, pp. 1–5].
697. Council Implementing Regulation (EU) 2019/2026 of 21 November 2019 amending Implementing Regulation (EU) No 282/2011 as regards supplies of goods or services facilitated by electronic interfaces and the special schemes for taxable persons supplying services to non-taxable persons, making distance sales of goods and certain domestic supplies of goods [OJ L 313, 4.12.2019, pp. 14–27].
698. Commission Implementing Regulation (EU) 2020/194 of 12 February 2020 laying down detailed rules for the application of Council Regulation (EU) No 904/2010 as regards the special schemes for taxable persons supplying services to non-taxable persons, making distance sales of goods and certain domestic supplies of goods [OJ L 40, 13.2.2020, pp. 114–124].
699. Commission Implementing Regulation (EU) 2021/965 of 9 June 2021 amending Implementing Regulation (EU) 2020/194 as regards the exchange of records held by taxable persons or their intermediaries and the designation of competent authorities responsible for coordinating administrative enquiries [OJ L 214, 17.6.2021, pp. 1–33].

Commission Implementing Decision 2021/942,[700] and on 26 July 2021 by Commission Implementing Regulation (EU) 2021/1218.[701]

In principle, the entire VAT e-commerce package was due to come into force on 1 January 2021. However, due to the COVID-19 pandemic, the Commission decided to postpone the implementation of the new rules. Although some Member States, such as Germany and the Netherlands, requested a postponement for one year,[702] it was eventually decided to change the date of entry into force of the new solutions by six months. The e-commerce VAT package, with minor exceptions, took effect from 1 July 2021.[703]

The purpose of the VAT e-commerce package, according to the above-mentioned Commission announcements, is to level the playing field between traditional commerce and e-commerce, eliminate distortions that work in favour of non-EU businesses, and reduce compliance costs and the complexity of VAT obligations for businesses.

In the case of the e-commerce model, it is likely that the OECD's preparatory work inspired the EU legislation, but the proposed changes could not have been based on the OECD report itself,[704] as it only appeared after the first part of the VAT e-commerce package came into force.[705] However, the EU rules in this regard are broadly in line with the OECD recommendations on the operation of the full VAT liability regime for platforms.[706]

In the VAT e-commerce package, the European legislator decided to adopt the intermediary model indicated by the OECD.[707] This choice seems reasonable given that more than 90% of online purchases by EU customers take place through intermediaries

700. Commission Implementing Decision (EU) 2021/942 of 10 June 2021 laying down rules for the application of Council Directive 2006/112/EC as regards the establishment of the list of third countries with which the Union has concluded an agreement on mutual assistance similar in scope to Council Directive 2010/24/EU and Council Regulation (EU) No 904/2010 [OJ L 205, 11.6.2021, pp. 80–81].
701. Commission Implementing Regulation (EU) 2021/1218 of 26 July 2021 amending Implementing Regulation (EU) No 79/2012 as regards the storage of and automated access to the information on the VAT exempted importations under the 'import scheme' [OJ L 267, 27.7.2021, pp. 12–13].
702. Messina (n. 556) 120–121.
703. Council Decision (EU) 2020/1109 of 20 July 2020 amending Directives (EU) 2017/2455 and (EU) 2019/1995 as regards the dates of transposition and application in response to the COVID-19 pandemic [OJ L 244, 29.7.2020, pp. 3–5]; Council Regulation (EU) 2020/1108 of 20 July 2020 amending Regulation (EU) 2017/2454 as regards the dates of application in response to the COVID-19 pandemic [OJ L 244, 29.7.2020, pp. 1–2]; Commission Implementing Regulation (EU) 2020/1318 of 22 September 2020 amending Implementing Regulations (EU) 2020/21 and (EU) No 2020/194 as regards the dates of application in response to the COVID-19 pandemic [OJ L 309, 23.9.2020, pp. 4–6]; Council Implementing Regulation (EU) 2020/1112 of 20 July 2020 amending Implementing Regulation (EU) 2019/2026 as regards the dates of application in response to the COVID-19 pandemic [OJ L 244, 29.7.2020, pp. 9–10].
704. OECD, *The Role of Digital Platforms in the Collection of VAT/GST on Online Sales* (n. 551).
705. Pollak (n. 339) 115.
706. For more on the similarities and differences between EU solutions and OECD guidelines, *see*: Dunja Nicole Lisa Jetten, *The VAT Liability of Digital Platforms: The EU Rules in the Light of the OECD Guidelines* (Lund University 2021).
707. OECD, *Addressing the Tax Challenges of the Digital Economy* (n. 548) 123–125.

involved in the transaction.[708] The solution adopted in the EU therefore places full liability for the collection and payment of VAT on platforms facilitating the supply of goods in certain cases.

In addition, as was the case with the digital model, the new legislation was also accompanied by the introduction of a mechanism to simplify VAT accounting. On 1 July 2021, the optional MOSS special procedure was significantly expanded, as reflected in its name, from which the word 'mini' disappeared and the OSS appeared.

The way this special procedure works has not been significantly modified. The OSS system allows certain taxable persons (including foreign taxable persons) to fulfil their EU VAT obligations in one Member State of their choice. This enables them to avoid having to register and account for VAT separately in each Member State where the place of taxation of their transactions is located.

Instead, the number of transactions that can be accounted for via this special procedure has increased. The OSS covers all types of services provided cross-border (not just TBE services as was the case with MOSS), EU B2C supplies of goods and distance sales of imported goods with an intrinsic value of EUR 150 or less. The latter type of transaction is accounted for through a new type of procedure in the OSS system, the so-called IOSS. When using IOSS, imports of low-value goods into the EU are exempt from VAT, which speeds up the supply of goods to the consumer.[709]

The platform, as a deemed supplier, will be able to benefit from the simplification under the OSS and IOSS procedure on the same terms as other taxable persons carrying out this type of transaction. In addition, unlike other taxable persons, the platform will also have the option to account under this procedure for VAT on domestic supplies of goods that it facilitates.

The Commission's approach of extending and modifying the existing VAT registration simplification regime appears to be in line with OECD guidelines. According to them, when a platform facilitates both the supply of goods and services within a particular jurisdiction, the simplified registration and compliance system should be used for both kinds of supplies, as this reduces the administrative and compliance costs.[710]

In addition, it is worth noting that the EC plans to further extend the OSS special procedure to further transactions (including the transfer of own goods). It is also

708. Messina (n. 556) 122–123.
709. As indicated by the OECD, one way to incentivize platforms to comply with the deemed supplier regime is to provide a fast-track processing pathway for goods covered by this system, as speedy delivery is crucial for e-commerce. The expedited procedure thus serves as a strong incentive for digital platforms to adhere to the deemed supplier regime for online sales related to the import of these goods. Implementing such a system is likely to also reduce the risk of fraud and non-compliance at the border. Additionally, platforms collecting and remitting VAT on low-value imported goods may reduce or eliminate the need for customs intervention, allowing them to fully allocate their resources to other key roles they perform, especially in ensuring the security and protection of the value chain (e.g., detecting and preventing the illegal and counterfeit flow of goods). OECD, *The Role of Digital Platforms in the Collection of VAT/GST on Online Sales* (n. 551) 31–32, 44–46.
710. *Ibid.*, 35–36.

possible that the use of IOSS will become mandatory for platforms as deemed suppliers facilitating distance sales of certain imported goods.[711]

4.2 Legal Basis

The main principles underlying the e-commerce model under EU law are regulated in Article 14a of the VAT Directive. According to the first paragraph of this provision, if a taxable person facilitates, through the use of an electronic interface such as a trading platform, platform, portal or similar means, the distance sale of goods imported from third territories or third countries in consignments of an intrinsic value not exceeding EUR 150, that taxable person is deemed to have received and supplied those goods himself. The second paragraph states, in turn, that where a taxable person facilitates, through the use of an electronic interface such as a trading platform, platform, portal or similar means, the supply of goods within the Community by a taxable person not established in the Community to a non-taxable person, the taxable person who facilitates that supply is deemed to have received and supplied those goods himself. This means that in the situations described above, the platforms will be deemed to be the suppliers and obliged to collect VAT on the sales they facilitate.

This provision was introduced by Council Directive (EU) 2017/2455 and came into force together with the VAT e-commerce package on 1 July 2021. According to recital 7 of this directive, its main objective is to ensure the effective and efficient collection of VAT and to reduce the administrative burden for vendors, tax administrations and consumers.[712] Recital 7 highlights that a major share of distance sales of goods, both supplied from one Member State to another and from third territories or third countries to the Community, are facilitated through the use of an electronic interface such as platforms. It was considered necessary to involve such entities in the VAT collection process by introducing a provision stating that they are the persons who are deemed to make those sales.

It is worth noting that Article 14a of the VAT Directive was not foreseen in the Commission's original 2016 legislative proposal.[713] It was added at the initiative of the EP during the work on this proposal in the Council of the EU.[714] Initially, according to Amendment 7, only platforms involved in distance sales of goods imported from third territories or third countries, the value of which did not exceed EUR 150, were to be

711. Proposal for a Council Directive amending Directive 2006/112/EC as regards VAT rules for the digital age (n. 382); it should be noted that the reform regarding the introduction of the mandatory IOSS is linked to the ongoing customs reform and is therefore unlikely to come into effect soon. Council of the EU, 'Statement by the Commission, Dated 8 May 2024, No 9680/24 ADD 1'.
712. These objectives were also outlined in the Explanatory Notes provided by the EC. European Commission, *Explanatory Notes on VAT E-Commerce Rules. Council Directive (EU) 2017/2455. Council Directive (EU) 2019/1995. Council Implementing Regulation (EU) 2019/2026* (n. 164) 12.
713. Bal (n. 566).
714. Messina (n. 556) 122–123; Pollak (n. 339) 109.

covered by the deemed supplier regime.[715] Finally, however, platforms facilitating certain EU supplies were also covered by the regime. It appears that the addition of this provision may have been prompted by the fact that some Member States in the EU[716] have, on their own, started to impose additional obligations (mainly joint and several liability for the payment of VAT) on operators of platforms facilitating e-commerce transactions. Recital 7 of Council Directive (EU) 2017/2455 points out that such arrangements put in place by individual Member States are proving insufficient to ensure the effective collection of VAT. It also appears that, in the long term, this could lead to regulatory fragmentation and a lack of uniformity in the application of EU VAT rules to e-commerce sector platforms.

The appearance of the proposal to introduce the deemed supplier regime as late as at the stage of the EU Council's work means that no analysis had been carried out on the possible impact of this solution on the platform sector (the Commission prepares an impact assessment of the planned regulation only for the original legislative proposals). This course of action may raise some procedural concerns, as it is difficult to consider the introduction of a completely new solution (covering e-commerce platforms by the deemed supplier regime) as a mere amendment to the proposed Directive. It is worth noting that, according to Article 17(2) of the EU Treaty,[717] only the Commission has the legislative initiative to introduce new rules (and in this case, it can be argued that a completely new rule came about at the initiative of the Council). In addition, Article 5 of the Protocol on the application of the principles of subsidiarity and proportionality[718] requires that a new draft legislative act be justified with regard to the principles of subsidiarity and proportionality (and in this case no such analysis was carried out in the impact assessment).

This way of conducting the legislative procedure for Article 14a of the VAT Directive seems to generate the risk that this provision may one day be challenged by taxable persons before the CJEU, as happened in the *Fenix* case.[719] In this case, however, the grounds would be different. Indeed, the preliminary question in the *Fenix* case was whether Article 9a IR in fact merely provides further detail in relation to the content of Article 28 of the VAT Directive but does not impose new obligations on platforms that are not provided for in the VAT Directive. In the case of Article 14a of the VAT Directive, there is no doubt that it imposes new obligations on platforms, and this provision has been in the VAT Directive from the outset. However, it is questionable whether a provision, imposing specific obligations on platforms, could have been

715. European Parliament, 'European Parliament Legislative Resolution of 30 November 2017 on the Proposal for a Council Directive Amending Directive 2006/112/EC and Directive 2009/132/EC as Regards Certain Value Added Tax Obligations for Supplies of Services and Distance Sales of Goods, P8_TA(2017)0471'.
716. Examples of such countries include Austria, France, Germany, and Italy. Their approaches differ from each other. Janssen (n. 479) 231.
717. Consolidated version of the Treaty on the Functioning of the European Union [OJ C 326, 26.10.2012, pp. 47–390].
718. Protocol (No 2) on the application of the principles of subsidiarity and proportionality [OJ C 115, 9.5.2008, pp. 206–209].
719. *Fenix International* (n. 504).

introduced at such a late legislative stage and without an assessment of its compliance with the principles of subsidiarity and proportionality.

It is also worth noting that, according to Article 14(2)(c) of the VAT Directive, a supply of goods is deemed to be the transfer of goods pursuant to a contract under which commission is payable on purchase or sale. The literature notes that this provision should be understood as follows: where a taxable person acting in his own name but on behalf of another person takes part in a supply of goods, he must be considered to have received and supplied those goods.[720] It is therefore similar to the structure in Article 28 of the VAT Directive; only it applies to undisclosed agents taking part in the supply of goods rather than services. It seems that, in theory, the EC could therefore 'provide further detail' in relation to Article 14(2)(c) of the VAT Directive in the IR, just as Article 9a of that Regulation provided further detail in relation to Article 28 of the VAT Directive. However, given taxable persons' doubts about the validity of this type of legislative exercise, it must be considered that the imposition of the deemed supplier regime on platforms in the new provision in the VAT Directive was a far better solution.

In addition, it should be pointed out that, even before Article 14a of the VAT Directive came into force, it became apparent that the new liability model would not be easy to implement for platforms. For this reason, some solutions have been introduced into the VAT e-commerce package to supplement and improve this model (mainly contained in Directive 2019/1995 and Regulation 2019/2026). These mainly concerned clarification of to which supply the dispatch or transport of goods should be attributed, indication of when the event giving rise to the tax obligation occurs, the right to deduct input VAT, the use by platforms of the special OSS procedure, definition of the meaning of the term 'facilitates', determination of when payment is accepted, limitation of platforms' liability, or a rebuttable presumption regarding the determination of the status of platform users. For this reason, the e-commerce model of the deemed supplier regime is far more extensive and complicated than the digital model discussed above.

4.3 Rationale for Using the E-commerce Model

4.3.1 The Subject Aspect

The provision of Article 14a of the VAT Directive covers taxable persons[721] who facilitate certain transactions through the use of an electronic interface such as a marketplace, platform, portal or similar means. The concept of 'interface' is not defined

720. Pollak (n. 339) 39–40; Terra and Kajus (n. 508).
721. In the doctrine, attention is drawn to the fact that platforms providing technical infrastructure for the delivery of illegal goods may also qualify as taxable persons under Article 14a of the VAT Directive. Pollak (n. 339) 120.

in the EU VAT legislation, but some guidance in this respect is provided by the non-legally binding explanatory notes[722] (Explanatory Notes 2020).

The definition of 'interface' in this document broadly corresponds to the definition of 'interface' given in the Explanatory Notes 2014, as used for the purposes of the digital model. The term 'electronic interface' is therefore a broad concept which should be understood as communication between two independent systems or a system and an end user with the help of a device or program. The term 'electronic interface' could encompass a website, portal, gateway, marketplace, API, etc.[723] However, as rightly pointed out in the literature, this definition does not explain what is meant by 'system' and what should be deemed to be 'two independent systems'.[724] The key point, however, seems to be whether all the technologies mentioned would allow to conclude the sale electronically.[725] What matters, therefore, is the effect rather than what a device or program was used by the taxable person.

The EC also clarified that the term 'similar means' was used to include current and future technologies that will allow to conclude the sale electronically.[726] Thus, the purpose of introducing an open catalogue was to enable it to evolve in line with new e-commerce developments. The EC has not applied a similar treatment to the digital model, but the concepts of telecommunications network, interface or portal contained therein are broad enough to seem to cover all existing technologies today and probably future ones as well.

Although Article 14a of the VAT Directive refers to operators of electronic interfaces (and electronic interfaces for the purposes of Article 14a of the VAT Directive are a broader concept than platforms), in the remainder of this chapter, the term 'platform operators' or 'platforms' will be used in order to be consistent in terminology with the rest of the book.

As was the case in the digital model, it matters less what technology the taxable person uses and more how such technology operates. In the case of the digital model, the platform had to take part in the supply of the service, and the meaning of this term was detailed in the Explanatory Notes 2014. In the case of the e-commerce model, the platform must 'facilitate' certain supplies of goods, a concept that is defined in Article 5b IR, although again, additional interpretative guidance is provided by the Explanatory Notes 2020.

The literature accepts that the scope of the term 'facilitation' is arguably broader than the similar term 'taking part in the supply of services', as used in Article 9a IR.[727]

722. European Commission, *Explanatory Notes on VAT E-Commerce Rules. Council Directive (EU) 2017/2455. Council Directive (EU) 2019/1995. Council Implementing Regulation (EU) 2019/2026* (n. 164).
723. *Ibid.*, 9.
724. Messina (n. 556) 124–125.
725. *Ibid.*
726. European Commission, *Explanatory Notes on VAT E-Commerce Rules. Council Directive (EU) 2017/2455. Council Directive (EU) 2019/1995. Counci l Implementing Regulation (EU) 2019/2026* (n. 164) 13.
727. Beretta (n. 344) 284–286; Marie Lamensch, 'Rendering Platforms Liable to Collect and Pay VAT on B2C Imports: A Silver Bullet?' (2018) 29 International VAT Monitor 48 https://doi.org/10.59403/3msxrka; Papis-Almansa (n. 662) 217–218.

However, in view of the fact that the presumption under Article 9a IR is regarded as being constructed so broadly, and that platforms seem almost unable to rebut this presumption,[728] it must be assumed that the distinction between the two terms is hardly of practical significance.

It is also worth noting that Article 14a of the VAT Directive applies when the conditions for a platform to be considered as facilitating a supply are met, without the need to further establish whether the platform is acting in its own name or on behalf of a third party. In other words, in contrast to the digital model, the e-commerce model also covers situations where the platform acts in the name of and on behalf of the supplier[729] (it is a disclosed agent).

Initially, the provisions of the VAT e-commerce package (adopted by the Council on 5 December 2017) did not include a definition of the term 'facilitate', and it was therefore unclear which platforms would face the new obligations. This concept was introduced into the package by Council Implementing Regulation (EU) 2019/2026, adopted on 21 November 2019, which introduced the provision of Article 5b into the IR.

According to Article 5b IR, the term 'facilitates' means the use of a platform to allow a customer and a supplier offering goods for sale through the platform to enter into contact which results in a supply of goods through that platform. This concept should therefore be considered to be defined in a very broad way. It requires first and foremost that the platform allows contact to be established, which corresponds to the function of platforms to provide a common ground on which buyers and sellers can communicate.[730]

The Explanatory Notes 2020 clarify that this concept encompasses situations where customers initiate the purchase process or make an offer for purchasing goods and underlying suppliers accept the offer via the platform (which is then reflected in the actual ordering and the checkout process being carried out by or with the help of the platform).[731] Given the literal wording of the provisions, however, it seems irrelevant which party initiates the communication process leading to the supply of the goods.

The provision of Article 5b IR expressly excludes only three situations from the term 'facilitates'. The platform operator is not facilitating a supply of goods where all of the following conditions are met: (i) the platform does not set, either directly or indirectly, any of the terms and conditions under which the supply of goods is made; (ii) the platform is not, either directly or indirectly, involved in authorizing the charge to the customer in respect of the payment made; (iii) the platform is not, either directly or indirectly, involved in the ordering or delivery of the goods. It is not clear why the EU legislator chose to formulate the list in a negative way when the same result could

728. Merkx (n. 573) 19.
729. *See also*: Papis-Almansa (n. 662) 218–219.
730. Lamensch and others (n. 104) 454–455.
731. European Commission, *Explanatory Notes on VAT E-Commerce Rules. Council Directive (EU) 2017/2455. Council Directive (EU) 2019/1995. Council Implementing Regulation (EU) 2019/2026* (n. 164) 18–19.

have been achieved with a positive formulation.[732] These conditions must be met cumulatively by the platform for it to be considered as not facilitating the supply. Even if a platform carries out only one of the above-listed activities, it may still be considered as the supplier.[733]

The Explanatory Notes 2020 provide detailed explanations and examples for each of the conditions indicated above. According to the document, the platform's setting, directly or indirectly, 'the terms and conditions under which the supply is made' means the platform's influence, in particular, on the obligations and rights of its users, as well as on other elements of the transaction. It is a concept that should be interpreted broadly and that goes beyond the contractual relationship and takes into account the economic situation and, in particular, the influence exercised by platforms or their contribution to the actual supply of the goods. In addition, the Explanatory Notes 2020 emphasize that the use of the words 'indirectly' and 'any' is meant to prevent artificial splitting of rights and obligations between the platform operator and the underlying suppliers.[734] The legal literature, however, points out that although, according to the Explanatory Notes 2020, the definition of 'the terms and conditions under which the supply is made' covers also the terms and conditions of use of the platform (including the terms and conditions of an account on the platform website), in view of the legal text, this condition is more likely to be thought of as referring only to the conditions relating to the delivery of goods or the payment for these goods.[735] According to some authors, including also the terms and conditions of use of the platform in this condition extends the scope of the regulation in question contrary to Article 14a of the VAT Directive.[736] It is worth noting, however, that in the case of the very similar condition of 'setting the general terms and conditions of services' of the digital model, the Explanatory Notes 2014 also indicated that it covered conditions to maintain a user account on the platform.[737] This interpretation was challenged by Fenix in proceedings initiated before the CJEU but was disagreed with by the Advocate General.[738] Ultimately, the CJEU did not explicitly indicate its position on this matter; however, indirectly, it can be inferred that it adopted a narrower understanding of this criterion.[739] As the condition of 'setting terms and conditions' is formulated analogously for the digital model and the e-commerce model, it should therefore be assumed that

732. Pollak (n. 339) 122.
733. European Commission, *Explanatory Notes on VAT E-Commerce Rules. Council Directive (EU) 2017/2455. Council Directive (EU) 2019/1995. Council Implementing Regulation (EU) 2019/2026* (n. 164) 19.
734. *Ibid.*, 19–21.
735. Janssen (n. 479) 232.
736. Merkx (n. 573) 20.
737. European Commission, *Explanatory Notes on the EU VAT Changes to the Place of Supply of Telecommunications, Broadcasting and Electronic Services That Enter into Force in 2015* (n. 498) 36.
738. 'Opinion of Advocate General Rantos Delivered on 15 September 2022 in Case C-695/20 Fenix International Limited v Commissioners for Her Majesty's Revenue and Customs' (n. 542), paragraph 82.
739. *Fenix International* (n. 504), paragraphs 83–84. *See also* further remarks on the subjective criteria for applying the digital model.

contrary to the 2020 Explanatory Notes, it should not cover in both cases the acceptance of the platform's terms of use.

However, as rightly pointed out in the literature, such a broad interpretation should not lead to 'unintentional' intermediation of platforms being covered by the deemed supplier regime.[740] These are situations where, through platforms designed for interaction, such as Facebook or online forums, for example, users begin to exchange or trade in goods (on their own, without the supervision of the platform).[741] In such cases, platforms could be considered as enabling the customer and the supplier to establish contact resulting in supply and therefore 'facilitate' such transactions. However, it must be agreed that it was clearly not the legislator's intention and that a distinction must be made between situations in which the actual ordering and/or checkout process is managed via the platform (in which case the platform is knowingly involved in the matching of buyers and sellers) and situations where customers initiate the purchase process or make an offer for purchasing goods themselves (unintended platform e-commerce).[742]

In the case of 'being involved in authorising the charge to the customer in respect of the payment made', the Explanatory Notes 2020 indicate that this condition refers to a situation where the platform operator can influence whether at what time or under which conditions the customer pays. This condition is therefore interpreted very broadly. For example, it is sufficient for the platform to communicate to the customer information about the payment, such as the price to be paid, any additional charges due, the time for the payment, and methods of payment. The platform operator authorizes the payment when it decides that the customer's account, credit or similar card can be debited/charged as payment for the supply or when he is involved in receiving the payment authorization message or the commitment for payment from the customer. This concept does not imply that the platform must effectively collect or receive the payment or that it should be involved in each step of the payment process.[743]

In the Explanatory Notes 2020, the concept of 'being involved in the ordering or delivery of goods' is also interpreted broadly. Indeed, this condition refers to a situation where the platform operator can influence in any way the ordering of goods; the platform need not even be involved in generating the purchase order. In turn, 'being involved in the delivery of goods' is not limited to the physical delivery of goods, which may or may not be arranged by the platform – it is sufficient that the platform can in any way influence the delivery of goods. The operator's involvement in the ordering or delivery process may be suggested by various features, for example, the fact that the

740. Lamensch and others (n. 104) 455–457.
741. Registered users on Facebook can become suppliers by using the social network as a platform for marketing and selling products or services. In such cases, users may also become VAT taxable persons in the same way as they would in the traditional market. Cristina Trenta, 'European VAT and the Digital Economy: Recent Developments' (2019) 17 eJournal of Tax Research 124.
742. Lamensch and others (n. 104) 455–457.
743. European Commission, *Explanatory Notes on VAT E-Commerce Rules. Council Directive (EU) 2017/2455. Council Directive (EU) 2019/1995. Council Implementing Regulation (EU) 2019/2026* (n. 164) 21–22.

platform provides the technical tool to take the order from the customer (typically the shopping cart/check-out process), communicates the confirmation and/or details of the order to the customer and to the underlying supplier, or charges to the underlying supplier a fee or commission based on the order's value.[744]

In this context, it is worth noting that the conditions contained in Article 5b IR, as well as its interpretation in the Explanatory Notes 2020, correspond to examples of the functions that, according to the OECD, may trigger the eligibility of a digital platform to the deemed supplier regime. These are: (i) controlling or setting the terms and conditions of the underlying transactions and imposing them on the other parties; (ii) being directly or indirectly involved in payment processing; (iii) being directly or indirectly involved in the delivery process or execution; and (iv) providing customer service (returns or refunds or assistance in grievance or dispute management procedures).[745] In addition, the conditions in question also appear to generally correspond to the conditions set out in Article 9a IR, which makes the presumption of the application of the deemed supplier regime in the digital model unrebuttable. It is sufficient that the platform meets at least one of the following conditions: (i) authorizes the charge to the customer, (ii) authorizes the supply of the services, or (iii) sets general terms and conditions for the supply of the services.

'Authorising the charge to the customer' in Article 9a IR appears to be an analogous condition to 'being involved in authorising the charge to the customer in respect of the payment made' in Article 5b IR, just as 'authorising the supply of services' appears to correspond to 'being involved in the ordering or delivery of goods' and 'setting the general terms and conditions of the supply of services' corresponds to 'setting the terms and conditions under which the supply of goods is made'. However, unlike Article 9b IR, the provision of Article 5b IR for each of the conditions in question specifies that these activities cover both direct and indirect involvement of the platform. It can therefore be concluded that Article 5b IR covers a broader spectrum of platform activities than Article 9b IR. However, as the presumption of Article 9a IR is considered to be almost impossible to rebut due to the broad formulation of its conditions, the fact that Article 5b IR appears to be defined in an even broader manner is unlikely to be of practical significance. However, such a move may further increase legal certainty for those applying the provision in question.

In addition, Article 5b IR provides for an exception to the rules indicated above. According to the third paragraph of this provision, Article 14a of the VAT Directive does not apply to a platform which only provides any of the following activities: (i) the processing of payments in relation to the supply of goods, or (ii) the listing or advertising of goods, or (iii) the redirecting or transferring of customers to other platforms where goods are offered for sale, without any further intervention in the supply.

The Explanatory Notes 2020 emphasize that if a platform operator carries out only one of the above-listed activities or several of them in combination, he will not be

744. *Ibid.*, 22–23.
745. OECD, *The Role of Digital Platforms in the Collection of VAT/GST on Online Sales* (n. 551) 73–74.

treated as the deemed supplier. It is also clear from the document that the aim is to exclude platforms that are not involved in any way in the delivery (which happens between the underlying supplier and the customer completely independently) because they would not in the normal course of business have knowledge of elements such as: (i) if and when a transaction was concluded, (ii) where the goods are located, (iii) where the goods are transported to, and without such information it would be impossible for the platform to comply with its VAT obligations as the deemed supplier.[746]

The literature notes – completely correctly – that the three excluded situations – processing payments, listing advertisements of goods and redirecting customers – seem a bit redundant as none of them seem to meet the main rule, which involves the platform allowing a customer and a supplier to make contact. Excluding these situations explicitly, however, probably provides more legal certainty.[747]

It is worth noting that the conditions set down in Article 5b IR essentially correspond to examples of functions that, according to the OECD, can exclude a platform from the deemed supplier regime. These occur when the platform: (i) only carries content (e.g., makes the internet network available for carrying content via Wi-Fi), or (ii) only processes payments, or (iii) only advertises offers, or (iv) only acts as a redirection platform.[748] Also, in this case, the OECD has indicated that the reason for excluding these platforms from the deemed supplier regime is that they do not have sufficient information to correctly account for VAT on the underlying transactions.[749]

What is missing from the conditions set out in Article 5b IR is an exemption for situations where the platform only carries content. However, such an exception has been made for the digital model. According to the Explanatory Notes 2014 and in the 2016 Guidelines, the participation of such platforms in the supply of services is insufficient for them to act as the deemed suppliers. It is not clear why a similar exemption was not included in Article 5b IR on the e-commerce model. However, it should be emphasized that, for this model, the platform's facilitation of transactions must result in the physical delivery of goods, so the mere digital carrying of content does not seem sufficient to achieve such an effect. It must be concluded that it was therefore not necessary to include this condition in the catalogue of Article 5b IR.

It is also worth noting that both the digital model and the e-commerce model exclude from the deemed supplier regime platforms that limit themselves to the processing of payments. The digital model, as opposed to the e-commerce model, does not explicitly exclude platforms whose functions are reduced to merely advertising goods or services, as well as platforms that merely redirect or transfer buyers to other platforms without any further involvement in the underlying transaction. It is difficult to see why the digital model does not contain analogous exceptions. While it seems that

746. European Commission, *Explanatory Notes on VAT E-Commerce Rules. Council Directive (EU) 2017/2455. Council Directive (EU) 2019/1995. Council Implementing Regulation (EU) 2019/2026* (n. 164) 23.
747. Lamensch and others (n. 104) 454–455.
748. OECD, *The Role of Digital Platforms in the Collection of VAT/GST on Online Sales* (n. 551) 73–74.
749. OECD, *Mechanisms for the Effective Collection of VAT/GST* (n. 550) 26.

such platforms should not be subject to the digital model anyway (as they do not have sufficient information to correctly account for VAT on the underlying transactions), the introduction of such exceptions could further increase legal certainty for those using this model.

In summary, the assessment of whether a platform facilitates a supply of goods should be made on a transactional basis (separately for each transaction).[750] At the same time, Article 5b IR defining the concept of 'facilitating' transactions appears to be worded broadly enough to cover most e-commerce platforms. In addition, it should be noted that the interpretation of this concept in the Explanatory Notes 2020 is also rather far-reaching and, as some authors have argued, even seems to go beyond what is literally provided for in Article 5b IR.[751]

Academic legal writers also point out that in practice platforms offer different levels of facilitation.[752] It may be related to the order phase (where platforms have a function to match vendors and customers and to build trust), or the execution phase (where platforms may be involved in shipment and payment), or the result phase (where platforms can take a role as regards dispute resolution or purchase protection). The further a platform's involvement in these phases, the higher the level of facilitation it offers. At the highest level, a platform is involved in all three phases of the transaction.[753] The coexistence of different levels of facilitation implies that e-commerce platforms may be able to comply with obligations relating to declaring and levying VAT only for some of their transactions.[754] However, the provisions of the VAT e-commerce package do not appear to take such differences into account, which may make it difficult to apply the new rules.

It is also worth noting that in practice platforms often collaborate with other platforms. Smaller and more specialized platforms may contract with more dominant platforms to provide particular services – such as payment processing.[755] It may also be the case that the user is assisted by two interfaces (one of which will be, for example, an online shop and the other a platform that translates that shop's website into another language).[756] In such situations, the question arises as to which platform will be deemed to be the supplier. As pointed out in the Explanatory Notes 2020, only one platform in a given transaction can be the facilitator and consequently the entity deemed to be the supplier, and that is the one via which the order is received and supply is made.[757] In order to determine this, it is first necessary to examine via which operator the sales contract is actually concluded with the consumer, thus through

750. Patric Ville, 'New VAT Rules on E-Commerce' (2021) 32 International VAT Monitor 6 https://doi.org/10.59403/2j9n13x.
751. Lamensch and others (n. 104) 455–457.
752. *Ibid.*, 447; Lamensch and others (n. 143).
753. Lamensch and others (n. 104) 451–452.
754. *Ibid.*, 450–451.
755. Julie E Cohen, 'Law for the Platform Economy' (2017) 51 U.C. Davis Law Review 133, 146–148.
756. Messina (n. 556) 126–127.
757. European Commission, *Explanatory Notes on VAT E-Commerce Rules. Council Directive (EU) 2017/2455. Council Directive (EU) 2019/1995. Council Implementing Regulation (EU) 2019/2026* (n. 164) 23–24.

which platform the consumer carries out the ordering or payment process.[758] It should be noted that a similar explanation is not included in the Explanatory Notes 2014 on the digital model.

Under the deemed supplier regime, the compliance burdens placed on platforms increase significantly. A measure that can be implemented to restore the balance is to adopt a provision that reduces or eliminates platforms' liability for mistakes resulting from reliance on inaccurate information if they can prove their good faith and their reasonable efforts to secure the accuracy and reliability of the information on which they acted.[759] In the OECD's view, the application of the principle of reducing or eliminating platforms' liability offers a balanced approach towards facilitating compliance.[760]

This is the role of Article 5c IR in the EU VAT system. This provision was introduced into the e-commerce VAT package by Council Implementing Regulation (EU) 2019/2026. According to recital 7 of this regulation, the purpose of this provision is to limit the liability of platforms as deemed suppliers when they act in good faith and meet certain conditions.

It should be noted that the platform, as the deemed provider, is liable for the fair accounting of the underlying transactions it facilitates. However, in reality, it is not the platform operator that does the transaction but the underlying supplier and the consumer. As rightly highlighted in the Explanatory Notes 2020, platforms typically do not own the goods, and the transfer of ownership happens between the underlying supplier and the consumer. As a result, the platform often does not have the necessary information to comply with VAT obligations and relies on information obtained from the underlying supplier, which may turn out to be incorrect. Thus, in order not to impose a disproportionate burden on platforms and to provide them with greater legal certainty, their liability for the payment of VAT was limited in pre-defined cases.[761]

According to Article 5c IR, the platform will therefore not be liable for the difference in VAT in respect of the supplies it facilitates and for potential penalties and interest for late payment provided all of the following conditions are met: (i) the platform is dependent on information provided by suppliers selling goods through the platform or by other third parties in order to correctly declare and pay the VAT on those supplies, (ii) that information is erroneous, and (iii) the platform can demonstrate that it did not and could not reasonably know that this information was incorrect.[762] This provision is sometimes referred to in the literature as the safe-harbour rules for

758. This interpretation appears similar to the solutions applied in Australia. In Australia, the deemed supplier is considered to be the first operator of the platform who receives or approves the provision or allows the delivery. Guglyuvatyy and Milogolov (n. 680) 33-36.
759. Scarcella (n. 391) 6-7.
760. OECD, *The Role of Digital Platforms in the Collection of VAT/GST on Online Sales* (n. 551) 36-37.
761. European Commission, *Explanatory Notes on VAT E-Commerce Rules. Council Directive (EU) 2017/2455. Council Directive (EU) 2019/1995. Council Implementing Regulation (EU) 2019/2026* (n. 164) 24.
762. In such a situation, it is possible to invoke the liability of the underlying supplier if the Member State has introduced national measures providing for their joint liability. Regarding future transactions, the electronic interface operator applies new, accurate information. *Ibid.*, 25.

platforms[763] or the diligent operator concept.[764] In order to invoke the limited liability provision, the platform must prove that all the necessary conditions have been met. The burden of proof therefore lies with the platform operator.[765]

The first condition relates to the platform's dependence on the information provided by suppliers or by other third parties. According to the legal literature, it remains unclear in which circumstances a platform should be considered to be dependent on this type of data, and where that condition is not fulfilled, the platform will be held liable even if it could demonstrate good faith.[766] In this context, it is worth noting that in practice, information chains are often incomplete,[767] and it may therefore be impossible for platforms to identify the responsible third party.[768]

Some, but rather general, guidance is provided in this respect by the Explanatory Notes 2020. While they do not refer to the notion of 'dependence' of platforms on information, they do indicate that they should make commercially reasonable and diligent efforts to collect all the necessary information from the underlying supplier so that it can fulfil its VAT obligations. This should be worked out as part of the existing commercial relationships, and if the underlying supplier persistently fails to provide the necessary information, the platform should take 'appropriate' action, which, however, the EC does not specify.[769]

Under the second condition, the information provided to the platform by the underlying supplier or third party must be incorrect. The scholarly literature highlights that, in practice, it is difficult for the platform to detect that the information provided by the underlying supplier is incorrect. Because of the platform's dependence on the supply of data by the underlying supplier, it is likely to find out that it should have declared VAT or declared an insufficient amount of VAT only after the competent tax authority has pointed this out to it.[770] In the case of this condition, it is also pointed out that this condition is vague whether it refers only to VAT or also to customs-related information, such as the customs status or physical location of the goods at the moment of sale.[771] For example, the scholarly literature highlights that the clause set out in Article 5c IR should not refer to situations of misuse of the IOSS number.[772]

763. Lamensch and others (n. 104) 462–464.
764. Easton (n. 33) 170–171.
765. European Commission, *Explanatory Notes on VAT E-Commerce Rules. Council Directive (EU) 2017/2455. Council Directive (EU) 2019/1995. Council Implementing Regulation (EU) 2019/2026* (n. 164) 26.
766. Papis-Almansa (n. 662) 220–221.
767. The physical flow of goods entails the coordination of various entities throughout the entire logistics chain of trade. Therefore, to identify goods, one would have to rely on information gathered by freight forwarders. However, such information is often passed from one agent to another, and detailed information may be lost along the chain. Messina (n. 556) 135–136.
768. *Ibid.*, 149–150.
769. European Commission, *Explanatory Notes on VAT E-Commerce Rules. Council Directive (EU) 2017/2455. Council Directive (EU) 2019/1995. Council Implementing Regulation (EU) 2019/2026* (n. 164) 26–27.
770. Pollak (n. 339) 206.
771. Messina (n. 556) 159.
772. Lamensch and others (n. 104) 465.

Platforms are also required to demonstrate that they did not and could not reasonably know that the information from the underlying supplier or third party was incorrect. It is not clear how the platforms are expected to demonstrate this negative fact.[773] The Explanatory Notes 2020 merely indicate that the platform operator needs to act in good faith and should exercise due commercial care, and whether this is indeed the case should be assessed not only based on the particular circumstances but also taking into account the internal organization of the platform and the information that can be available to it.[774] According to the wording of the Explanatory Notes 2020, the limited liability clause takes into account the differences between platform operators and accepts that the notion of due commercial care may vary depending on the size of the platform, its business model, the volume of transactions, the number of underlying suppliers, etc. The deemed supplier rule should not put a disproportionate burden on platform operators and does not aim to require a widespread standard of checks to be performed for every supply, which might put a heavier burden on smaller platforms and might ultimately lead to certain larger platforms obtaining an even larger market share.[775]

The Commission has also suggested that some theoretical guidance relating to the good faith of taxable persons can be found in the jurisprudence of the CJEU.[776] According to the scholarly literature, the cases cited by the Commission can be divided into two groups: (i) the ECJ's jurisprudence on the right to deduct VAT and (ii) the ECJ's jurisprudence concerning the good faith exemption upon export to third countries.[777]

The ECJ's jurisprudence on the right to deduct VAT are cases in which the ECJ is demanded to strike a balance in terms of proportionality between the objective to prevent tax evasion, avoidance and abuse on the one hand and the right of taxable persons to deduct input VAT on the other.[778] On the issue of good faith relating to the exemption upon export to third countries, the Commission referred to the CJEU's judgment in the *Netto Supermarkt* case.[779] There, the CJEU held that in the case of an exemption when exporting to a third country, a liability regime that would not allow the exporter any good faith justification would be disproportionate. The citation of this judgment by the EC in the Explanatory Notes 2020 is regarded as controversial, as the

773. *Ibid.*, 462–464.
774. European Commission, *Explanatory Notes on VAT E-Commerce Rules. Council Directive (EU) 2017/2455. Council Directive (EU) 2019/1995. Council Implementing Regulation (EU) 2019/2026* (n. 164) 27–28.
775. *Ibid.*
776. The referenced CJEU judgments are: *Santogal M-Comércio e Reparação de Automóveis Lda v. Autoridade Tributária e Aduaneira* [2017] CJEU C-26/16, paragraphs 71–72; *Mecsek-Gabona Kft v. Nemzeti Adó- és Vámhivatal Dél-dunántúli Regionális Adó Főigazgatósága* [2012] CJEU C-273/11 31, paragraph 48; *LVK - 56 EOOD v. Direktor na Direktsia 'Obzhalvane i upravlenie na izpalnenieto' - Varna pri Tsentralno upravlenie na Natsionalnata agentsia za prihodite* [2013] CJEU C-643/11, paragraph 63; *Netto Supermarkt GmbH & Co OHG v. Finanzamt Malchin* [2008] CJEU C-271/06, paragraphs 24–25, 27; *Gábor Tóth v. Nemzeti Adó- és Vámhivatal Észak-magyarországi Regionális Adó Főigazgatósága* [2012] CJEU C-324/11, paragraph 45.
777. Messina (n. 556) 150–151.
778. *Ibid.*, 152–155.
779. *Netto Supermarkt GmbH & Co. OHG v. Finanzamt Malchin* (n. 772).

scholarly literature points out that it concerned the VAT system that was significantly modified after the introduction of the VAT e-commerce package.[780]

It is worth noting that the EU legislator's approach to limiting the liability of platforms as deemed suppliers is in line with the OECD guidelines. Indeed, in the OECD's view, platforms can reasonably be expected to implement appropriate measures to ensure the accuracy and reliability of the information on which the determination of their taxation is based. This also applies to cases when the information collected is obtained from underlying suppliers or third parties. Jurisdictions may consider implementing a provision that reduces or eliminates platforms' liability for mistakes resulting from reliance on inaccurate information if they can supply evidence of their good faith and of their reasonable efforts to secure the accuracy and reliability of the information on which they acted. What is considered as 'reasonable efforts' is for tax authorities to decide and is likely to depend on circumstances.[781]

Concerns have been expressed in the literature that the provision of Article 5c IR, worded in this way, will either hinder the effective collection of VAT or impede the fair collection of VAT. If the platform is easily released from its obligation to pay additional VAT, the provision will hinder the effective collection of VAT, and if too strict approach is applied, the platform will be held liable even in situations where it has acted in good faith.[782] However, while the literature emphasizes that clear guidance is called for to provide platforms with more certainty in relation to how any measures they take interact with their liability,[783] as the Explanatory Notes 2020 rightly point out, since every case can be different, it is not possible to provide well-defined guidelines in this respect.[784] The reasonable efforts of a platform must therefore be assessed on a case-by-case basis depending on the specific operator and its resources.

It should also be noted that the EU legislator has not chosen to introduce a similar regulation limiting the liability of platforms in the digital model. This is probably due to the different specificity of the transactions which include the digital model and the e-commerce model. It appears that in the case of the e-commerce model, platforms may depend more on the reliability of information provided by third parties due to the need for physical delivery of goods. Platforms typically do not hold the goods, and the transfer of goods happens between the underlying supplier and the consumer, often involving different freight forwarders or carriers. The digital model, however, involves electronically transmitted services, which means that similar problems are unlikely to occur in this case.

For the purposes of applying Article 14a of the VAT Directive, it is also irrelevant whether the platform is operated by an EU operator or a third-country entity. However, it is worth noting that enforcement of compliance might be more challenging against

780. For more detailed information on this topic, refer to: Messina (n. 556) 155–159.
781. OECD, *The Role of Digital Platforms in the Collection of VAT/GST on Online Sales* (n. 551) 33–34.
782. Merkx (n. 573) 23–25.
783. Easton (n. 33) 170–171.
784. European Commission, *Explanatory Notes on VAT E-Commerce Rules. Council Directive (EU) 2017/2455. Council Directive (EU) 2019/1995. Council Implementing Regulation (EU) 2019/2026* (n. 164) 26.

platform operators from third countries.[785] The key problem is the mismatch between this substantive jurisdiction and any (effective) enforcement jurisdiction, particularly in the VAT realm, as decisions about the tax must be made for every transaction, not just on an annual basis.[786] Legal literature highlights that platforms can be located anywhere in the world, and the grip of EU tax authorities on platforms located outside the EU is limited (so there is a risk that EU trade in goods through platforms will shift to platforms located outside the EU, which could have a negative effect on the effectiveness of EU rules).[787] However, when implementing a system based on the principle of VAT taxation at destination, the effectiveness of this mechanism always depends on the willingness of non-resident businesses to fulfil their obligations to register and account for VAT in the EU. In such a case, 'substantive jurisdiction' for taxation is imposed, but there is still no jurisdictional basis for enforcing EU rules against non-EU vendors. This explains why the EU legislator, in an attempt to close this loophole, introduces a model of shifting tax liability from such vendors to platforms.[788] This is because it is easier to get a smaller number of foreign platforms to comply as deemed suppliers than it is to get millions of foreign underlying suppliers to comply.

Given the problem of possible enforcement of tax obligations from foreign operators, it is rightly advocated that international administrative cooperation in this area should be further promoted and strengthened and that national tax authorities might consider introducing additional (reasonable and proportionate) safeguards to reduce risks of non-compliance.[789]

4.3.2 *The Object Aspect*

The provision of Article 14a of the VAT Directive applies if the platform only facilitates two types of transactions: (i) distance sales of goods imported from third territories or third countries in consignments of an intrinsic value not exceeding EUR 150 (Article 14a(1) of the VAT Directive) and (ii) the supply of goods within the Community by a taxable person not established within the Community to a non-taxable person (Article 14a(2) of the VAT Directive).

DSIG is defined in Article 14(4)(2) of the VAT Directive. According to this provision, this concept means supplies of goods dispatched or transported by or on behalf of the supplier, including where the supplier intervenes indirectly in the transport or dispatch of the goods, from a third territory or third country, to a customer in a Member State, where the following conditions are jointly met:

785. OECD, *The Role of Digital Platforms in the Collection of VAT/GST on Online Sales* (n. 551) 28–29.
786. Millar (n. 384) 9.
787. Lamensch and others (n. 104) 475–477.
788. Messina (n. 556) 122–123.
789. OECD, *The Role of Digital Platforms in the Collection of VAT/GST on Online Sales* (n. 551) 28–29.

(a) the supply is carried out for a taxable person or a non-taxable legal person whose intra-Community acquisition of goods is not subject to VAT or for any other non-taxable person (B2C transactions);
(b) the goods supplied are neither new means of transport nor goods which are assembled or installed, with or without a trial run.

For this transaction (unlike Article 14a(2) of the VAT Directive discussed below), it is irrelevant whether the underlying supplier is established within or outside the EU. However, it is essential that the consignments are delivered from a third country. In addition, the platform will only become an entity deemed to be a supplier if the value of consignments delivered via DSIG does not exceed an intrinsic value of EUR 150.[790] This is the value adopted in the EU for low-value goods due to the fact that the EUR 150 threshold is the value up to which goods are exempt from customs duty, meaning that only VAT is due on these consignments.[791] This approach is in line with OECD observations which show that tax authorities mainly consider the deemed supplier regime for imports of goods below the *de minimis* customs threshold. Indeed, the operation of a dual collection regime could create risks for double taxation of VAT in some limited circumstances (e.g., where the value of an imported good is calculated differently for customs purposes than for VAT compliance purposes or where the platform collects VAT on a sale of multiple low-value goods to a single customer and then chooses to transport these goods in a single consignment that is then valued above the *de minimis* customs threshold).[792] However, it should be noted that this situation may soon change. On 17 May 2023, the Commission published a proposal for a council directive amending the VAT Directive as regards VAT rules relating to taxable persons who facilitate DSIG and the application of the special scheme for distance sales of goods imported from third countries and other special arrangements for declaration and payment of VAT on imports.[793] Under this proposal, the EUR 150 threshold will be removed from Article 14a of the VAT Directive and from the scope of supplies covered by the IOSS, as well as from other special arrangements. This will make the deemed supplier regime cover a much higher volume of transactions.

790. Intrinsic value means: (a) for commercial goods: the price of the goods themselves when sold for export to the customs territory of the Union, excluding transport and insurance costs, unless they are included in the price and not separately indicated on the invoice, and any other taxes and charges as ascertainable by the customs authorities from any relevant document(s); (b) for goods of a non-commercial nature: the price which would have been paid for the goods themselves if they were sold for export to the customs territory of the Union. Commission Delegated Regulation (EU) 2015/2446 of 28 July 2015 supplementing Regulation (EU) No 952/2013 of the European Parliament and of the Council as regards detailed rules concerning certain provisions of the Union Customs Code [OJ L 343, 29.12.2015, pp. 1–557], Article 1(48).
791. European Commission, Directorate General for Taxation and Customs Union and others, *VAT in the Digital Age: Final Report. Volume 3, Single Place of VAT Registration and Import One Stop Shop* (Publications Office 2022) 16.
792. OECD, *The Role of Digital Platforms in the Collection of VAT/GST on Online Sales* (n. 551) 46–47.
793. Proposal for a Council Directive amending Directive 2006/112/EC as regards VAT rules relating to taxable persons who facilitate distance sales of imported goods and the application of the special scheme for distance sales of goods imported from third territories or third countries and special arrangements for declaration and payment of import VAT 2023 [COM(2023) 262].

Additionally, a 'deemed importer' solution will be introduced. Currently, customs clearance procedures for e-commerce packages are typically handled by couriers or consumers. However, if the planned changes are implemented, the responsibility for completing these procedures will shift to e-commerce platforms, termed as 'deemed importers'. Economic operators will be designated as such if they engage in distance sales of goods to be imported into the EU from third countries and are authorized to use the IOSS.[794]

The Commission plans for these changes to come into force on 1 March 2028, although, as noted in scholarly discussions, meeting this deadline seems improbable.[795]

The supply of goods within the Community, as referred to in Article 14a(2) of the VAT Directive, concerns both domestic supplies and ICDS. This transaction is defined in Article 14(4)(1) of the VAT Directive. According to this provision, this concept means supplies of goods dispatched or transported by or on behalf of the supplier, including where the supplier intervenes indirectly in the transport or dispatch of the goods, between Member States, where the following conditions are jointly met:

(a) the supply is carried out for a taxable person or a non-taxable legal person who is not required to account for intra-Community acquisitions of goods or for any other non-taxable person (B2C transactions);
(b) the goods supplied are neither new means of transport nor goods which are assembled or installed, with or without a trial run.

The conditions set out in points (a)–(b) correspond to those set out in the definition of DSIG. However, it is worth noting that the provision of Article 14(4)(1)(a) may change effective from 1 January 2025, and the ICDS will additionally cover the sale of second-hand goods, works of art, collectors' items and antiques.[796]

Furthermore, unlike DSIG facilitated by platforms, the value of the goods to be supplied within the Community is irrelevant. However, they must already be within the Community or be marketed there.

It should be noted that for this transaction, the platform will only become a deemed supplier if its underlying supplier is established outside the EU. This solution takes into account the OECD guidelines, according to which consideration should first be given to introducing the deemed supplier regime for supplies made by an underlying supplier that is established within a foreign tax jurisdiction. This is because, in this case, enforcement against (potentially millions) underlying suppliers may be more

794. For a more extensive discussion on this topic, refer to: Sergio Messina, 'EU "Distance Sales of Goods Imported" and Customs Duties: Mind the Link' (2024) 35 International VAT Monitor https://doi.org/10.59403/2d6vj6q; Martijn L Schippers, 'Proposals to Reform the EU Customs Union' (2023) 32 EC Tax Review 253 https://doi.org/10.54648/ecta2023031.
795. Schippers (n. 790), 261–262.
796. Proposal for a Council Directive amending Directive 2006/112/EC as regards VAT rules for the digital age (n. 382); in the latest compromise text, however, this idea was abandoned. Draft Council Directive amending Directive 2006/112/EC as regards VAT rules for the digital age – compromise text 8 May 2024 (n. 382).

challenging for the tax authorities.[797] However, the OECD notes that such an arrangement may create compliance complexities for platforms (e.g., the need to operate compliance processes that distinguish between domestic and foreign suppliers) and audit challenges for tax administrations (e.g., checking the location of underlying suppliers).[798] In the OECD's view, these considerations might support the application of the full deemed supplier regime to all the relevant transactions, irrespective of the location of the underlying supplier.[799]

It is possible that such a solution will soon be introduced by the legislator into the EU VAT system with effect from 1 January 2025. Under the planned Article 2(2) of the legislative proposal,[800] the requirement for the underlying supplier to be established in a third country will disappear from Article 14a(2) of the VAT Directive. In its extended scope, the deemed supplier principle will therefore apply to all supplies of goods within the EU made through the platform, regardless of where the supplier is established.[801] It is worth noting that, in doing so, the EU legislator also plans to abolish the requirement that the consumer of the services must not be a taxable person. Thus, the deemed supplier regime in the future could apply to all supplies of goods within the EU regardless of the status of the consumer (both B2B[802] and B2C transactions). In the proposal, however, the EU legislator provides for one exception. Under the planned Article 14a(4) of the VAT Directive, where a platform, established only in one Member State, facilitates supplies of goods only in that Member State without dispatch or transport, or with dispatch or transport which begins and ends in that Member State,

797. OECD, *The Role of Digital Platforms in the Collection of VAT/GST on Online Sales* (n. 551) 29.
798. *Ibid.*
799. *Ibid.*
800. Proposal for a Council Directive amending Directive 2006/112/EC as regards VAT rules for the digital age (n. 382).
801. This solution raises concerns among entrepreneurs. It is pointed out that while the existing regulations have proven effective in increasing compliance with VAT rules, it is doubtful whether the same success can be expected when applying them to intra-EU transactions. These sales are already subject to tax enforcement, just like any other domestic or EU sale. At the same time, there are still gaps in enforcing the law regarding platform operators based in third countries, meaning that large platforms operating outside the EU are effectively not pursued. As a result, the new obligations would create a competitive disadvantage for EU platforms and sellers compared to platforms outside the EU. Ecommerce Europe, 'Position Paper 3 April 2023. Ecommerce Europe's Feedback on the VAT in the Digital Age Proposal'.
802. In the literature, the extension of Article 14a of the VAT Directive to B2B supplies is described as 'surprising'. According to the impact assessment and the study preceding the ViDA proposals, the focus was solely on B2B2C supplies (e.g., dropshipping). Therefore, more information is expected regarding the reasons for taking this step in the proposal's justification and in the impact assessment. Madeleine Merkx and others, 'VAT in the Digital Age Package: Singling Out the Single VAT Registration' (2023) EC Tax Review 179 https://doi.org/10.2139/ssrn.4504784; it is also emphasized that most platforms operating in the B2B sector are typically not involved in the transport of goods. This means they would have to obtain relevant evidence from the supplier or customer and rely on their diligence to provide complete information on time (otherwise, they risk losing the benefit of the intra-Community supply exemption). If new reporting requirements are implemented, this would need to be done within very tight deadlines, which could be challenging for the platforms: Lamensch and others (n. 143).

that taxable person will not be deemed to have received and supplied those goods.[803] Local platforms facilitating the domestic sales of goods would therefore be excluded from the deemed supplier regime. However, it is important to note that some Member States are opposed to this solution, making it difficult to assess the likelihood of its implementation.[804]

Furthermore, in the view of the EU legislator, the deemed supplier regime could apply to situations where there is a transfer of the taxable person's own goods to another Member State. It is therefore planned to add paragraph 3 to Article 14a of the VAT Directive. Under the draft of this provision, a platform would be treated as a deemed supplier if it facilitated transfer by the taxable person of: (i) goods other than capital goods to another Member State in accordance with Article 17(1) of the VAT Directive (transfer by a taxable person of goods forming part of his business assets), or (ii) goods in relation to which there is no full right of deduction in that Member State. It therefore appears that, in practice, the planned provision would primarily cover platforms that store goods belonging to the underlying suppliers in their logistics centres (fulfilment warehouses). Currently, the transfer of a taxable underlying supplier's own goods to another Member State, *inter alia*, for the purposes of its e-commerce activities, triggers the need for that supplier to register in the Member States from and to which the goods are transferred, even if such transfer is facilitated by the platform.[805] If the planned provision were to enter into force, underlying suppliers would avoid this obligation. This solution was met with initial approval from the legal commentators[806] and entrepreneurs.[807] It is pointed out that with this solution, platforms that offer warehousing services will have information available about the location of the goods, whereas suppliers will have to rely on the information from the platform. This provision would therefore ensure fair and efficient collection of VAT because it puts the burden on bigger market players that have the information available instead of smaller market players that rely on information from a third party.[808] However, as indicated in the literature, this solution is not without its drawbacks. First, it is unclear whether the deeming provision would cover both transfers of goods decided and organized by the supplier and those decided and organized by the platform. Additionally, there is a need to adopt a new definition of 'facilitation' specifically for the context of goods transfer.[809]

It is worth noting that the transactions that are currently covered by the deemed supplier regime in the e-commerce model are related to third countries. For DSIGs with a value not exceeding EUR 150, the goods must be imported into the Community from third countries, and for EU supplies, the underlying supplier should be established in

803. Proposal for a Council Directive amending Directive 2006/112/EC as regards VAT rules for the digital age (n. 382).
804. Council of the EU, 'VAT in the Digital Age Package – Policy Debate, 9749/23'.
805. Proposal for a Council Directive amending Directive 2006/112/EC as regards VAT rules for the digital age (n. 382).
806. Merkx and others (n. 798) 180.
807. Ecommerce Europe (n. 797).
808. Merkx (n. 573) 27.
809. Lamensch and others (n. 143).

a third country. This shaping of the rules appears to have been primarily intended to improve the level playing field for EU and non-EU vendors. In addition, it should be noted that if platforms were not responsible for enforcing EU VAT rules against non-EU underlying suppliers, then the responsibility for prosecuting unreliable suppliers would fall on Member States, which, as past practice shows, is not effective. However, the current direction in which changes to the rules on the deemed supplier regime are planned shows that the EU legislator's assessment is that it may also cover other supplies of goods not linked to third countries.

It should be noted that, finally in the latest compromise text, the EC decided only to make changes to Article 14a(2) of the VAT Directive.[810] It was thus clarified that a platform will be deemed the supplier for intra-Community supplies made by an underlying supplier from outside the EU if the recipient is a taxable person, a non-taxable legal person whose intra-Community acquisitions of goods are not subject to VAT pursuant to Article 3(1), or any other non-taxable person. In the area of transfer of own goods, it was decided to introduce only a new OSS scheme in line with the original proposal. However, there is no exclusion for capital goods where the owner is entitled to full VAT recovery.

Moreover, the EC is obliged, at the latest by 1 July 2027, to present to the EP and to the Council, on the basis of information obtained from the Member States, an assessment report on the functioning of the deemed supplier rule and, where appropriate, submit a legislative proposal for its further extension. It appears that Member States will first want to assess the results of the deemed supplier regime before deciding on its further extension. This cautious approach seems appropriate given that the deemed supplier regime is quite burdensome for platforms.

With regard to the type of transaction covered by the deemed supplier regime, the OECD indicates that where different VAT rules are applied in a jurisdiction for B2B and B2C supplies (e.g., different rules for determining the place of taxation), knowing the status of the customer is indispensable for determining the correct VAT treatment of the supply. In this regard, the OECD suggests that when implementing the deemed supplier regime for platforms, tax authorities should indicate how to make the distinction between the B2B and B2C supplies.[811]

Such distinction is also important from the point of view of the EU e-commerce model, as a platform will only be a deemed supplier if the transactions it facilitates are B2C (the underlying supplier must be a VAT taxable person, and the consumer must be a private individual or a person so treated). The EU legislator recognized this problem and, in order to provide platforms with greater legal certainty and to free them from the disproportionate burden of verifying the status of the seller and the buyer,[812] Article 5d was introduced into the IR. This provision states that a platform that is a deemed

810. Draft Council Directive amending Directive 2006/112/EC as regards VAT rules for the digital age – compromise text 8 May 2024 (n. 382).
811. OECD, *The Role of Digital Platforms in the Collection of VAT/GST on Online Sales* (n. 551) 32–33.
812. European Commission, *Explanatory Notes on VAT E-Commerce Rules. Council Directive (EU) 2017/2455. Council Directive (EU) 2019/1995. Council Implementing Regulation (EU) 2019/2026* (n. 164) 26.

provider, unless it has information to the contrary, regards: (i) the person selling the goods through the electronic interface as a taxable person (presumption of the status of the seller) and (ii) the person buying those goods as a non-taxable person (presumption of the status of the buyer).

According to the Explanatory Notes 2020, if the underlying supplier or buyer indicates to the platform in what capacity they act, the platform should consider them as a taxable person or non-taxable person according to their declaration, unless it has information to the contrary. However, the platform operator should have a process in place to verify the status of the underlying supplier. It was also emphasized that the absence of the VAT identification number or tax reference number does not automatically mean that the underlying supplier is not a taxable person.[813] Regarding the customer, the platform may assume that if no VAT number or comparable tax number is provided, it is a private customer, unless the platform has information to the contrary.[814]

While the approach of the EU legislator may be considered reasonable, it is still not clear what level of scrutiny is required from the platforms in order to rebut that presumption.[815] In addition, platforms should also set up a procedure to rebut the presumptions, which entails new obligations and costs for them.[816] The literature also points out that requiring platforms to regard the supplier as a taxable person (unless they have information to the contrary) creates the risk that C2C transactions will be caught unintentionally by the deeming provision – in which case transactions that would normally not be subject to VAT would be taxed.[817]

4.4 Mode of Operation

The OECD proposes the following mechanics for the operation of the deemed supplier model for e-commerce sector platforms:

(1) The platform assumes full VAT liability as if it has affected the underlying sale to the customer itself.

(2) The underlying supplier is in principle relieved from any VAT obligations on the supply to the customer to avoid double taxation; however, the deemed supplier regime should not affect the underlying supplier's right to deduct VAT. Tax authorities may consider treating the supply by the underlying supplier as zero-rated or implementing a reverse-charge regime where this is compatible with the domestic VAT rules (alternatively, tax authorities could also consider disregarding the supply by the underlying supplier for VAT purposes; however, such solution could, for example, create complexity in respect of the supplier's right to deduct the associated VAT).

813. *Ibid.*
814. Janssen (n. 479) 233–234.
815. Papis-Almansa (n. 662) 220–221.
816. Lamensch and others (n. 104) 460.
817. Merkx (n. 573) 26.

(3) In order to avoid a break in the staged collection chain, the platform may be treated as having received the supply from the underlying supplier and having supplied it onwards to the customer (the fiction of two supplies).

(4) Each of these supplies is then subject to the appropriate VAT rules, including invoicing and reporting requirements. Such an approach allows the underlying supplier and the platform to process the sale for VAT purposes, including the deduction of the associated input VAT by the underlying supplier.

(5) The consumer can pay for his or her purchase on the platform or with the supplier. If the payment is made directly to the platform, the platform will remit VAT from it at the appropriate rate. If payment is made to the underlying supplier, the platform will have to recuperate the amount needed to pay VAT from the underlying supplier in order to pass it on to the tax authorities. In the latter case, tax authorities are encouraged to consider implementing an appropriate bad debt relief arrangement to limit the potential risk of default by underlying suppliers in remitting the VAT to the platform, provided that the platform has made reasonable efforts to ensure compliance.[818]

The EU digital model is based on these solutions. In applying the deemed supplier regime, the platform that facilitates the supply is deemed to have received and delivered the supplied goods itself. In practice, this means that a single supply from the underlying supplier selling goods via the platform to the end consumer (the underlying B2C delivery) is split into two supplies: (i) a supply from the underlying supplier to the platform (the platform is deemed to 'purchase' the goods from the underlying supplier) and (ii) a supply from the platform to the end consumer (the platform is deemed to resell the 'purchased' goods to the consumer).[819] In other words, the fiction of two consecutive supplies of goods is created, one between the actual supplier and the platform and the other between the platform and the end consumer. This fiction is limited to VAT liabilities only and does not apply to any other aspects of platforms' liability, such as product liability. According to some authors, the new rules' disregard for economic reality raises doubts as to whether they comply with the basic principles of the European VAT system.[820]

The first transaction (from the underlying supplier to the platform) is considered a B2B supply, which is treated as a supply without transport (Article 36b of the VAT Directive).[821] Where this is a DSIG with a value not exceeding EUR 150, such supply happens outside the EU. Consequently, the B2B supply between the underlying

818. OECD, *The Role of Digital Platforms in the Collection of VAT/GST on Online Sales* (n. 551) 24–25.

819. European Commission, *Explanatory Notes on VAT E-Commerce Rules. Council Directive (EU) 2017/2455. Council Directive (EU) 2019/1995. Council Implementing Regulation (EU) 2019/2026* (n. 164) 14–15.

820. Barr and others (n. 652) 50.

821. It is worth noting that without this additional provision (added to the VAT e-commerce package in 2019), transactions involving transport would have to be determined based on existing CJEU case law, and in many cases, this would undermine the intended results of Article 14a of the VAT Directive. Papis-Almansa (n. 662) 219–220.

supplier and the platform operator will be outside the scope of VAT. It also means that this transaction does not require an invoice.[822] If it is an EU supply (either an ICDS or a domestic supply), it will be taxed in the Member State where the goods are located at the time of supply. This supply is exempt from VAT, with the right of deduction vested in the underlying supplier (Articles 136a and 169(b) of the VAT Directive). The underlying supplier must invoice the platform in accordance with the rules of the Member State where the supply takes place.[823]

Furthermore, it seems that if the payment is not intermediated by the platform, the amount of VAT should be remitted by the underlying supplier to the platform and the transaction should be outside the scope of VAT, as well as neutral for other fiscal and accounting purposes. A similar position is expressed by the EC with regard to the service model discussed below.[824] This solution should also be applicable to the e-commerce model.

The second transaction (from the platform to the consumer) is considered a B2C supply, to which transport is assigned. Regardless of whether it is an ICDS or DSIG supply, taxation will take place in the country of the recipient. It should be noted that for B2C transactions, the VAT Directive does not provide for an obligation to issue an invoice, but the Member States may impose such an obligation (or an invoice may be required for customs clearance). Assuming that an invoice will be issued, according to Explanatory Notes 2020,[825] the following options are possible regarding the invoicing obligation:

(1) Where the underlying transaction is a DSIG with a value not exceeding EUR 150 and where the place of supply is within the EU and the platform uses the IOSS, then, in accordance with Article 219a of the VAT Directive, the invoicing rules of the Member State of identification (the Member State where the platform has registered for the special scheme) will apply. When the platform does not use the IOSS, then the rules of the Member State where the DSIG takes place will apply.

(2) Where the underlying transaction is a domestic supply and the platform uses the OSS, then, in accordance with Article 219a of the VAT Directive, the invoicing rules of the Member State of identification will apply. When the platform does not use the OSS, the rules of the Member State where the supply takes place will apply.

(3) When the underlying transaction is an ICDS and the platform uses the OSS, then, pursuant to Article 220(1)(2) of the VAT Directive, there is no legal obligation to issue an invoice for this B2C supply. When the platform issues

822. European Commission, *Explanatory Notes on VAT E-Commerce Rules. Council Directive (EU) 2017/2455. Council Directive (EU) 2019/1995. Council Implementing Regulation (EU) 2019/2026* (n. 164) 15–18.

823. *Ibid.*

824. European Commission, Directorate General for Taxation and Customs Union and others (n. 6) 115–116.

825. European Commission, *Explanatory Notes on VAT E-Commerce Rules. Council Directive (EU) 2017/2455. Council Directive (EU) 2019/1995. Council Implementing Regulation (EU) 2019/2026* (n. 164) 15–18.

an invoice, the invoicing rules of the Member State of identification (Article 219a of the VAT Directive) will apply.

When the underlying transaction is an ICDS and the platform does not use OSS, then there is an obligation to issue an invoice. In this case, the invoice to the consumer must be issued by the platform in accordance with the invoicing rules of the Member State where the supply takes place.

As is rightly pointed out in the legal literature, from the perspective of the provisions on platforms' liability for collection of VAT, the treatment of the B2C transaction, between the platform and the consumer, as a deemed supply is crucial. The analogous treatment of the B2B transaction between the principal supplier and the platform is a logical consequence motivated by the objective of maintaining normal operation of the system where VAT is collected at every stage of the production-distribution chain.[826]

The mechanics of Article 14a of the VAT Directive are illustrated in Figure 3.3.

Figure 3.3 Mode of Operation of Article 14a of the VAT Directive

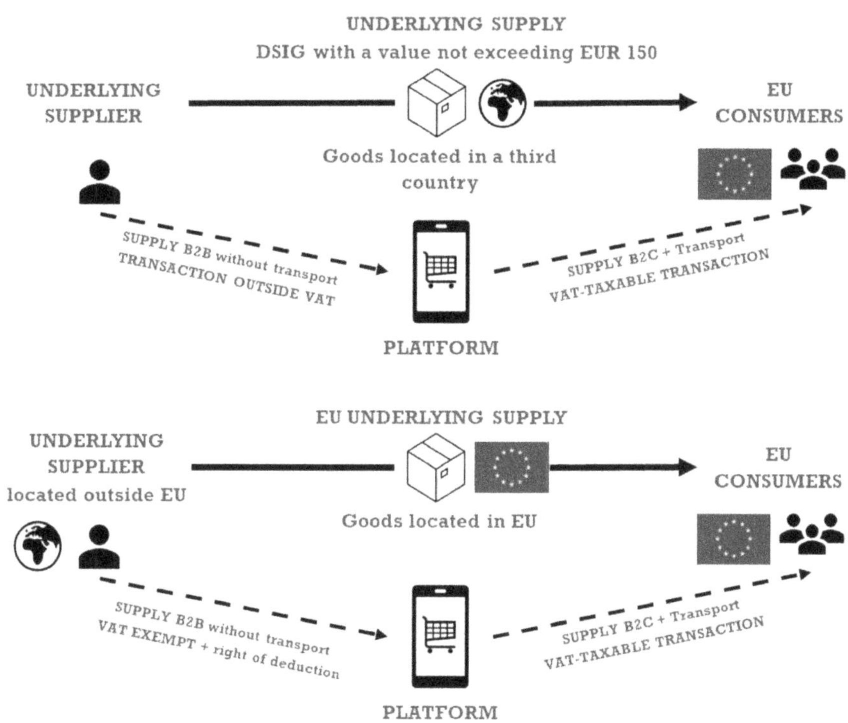

Source: Own compilation.

826. Papis-Almansa (n. 662) 220.

Another crucial element of the deemed supplier regime is the definition of the taxing point, i.e., the time at which the platform will be required to account for VAT. As the OECD points out, a platform that is not an actual supplier will not always have all the information that is required to determine the taxing point according to standard rules. Even if the platform has such information, it is likely to create an undue burden for platforms to make that individual determination for each of the potentially millions of supplies.[827] Therefore, in the OECD's view, the practical solution is to define the taxing point at the time at which the confirmation of the payment is received by or on behalf of the underlying supplier. This is the time at which the payment has been accepted or authorized by or on behalf of the underlying supplier (this does not necessarily mean that the actual money transfer has been made).[828]

The EU legislator shared this view and, for the deemed supplier regime, introduced an exception to the general rule of tax chargeability.[829] Under Article 66a of the VAT Directive, the platform is liable for declaring and paying VAT which becomes due when the underlying supplier accepts payment. This provision is further elaborated in Article 41a IR, which states that the time when the payment has been accepted means the time when the payment confirmation, the payment authorization message or a commitment for payment from the customer is received by or on behalf of the underlying supplier, regardless of when the actual payment of money is made, whichever is the earliest.

No similar regulation has been introduced for the digital model, although, as the OECD points out, moving the taxing point to the time of confirmation of payment both for the supply of services and for the supply of goods may simplify compliance under the deemed supplier regime, notably for platforms that intervene in the online supply of both goods and services.[830]

It should be noted that in many respects the mechanics of the e-commerce model are similar to those of the digital model – in both cases, there is a legal fiction of two identical consecutive supplies, and a liability is placed on the platform to account for VAT from the transaction to the end consumer.

However, the structure adopted in the e-commerce model is somewhat different from the solutions of the digital model. According to established legal views and case law under Article 28 of the VAT Directive, the activities of platforms are not separated from the tangible services on which their intermediation is based (the service provided

827. OECD, *The Role of Digital Platforms in the Collection of VAT/GST on Online Sales* (n. 551) 34–35.
828. *Ibid.*
829. In legal doctrine, it is pointed out that to avoid the negative impact of new regulations on platform liquidity (not all platforms are involved in the payment process and therefore may not receive funds from the underlying supplier to cover VAT costs), the EU legislator could indicate that the moment of chargeable event for the purposes of applying Article 14a of the VAT Directive is when the VAT payment has actually been received by the platform. However, such a derogation would be highly vulnerable to abuse. If a platform user did not pay its VAT, the chargeable event would not occur, and the platform would not have to pay VAT to the relevant tax authorities. Pollak (n. 339) 178.
830. OECD, *The Role of Digital Platforms in the Collection of VAT/GST on Online Sales* (n. 551) 35–36.

by an undisclosed agent is integrated into the commissioned service).[831] This means that in the digital model, there is no separate service supplied by the platform - its commission is included in the tax base of the underlying service. The platform therefore charges VAT on the total price of the service, which consists of the underlying transaction price and the agreed intermediation fee.

In the e-commerce model, this issue is controversial. Some legal writers are of the opinion that, as in the digital model, the platform does not provide another service to its users for VAT purposes - the commission could therefore be included in the tax base.[832] However, according to some authors, the platform still provides a separate service to the supplier or the consumer.[833] This would mean that the platform, as a deemed supplier, would separately remit VAT on the underlying transaction and VAT on its intermediation service.

Clarification of this issue by the EC, e.g., in explanatory notes or guidelines from the VAT Committee, would be welcome.

5 THE SERVICE MODEL

5.1 Historical Background

A number of countries have chosen to introduce the deemed supplier regime for platforms that intermediate the supply of digital services and facilitate certain supplies of goods (the digital model and the e-commerce model) in the expectation that this arrangement will support the efficient collection of VAT. Their experience seems to confirm that the new rules have met expectations.[834] This has led to the consideration of extending this regime to more types of transactions present in the platform economy. Already in 2019, the OECD indicated that it appeared possible to extend this solution to platforms providing non-electronic types of services, and both tax authorities and the business community identified a clear need for further internationally agreed standards and guidance in this regard.[835]

As indicated in the first chapter, platforms are at the forefront of delivering new solutions for the delivery of services that involve a certain level of physical presence, for example, such as accommodation, transportation, food delivery or house cleaning. While these services are often traditional in nature, the service provider and the buyer are brought together through platforms which harness new technologies.[836] As pointed out by the OECD, the development of the platform economy may create regulatory pressures related to VAT treatment, particularly in the accommodation and transport

831. Zechner (n. 368) 181.
832. Pollak (n. 339) 185–186.
833. Ad van Doesum, 'Een Faciliterend Online Goederenplatform Is Nog Geen Commissionair' (2020) Weekblad Fiscaal Recht; Merkx (n. 573) 20.
834. OECD, *The Role of Digital Platforms in the Collection of VAT/GST on Online Sales* (n. 551) 29–30.
835. *Ibid.*
836. *Ibid.*, 19.

sectors, which together represent around 90% of the total market value of the platform economy worldwide and are expected to have high growth rates in the coming years.[837]

The main problem in this respect appears to be the inadequacy of the current VAT legal frameworks to provide a level playing field for traditional businesses competing with those offering services through platforms. As indicated in the literature, the lack of sharing economy-specific regulations results in: (i) under-collection of tax from suppliers using platforms and (ii) tax breaks for platforms giving them an unfair competitive advantage over counterparts in the more tightly regulated traditional sectors.[838] In particular, the growing popularity of using platforms to provide accommodation creates a number of VAT compliance challenges. An important issue in this area is the involvement of a large number of small entrepreneurs and individuals in transactions carried out through platforms (more on this in the first chapter). Supplies made by such small underlying suppliers through the platform are often not subject to VAT. In the case of the STR market, property owners operating on a small-scale basis are likely not required to collect VAT, taking advantage of the SME exemption. Other property owners that operate on a larger scale – offering multiple properties for rent on a regular basis – may not be aware of their requirement to register for and collect VAT.[839] In the past, this competitive advantage was minimal due to the limited reach and resources of small suppliers. Until recently, therefore, they were considered to have no effect on market competition with VAT-registered businesses (such as hotels). However, platforms, through economies of scale and network effects (discussed in detail in the first chapter), have introduced new business models that are changing this situation, enabling small suppliers to directly compete with traditional VAT-registered businesses.[840] The benefits to the individual supplier of using the technological, commercial and legal infrastructure provided by the platform therefore put it in a comparable position to a traditional business, but unlike a traditional business, it is not usually liable to pay VAT. As pointed out in the legal literature, such an individual supplier, by operating through a platform rather than following more conventional business routes, has chosen – at least implicitly – to be a 'full-fledged' supplier and, as such, should bear the related tax obligations.[841] It is worth noting that in the EC's public consultation, more than 70% of respondents from the 'traditional' STR sector said they were suffering from a distortion of competition with firms offering the same services

837. OECD, *The Impact of the Growth of the Sharing and Gig Economy on VAT/GST Policy and Administration* (n. 47) 14–15.
838. Clement Okello Migai, Julia de Long and Jeffrey P Owens, 'The Sharing Economy: Turning Challenges into Compliance Opportunities for Tax Administrations' (2019) 16 Journal of Tax Research 395.
839. Department of Finance Canada, 'Fall Economic Statement 2020. Supporting Canadians and Fighting COVID-19'.
840. European Commission, 'Impact Assessment Report, SWD(2022) 393 Final' (n. 362).
841. Beretta (n. 344) 303.

via platforms.[842] This has led to the need to regulate this situation, which also involves more involvement of platforms in VAT collection.

According to the OECD, there are many opportunities for platforms to get involved in this process.[843] One of them, the most far-reaching one, is the introduction of the deemed supplier regime which would make the platform solely and fully liable for assessing, collecting and remitting the VAT on the underlying services it facilitates, as if it had provided the service itself.[844] As was the case with the digital model and the e-commerce model, the OECD additionally recommends the use of a simplified registration system as an element to enhance and facilitate compliance by non-resident platforms.[845] According to the OECD, the introduction of the deemed supplier regime would result in: (i) a significant reduction of costs for tax administrations (the authorities' efforts could be focused on a relatively limited number of platforms instead of on the continuously growing number of often small underlying suppliers); (ii) an enhancement in the overall level of compliance, as platforms, particularly the largest ones, are often better placed to comply than underlying suppliers; (iii) a broadening of the tax base by formalizing activities that have remained outside the scope of VAT; and (iv) a reduction in distortions of competition.[846]

For this reason, an increasing number of jurisdictions have implemented or are considering implementing[847] a system that places full liability for the collection of VAT on platforms that intermediate services (other than electronic services). Such a system has, for example, been implemented in Canada. From 1 July 2021, the deemed supplier regime has been introduced into Canada's GST tax regime (where GST is the equivalent to EU VAT). The regime is applied to the supply of accommodation (the rental of a residential complex, unit, or part thereof, thus excluding the rental of commercial properties such as hotels) operated by a platform if the landlord is unregistered for GST tax purposes in Canada.[848] For this reason, Airbnb encourages hosts operating in Canada to provide the platform with their GST IDs. If they fail to do so, Airbnb collects and remits this tax in addition to the basic price per night, cleaning fee and guest service charge for each listing located in Canada.[849] The regime applies to platforms

842. European Commission, 'How Bringing VAT into the Digital Age Can Help Restore a Level Playing-Field in the Hospitality Sector', https://taxation-customs.ec.europa.eu/news/how-bringing-vat-digital-age-can-help-restore-level-playing-field-hospitality-sector-2023-03-31_en accessed 20 May 2023.
843. OECD, *The Impact of the Growth of the Sharing and Gig Economy on VAT/GST Policy and Administration* (n. 47) 58–60.
844. *Ibid.*, 60.
845. *Ibid.*, 80–81.
846. *Ibid.*, 77–78.
847. *See*, for example: Mohamed Alaradi and Bastiaan Moossdorff, 'The Role of Digital Platforms in Collecting VAT in Selected Countries in the Middle East' (2024) 35 International VAT Monitor https://doi.org/10.59403/rk09jc.
848. European Commission, Directorate General for Taxation and Customs Union and others (n. 6) 108.
849. 'Dlaczego Airbnb prosi o podanie informacji dotyczących Twojego kanadyjskiego GST – Centrum Pomocy Airbnb' (*Airbnb*), https://www.airbnb.pl/help/article/3198 accessed 4 December 2022.

that facilitate or expect to facilitate in a 12-month period taxable supplies of accommodation with a value exceeding USD 30,000.[850] According to the Canadian supplier, this legislative intervention was needed to improve GST compliance and provide a level playing field across the accommodation sector.[851]

It is worth noting that the draft amendments to the EU rules on the liability of STR intermediating platforms are very similar to Canadian solutions.[852] Indeed, the Canadian regulations were intended to address the same problems currently faced by the EU, in particular the difficulty of enforcing VAT compliance in the platform economy, putting traditional business models at a disadvantage and leading to VAT inequality and VAT neutrality.[853]

To address this challenge in 2020, the EC announced an action plan for fair and simple taxation supporting the economic recovery,[854] as part of the priority of 'adapting EU regulation to the digital age' adopted by the EC for 2019–2024.[855] Among the actions listed there is the adaptation of the VAT framework to the platform economy, which envisaged examining the role platforms can play in securing the collection of this tax. The Council welcomed the initiative announced by the Commission to examine the need to adapt the VAT framework to the platform economy.[856]

The Commission's analysis resulted in the publication of 'VAT in the Digital Age (ViDA)' legislative package on 8 December 2022, which proposed several measures to modernize the EU VAT system.[857] This package consists of drafts of three pieces of legislation introducing changes to the EU VAT system: (i) proposal amending the VAT Directive,[858] (ii) proposal amending Regulation 282/2011,[859] and (iii) proposal amending Regulation 904/2010.[860]

One of the objectives of the ViDA package is, *inter alia*, to address the challenges of the platform economy by updating the VAT rules in order to address the issue of equal tax treatment, to clarify the rules on the place of supply of services and to enhance the role of platforms in the collection of VAT when they facilitate the supply

850. Department of Finance Canada (n. 835).
851. *Ibid.*
852. European Commission, 'Impact Assessment Report, SWD(2022) 393 Final' (n. 362) 64.
853. European Commission, Directorate General for Taxation and Customs Union and others (n. 6) 108.
854. European Commission, 'An Action Plan for Fair and Simple Taxation Supporting the Recovery Strategy, COM(2020) 312 Final' (n. 45).
855. European Commission, 'Priorities of the European Union 2019–2024', https://european-union.europa.eu/priorities-and-actions/eu-priorities/european-union-priorities-2019-2024_en accessed 12 May 2023.
856. Council of the EU, 'Council Conclusions on Fair and Effective Taxation in Times of Recovery, on Tax Challenges Linked to Digitalisation and on Tax Good Governance in the EU and beyond, FISC 226 ECOFIN 1097'.
857. European Commission, 'VAT in the Digital Age', https://taxation-customs.ec.europa.eu/taxation-1/value-added-tax-vat/vat-digital-age_en accessed 1 May 2023.
858. Proposal for a Council Directive amending Directive 2006/112/EC as regards VAT rules for the digital age (n. 382).
859. Proposal for a Council Implementing Regulation amending Implementing Regulation (EU) No 282/2011 as regards information requirements for certain VAT schemes [COM/2022/704 final].
860. Proposal for a Council Regulation amending Regulation (EU) No 904/2010 as regards the VAT administrative cooperation arrangements needed for the digital age [COM/2022/703 final].

of short-term accommodation rental or passenger transport services.[861] Under the new rules, platform operators in these sectors will become liable for collecting and remitting VAT to the tax authorities when their users are not VAT taxable persons.

It should be noted that the ViDA package does not foresee the introduction of a new mechanism to simplify registration obligations and VAT accounting (as was the case with the digital model and the e-commerce model). However, it is worth noting that already from 1 July 2021, the optional OSS simplification procedure includes the possibility to account for all services, including accommodation. It therefore appears that there was no need to amend the legislation in this respect.

The ViDA package is currently undergoing legislative work in the EU Council. The first meeting in the Council took place under the Czech Presidency on 12 December 2022, during which the Commission services gave a detailed presentation of the regulations' impact assessment. Negotiations resumed in January 2023 under the Swedish Presidency. Negotiations continued during the Spanish and Belgian presidencies (second half of 2023 and first half of 2024), both of which identified the ViDA package as a top priority.[862] According to this package, the planned changes in Pillar 2 (area of platform economy) would come into force on 1 July 2027.[863] It should be noted that the ViDA reforms were presented at the ECOFIN meeting on 14 May but failed to receive political agreement from the Finance Ministers.[864] Also, at the ECOFIN meeting that took place on 21 June 2024, no agreement was reached because, once again, Estonia's objection to the proposed rules for Pillar 2 halted the legislative process.[865] Estonia primarily raised the issue that the proposed deemed supplier rules would violate the principle of VAT neutrality, as the service supplier will not be able to deduct input VAT (e.g., VAT would be charged on the apartment rental, but the property owner would not be able to reclaim the VAT they paid on their own purchases[866] – this problem is discussed in detail in section 5.4 below). It is worth noting that Estonia's comments were not reflected in the June compromise text, which only underwent

861. Proposal for a Council Directive amending Directive 2006/112/EC as regards VAT rules for the digital age (n. 382).
862. European Commission, 'VAT Expert Group No 111: Summary Minutes 33rd Meeting 14 March 2023, Taxud.c.1(2023)3335919'; 'The Belgian Presidency Programme', https://belgian-presidency.consilium.europa.eu/en/programme/the-belgian-presidency-programme/ accessed 12 January 2024.
863. The initial implementation date for Pillar 2 was set for 1 January 2025. However, postponing this deadline to 1 January 2026 or 2027 was suggested. European Parliament, 'Amendments to Directive 2006/112/EC as Regards VAT Rules for the Digital Age, 2022/0407(CNS)'; in the latest compromise text, the proposed date is set for 1 July 2027. Draft Council Directive amending Directive 2006/112/EC as regards VAT rules for the digital age – compromise text 8 May 2024 (n. 382).
864. *See also*: Richard Asquith, 'EU ViDA Agreement Delayed' (14 May 2024), https://www.vatcalc.com/eu/eu-vat-in-the-digital-age-vida-adopted-by-ec/ accessed 30 May 2024.
865. *See also*: Richard Asquith, 'VAT in the Digital Age Won't Return to ECOFIN for Agreement Till October or November 2024' (9 July 2024), https://www.vatcalc.com/eu/eu-vat-in-the-digital-age-vida-adopted-by-ec/ accessed 23 July 2024.
866. *See also:* Bal A, 'VAT and Platform Economy: Unanswered Questions and an Uncertain Future' (*Forbes*), https://www.forbes.com/sites/aleksandrabal/2024/06/23/vat-and-platform-economy-unanswered-questions-and-an-uncertain-future/ accessed 25 July 2024.

slight modifications in Article 28a, point 5 of the VAT Directive compared to the May text. Therefore, the comments made based on the May compromise text remain valid.

It is expected that during the latter half of 2024, the Hungarian presidency will strive to achieve agreement on the ViDA proposal.

5.2 Legal Basis

The EU legislator, unlike the Canadian legislator, has chosen to extend the ViDA package not only to platforms facilitating accommodation services but also to platforms facilitating passenger transport. In recital 22 of the proposal amending the VAT Directive, the EU legislator explained that the platform economy led to an unjustified distortion of competition between supplies made through platforms and those made in the traditional economy.[867] In his assessment, this distortion has been most acute in the two largest sectors of the platform economy, namely the STR sector and the passenger transport sector[868] (these two sectors together accounts for more than half of the total value of the platform economy).[869]

By applying the deemed supplier regime to these two sectors, the EU legislator also appears to be following the OECD's suggestion that, within the platform economy, it is accommodation and transport services that currently create the most urgent pressure on VAT policy and require the most urgent legislative intervention.[870] It is worth noting that the Commission has, however, considered other solutions to this issue (options C and E).[871] Under option C, the deemed supplier regime would only be applied to selected transactions within the accommodation and transportation sectors (and would therefore be narrower in scope than that outlined in the proposal). However, the adoption of this option could lead to some complications related to the need to assess on a case-by-case basis whether a particular transaction would meet the criteria for triggering the deemed supplier regime. In addition, should other business models emerge within these sectors in the future, they might not meet the criteria for the application of this regime to them. Under option E, it is assumed that the deemed supplier regime would cover all services supplied through platforms, not just within the accommodation and transport sectors (and would therefore be broader in scope than what was ultimately presented in the proposal). However, this option was questionable because of its proportionality.[872]

867. Proposal for a Council Directive amending Directive 2006/112/EC as regards VAT rules for the digital age (n. 382).
868. Finally, the EC clarified that it pertains to the sector of passenger transport by road. Draft Council Directive amending Directive 2006/112/EC as regards VAT rules for the digital age – compromise text 8 May 2024 (n. 382).
869. European Commission, 'Impact Assessment Report, SWD(2022) 393 Final' (n. 362).
870. OECD, *The Impact of the Growth of the Sharing and Gig Economy on VAT/GST Policy and Administration* (n. 47) 14–15.
871. European Commission, Directorate General for Taxation and Customs Union and others (n. 6) 104–105.
872. *Ibid.*, 108.

The mid-way solution adopted by the EC seems appropriate, given that the introduction of the deemed supplier regime is a radical change compared to the current VAT regime. Limiting the application of this solution to only two sectors will allow its effects to be observed only in certain markets, potentially facilitating its introduction for all services within the platform economy in the future. Furthermore, as the EC points out, focusing on the accommodation and passenger transport sectors, where the issue of VAT inequality is most acute, ensures the proportionality of this solution.[873] It should also be noted that the STR and passenger transport sectors account for almost 70% of the activity carried out within the service sector platform economy, which means that with relatively little control activities on the part of the administration, a large increase in VAT collection will be achievable.[874]

Given the theme of this book, dedicated to the STR platform economy, only solutions relating to platforms operating in this sector will be discussed below.

The main principles underlying the service model are regulated in the proposed Article 28a of the VAT Directive. According to this provision, notwithstanding Article 28 of the VAT Directive, a taxable person who facilitates, through the use of an electronic interface such as a platform, portal, or similar means, the supply of short-term accommodation rental services, as referred to in Article 135(3) of the VAT Directive, or passenger transport, will be deemed to have received and supplied those services themselves where the person providing those services is one of the following: (a) a non-established person who is not identified for VAT purposes in a Member State; (b) a non-taxable person; (c) a taxable person carrying out only supplies of goods or services in respect of which VAT is not deductible; (d) a non-taxable legal person; (e) a taxable person subject to the common flat-rate scheme for farmers; (f) a taxable person subject to the special scheme for small enterprises.

In the compromise text, Article 28a of the VAT Directive has been given slightly different wording. According to this provision, a taxable person who facilitates, through the use of an electronic interface such as a marketplace, platform, portal, or similar means, the supply, within the Union, of STR services, namely the uninterrupted rental of accommodation to the same person for a maximum of 30 nights, shall be deemed to have received and supplied those services themselves unless the person providing those services has: (a) provided to the taxable person facilitating the supply their VAT identification number for VAT purposes and (b) declared to the taxable person facilitating the supply that he will charge any VAT due on that supply.[875]

873. Proposal for a Council Directive amending Directive 2006/112/EC as regards VAT rules for the digital age (n. 382).
874. Fernando Matesanz, 'IVA La Vida. Primera Parte. IVA y Economía Colaborativa', https://www.legaltoday.com/opinion/blogs/fiscal-y-legal/blog-sobre-tributacion-indirecta/iva-la-vida-primera-parte-iva-y-economia-colaborativa-2023-01-02/ accessed 23 March 2023.
875. Draft Council Directive amending Directive 2006/112/EC as regards VAT rules for the digital age – compromise text 8 May 2024 (n. 382).

However, this does not change the essence of the regulation. The above means that when the underlying supplier (host offering an apartment for rent) does not charge VAT, the digital platform will charge this tax to the consumer and will account for this tax. The digital platforms will be deemed to be the supplier and obliged to collect VAT on the supplies they facilitate. Therefore, this solution will not simultaneously impose a burden on the listed underlying suppliers, as they will still not be required to register and account for VAT themselves.

It is noteworthy that, at this stage, the legislative process for the service model does not raise the controversy that occurred when the digital model and the e-commerce model were introduced into the EU legal order. In contrast to the digital model, the provision imposing liability on platforms is found in the proposal for the VAT Directive (Article 28a) and not in the proposal for IR (only further elements on the practical application of this measure are found in this regulation). It seems that, in theory, the EC could 'provide further detail' in relation to Article 28 of the VAT Directive in IR, just as in the digital model Article 9a of that Regulation provided further detail in relation to Article 28 of the VAT Directive. However, given doubts about the validity of this type of legislative exercise raised in the *Fenix* case,[876] it must be considered that the imposition of the deemed supplier regime on platforms in the new provision in the VAT Directive was a far better solution. In this way, the EU legislator avoids the risk that the provision will be challenged on the grounds that it is misplaced in an inadequate piece of legislation. The structure of the service model therefore resembles the structure of the e-commerce model more than the digital model - the provision imposing liability on platforms is in a new provision in the proposal amending the VAT Directive and a number of technical adjustments and clarifications in the proposal for IR. However, unlike the e-commerce model, the provision imposing the deemed supplier regime on STR platforms is included in the ViDA package from the outset and is accompanied by a detailed regulatory impact assessment. In this way, the EU legislator avoids the potential controversy of introducing provisions imposing specific obligations on platforms at a late legislative stage and without assessing their compliance with the principles of subsidiarity and proportionality.

5.3 Rationale for Using the Service Model

5.3.1 The Subject Aspect

The proposed Article 28a of the VAT Directive, in its original wording, applies to taxable persons who facilitate the supply of STR services through the use of an electronic interface such as a platform, portal or similar means. This provision is therefore structured in virtually the same way as Article 14a of the VAT Directive, but

876. *Fenix International* (n. 504).

its list of examples of an electronic interface is shorter and does not include the concept of a marketplace. However, the catalogue of examples of an 'electronic interface' in the proposed Article 28a remains open, as is the case with Article 14a of the VAT Directive. The difference can therefore be considered to be of rather little practical significance, especially as it is difficult to pinpoint the actual difference between the terms 'platform' and 'marketplace' (these terms are not defined under the VAT system rules).

It should be noted that, in the compromise text, the word 'marketplace' was added to the list in Article 28a of the VAT Directive, which is a welcome addition, as the original wording introduced some above-mentioned ambiguity.[877]

Given the similarities between Article 14a and the proposed Article 28a of the VAT Directive, it appears that the interpretation of the concept of 'electronic interface' under the services model will be similar to that under the e-commerce model. This means the meaning of this term is broad and should be understood to encompass communication between two independent systems or a system and an end user with the help of any device or program. Irrespective of the device or program used, the result of this communication should be the conclusion of a contract by electronic means. As was the case with the e-commerce model, the use of the term 'similar means' seems intended to take into account current and future technologies so that the proposed Article 28a of the VAT Directive evolves alongside new solutions developing in the platform economy.

Although the proposed Article 14a of the VAT Directive refers to operators of electronic interfaces (and electronic interfaces for the purposes of this provision are a broader concept than platforms), in the remainder of this chapter, the term 'platform operators' or 'platforms' will be used in order to be consistent in terminology with the rest of the book.

As was the case in the digital model and the e-commerce model, it matters less what technology the taxable person uses and more how such technology operates. In the case of the digital model, the platform must take part in the supply of the service, and the meaning of this term is not elaborated in IR. In the case of the e-commerce model, the platform must facilitate certain supplies of goods, and this concept is defined in Article 5b IR. The service model is closer to the e-commerce model, as, according to the proposed provisions, the platform must also 'facilitate' the supply of certain services, and this concept is to be defined in Article 9b IR.

According to the proposed Article 9b IR, the term 'facilitates' means the use of a platform to allow a customer and an underlying supplier to enter contact which results in a supply of accommodation services through that platform. This concept, as is the case in the e-commerce model, should therefore be considered to be defined in a very broad way, as it only requires the platform to provide a shared space where the guest and host can communicate.

877. Draft Council Directive amending Directive 2006/112/EC as regards VAT rules for the digital age – compromise text 8 May 2024 (n. 382).

The proposed Article 9b IR expressly excludes only three situations from the term 'facilitates'. The platform operator is not facilitating a supply of STR services where all of the following conditions are met: (i) the platform does not set, either directly or indirectly, any of the terms and conditions under which the supply of services is made; (ii) the platform is not, either directly or indirectly, involved in authorizing the charge to the customer in respect of the payment made; (iii) the platform is not, either directly or indirectly, involved in the supply of the services. The use of the wording 'all' means that these conditions must be met cumulatively by the platform for it to be considered as not facilitating the supply of services. Even if a platform meets at least one of the above-listed conditions, it may still be considered as the supplier.

It should be noted that the proposed Article 9b IR contains a virtually identical list of conditions to Article 5b IR, which deals with the e-commerce model, and a very similar list of conditions to that contained in Article 9a IR, which deals with the digital model. Therefore, the interpretation of Article 5b of the IR in the Explanatory Notes 2020 and of Article 9a IR in the Explanatory Notes 2014 can be applied by analogy to the service model in question.

This means that the platform's setting, directly or indirectly, 'the terms and conditions under which the supply is made' will mean the platform's influence on the obligations and rights of its users, as well as on other elements of the transaction. This will also be a concept that needs to be interpreted narrowly (rather, it will not cover the controversial terms and conditions of use of the platform). This condition will go beyond the contractual relationship and will take into account the economic situation and, in particular, the influence exercised by the platforms or their contribution to the actual supply of the supply services. The use of the words 'indirectly' and 'any' is also likely in this provision to avoid an artificial division of rights and obligations between the platform operator and the underlying suppliers.

It seems that also in the case of the service model, there will be a risk of the application of the deemed supplier regime to 'unintentional' intermediation of platforms. These are situations when on platforms designed for interaction, such as Facebook, users post adverts offering accommodation services.[878] In such cases, platforms could be considered as enabling guests and non-taxable hosts to establish contact, resulting in the supply of such service and therefore 'facilitating' such transactions. However, also in the case of the service model, it should be emphasized that this definitely does not seem to be the intention of the legislator and that a

878. An example of this can be the Facebook group 'Host A Sister', which was started in 2019. This group offers women a safe place to travel and connect with each other. Today, it has become a community with more than half a million members across all continents. 'Host a Sister – Connecting Sisters Around The Globe' (*Host A Sister*), https://hostasister.global/ accessed 4 March 2024.

distinction should be made between situations where the actual transaction process is managed through the platform (the platform is intentionally involved in matching a host and a guest) and situations where users are actually acting on their own without involving the platform in their mutual interactions.

The another condition of 'being involved in authorising the charge to the customer in respect of the payments made' is also likely to be interpreted very broadly, referring to a situation where the platform operator can influence whether, when and under what terms and conditions the purchaser pays the charge (e.g., it is sufficient for the platform to provide the purchaser with payment information such as the price, any additional charges, the time for the payment, and methods of payment). This condition will not imply that the platform has to effectively collect or receive the payment or that it should be involved in each step of the payment process. It is noteworthy that, in contrast to the analogous condition in Article 5b IR, the legislator uses the wording 'payments' in the plural and not 'payment' in the singular. This treatment makes the condition of the proposed Article 9b IR appear to have a broader meaning. It is possible that the use of the singular number of the word 'payment' in Article 5b IR has led to questions of construction, for example, in the case of instalment payments in the authorization of which the e-commerce platform was involved. If this was the case, these doubts would be eliminated, at least for the service model.

Similarly, the concept of 'being involved in the provision of service' will also be subject to a broad interpretation. This is because this condition will refer to a situation where the platform operator influences the supply of services in any way, directly or indirectly. The platform operator's involvement in the delivery of accommodation service may be suggested by various features, for example, the fact that the platform provides the technical tool to take the order from the customer (typically the shopping cart/check-out process), communicates the confirmation and/or details of the order to the host and guests, or charges them a fee or commission based on the order's value.

In addition, Article 9b IR, as Article 5b IR, provides for an exception to the rules indicated above. According to the second paragraph of this provision, Article 28a of the VAT Directive will not apply to an STR platform which only performs any of the following activities: (i) the processing of payments in relation to the supply of accommodation services, or (ii) the listing or advertising of such services, or (iii) the redirecting or transferring of customers to other platforms through which accommodation services are offered for sale, without any further intervention in the supply of such services.

In the explanatory memorandum of the proposal, the EU legislator pointed out that certain providers, including those that only provide listings, should be explicitly excluded from the measure because they do not enter direct competition with the traditional sectors.[879] It seems that the legislator was referring in this clarification not to the suppliers but to the platforms that merely provide listings. This is indicated by the fact that the word 'listing' only appears in the proposed Article 9b IR, which does not refer to actual suppliers but to platforms deemed to be suppliers.

It should be noted that the proposed Article 9b IR contains a virtually identical list of exceptions as Article 5b IR, which deals with the e-commerce model. Therefore, the interpretation of Article 5b IR in the Explanatory Notes 2020 can be applied by analogy to the service model in question. This means that also under this model if a platform operator carries out only one of the listed activities or several of them in combination, he will not be treated as the deemed supplier. It is worth noting that also in this case, the conditions from the proposed Article 9b IR essentially correspond to examples of functions that, according to the OECD, can exclude a platform from the deemed supplier regime. In fact, on this point, the OECD refers explicitly to its 2019 report,[880] which is discussed in more detail in the section on the e-commerce model. The OECD pointed out also this time that platforms that only exchange[881] or advertise services, or only process payments or only provide technical means (e.g., internet bandwidth), are unlikely to be able to comply with the full liability regime and may therefore be excluded from its scope.[882]

When relating the condition of 'facilitation', as set out in the proposed Article 9b IR, to the STR platform models discussed (represented by platforms such as Airbnb, Booking.com, Couchsurfing and HomeExchange), it should be noted that they are formulated in such general terms that they should cover them all. Indeed, the platforms analysed enable guests and hosts to get in touch, define (also indirectly) the terms and conditions of accommodation services, or mediate matters of payment between a host and a guest. None of them is a platform that merely supplies a service for processing payments, advertising or transferring visitors to other platforms.

Table 3.1 presents a list of indications to be taken into account in order to determine whether STR platforms facilitate the supply of services in line with the proposed Article 28a of the VAT Directive.

879. Proposal for a Council Implementing Regulation amending Implementing Regulation (EU) No 282/2011 as regards information requirements for certain VAT schemes (n. 855).

880. OECD, *The Role of Digital Platforms in the Collection of VAT/GST on Online Sales* (n. 551) 73–74.

881. As an example, the OECD mentions a click-through/shopping referral platform. Such a platform solely directs potential customers to a seller's website through software, an internet link, or similar means, facilitating the discovery, promotion, or listing of goods for sale. The transaction between the customer and seller is completed without any direct or indirect involvement of the digital platform in setting the terms of the underlying supply or in the payment or delivery process. OECD, *The Impact of the Growth of the Sharing and Gig Economy on VAT/GST Policy and Administration* (n. 47) 115.

882. *Ibid.*, 80.

Table 3.1 List of Indications to Be Taken into Account in Order to Determine Whether STR Platforms Facilitate the Supply of Services

	Criteria	*Airbnb*	*Booking.com*	*Couchsurfing*	*HomeExchange*
		airbnb	Booking	couchsurfing	
1	The platform enables the customer and the underlying supplier to establish contact, resulting in the supply of STR services	V	V	V	V
2	The platform directly or indirectly specifies the conditions under which the services are provided	V	V	V	V
3	The platform directly or indirectly participates in approving the consumer's charge related to the payments made	V	V	V	V
4	The platform directly or indirectly participates in the process of providing STR services	V	V	V	V
5	The platform only processes payments related to the provision of STR services	X	X	X	X
6	The platform only advertises services	X	X	X	X
7	The platform only redirects or transfers consumers to other platforms	X	X	X	X

Source: Own compilation.

In summary, the proposed Article 9b IR defining the concept of 'facilitating' transactions appears to be worded broadly enough to cover most existing business models of accommodation sector platforms.

It is also worth noting that, as indicated in the first chapter, it is not uncommon that multiple actors intervene in the supply of tourism services. In such situations, the question arises as to which of these actors will be deemed to be the supplier. For example, meta-search engines play a significant role in the economy of STR platforms. These engines enable the comparison of prices and availability across different properties, redirecting customers to partner booking sites for finalizing transactions. Meta-search engines can only provide users with information about potential transactions and direct them to the respective platform for completion. However, some meta-search engines allow direct bookings, earning commissions for these transactions.[883] While meta-search engines that merely provide information and redirect users to the relevant platforms should be excluded from the deemed supplier regime under the proposed Article 9b(2)(c) IR, there are some doubts about meta-search engines that charge a commission for doing so.

It seems that also in this case the EU legislator should clarify, as he did in the Explanatory Notes 2020, that only one platform for a given transaction can be the facilitator and consequently the deemed supplier. This will be the platform through which the order is taken, and the accommodation service is supplied. In order to determine this, it is first necessary to examine via which operator the contract will be actually concluded with the consumer and thus through which platform the consumer carries out the ordering or payment process.

A very important issue is also the liability of platforms for errors resulting from reliance on erroneous information provided by hosts. In such a situation, platforms, as is the case in the e-commerce model, should not be held liable for the payment of the VAT due if they can demonstrate that they could not reasonably have known that the information was incorrect. For this reason, the legal literature advocates the introduction of clauses exempting the liability of platforms that can prove that they acted in good faith or made reasonable efforts to ensure compliance by their own underlying suppliers.[884]

The EU legislator has recognized this problem and introduced a regulation limiting the liability of STR platforms in the proposed Article 9d IR. According to this provision, where, based on the information provided by the underlying supplier, the platform does not act as a deemed supplier, it will not be liable to pay the VAT due should it be subsequently found that it should have been deemed to be a supplier provided all the following conditions are met: (a) the platform is solely dependent on the information provided by the underlying supplier, (b) the information so provided is erroneous, (c) the platform can prove that it did not know and could not reasonably have known that information was erroneous.

In order to invoke the limited liability provision, the platform will have to prove that all the necessary conditions have been met. The burden of proof, as in the e-commerce model, will therefore fall on the platform operator.

The first condition relates to the platform's dependence on the information provided by suppliers or by other third parties. In contrast to Article 5c IR, the EU legislator here uses the wording that 'the platform is solely dependent on the information (...)' rather than that it is simply 'dependent on information'. This seems to mean that the platform cannot even be allowed to obtain from sources other than the host the information it needs to determine whether it is a deemed supplier. This makes the condition unduly restrictive for platforms which would have to demonstrate not only that they are dependent on the information provided by the underlying providers but also that this dependence is total. Thus, even if the platform had demonstrated

883. Pawlicz, (n. 63) 95–99.
884. Beretta (n. 344) 298–301.

good faith and made commercially reasonable efforts to obtain all necessary data from the hosts, this would still be insufficient for potential exemption from liability.

It should be noted that in the latest compromise text, the EU legislator has opted to omit the word 'solely'. Considering the aforementioned uncertainties, this decision is to be welcomed.[885]

Under the second condition, the information 'so provided'[886] to the platform by the underlying supplier must be incorrect. This condition is therefore somewhat narrower than the analogous condition set out in Article 5c IR which stated that the information provided by the underlying supplier or third party must be incorrect. This is likely to be due to the nature of e-commerce transactions where the platform's dependence on third-party information due to the need to transport goods (e.g., forwarding agents, postal operators, couriers) is greater than in the case of STR transactions. Nevertheless, this means that the platform will not have legal protection if it assumes that it is not obliged to pay VAT but, based on the third-party information, it could have established that it is indeed obliged to pay.[887]

In addition, platforms are also expected to prove that they did not know and could not have reasonably known that the information from the underlying supplier was incorrect. This is a very similar condition to that provided in the e-commerce model, although under Article 5c IR, it is sufficient for platforms to merely demonstrate a lack of knowledge and reasonable possibility of obtaining it. Nonetheless, it appears that, again, the comments in the Explanatory Notes 2020 may prove useful. This means that, also under the service model, the platform operator needs to act in good faith and should exercise due commercial care, and whether this is indeed the case should be assessed not only based on the particular circumstances but also taking into account the internal organization of the platform and the information that can be available to it. In addition, the deemed supplier regime should not disproportionately burden platform operators, so the exercise of due commercial care should be assessed taking into account differences depending on the size of the platform, its business model, the volume of transactions, the number of underlying suppliers, etc.

Although the conditions for excluding platform's liability set out in the proposed Article 9d IR are very similar to the conditions set out in Article 5c IR, it is important to note the differences between the consequences for platforms set out by the two articles. In the case of Article 5c IR, the fulfilment of the conditions set out therein makes the e-commerce platform not liable for the payment of VAT in excess of the VAT which it declared and paid on these supplies. In contrast, in the case of the proposed Article 5d IR, the STR platform will not be obliged to pay the VAT due at all in the event that it is later found that it should not have been deemed a supplier. It is likely that this difference is due to the fact that the planned service model will mostly cover transactions that are currently outside the EU VAT system, and which, when supplied

885. Draft Council Implementing Regulation amending Implementing Regulation (EU) No 282/2011 as regards information requirements for certain VAT schemes – compromise text 8 May 2024 [2022/0410 (NLE)].
886. It should be noted that in the latest compromise text, the EU legislator has opted to omit the word 'so', which seems to have little practical significance. *Ibid.*
887. Merkx and others (n. 381) 137.

without the intermediation of platforms, will not be subject to VAT at all (more on this in the section on the subject aspect of the service model in question). Therefore, it is difficult for the platform in this case to be liable for the potential difference in taxation when this VAT will not be there.

It further follows from the wording of the proposed Article 9d IR that the exclusion of liability of a platform only applies if it erroneously failed to act as a deemed supplier by relying on information obtained from the underlying supplier. The question arises whether the STR platform can exclude its liability when, although it deems itself as a supplier, it incorrectly accounts for the tax because of incorrect data provided by the host. Based on the current wording of Article 9d IR, it appears that it cannot do so. The literature indicates that a platform will not be protected if it has rightly assumed that it is a deemed supplier but relies on erroneous or incomplete information from the underlying supplier to pay the correct amount of VAT. The same will be true if the underlying supplier provides the platform with a VAT number, misleading it as to its status – it must be assumed that the supplier has not provided incorrect information but has provided correct information that it should not have provided.[888]

Thus, despite their apparent similarity, the proposed Article 9d IR and Article 5c IR exclude liability of platforms in different situations.[889] However, there seems to be no reason for the EU legislator to differentiate between e-commerce sector platforms and accommodation sector platforms in this respect. It is even pointed out that in the case of the STR platform economy, the risk of relying on incorrect information is greater than in the e-commerce sector since in this case the actual parties to the transaction (host and guest) will have 'offline contacts'. Hence, they may, for example, agree on paying EUR 50 for a service through communication tools provided by the platform, but when the supplier provides the service, the customer pays EUR 100 in cash.[890] Application of the 'good faith' protection could be a possible compromise solution to this issue, as it has been in the context of the e-commerce.[891] Thus, the proposed Article 9d IR should also cover the situation where an STR platform deems itself to be a supplier but, relying in good faith on erroneous data obtained from the host, incorrectly accounts for VAT. Then, the platform would not be liable for the payment of VAT in excess of the VAT which it declared and paid on these services.[892] Similarly, Article 5c IR should cover the situation where an e-commerce platform, acting in good faith, does not deem itself as a supplier by relying on erroneous data obtained from the underlying supplier – in which case such a platform would not be liable to pay the VAT due if it is later discovered that it should have been deemed to be a supplier.

---

888. *Ibid.*
889. *See also*: Lamensch and others (n. 143); Emilia Teresa Sroka, 'Comparing Deemed Supplier Regimes: E-Commerce and Short-Term Rental/Passenger Transport Platforms in the EU VAT System' (2024) CIDEEFF – Centre for Research in European, Economic, Fiscal and Tax Law, https://www.cideeff.pt/pt/publicacoes/working-papers/comparing-deemed-supplier-regimes-e-commerce-and-short-term-rentalpassenger-transport-platforms-in/6264/ accessed 3 April 2024.
890. European Commission, 'VAT Expert Group No 095: VAT Treatment of the Sharing Economy, Taxud.c.1(2020)5816454' (n. 338).
891. *Ibid.*
892. *See also*: Merkx and others (n. 381) 137.

In the absence of separate provisions in this regard, it also appears that platforms benefiting from the SME exemption, as is the case in Canada,[893] will not be deemed suppliers. However, a question arises as to whether the platform will be required to take into account the value of the underlying transactions it facilitates when calculating the threshold for this exemption. The EC proposes that when assessing its turnover, the platform must include the value of the underlying supplies it facilitates.[894]

The envisaged provision of Article 28a of the VAT Directive (as well as Article 9a IR and Article 14a of the VAT Directive) does not contain restrictions as to the status of the platform operator, so it should not matter whether the platform is operated by an EU resident or a third-country entity. In practice, this leads to a problem related to the potential enforcement of liabilities from foreign resident platforms. It is questionable whether tax authorities in the EU are able to effectively collect VAT from non-EU operators.[895] This issue seems particularly relevant in the STR platform economy. This is because the underlying suppliers (such as hosts) are often in the tax jurisdiction where the property is located and may already be registered for VAT there. However, if it is the non-resident platform that has the status of a deemed supplier, the tax authorities will have to perform enforcement procedure in the foreign tax jurisdiction. This situation is somewhat different from that of platforms facilitating the sale of goods or digital products, as in these sectors, the platform economy often includes underlying vendors selling from various locations around the world to a single location[896] (e.g., Chinese vendors sell goods to the EU market through the platform). Because of this, in the case of the STR platform economy, the tax authorities may wish to carefully weigh the risks and benefits of shifting the VAT collection liability from the individual hosts that are often residents in a specific jurisdiction onto foreign STR platforms.[897] It is rightly pointed out that from a level playing field perspective, one cannot have a rule which only requires EU platforms to collect VAT and not non-EU platforms.[898] In this context, however, it is worth noting that about 73% of all service sector platforms surveyed in the analysis commissioned by the EC had an establishment located in the EU, and of the largest platforms, more than half had a global headquarters in the EU, or a branch or subsidiary overseeing EU operations.[899] It therefore appears that the

893. In the Canadian system, there is a threshold of CAD 30,000, which is approximately EUR 20,000. If a platform does not expect to facilitate supplies exceeding this amount, it is not obligated to register for GST and declare GST on its supplies. It is important to highlight that the CAD 30,000 threshold serves as the general SME threshold, under which businesses are not mandated to register for or declare their GST. European Commission, 'Group on the Future of VAT No 122: VAT and the Platform Economy - Focus on Specific Issues - Follow up, Taxud.c.1(2022)3461477'.
894. *Ibid.*
895. European Commission, 'VAT Expert Group No 095: VAT Treatment of the Sharing Economy, Taxud.c.1(2020)5816454' (n. 338) 095.
896. OECD, *The Impact of the Growth of the Sharing and Gig Economy on VAT/GST Policy and Administration* (n. 47) 62.
897. *Ibid.*
898. European Commission, 'VAT Expert Group No 095: VAT Treatment of the Sharing Economy, Taxud.c.1(2020)5816454' (n. 338) 095.
899. European Commission, Directorate General for Taxation and Customs Union and others (n. 6) 34.

problem of enforcing the obligations of platforms from third countries will not happen often.

5.3.2 The Object Aspect

The envisaged provision of Article 28a of the VAT Directive applies if the platform facilitates the supply of STR services referred to in Article 135(3) of the VAT Directive.[900] According to the draft of this article, an uninterrupted rental of accommodation for a maximum of 45 days with or without the provision of other ancillary services will be regarded as having a similar function to the hotel sector.[901]

As the EU legislator explains in the planned recital 25 to the draft amending the VAT Directive: 'Some Member States rely upon Article 135(2) of the VAT Directive to apply a VAT exemption to short-term accommodation rental, while others do not. In order to ensure equal treatment and consistency, whilst continuing to address the distortion of competition in the accommodation sector, it should be clarified that this exemption does not apply to short-term accommodation rentals. The criteria used to identify short-term accommodation rentals, which shall be regarded as having a similar function to the hotel sector, are only to be applied for the purposes of this Directive and are without prejudice to the definitions used in other Union legislation. This Directive therefore does not create an EU definition of short-term accommodation rentals.'[902]

The fact that the supply of STR services is considered to be an activity in a sector similar to the hotel industry means that it does not qualify for VAT exemption under Article 135(1) of the VAT Directive. As pointed out in the literature, a number of Member States are currently exempting accommodation due to the high costs of administering a large number of suppliers in exchange for small amounts of VAT.[903] Member States follow two approaches: (i) letting of residential property is generally exempt; or (ii) letting of residential property is exempt, unless the supplier also provides additional services (e.g., cleaning, breakfasts, bedding), which would qualify the supply as accommodation services.[904] The legal literature highlights that Member States should continue to have a margin of discretion in the case of lettings lasting 46

900. The lack of a definition of STR services in Article 28a of the VAT Directive itself is viewed negatively – it is noted that Article 28a of the VAT Directive uses the term 'short-term accommodation rental', which is not used in the same way in Article 135(3) of the VAT Directive, making it unclear whether STR is indeed limited to a maximum of 45 days. Merkx and others (n. 381) 135.

901. It should be noted that the proposed solution in this regard differs from analogous Canadian regulations, where short-term accommodation subject to taxation includes renting out a residential complex or unit (or part thereof) to an individual for a period of less than one month, where the price exceeds USD 20 per day. Department of Finance Canada (n. 835).

902. Proposal for a Council Directive amending Directive 2006/112/EC as regards VAT rules for the digital age (n. 382).

903. Richard Asquith, 'EU Platform Economy Issues on Full Liability Model – VAT in the Digital Age' (11 May 2022), https://www.vatcalc.com/eu/eu-platform-economy-issues-on-fully-liability-model-vat-in-the-digital-age/ accessed 28 November 2022.

904. European Commission, Directorate General for Taxation and Customs Union and others (n. 6) 113–115.

days or longer – national legislation applying a longer term to distinguish between exempt leases and taxable lettings should still be allowed.[905]

Given the current divergence in the application of the exemption for letting of residential property, in the view of the legal writers, the proposed solution can be welcomed as an improvement.[906] The approach chosen by the EC, based solely on the time criterion, should be assessed positively – it seems easy to apply and enforce in practice. However, it is worth noting that the proposed length (45 days) raises some concerns.[907] In addition, given that many countries are now exempting this type of letting, it seems that reaching an agreement at Community level on this issue will be extremely difficult.[908] In addition, France, Greece, Spain and Italy take the view that when the host does not provide any of the services complementary to the hotel industry, such as those of a restaurant, cleaning, washing clothes or similar activities, the services should still be exempted from VAT – so it is possible that there will be some opposition to this proposal by these Member States.[909]

The possible continuation of the exemption would have a negative impact on revenues resulting from the application of the deemed supplier regime – where accommodation is exempt, this could lead to less revenue and even generate VAT revenue losses.[910] Assuming that the proposed deemed supplier regime comes into effect with the exemption in question, it is estimated that the increase in revenue across the EU-27 could be as high as EUR 518 to EUR 748 million between 2025 and 2032.[911]

It should be noted that in the latest compromise text, the EU legislator has made certain changes regarding the definition of STR services.[912] First, rental services should now be considered to have a similar function to the hotel sector when they are uninterrupted, provided to the same person, and for a maximum of 30 nights instead of 45. This numerical adjustment has been directly incorporated into Article 28a of the VAT Directive. Considering the concerns raised earlier, this change should be regarded rather positively.

Additionally, in Article 135(2) of the VAT Directive, it has been added that the uninterrupted rental of accommodation to the same person for a maximum of 30 nights shall be regarded as having a similar function to the hotel sector, subject to criteria,

905. Merkx and others (n. 381) 135.
906. Nevia Čičin-Šain, 'Newly Proposed VAT Rules for Sharing Economy Platforms – Some Fine-Tuning Needed?' (*Kluwer International Tax Blog*, 22 March 2023), https://kluwertaxblog.com/2023/03/22/newly-proposed-vat-rules-for-sharing-economy-platforms-some-fine-tuning-needed/ accessed 4 April 2023.
907. Business representatives point out that the proposed 45-day period in Article 135(3) of the VAT Directive should be shortened, as in practice, guests do not rent holiday accommodation for such a long duration. CFE Tax Advisers Europe, 'Opinion Statement FC 6/2023 – Further CFE Comments on the EU Commission's VIDA Proposals of 8 December 2022'.
908. Matesanz, 'IVA La Vida. Primera Parte. IVA y Economía Colaborativa' (n. 868).
909. Javier Sanchez Gallardo and Gorka Echevarría, 'The Platform Economy Will Have Its Own VAT Regime in 2025' (2023) 34 International VAT Monitor, ibfd.org accessed 7 August 2023 https://doi.org/10.59403/3nmrjn6.
910. European Commission, Directorate General for Taxation and Customs Union and others (n. 6) 113–115.
911. *Ibid.*, 141–143.
912. Draft Council Directive amending Directive 2006/112/EC as regards VAT rules for the digital age – compromise text 8 May 2024 (n. 382).

conditions, and limitations to be determined by Member States. As indicated in the updated recital 25, to adapt to different national specificities of the sector, Member States should have the possibility to subject short-term accommodation rental services to certain criteria, conditions, and limitations according to their national laws.

This change should be viewed somewhat negatively, as instead of a single, straightforward criterion based on the number of days, it allows for the introduction of numerous subjective criteria by Member States. This may contribute to further fragmentation of the accommodation sector in the EU. Again, it should be stressed that currently, regulatory fragmentation and selectively applied VAT exemption rules, particularly in the accommodation sector, do not seem to have a positive impact on VAT harmonization and consequently on the competitiveness of the EU market. The ViDA package presents an excellent opportunity to somewhat harmonize VAT taxation rules in this area within the EU. Therefore, this project should not contribute to maintaining or deepening the fragmentation of EU VAT legislation in this area.[913] Furthermore, if the deemed supplier solution is adopted, EU lawmakers and national governments must prioritize the operational ease of platforms. These platforms should have standardized regulations across all Member States, eliminating the need to navigate individual exemptions and national provisions that often lead to complex interpretations on a case-by-case basis.[914]

What is very distinctive about the service model is the type of underlying transactions it covers. These can be referred to, in simple terms, as C2C and C2B transactions or, more precisely, transactions from entities that do not charge VAT for various reasons (the catalogue of which is included in the proposed Article 28a of the VAT Directive) to customers who have or do not have the status of VAT taxable persons.

Under the service model, the question of the status of the underlying suppliers is therefore relevant. According to the planned Article 28a of the VAT Directive, these will only include entities that currently remain outside the EU VAT system (non-established persons who are not identified for VAT purposes in a Member State and non-taxable persons),[915] as well as those belonging to the so-called Group of Four.[916] The Group of Four includes: (i) taxable persons carrying out only supplies of goods or services in respect of which VAT is not deductible; (ii) non-taxable legal persons; (iii) taxable persons subject to the common flat-rate scheme for farmers; and (iv) taxable persons subject to the SME scheme.[917] All underlying suppliers to whom the proposed Article

913. *See also*: Marta Papis-Almansa and Emilia Teresa Sroka, 'Questioning the Proportionality of the ViDA Rules on the Platform Economy: Are We Veering Off Course?' (2024) 35 International VAT Monitor https://doi.org/10.59403/3ajrqgg.
914. *Ibid.*
915. In doctrine, this category of entities is considered particularly uncertain because the issue of who qualifies as a non-taxable person may vary among individual Member States and be subject to different interpretations. Gallardo and Echevarría (n. 903).
916. European Commission, Directorate General for Taxation and Customs Union and others (n. 6) 105–106.
917. It is worth noting that the approach where VAT is collected by digital platforms on behalf of all suppliers, even if their turnovers are below the current registration threshold (as in the case of SME), is argued to be analogous to the current treatment of low-priced imports through

28a of the VAT Directive applies will be referred to as the 'Group of Six'. This is illustrated in Figure 3.4.

Figure 3.4 Underlying Suppliers Covered by Proposed Article 28a of the VAT Directive

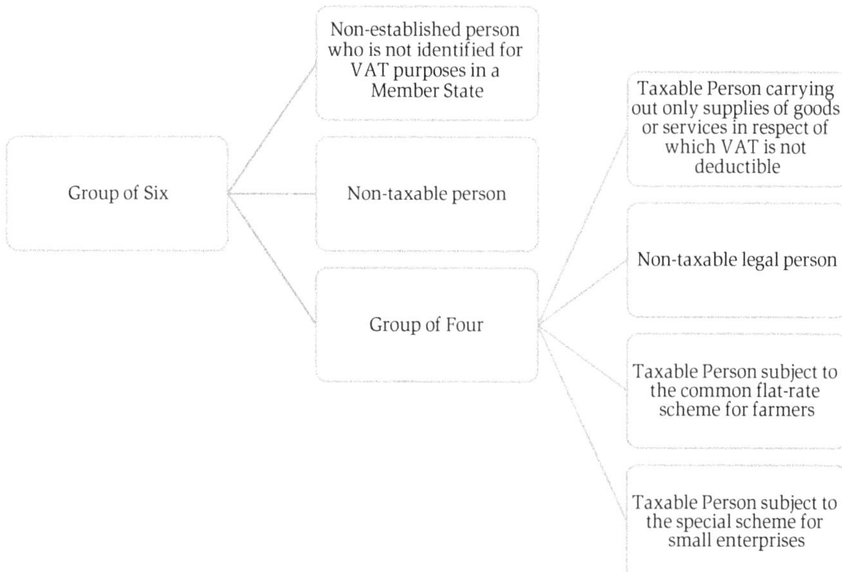

Source: Own compilation.

In the view of the EU legislator, it is precisely these actors, due to the fact that they operate via platforms and at the same time are not subject to standard VAT taxation, that compete with traditional accommodation suppliers who are qualified as VAT taxable payers. At the same time, self-collection of VAT by such hosts would be burdensome, especially when they are private operators,[918] and collection of VAT by an intermediation platform would be a safer option, especially when the host is not established in the EU.[919] In addition, the inclusion of the Group of Four is intended to prevent the risk of an arbitrage once the deemed supplier regime is in place, therefore ensuring that these arrangements are more future-proof.[920]

e-commerce platforms (e.g., Amazon and AliExpress). Andrew MC Smith, 'New Zealand. Extending the Tax Net to the Gig Economy' (2023) 29 Asia-Pacific Tax Bulletin.

918. Many small service providers are not even aware that they may be subject to VAT for the services they offer, and even if they are aware, it is very difficult for them to determine the VAT treatment of their activities. Matesanz, 'IVA La Vida. Primera Parte. IVA y Economía Colaborativa' (n. 868).

919. Proposal for a Council Directive amending Directive 2006/112/EC as regards VAT rules for the digital age (n. 382).

920. European Commission, Directorate General for Taxation and Customs Union and others (n. 6) 105–106.

The catalogue of underlying suppliers included in the Group of Six is closed. This means that if the underlying services are supplied by other entities that are outside this catalogue (primarily taxable persons who are subject to standard VAT taxation), the platform will not become a deemed supplier in such a situation. It is also irrelevant whether the underlying suppliers are established in the jurisdiction where the underlying transaction is taxed or, instead, whether the transactions are handled by a foreign host.

It should be noted that some Group of Six suppliers have the option to opt out of the deemed supplier regime. As pointed out in the legal writings, this option applies to a supplier established outside the EU who can register in the EU as a VAT taxable person and to a supplier subject to the SME scheme or the flat-rate scheme for farmers who can choose to account under the normal VAT rules. Such a solution will not be possible for non-taxable legal persons unless a Member State implements Article 12 of the VAT Directive, according to which a person carrying out occasional transactions[921] should be considered a taxable person.

The deemed supplier regime therefore requires platforms to check the VAT status of their underlying suppliers. This requirement could potentially place a very heavy burden on platforms, as it requires distinguishing between those required to register for VAT and those not required to do so, which appears to significantly increase their costs.

The EU legislator has recognized this problem and, in order to make the service model provisions workable in practice, has proposed a way for platforms to determine the status of underlying providers. According to the proposed Article 9c IR, the deemed supplier regime will apply where the person providing the STR service does not provide the platform with a valid VAT identification number. As the EU legislator points out, the platform is not obliged to carry out a detailed verification of this number.[922] In practice, this means that when the underlying supplier uses the platform and does not provide the platform with a VAT number, the platform will take on the role of the deemed supplier. If this is not the case (i.e., when the underlying supplier provides its VAT number to the platform), the deemed supplier system will not apply and so the host will account for VAT.

It should be noted that the Group of Four includes entities that may have a VAT number (in some Member States, SMEs are identified for VAT purposes[923] or obtain

921. Merkx and others (n. 381) 134–135.
922. Proposal for a Council Directive amending Directive 2006/112/EC as regards VAT rules for the digital age (n. 382).
923. Member States can, under Article 292b of the VAT Directive, release small enterprises applying the exemption within their Member State from the obligation to be identified by means of an individual number (a VAT number). However, there are instances, where a Member State will allocate a number to an exempt small enterprise – either because they do so as a matter of course for domestic suppliers or because the exempt small enterprise wishes to avail itself of the special scheme in another Member State (in which case the number will have an 'EX' suffix). While it would be easy for a platform to identify an exempt small enterprise if it has the 'EX' suffix, it would not be the case if exempt small enterprises were given VAT numbers similar to those used by other businesses. European Commission, 'VAT Expert Group No 107: VAT and the Platform Economy – Focus on Specific Issues, Taxud.c.1(2020)4162479'.

this number for a specific purpose, e.g., because of participation in a reverse-charge transaction).[924] This raises the risk that some underlying suppliers who are exempt from VAT but have a VAT number will transfer it to the platform without declaring that they are a member of the Group of Four. This will make the deemed supplier regime inapplicable, and, consequently, these underlying suppliers will be able to provide VAT-exempt services, with a price advantage for their consumers equal to the applicable VAT rate.[925] This may lead to an unjustified increase in the number of requests for VAT identification numbers by SMEs.

The second paragraph of the proposed Article 9c IR refers to this situation. According to this provision, where the underlying supplier has a VAT identification number and at the same time belongs to the Group of Four, such VAT identification number will not be communicated to the platform. However, the EU legislator has not foreseen any consequences in the proposed legislation for underlying suppliers who do not comply with this ban. However, such sanctions may be imposed by individual Member States.[926]

As rightly pointed out in the legal literature, this prohibition appears to conflict with Article 55 IR and the requirements imposed on the platform by the DAC7 Directive.[927] Article 55 IR requires taxable persons and non-taxable legal persons liable to account for VAT under Article 196 of the VAT Directive (reverse charge), in respect of services received, to communicate their VAT number to those supplying goods or services to them as soon as it is obtained. The DAC7 Directive requires platform operators to collect VAT numbers from their 'reportable vendors', i.e., among others, from those who let properties through them.

Furthermore, where a host communicates its VAT number to a platform despite being part of the Group of Four, it does not appear that the platform will be able to exclude its liability under the proposed Article 9d IR. Indeed, as pointed out in the legal literature, a valid VAT number should not qualify as 'erroneous' information, which is one of the three requirements that need to be fulfilled cumulatively for the proposed Article 9d IR[928] to apply. It therefore seems that the EU legislator should modify the wording of the proposed Article 9d IR, so that also in this situation the platform is not liable, or clarify in the explanatory notes that the unjustified communication of the VAT number by the host is 'misinformation' within the meaning of this provision.

It should be mentioned that the EU legislator also considered another variant of the presumption in question, according to which, in addition to communicating (or not) a VAT number, the underlying supplier would also make a declaration, to be updated periodically, that he does not belong to the Group of Four.[929] As rightly pointed out by legal writers, whether relying on the truthfulness of such statements would be

924. European Commission, Directorate General for Taxation and Customs Union and others (n. 6) 111-112.
925. *Ibid.*, 151-153.
926. Merkx and others (n. 381) 134.
927. Čičin-Šain (n. 900).
928. *Ibid.*
929. European Commission, Directorate General for Taxation and Customs Union and others (n. 6) 111-112.

a reliable method remains questionable.[930] At the same time, this two-tier system could lead to over-complexity of the deemed supplier regime without achieving greater credibility.

It also appears that the tax authorities can play a role in ensuring the compliance of the proposed solutions by carrying out *ex post* audits, comparing the information communicated by the Group of Six with the information collected by the platform.[931] In particular, information received on transactions facilitated by the platform, but which is not subject to the deemed supplier regime, would need to be checked against national taxable persons databases. Such audits should be accompanied by an information campaign by platforms and tax authorities that would inform about such audits and their consequences.[932] As the EC rightly points out, it is not the role of the platform to police the SME exemption scheme and in particular whether they reach the thresholds that entitle them to apply this exemption; this role continues to be carried out by the Member States.[933] However, platforms could, on a voluntary basis, inform their users that they are approaching or exceeding the relevant thresholds, which are likely to require those entities to register and account for VAT in a particular Member State.

It is also worth noting that, in practice, establishing the true identity of the host (whose status determines whether the platform is subject to the deemed supplier regime) may prove to be a problem.[934] As the OECD points out, one of the problems of the STR sector in the platform economy is that the identity of the underlying supplier may not always be readily available to the platform. This is, for instance, the case where a property is managed and advertised by a professional agent on behalf of its owner.[935] As mentioned in the first chapter, an integral part of the STR platforms' economy is occupied by the so-called super-listers, entities that manage bookings for individuals who do not have the expertise or time for such activities.[936] Super-listers professionally handle operational aspects of rentals for the hosts who engage them in exchange for commissions. Hosts using this type of intermediary often do not even know which platforms list their properties, receiving only rental fees less a management commission.[937] Sometimes super-listers act as so-called undisclosed agents advertising properties in their own name but acting on behalf of 'hidden' owners.[938] The question therefore arises: what consequences will arise if a host belonging to the Group of Six is replaced by a professional intermediary (a VAT taxable person) when

930. Čičin-Šain (n. 900).
931. European Commission, Directorate General for Taxation and Customs Union and others (n. 6) 111–112.
932. *Ibid.*, 151–153.
933. European Commission, 'VAT Expert Group No 107: VAT and the Platform Economy – Focus on Specific Issues, Taxud.c.1(2020)4162479' (n. 917).
934. *See also*: Sroka (n. 883).
935. OECD, *The Impact of the Growth of the Sharing and Gig Economy on VAT/GST Policy and Administration* (n. 47) 75.
936. Bakker, Hendrica and Twining-Ward (n. 50) 23.
937. OECD, *The Impact of the Growth of the Sharing and Gig Economy on VAT/GST Policy and Administration* (n. 47) 102–103.
938. *Ibid.*, 29.

the intermediary himself registers on the platform and communicates to the platform his VAT number? Given the prevalence of such practices in the accommodation sector, it seems that the EU legislator should consider how to treat this situation for VAT purposes and whether the deemed supplier regime applies in these situations. It might be helpful in this respect to refer to the proposed regulation on data collection and sharing relating to services[939] (assuming it comes into force). This regulation proposes that hosts provide their data and information on the units they offer under STR services to the competent authorities. Public authorities in each Member State will keep registers of people renting units and assign them an identification number, and platforms will be required to oblige hosts to provide them with this number. Platforms should also ensure that STR services are not offered when there is no host identification number.[940] In such a situation, platforms could conclude that those communicating a number to them are the relevant underlying suppliers and check their tax status. Unfortunately, this certainty would not be available to platforms intermediating free-of-charge STR services, as the proposed changes are intended to apply only to STR services provided for consideration. It is also worth noting that this regulation is not intended to ensure tax compliance and that the EC excludes any future use of personal data processed under the regulation for law enforcement or tax and customs purposes.[941] Interpretative doubts may therefore arise as to whether the platform will be able to use the number communicated to it to correctly fulfil its obligations as a deemed supplier under EU VAT law. It would be desirable for the EC to clarify this issue.

Ultimately, however, the EU legislator decided to overhaul the aforementioned solutions. In the compromise text, they abandoned the concept of the Group of Six and directly specified in Article 28a of the VAT Directive that the deemed supplier regime applies unless underlying suppliers: (a) provided their identification number for VAT purposes to the platform issued in the Member States where the supply occurs, or the identification number allocated to them (Member States may require the platform to validate the identification number for VAT purposes using appropriate means established in accordance with national law); (b) declared to the platform that they will charge any VAT due on that supply.[942]

939. Proposal for a regulation of the European Parliament and of the Council on data collection and sharing relating to short-term accommodation rental services and amending Regulation (EU) 2018/1724 (n. 309).

940. The registration system for hosts is considered an effective tool in combating abuses in the STR market. It is noted that such a system was introduced in Greece in 2016, and through cooperation with platforms like Booking, Expedia, Airbnb, and HomeAway, it led to the removal of properties without registration numbers since 2022. European Commission, 'Developing a Responsible, Fair and Trusted Single Market for Short-Term Rental Services. Workshop 1: Enhancing Transparency on Short-Term Accommodation Rentals in the EU. 22 October 2021 – Conclusions, GROW.G.3/CD' (n. 434).

941. It is worth noting that, concerning tax compliance, there has been consideration for implementing a simple, centralized registration system for accommodation service providers. Such a central registry would enable tax authorities to conduct easier and more targeted controls to enforce compliance with tax obligations by STR service providers. European Commission, Directorate General for Internal Market, Industry, Entrepreneurship and SMEs, VVA, and Spark Legal Network (n. 48) 49.

942. Draft Council Directive amending Directive 2006/112/EC as regards VAT rules for the digital age – compromise text 8 May 2024 (n. 382).

This naturally led to changes in Article 9c and 9e IR.[943] Article 9c IR specifies that the taxable person supplying the service must provide the identification number for VAT purposes or the number allocated in accordance with specific articles to the facilitating taxable person only once, unless there is a change in their taxable activity. According to Article 9e IR, for the purposes of determining the place of supply of the facilitation service of platforms, the taxable person shall regard the person to whom those services were supplied as a non-taxable person where that person to whom those services were supplied does not provide a VAT identification number, unless that taxable person has information to the contrary. In the new Article 9g IR, it was also clarified that, with regard to short-term accommodation rental services, the special scheme SME can apply only to the taxable person deemed to have supplied those services.

These changes indeed seem to simplify and clarify the rules for applying the deemed supplier regime. However, as rightly pointed out in the doctrine, this solution may encounter some practical difficulties. Currently, the verification of a customer's VAT number relies on the VAT Information Exchange System (VIES) database, which has its limitations and often experiences periods of downtime due to high usage or maintenance. To ensure efficient and reliable verification of VAT numbers, it seems essential for VIES to support bulk validation real-time updates and minimize downtime.[944]

In turn, the changes proposed in points 4 and 5 of Article 28a of the VAT Directive should be assessed rather negatively. According to these regulations, Member States have the right to exclude entities participating in the special SME scheme from the scope of the deeming supplier rule, allowing them to continue exempting VAT on services provided by such suppliers. This means platforms will not have to collect VAT on STR services provided by such small businesses. Member States should inform the VAT Committee about this exclusion, and the EC shall publish a comprehensive list of the means used by those Member States exercising this option.

It is worth noting that in the compromise text from May 2024, a Member State wishing to exercise the opt-out option was obligated to provide the means by which the supplier of STR services shall indicate to the platform that his supplies fall under the special scheme (updated Article 28a, point 5). In recital 24, it was emphasized that Member States should ensure that the platform can easily identify that the underlying supplier is operating under the special scheme for SME, for example, by providing for the use of a specific identification number, or an electronic certificate indicating that the underlying supplier is using the special SME scheme, or any other means which allows for the easy verification of this status.[945] In the compromise text from June 2024,

943. Draft Council Implementing Regulation amending Implementing Regulation (EU) No 282/2011 as regards information requirements for certain VAT schemes – compromise text 8 May 2024 (n. 879).
944. Bal A, 'VAT in the Digital Age: Impact of Revised Proposals on EU Businesses' (*Forbes*), https://www.forbes.com/sites/aleksandrabal/2024/05/12/vat-in-the-digital-age-impact-of-revised-proposals-on-eu-businesses/?sh=f994c06188cb accessed 25 July 2024.
945. Draft Council Directive amending Directive 2006/112/EC as regards VAT rules for the digital age – compromise text 8 May 2024 (n. 382).

this requirement was removed, and recital 24 indicates only that the exercise of the opt-out option by a Member State should not cause any additional undue administrative burden on the person providing the supply of STR services or the platform.[946] This change makes it even easier for Member States to exercise the opt-out option, as, in practice, it would only involve notifying the VAT Committee.

As rightly pointed out in the literature, the solution allowing Member States to opt out from the deemed supplier rule appears highly detrimental, not only from the perspective of platforms, which would likely struggle to automate the VAT reconciliation process for their underlying suppliers in such a scenario (due to the need to consider national discretionary provisions requiring individual interpretation in each case), but also in terms of harmonizing the entire EU VAT tax system. Such a solution is likely to undermine the very purpose of introducing the deemed supplier regime for accommodation platforms, which is to level the playing field between traditional businesses and entities operating through platforms.[947]

5.4 Mode of Operation

According to the OECD, there are two variations of the deemed supplier model for STR platforms: (i) in the first variation, the deemed supplier regime would apply only in cases where the underlying supplier is regarded as a taxable person for VAT purposes under national law,[948] (ii) in the second variation, the regime applies irrespective of the status of the underlying supplier. In both variations, the platform can be seen as an entity that purchases services from the underlying supplier and supplies them onwards to the end customer.[949] This means that the platform is solely and fully liable for assessing, collecting and remitting VAT on the activities it facilitates. At the same time, the underlying supplier is in principle relieved from any VAT obligations on the supply of services to its customer.[950] The OECD further stressed that this liability regime should be limited to VAT liabilities only and should not affect any other liability aspects for platforms beyond the VAT.[951]

The EU service model is based on the second variation identified by the OECD but in a slightly narrowed version. Under this model, platforms are to be required to assess VAT when the underlying supplier does not charge VAT. This model therefore does not cover transactions where the underlying supplier is subject to standard taxation for VAT purposes.

946. Draft Council Directive amending Directive 2006/112/EC as regards VAT rules for the digital age – compromise text 19 June 2024 [2022/0407(CNS)].
947. Papis-Almansa and Sroka (n. 907).
948. However, in this case, the OECD points out that additional complexity may arise from shifting VAT compliance responsibilities from suppliers who already pay VAT to the platform. To mitigate such risks, limiting the scope of the deemed supplier regime to base suppliers below a certain threshold could be considered (although this would necessitate monitoring supplier thresholds). OECD, *The Impact of the Growth of the Sharing and Gig Economy on VAT/GST Policy and Administration* (n. 47) 77–79.
949. *Ibid.*, 60.
950. *Ibid.*, 76–77.
951. *Ibid.*, 76.

However, in terms of its mechanics, the proposed service model replicates the solutions proposed in the e-commerce model.[952] This means that the fiction of two consecutive services will be created, one between the actual supplier (host) and the platform and the other between the platform and the end consumer. This fiction will be limited to VAT liabilities only.

The first transaction (from the underlying supplier to the platform), under the proposed Article 136b of the VAT Directive, will be exempt from VAT, but unlike the e-commerce model, without the right to deduct. As the EC points out, this is justified on various grounds. First, it should be noted that the underlying suppliers covered by the deemed supplier regime do not currently deduct VAT. Second, individuals would have to register for VAT deduction and, in the case of shared assets, allocate the costs charged between private and commercial uses of the property, which could prove very difficult. In addition, the solution adopted prevents occasional suppliers from registering for VAT just before the start of renovation work and then abandoning them only to obtain a large input VAT deduction. The EC also stressed that the exercise of the right of deduction is often conditional on fuller compliance with VAT disclosure obligations that are not imposed on the underlying suppliers covered by the deemed supplier regime.[953]

Such an arrangement, however, requires the underlying supplier to raise the price requested for providing the service, without the option to deduct VAT that traditional suppliers have, and with this, it is more than likely that the competitive advantage over traditional sectors will not disappear but may be reversed.[954] This new rule, instead of contributing to an equal treatment between traditional and platform-based providers, introduces a discriminatory treatment of these suppliers using platforms' intermediation who potentially compete with traditional businesses – that approach seems alien to the purpose and logic of VAT.[955] Furthermore, the impossibility to deduct VAT that the individual underlying supplier has paid on its inputs leads to VAT cascading. Such risks are pointed out, among others, by business representatives.[956] The academic legal writers point to various possible strategies for removing the amounts of undeducted VAT and thus avoiding its cascading[957] (although not flawed).[958] In New Zealand, three possible options regarding credits for GST incurred

952. Matesanz, 'IVA La Vida. Primera Parte. IVA y Economía Colaborativa' (n. 868).
953. European Commission, Directorate General for Taxation and Customs Union and others (n. 6) 143–147.
954. Gallardo and Echevarría (n. 903).
955. Papis-Almansa and Sroka (n. 907).
956. Bolt and others, 'Letter to the Swedish Presidency Dated May 31, 2023: Urgent Need to Review the EU's Proposed VAT Platform Rules'; BusinessEurope, 'VAT in the Digital Age – BusinessEurope Reply to the Public Consultation', https://www.businesseurope.eu/publications/vat-digital-age-businesseurope-reply-public-consultation accessed 9 May 2023; European Travel Agents' and Tour Operators' Association, 'Feedback on the ViDA Regulation Proposal 4.04.2023'.
957. For instance: (i) the underlying transaction can be zero-rated, (ii) a reduced rate can be introduced for output transactions made by platforms, (iii) a flat-rate input VAT compensation scheme can be enacted. Beretta (n. 344) 314.
958. For example, according to the doctrine, allowing the platform to deduct VAT on purchases made by the underlying suppliers would not solve the issue, as these purchases are often used

by suppliers on their inputs were considered,[959] and finally a flat-rate credit approximating the recoverable input tax was offered (platforms charge a 15% GST, of which they return 8.5% to the service provider, resulting in only 6.5% of the charged GST being collected).[960] The EU legislator, however, has not chosen to introduce any of these solutions. However, there is a view in the literature that the EC's proposed regulation seems acceptable, taking into account the CJEU's conclusions in the *Avon* case[961] and the fact that the platform has the possibility to use a different business model that does not include the services provided by the Group of Six.[962] In order to ensure greater flexibility and neutrality, the Commission could require EU Member States to regard non-taxable legal persons as taxable persons under Article 12 of the VAT Directive – thus giving these persons the option to choose whether to claim the SME scheme exemption or to account under the normal rules and thus be able to claim a VAT deduction.[963]

Furthermore, it is pointed out that if the payment is not intermediated by the platform, the amount of VAT should be remitted by the underlying supplier to the platform, and the transaction should be outside the scope of VAT, as well as neutral for other fiscal and accounting purposes.[964]

The second transaction (from the platform to the consumer of the service) is subject to VAT, so the taxation rules and rates that apply to the supply of STR services will apply. In addition, the proposed Article 172a of the VAT Directive clarifies that where a platform has received and supplied services in accordance with Article 28a of the VAT Directive, these supplies do not affect its right to deduct, whether or not they are subject to VAT deduction. This regulation appears to be aimed at providing

---

for both business and personal purposes, making it challenging for the platform to monitor and prevent potential fraud. Similarly, implementing a flat-rate deduction is not feasible because setting a realistic flat-rate across various sectors and business models within the platform economy would be difficult. While a flat-rate per sector is a possibility, it would introduce more complexity and raise issues regarding delineation. Merkx and others (n. 381) 140–141.

959. The first was to file a GST return claiming GST input credits in the same way as other GST-registered suppliers. The second was to adopt a 'flat-rate' scheme, where suppliers collect GST at a predetermined rate that assumes a certain proportion of GST input credits relative to sales and no credit is given for GST paid. The third option was to refund GST on costs as part of unregistered suppliers' annual tax returns. Smith (n. 911).

960. Bal (n. 866).

961. The representatives of Avon, covered by the SME exemption, delivered goods to consumers, while the company supplied them with goods below the retail price. Specific UK regulations imposed a VAT payment obligation on Avon based on the price charged by the representatives. The company challenged these regulations, noting that the VAT deduction from the purchases of demonstration items by the representatives was not taken into account, which, in its view, violated the principles of proportionality, equal treatment, tax neutrality, and led to an unfavourable competitive situation between Avon and businesses using traditional sales methods, which were not burdened with VAT. However, the CJEU ruled that this measure was appropriate and necessary because its purpose was to prevent tax avoidance and address specific problems caused by the direct selling system (i.e., the system used by Avon). *Avon Cosmetics Ltd v. The Commissioners for Her Majesty's Revenue and Customs* [2017] CJEU C-305/16.

962. Merkx and others (n. 381) 140–141.

963. *Ibid.*

964. European Commission, Directorate General for Taxation and Customs Union and others (n. 6) 115–116.

platforms with greater legal certainty in this matter. Therefore, regardless of whether the underlying supply is exempt or taxed for VAT, this will not be taken into account in determining the platform's right to deduct.[965]

This provision seems to confirm that the underlying service and the service supplied by the platforms should be accounted for separately. Given the similarity between the service model and the e-commerce model, it can therefore be assumed that, also in the case of the e-commerce model, the platform continues to supply separate services to the supplier or consumer (making the platform available) for a fee. Thus, unlike in the digital model, in the e-commerce model and the service model, the underlying supply and the platform service would not be merged.

In adopting this view, it should be noted that the EU legislator considered that the distinct service provided by the platform should be regarded as an intermediation service.[966] According to the proposed Article 46a of the VAT Directive, the place of supply of the facilitation service provided to a non-taxable person by a platform, portal or similar means will be the place where the underlying transaction is supplied in accordance with the VAT Directive. This regulation should be viewed positively, as it will allow a uniform application of the rules on the place of supply of platform services. Nevertheless, the suggestion that the platform's facilitation service continues to exist alongside the legal fiction of two consecutive supplies has met with doctrinal opposition, which points out that it creates unnecessary complexity and inconsistency within the VAT system.[967]

The mechanics of the proposed Article 28a of the VAT Directive are illustrated in Figure 3.5.

Figure 3.5 Mode of Operation of the Proposed Article 28a of the VAT Directive

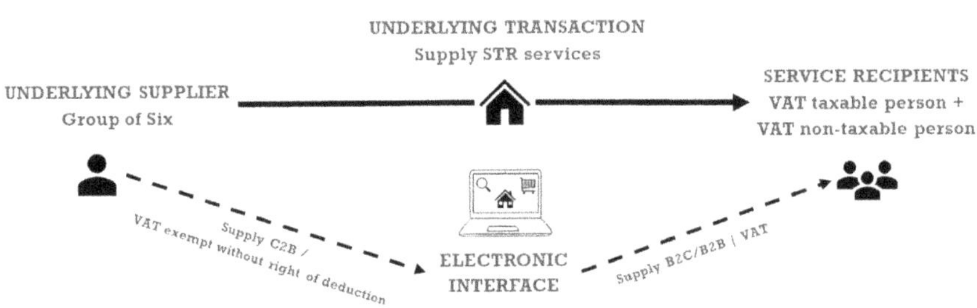

Source: Own compilation.

Unlike in the case of the e-commerce model, in the case of the service model, the Commission has not chosen to introduce specific arrangements for the moment when tax liability arises. Therefore, the general principles set out in Articles 63, 64 and 65 of the VAT Directive will apply.

965. Merkx and others (n. 381) 136–137.
966. Proposal for a Council Directive amending Directive 2006/112/EC as regards VAT rules for the digital age (n. 382).
967. Bal (n. 866).

It should also be noted that the plans to introduce a new regime may complicate the situation for tour operator platforms that benefit from a special TOMS. In order to avoid a potential conflict of regulations, the EU legislator decided that the TOMS would not apply to supplies made based on Article 28a of the VAT Directive (the proposed Article 306(3) of the VAT Directive). Therefore, a transaction for which a platform is the deemed supplier cannot be subject to the special scheme for travel agents. The EC, in recital 26 of the compromise text, also clarified that travel agents should not be included in the 'deemed supplier' rule.[968]

Despite this regulation, it is pointed out that there are still some issues regarding the relationship of these two regimes that need to be clarified. The Commission is currently analysing: (i) the scope of the services supplied to the platform and whether they can be regarded as supplies by a taxable person in the provision of travel facilities and (ii) the differentiation between STR platforms and OTAs.[969] The Commission notes that the TOMS usually applies where there is more than one supply that are 'packaged' together by the travel agent and sold as a single supply to the customer.[970] Many of the supplies which are facilitated by STR platforms would be single supplies only. While the CJEU has held, in C-552/17 *Alpenchalets Resorts*,[971] that the mere supply of holiday accommodation rented from another taxable person can be considered as a single supply under the special scheme for TOMS (this position was upheld by the judgment in C-108/22),[972] it is questionable as to whether the platform actually 'rents' the accommodation when it is deemed to be the supplier (it is in fact a facilitation service which is leading to the fiction of a deemed supply).[973] Nevertheless, in the EC's view, it would be necessary to add clarity to the legislation.

Furthermore, the VAT Directive does not define a travel agent, and the definition of electronic interfaces, as mentioned above, is very broad. So, in practice, the deemed supplier regime could apply even to OTAs. This would result in the undesirable situation where OTAs would be prevented from benefiting from the TOMS. However, the TOMS should not represent an escape route that would defeat the objectives of the

968. Draft Council Directive amending Directive 2006/112/EC as regards VAT rules for the digital age - compromise text 8 May 2024 (n. 382).
969. Asquith, 'EU Platform Economy Issues on Full Liability Model - VAT in the Digital Age' (n. 897).
970. European Commission, 'Group on the Future of VAT No 122: VAT and the Platform Economy - Focus on Specific Issues - Follow up, Taxud.c.1(2022)3461477' (n. 887).
971. *Alpenchalets Resorts GmbH v. Finanzamt München Abteilung Körperschaften* [2018] CJEU C-552/17.
972. The service provided by a taxable person, which consists in purchasing accommodation services from other taxable persons and reselling them to other economic operators, is covered by the special VAT scheme applicable to travel agents, even though those services are not accompanied by ancillary services. *Dyrektor Krajowej Informacji Skarbowej (TVA - Agrégateur de services hôteliers)* [2023] CJEU C-108/22; in the assessment of the doctrine in this matter, the CJEU made a practical decision to facilitate the taxable person's economic activity. However, this decision likely sparked controversy in certain Member States where TOMS application typically requires dealing with a 'complex' service, involving a bundle of multiple supplies. Fernando Matesanz, 'Present and Future Challenges of the Special VAT Scheme for Travel Agents' (2024) 35 International VAT Monitor 73 https://doi.org/10.59403/1n40s75.
973. European Commission, 'Group on the Future of VAT No 122: VAT and the Platform Economy - Focus on Specific Issues - Follow up, Taxud.c.1(2022)3461477' (n. 887).

deemed supplier regime.[974] However, platforms wishing to use the TOMS in this way would likely have to significantly change their business models and face significant legal consequences beyond the VAT sphere, including contractual liability of the supplier.[975]

The situation is further complicated by the fact that the EC has announced that it will propose an amendment to the VAT Directive in 2022/2023 to simplify the special scheme for travel agents and ensure a level playing field within the EU, taking into consideration the competitiveness of EU travel industry.[976] However, work has only just begun, so it is difficult to say when the new legislative proposal will actually arrive and how it will affect the complexity of the obligations of tourism sector platforms and the potential conflict with the deemed supplier regime.

6 SUMMARY

In essence, the deemed supplier regime is a mechanism introduced into the VAT system whereby the platform mediating the underlying transaction is liable to account for it for VAT purposes. This liability is therefore shifted from the supplier or underlying supplier to the platform.

The development of the platform economy has led the EU legislator to choose to include certain platforms in the VAT collection process, imposing the deemed supplier regime on them. This process occurred gradually and was correlated with the development of the platform economy within the EU. Initially, the platforms primarily facilitated users' distribution of various digital content. When there was a strong increase in this type of supply, this led to problems with VAT taxation, notably no VAT collection or an inappropriately low amount of VAT collection. In response, the EU legislator decided to introduce a rebuttable presumption in 2015, whereby platforms became liable for collecting VAT 'on behalf of' their actual suppliers in certain circumstances (the digital model of the deemed supplier regime).

In parallel, the e-commerce sector of the platform economy was thriving. Platforms intermediating the sale of goods enabled small consignments to be easily imported into the EU, resulting in, among other things, unfair competitive pressures on EU retailers in terms of VAT. This factor led the EU legislator to decide in 2021 to impose on platforms facilitating the supply of goods full liability for collecting VAT on the underlying supplies in certain cases (the e-commerce model of the deemed supplier regime).

The development of new technologies has also made it possible for platforms to mediate the supply of services in the real world, particularly in the area of accommodation. The growing popularity of this solution has begun to provide a competitive advantage for private operators and small businesses not paying VAT, as opposed to

974. European Commission, Directorate General for Taxation and Customs Union and others (n. 6) 115-116.
975. *Ibid.*, 151-153.
976. European Commission, 'An Action Plan for Fair and Simple Taxation Supporting the Recovery Strategy, COM(2020) 312 Final' (n. 45).

traditional suppliers (such as hotels) who are required to pay this tax. For this reason, the EU legislator plans to adopt solutions in 2027 according to which STR platforms will, in certain cases, bear the full liability for collecting VAT on underlying transactions when their hosts are not required to do so (the service model of the deemed supplier regime).

The EU legislator's approach means that platforms intermediating different transactions are not treated similarly. However, the difference in treatment may be justified because, as the CJEU points out, the EU legislator may take a step-by-step approach when introducing complex schemes.[977] The introduction of the digital model appears to have been only the first step in implementing a new policy to engage platforms in the collection of VAT on underlying transactions in order to simplify, strengthen and increase neutrality in the internal market.[978]

All three EU deemed supplier regime models are based on solutions proposed by the OECD which has analysed the different roles that platforms of the digital services sector,[979] the e-commerce sector,[980] and the accommodation and transport sectors[981] can play in VAT collection. OECD reports have no binding force, nor do they refer exclusively to the European VAT system. They should therefore not be taken into account when interpreting EU rules. Nevertheless, given the importance of coordinating an international approach to the VAT treatment of platform economies, the OECD proposals seem a good starting point for EU legislative work in this area.

977. *Société Arcelor Atlantique et Lorraine and Others v. Premier ministre, Ministre de l'Écologie et du Développement durable and Ministre de l'Économie, des Finances et de l'Industrie* [2008] CJEU C-127/07.
978. *See also*: Pollak (n. 339) 294–295. Nevertheless, in the author's opinion, the introduction of the e-commerce model represented the first step in implementing a new policy.
979. OECD, *Mechanisms for the Effective Collection of VAT/GST* (n. 550).
980. OECD, *The Role of Digital Platforms in the Collection of VAT/GST on Online Sales* (n. 551).
981. OECD, *The Impact of the Growth of the Sharing and Gig Economy on VAT/GST Policy and Administration* (n. 47).

CHAPTER 4

Evaluation of the Operation and Comparison of the EU Deemed Supplier Regime Models in the Context of STR Platforms

1 BACKGROUND

The development of the platform economy has prompted the EU legislator to introduce new solutions into the VAT system to ensure fair and efficient taxation of transactions made through platforms. One is the introduction of a special deemed supplier regime which shifts the liability for accounting for VAT from underlying suppliers to platforms. The third chapter discusses in detail the three models of the deemed supplier relating to platforms under the European VAT system: the digital model governed by Article 9a IR, the e-commerce model governed by Article 14a of the VAT Directive, and the service model to be governed by Article 28a of the VAT Directive assuming the amendments proposed by the EC come into force.

The purpose of this chapter is to assess the functioning of these models. The chapter will explore how these solutions affect or could potentially affect (in the case of the service model) entrepreneurs and, above all, platforms. In addition, the point of view of the administrative authorities regarding the issue at hand will be analysed.

This chapter will also compare the deemed supplier regime models from the perspective of the STR sector of the platform economy and will analyse whether the digital and e-commerce models could potentially apply to STR platforms. This will be followed by a general assessment of the functioning of the deemed supplier regime in the EU VAT system.

2 EVALUATION OF OPERATION OF THE EU MODELS OF THE DEEMED SUPPLIER REGIME

Turning to the assessment of the functioning of the deemed supplier regime models presented, it should be noted that this may vary depending on the status of the actors involved. To assess the different models, it is therefore necessary to consider how they can be viewed from the perspective of both the legislator and entrepreneurs (primarily platforms).

2.1 Evaluation of the Operation of the Digital Model

The development of the platform economy raises questions as to whether, and to what extent, the rules drafted for more traditional ways of doing business apply to new business models. It should be noted that the current law – supplemented by traditional rules of interpretation and developments in case law – does not cease to have effect simply because new technologies were not foreseen by their authors.[982] The relationship between Article 28 of the VAT Directive and Article 9a IR appears to be a good example of this phenomenon. The provision of Article 28 of the VAT Directive was already in place before the advent of the platform economy. With the emergence of new business models, questions have arisen as to whether and how to apply Article 28 of the VAT Directive to them. For this reason, the European legislator has chosen to clarify this provision in Article 9a IR but makes it applicable only to platforms intermediating in the supply of digital services.

Depending on the business model adopted, entrepreneurs have ambiguous opinions regarding the assessment of the functioning of the presumption established in Article 9a IR. As indicated in the report commissioned by the EC,[983] the following approaches can be distinguished in this regard:

(1) Companies providing their services through intermediaries.
For this type of companies, the introduction of the presumption was a good solution, mainly because they often have little contact with final consumers, which translates into difficulties in correctly calculating and collecting VAT. Therefore, in their view, Article 9a IR facilitates the application of the rules, although in some situations it is not easy to assess who is 'taking over' the tax obligations. In addition, companies have pointed out that when they deal with smaller platform operators, the contracts are usually not very clear or are out of line with reality.[984] Businesses have also expressed concerns about the possibility of being held liable by the tax authorities in cases when an

982. Brescia (n. 246) 159–160.
983. European Commission, Directorate General for Taxation and Customs Union and Deloitte (n. 601) 74–75, 199–201.
984. For example, there were situations where the agreement stated that the operator only allowed the use of its platform for content sales, while in reality, it also controlled the fees charged to the customer and defined the general terms of service.

intermediary (especially one not established in the EU) fails to pay the VAT due, despite its status as a deemed supplier.

(2) Intermediaries covered by the presumption (excluding telecommunications companies).
Some intermediaries (especially the larger ones) welcomed the introduction of the presumption, as it confirmed a practice that had already been in place in the market (these platforms often already acted as undisclosed agents even though the rules in force in this regard were not always clear). Although the cost of complying with the new rules proved to be high, they were well equipped to deal with the complexity of potentially having clients in 28 different Member States. However, for less typical platforms,[985] the introduction of Article 9a IR proved to be a challenge for which they had to incur additional expenses. It was pointed out that increased compliance costs for intermediaries might increase costs for platform users (the platform will increase its commission due to the new obligations). These platforms still offer their suppliers the opportunity to sell their services to a very wide audience.

(3) Telecommunications companies, potentially covered by the presumption.
Companies that allow consumers to purchase electronically supplied services by adding the price of the service to the bill for mobile telephone service have pointed out that in practice they quite often try to rebut the presumption. Depending on the Member State, however, they face different approaches to this issue. Some countries take the approach that such entities are always covered by the presumption, but others are not so restrictive.

However, it is generally accepted that Article 9a IR has increased legal certainty for entrepreneurs.[986] In the context of the platform economy, this is particularly important because, as pointed out in the literature, confusion surrounding rights and obligations discourages investments in this area.[987]

In addition, in the EC's perspective, this type of collection model using platforms for VAT accounting considerably simplifies the administrative burden for the underlying suppliers, especially smaller companies.[988] This is a helpful instrument for them to be able to deal with their tax obligations since its application greatly enhanced their VAT.[989] Indeed, these companies do not need to identify the location of each of these individual customers and comply with the different sets of VAT legislation in all the Member States – it is up to the platforms falling under the presumption of Article 9a

985. Entities were not initially created with the intention of establishing a platform (e.g., initially operated solely as social networks); however, in practice, their business models met the criteria of Article 9a IR. European Commission, Directorate General for Taxation and Customs Union and Deloitte (n. 601) 201–202.
986. Amand (n. 489) 242–243.
987. Smorto (n. 111) 112–113.
988. European Commission, Directorate General for Taxation and Customs Union and Deloitte (n. 601) 11.
989. *Ibid.*, 82.

IR.[990] In a way, this presumption seems to encourage smaller operators to carry out their business activities through platforms. According to the business input, trading through platforms is used widely by small businesses, as despite the cost of using such a platform, they find the burden of the place of supply determination and compliance (e.g., through MOSS) even higher.[991] Platforms, especially the larger ones, are also often much better equipped to handle a large number of clients, to determine the location of the customers, and to comply with relevant VAT rules, having usually set up powerful automated processes.[992] Therefore, the presumption established in Article 9a IR does not appear to place a disproportionate burden on platforms since it reflects their business models and often the existing VAT accounting practice.[993]

2.2 Evaluation of the Operation of the E-commerce Model

The rapid growth of e-commerce has made the EU legislator decide to introduce new solutions into the European VAT system. One element of the reform was to put operators of platforms facilitating certain supplies of goods under full liability for accounting for VAT on these transactions, shifting this obligation from the underlying suppliers to the platforms.

It is important to note that legislative intervention at EU level has had a positive impact on the harmonization of the rules regarding the obligations of e-commerce sector platforms. Even before the introduction of the deemed supplier regime, some Member States had already started to introduce individual solutions for the liability of platforms to account for underlying supplies. For example, Austria, the UK (even before Brexit) and Germany implemented secondary platform liability, whereby in certain circumstances platforms were liable for unpaid VAT by the supplier if the supplier did not fulfil its obligations.[994] The literature indicates that national liability regimes are likely to remain in place, but this raises questions from a proportionality perspective (if, in theory, all Member States were to introduce their own domestic liability regimes, the burden on platforms would become so great that it would seem impossible for them to be compliant).[995] It is rightly advocated that the already existing domestic rules in this regard should be abolished or linked to the EU harmonized rules.[996]

As the EC points out in its first preliminary assessment of the validity of the e-commerce VAT package, the reform bolsters compliance with VAT rules as it streamlines the VAT obligations of thousands of underlying sellers.[997] IOSS registration data shows that all major platforms have registered to use the import scheme. Early

990. *Ibid.*, 199.
991. *Ibid.*, 89.
992. *Ibid.*, 72–73.
993. *Ibid.*, 203–204.
994. Janssen (n. 479) 236.
995. *Ibid.*, 238–239.
996. *Ibid.*
997. Annex No 6 'E-commerce evaluation' to: European Commission, 'Impact Assessment Report, SWD(2022) 393 Final' (n. 362).

analysis also shows that the eight largest companies registered with IOSS accounted for approximately 91 % of all transactions reported for import into the EU via IOSS (EC data also shows that IOSS' capacity to counter fraud and VAT losses due to undervaluation generated additional revenue of approximately EUR 270 million VAT in the six months of the functioning of the VAT e-commerce package).[998] Member States collected almost EUR 20 billion in VAT revenue in 2022 via the new OSS and IOSS systems (Member States collected more than EUR 17 billion through the expanded OSS portal, in addition to collecting EUR 2.5 billion in VAT revenues on e-commerce imports).[999] In the EC's view, these statistics highlight the positive impact that the deemed supplier regime has had on compliance. As a result of the new regulations, efforts to ensure compliance are now focused on a much smaller number of large players in the market, who account for most low-value imports into the EU. This is beneficial for the tax authorities who only must monitor a limited number of taxable persons for the supply of goods via platforms, leading to VAT being more easily collected by them.[1000] The data also shows that, overall, VAT revenue collected via the new systems has seen a 26% increase compared to the 2021 figures.[1001] This demonstrates the success of the reform and appears to justify plans to cover by the deemed supplier regime in the e-commerce model new transactions.[1002] However, it should be noted that the VAT e-commerce package consisted of a number of measures, one of which was the deemed supplier regime, so it is difficult to assess what effect this one particular element of the larger reform has had.

As the burden of VAT on the supply of goods is shifted to the platforms, the underlying suppliers are seen as the 'big winners' of the introduction of Article 14a of the VAT Directive in addition to the tax authorities.[1003] With the introduction of the reform, the number of their VAT accounting obligations has decreased significantly. However, as pointed out in the legal literature, it is not entirely clear why the EU legislator has not abolished in its entirety (or at least provided Member States with the possibility to do so) the obligation to register taxable persons for VAT purposes and to submit VAT returns for the underlying suppliers when this tax does not become due because of the application of Article 14a of the VAT Directive.[1004]

998. European Commission, 'New EU VAT Rules for E-Commerce: Updated Revenue Figures Point to a Successful Implementation', https://taxation-customs.ec.europa.eu/news/new-eu-vat-rules-e-commerce-updated-revenue-figures-point-successful-implementation-2022-05-23_en accessed 9 May 2023.

999. *Ibid.*

1000. Pollak (n. 339) 296.

1001. European Commission, 'New EU VAT Rules for E-Commerce' (n. 987).

1002. It is also worth noting that in Australia, where similar solutions to those in the EU have been in place since 1 July 2018, the Australian legislature also positively assessed the new arrangements. According to the Australian government, the primary benefits of this collection mechanism include enhanced tax neutrality, competitive fairness for Australian retailers, additional government revenue, and relatively minimal administrative costs. In contrast to the border model, this approach incurs lower administrative expenses for the government and helps avoid potential delays and disruptions in goods delivery for consumers. Guglyuvatyy and Milogolov (n. 680) 33.

1003. Pollak (n. 339) 263.

1004. *Ibid.*

While undoubtedly shifting the obligation to account for VAT to platforms in certain circumstances is a great convenience for entrepreneurs trading through them, it is certainly the case that the new rules do not make accounting easier for the platforms themselves. As is rightly pointed out in the literature, to comply with the new obligations, platforms must closely monitor the underlying supplies that take place through them.[1005] Platforms need to be able to determine what the value of the supply is (above or below EUR 150), where the goods are at the time of supply and whether the underlying suppliers are established within the EU and prepare their systems to meet the new invoicing requirements. This requires close cooperation with the underlying suppliers who should communicate the relevant information to the platforms, and the platforms should check it and take action in case of error or insufficient data.[1006] The literature also highlights the risk for platforms associated with tax authorities seeking to recover VAT from the platform whenever their IOSS numbers have been fraudulently used. This issue arises because the import exemption is granted when a valid IOSS number is included in the import declaration. In practice, it is no secret that the IOSS numbers of major platforms can be found online and are being abused by dishonest traders.[1007] Currently, there seems to be no effective means for platforms to prevent this fraud.[1008] Furthermore, from the operational point of view, it also seems clear that no platform can risk not monitoring payments – when platforms are required to pay VAT, they should be able to deduct it to avoid the need for early funding. This means that, in practice, payments will go through them and not directly through the underlying suppliers, as otherwise the platforms would have to constantly go after the underlying suppliers about transferring to them the funds to pay VAT.[1009] Although full control of underlying deliveries and payments is already in place on the most established platforms, the new deemed supplier regime will impact those platforms that, in line with their business model, do not have this level of control.[1010] It should also be considered that this may lead to blurring the boundary between platforms and financial institutions (payment institutions). In particular, a platform deemed to be a supplier and making simultaneous payments between two parties to the underlying transaction, in addition to being required to account for that transaction for VAT

1005. Scarcella (n. 391) 14.
1006. Lamensch and others (n. 104) 459.
1007. It is worth noting that the EC, in the ViDA package, plans to introduce paragraph 1a to Article 143, according to which the Commission shall adopt an implementing act to introduce special measures to prevent certain forms of tax evasion or avoidance by, *inter alia*, linking the unique consignment number with the corresponding VAT identification number. This solution raises some concerns in the doctrine regarding whether the added protection against fraud might exceed the associated compliance burden. Allocating a unique transaction number to each transaction may be considered an additional burden. Lamensch and others (n. 143).
1008. *Ibid.*
1009. In this context, it is worth noting the solution in Japan, where the Platform Taxation Regime applies only if the underlying supplier receives consideration for their electronic services through the digital platform. This requirement excludes cases where platform operators would have difficulty passing on the consumption tax burden effectively to the supplier because the platform is not an intermediary in the payment flow from the consumer to the supplier. Masuda (n. 656) 106.
1010. Lamensch and others (n. 104) 459–460.

purposes, could also be required to report information on those payments to the tax authorities based on the Payment Service Providers Reporting Directive,[1011] which would inevitably increase its operating costs.[1012] There is also a risk that if the new obligations force platforms to change their business model, but users will not want to pay for this, this could mean that the platform will be making losses, which will threaten its existence. The same is true for situations when the platform needs to obtain a lot of information from suppliers in an environment where they can easily switch to another platform.[1013]

In light of these risks, we should expect to see a change in the business models of platforms which may, for example, choose to arrange shipping themselves for all transactions they facilitate. Platforms may also be reluctant to offer goods from underlying suppliers established in third countries, as this could trigger the deemed supplier regime.[1014] One may wonder whether such a disruption of their existing business models is desirable,[1015] and raises the question of to what extent it is proportionate.[1016]

It is worth noting, however, that in Australia, despite initial concerns,[1017] large international suppliers of digital services and products have expressed a willingness to comply with the GST rules which require platforms to register and bear tax liability for intangible supplies and imports of low-value goods. There is also no evidence that offshore platforms have left the Australian market due to their new obligations.[1018] This is also a good signal for the EU market.

In addition, it is pointed out that the adopted regulations do not provide for measures enabling the enforcement of compliance by non-EU suppliers and platforms.[1019] In the absence of enhanced international cooperation with third countries, the enforceability of the new VAT rules on e-commerce may, thus, become rather problematic.[1020] It is therefore right to call for stronger cooperation between customs and tax authorities of the different Member States[1021] and for enhanced international

1011. On 18 February 2020, a new set of regulations was adopted, requiring payment service providers to record certain information about payment transactions and report this information to the tax authorities of EU Member States starting from 1 January 2024. Council Directive (EU) 2020/284 of 18 February 2020 amending Directive 2006/112/EC as regards introducing certain requirements for payment service providers [OJ L 62, 2.3.2020, pp. 7-12].
1012. Giorgio Beretta and Mariken van Hilten, 'The New VAT Record Keeping and Reporting Obligations for Payment Service Providers' (2020) 31 International VAT Monitor 181 https://doi.org/10.59403/1b22nh3.
1013. Lamensch and others (n. 104) 475–477.
1014. Pollak (n. 339) 311.
1015. Lamensch and others (n. 104) 462–464.
1016. Pollak (n. 339) 296–297.
1017. In their submissions to the Australian Senate Economics Legislation Committee, platforms such as eBay, Alibaba, and Etsy expressed concern that they would be held responsible for GST on goods they never owned or tracked, suggesting that the introduced system would be complex and costly to administer, and it is likely that its costs will be passed on to consumers. Guglyuvatyy and Milogolov (n. 680) 41.
1018. *Ibid.*, 33.
1019. Papis-Almansa (n. 662) 221–222.
1020. Beretta and van Hilten (n. 1000) 173.
1021. Scarcella (n. 391) 14.

administrative cooperation, including relevant arrangements in the customs area.[1022] It is also important to have more alignment between national approaches (Member States may decide that an entity other than the one liable for the payment of VAT, for example, the platform operator, will be jointly and severally liable for this). It is not clear how the rules applicable to national platforms can be linked to the conditions imposed on them under the EU deemed supplier regime.[1023]

For this reason, the EU legislator should continue to work on further changes and tools to better achieve the intended objectives, as well as regularly review any criteria used to define the eligibility of platforms for the deemed supplier regime to ensure their effectiveness.[1024]

2.3 Evaluation of the Operation of the Service Model

The introduction of the service model can be seen as a replication of the strategy introduced as part of the VAT e-commerce package. As with the e-commerce model, the plan to introduce harmonized solutions at Community level for the STR sector of the platform economy should be welcomed.[1025] Otherwise, Member States might start acting unilaterally or adding obligations to solutions developed at EU level, which could lead to disruption and complications for businesses, including STR platforms.

In addition, according to the EU legislator, the adoption of the service model should result in a significant increase in VAT revenue.[1026] This is due to two factors. First, the VAT tax base will be broadened – several transactions that are currently exempt or outside the scope of the VAT system will be taxed. The introduction of the deemed supplier regime for STR and transport services is expected to increase VAT revenues across the EU.[1027] Member States would be expected to collect additional VAT revenues of EUR 6.6 billion per year over a 10-year period.[1028] Second, the burden of compliance will be shifted from small suppliers to the platform, making it easier for Member States to control transactions.[1029] Despite all the uncertainties, it can be expected that the reduction of the number of taxable persons in charge of paying VAT from millions of providers to thousands of platforms will markedly increase the ability of tax administrations to monitor VAT obligations.[1030]

1022. OECD, *The Role of Digital Platforms in the Collection of VAT/GST on Online Sales* (n. 551) 48–49.
1023. Janssen (n. 479) 231.
1024. Scarcella (n. 391) 6.
1025. As indicated in the literature, considering the impact of the platform economy on the internal market as a whole, the EU has competence to regulate the platform economy of the services sector. Finck (n. 17) 263–265.
1026. European Commission, 'Impact Assessment Report, SWD(2022) 393 Final' (n. 362).
1027. European Commission, Directorate General for Taxation and Customs Union and others (n. 6) 134–135.
1028. European Commission, 'How Bringing VAT into the Digital Age Can Help Restore a Level Playing-Field in the Hospitality Sector', (n. 838).
1029. European Commission, 'Impact Assessment Report, SWD(2022) 393 Final' (n. 362).
1030. European Commission, Directorate General for Taxation and Customs Union and others (n. 6) 140; Pollak (n. 339) 296.

It is also pointed out that indirect benefits of enhanced compliance are very likely because the understatement of turnover to remain below the VAT threshold,[1031] which is one of the main sources of non-compliance in the platform economy, will no longer lead to the evasion of the VAT due on their supplies.[1032] Even a low increase in compliance (5 percentage points) would generate between EUR 1 and EUR 3 billion in additional VAT revenue per year between 2023 and 2032, a moderate increase (10 percentage points) between EUR 2 and EUR 6 billion, and a high increase (20 percentage points) between EUR 4 and EUR 11 billion.[1033] In addition, clarifying the existing VAT rules for the platform economy will increase legal certainty, which should result in a reduction of the current VAT burdens, estimated at around EUR 1.9 billion.[1034]

It should be also noted that the service model of DSR indirectly addresses issues associated with the growth of platform economies in the STR sector, as described in the second chapter. This model ensures that hosts operating through platforms, regardless of whether they are considered taxable persons or not, will be subject to VAT. Consequently, this should eliminate any competitive advantage they may have over traditional VAT-registered entrepreneurs. Furthermore, assuming that Article 28a of the VAT Directive will function in a similar manner to Article 28, the service of intermediation provided by the platform would 'disappear' for VAT purposes as it becomes integrated with the underlying service.[1035] This indirectly resolves the issue related to the nature of services facilitated by STR platforms.

At this stage, it is difficult to anticipate whether the implementation of the new deemed supplier regime into the EU VAT system will have the desired effect. In the EP's view, the deemed supplier regime is not suitable for services at all, especially for services provided within the EU.[1036] Nevertheless, it is pointed out that in Canada, where similar solutions have been adopted, they have successfully contributed to levelling the playing field.[1037]

1031. As indicated in the doctrine, failure to register typically happens, although not exclusively, when small businesses have annual turnovers slightly above the registration threshold. This form of evasion is particularly prevalent among businesses mainly involved in B2C transactions, as they lack an incentive to request invoices. Rita de la Feria and Anculien Schoeman, 'Addressing VAT Fraud in Developing Countries: The Tax Policy-Administration Symbiosis' (2019) 47 Intertax 953 https://doi.org/10.54648/taxi2019096.
1032. European Commission, Directorate General for Taxation and Customs Union and others (n. 6) 157–159.
1033. *Ibid.*, 140.
1034. European Commission, 'Impact Assessment Report, SWD(2022) 393 Final' (n. 362).
1035. According to the legal doctrine, the wording of proposed Article 46a of the VAT Directive suggests that the facilitation service by the platform exists in addition to the deemed supply of the accommodation services. This, however, does not clearly stem from the wording of Article 28a of the VAT Directive, the disposition of which almost literally copies Article 28 of the VAT Directive. Based on arguments of coherence of the system, the authors submit that Article 28a of the VAT Directive should be interpreted as resulting in the same legal consequences as Article 28 of the VAT Directive. Papis-Almansa and Sroka (n. 907).
1036. European Parliament, 'Amendments to Directive 2006/112/EC as Regards VAT Rules for the Digital Age, 2022/0407(CNS)' (n. 859).
1037. European Commission, 'How Bringing VAT into the Digital Age Can Help Restore a Level Playing-Field in the Hospitality Sector' (n. 838).

The proposed changes will certainly also have a direct impact on platforms and underlying suppliers, as well as an indirect impact on traditional suppliers.

Platforms may have several objections to the proposed model of the deemed supplier regime. These broadly coincide with the concerns raised about the e-commerce model, i.e.: (i) the need for platforms to put in place IT infrastructure to ensure the proper functioning of the regime and the need to adapt business and payment models that are not adapted to the new obligations;[1038] (ii) the need to handle new information obligations or to extend the scope of the existing ones, in particular for platforms to handle VAT numbers and to confirm the status of the underlying suppliers;[1039] and (iii) the need for platforms in some cases to obtain a valid VAT registration in a Member State other than the country of their establishment.[1040]

However, as with the e-commerce model, it is pointed out that platforms are highly automated and can therefore cope with VAT obligations quite easily.[1041] In addition, the underlying transactions are likely to be recorded and annotated by the platforms already in the present situation; hence, the additional burdens are unlikely to involve the creation of new IT procedures but probably the adaptation of the existing ones.[1042] Many platforms (such as Airbnb and HomeExchange) are involved in receiving and processing payments made by their users and can therefore be said to have effective means to collect and remit VAT.[1043] The need for platforms to obtain new VAT registrations can be a significant burden, given that obtaining and operating a foreign VAT number can cost up to EUR 20,000 per year. However, platforms can use the OSS to minimize this cost.[1044]

The deemed supplier regime will also change the situation for some of the hosts providing accommodation services through platforms who belong to the underlying suppliers that do not charge VAT. While the compliance costs of the platforms are expected to increase, these are expected to be overcompensated by compliance cost savings on the side of the underlying suppliers.[1045] The new regulations are expected to increase VAT collection without placing an undue burden on small suppliers.[1046] These suppliers will not be required to register and account for VAT itself, thus bearing no additional burden.[1047]

1038. Asquith, 'Co-Opting Gig & Sharing Platforms as Tax Collectors' (n. 440).
1039. European Commission, Directorate General for Taxation and Customs Union and others (n. 6) 150–151.
1040. To comply with these new VAT obligations, platforms will need to register in all Member States where they engage in transactions, or alternatively, register in one Member State to apply the OSS system. Gallardo and Echevarría (n. 903).
1041. Evans and Krever (n. 675) 147.
1042. European Commission, Directorate General for Taxation and Customs Union and others (n. 6) 150–151.
1043. Beretta (n. 344) 298–301.
1044. European Commission, Directorate General for Taxation and Customs Union and others (n. 6) 150–151.
1045. European Commission, 'VAT Expert Group No 095: VAT Treatment of the Sharing Economy, Taxud.c.1(2020)5816454' (n. 338).
1046. Thang and Shatalow (n. 422) 436.
1047. European Commission, 'Impact Assessment Report, SWD(2022) 393 Final' (n. 362).

In addition, the potential burden of providing a VAT number or declaring not having one is likely to be limited. It is acknowledged that for registered taxable persons, the communication of a VAT number would not be an additional requirement, and for non-taxable persons, it would probably mean giving a few additional click-approved statements during the registration process confirming their status as non-taxable persons.[1048]

However, according to platforms, collecting any further information from individuals for tax purposes often deters them from the signing-up process and consequently undermines their own growth – many of the most successful marketplaces are built on the freelance model, and imposing VAT obligations could severely curtail or even terminate their activities.[1049] In addition, the supplies made by the underlying suppliers that do not charge VAT will become subject to VAT, which could have a significant negative impact on the earnings or margins of these suppliers and create a disincentive for them to use the platforms.[1050] At the same time, the accommodation services provided by these underlying suppliers will continue to be untaxed by VAT if they are not supplied through platforms, which could put the platforms' business model at a potential disadvantage. The additional VAT may result in an increase in the prices for final consumers, thereby reducing the demand for accommodation services offered via platforms, and it may also contribute to a drop in earnings for hosts, thus diminishing the attractiveness of the STR market.[1051] It is therefore possible that some entities from the group of the underlying suppliers that do not charge VAT will move all or part of their business to the traditional direct sale channel to retain their VAT exemption.[1052] This situation does not appear to be beneficial from a labour market point of view. Studies show that the jobs created by the platform economy cannot be fully substituted by traditional channels.[1053]

It is also worth noting that under the new model of the deemed supplier, the underlying supplier that does not charge VAT will not be entitled to deduct input VAT, whereas other entities operating through platforms, and being VAT registered, will be entitled to do so. This will put these underlying suppliers at a competitive disadvantage. Therefore, it is noted that it is likely that some entities from the group of the underlying suppliers that do not charge VAT will decide to register their activities as VAT taxable persons to gain the right to deduct input tax.[1054] However, this will mean

1048. The burden may be small but not insignificant for VAT-exempt taxpayers who may be required to familiarize themselves with the new requirement, submit periodic declarations, and potentially some supporting documents if requested. However, it is unlikely that such a declaration would require more than one to two hours in the first year, and significantly less for annual confirmations. The cost of one event would therefore be EUR 18–36. European Commission, Directorate General for Taxation and Customs Union and others (n. 6) 150–151.

1049. Asquith, 'Co-Opting Gig & Sharing Platforms as Tax Collectors' (n. 440).

1050. OECD, *The Impact of the Growth of the Sharing and Gig Economy on VAT/GST Policy and Administration* (n. 47) 77–79.

1051. European Commission, Directorate General for Taxation and Customs Union and others (n. 6) 147–150.

1052. *Ibid.*, 143–147.

1053. Niemniej wskazuje się równiez, ze zmiany w zakresie VAT wpływają na rynek pracy tylko w niewielkim stopniu. *Ibid.*, ss 147–150.

1054. *Ibid.*, 157–159.

the need to bear additional VAT compliance costs.[1055] This choice appears to depend on the trade-off between the benefits from input tax deduction and the additional VAT compliance costs. It is understood that this becomes likely above a certain turnover threshold, amounting to no less than EUR 10,000 per year.[1056]

With the above in mind, there seems to be a risk that if non-professional hosts are automatically treated as professionals, this may dissuade them from providing STR services through platforms.[1057] However, despite the inconvenience of introducing the deemed supplier regime, it is pointed out that small suppliers would still enjoy the simplifications associated with their VAT status while benefitting from the platform's network effects.[1058]

The proposed solutions will also have an indirect impact on hosts operating through platforms that are not underlying suppliers that do not charge VAT and therefore not covered by the deemed supplier regime and on traditional suppliers such as hotels and guesthouses. Both these groups are engaged in the business of providing accommodation services and are generally subject to VAT on this. Therefore, their competitive situation, at least under the EU VAT system, is comparable. However, these entities have to compete with the underlying suppliers that do not charge VAT, operating through platforms, which does not have to pay this tax.[1059] It is pointed out that the services provided by traditional suppliers and these entities are in fact very similar and in many cases meet the same needs in the same market.[1060] It can therefore be considered that the introduction of the deemed supplier regime will ensure that this competitive advantage is eliminated.

It is worth noting that ensuring a level playing field between the traditional economy and the platform economy is a very important issue.[1061] With the deemed supplier regime, all services offered by the STR platform economy will be subject to VAT, which will eliminate the existing tax-induced advantage of hosts using platforms who were previously untaxed over traditional suppliers.[1062]

1055. *Ibid.*, 143–147.
1056. *Ibid.*
1057. European Commission, Directorate General for Internal Market, Industry, Entrepreneurship and SMEs, VVA, and Spark Legal Network (n. 48) 51–52.
1058. European Commission, Directorate General for Taxation and Customs Union and others (n. 6) 157–159.
1059. In Europe, the cost of accommodation booked through a platform can be on average 8% to 17% cheaper than the average daily rate of a regional hotel, and up to 70% of underlying service providers using the platform are not registered for VAT purposes (although this varies depending on the type of platform). Proposal for a Council Directive amending Directive 2006/112/EC as regards VAT rules for the digital age (n. 382).
1060. Matesanz, 'IVA La Vida. Primera Parte. IVA y Economía Colaborativa' (n. 868).
1061. According to the majority of respondents assessing the ViDA initiative, ensuring equal opportunities between traditional and platform economies (uniform treatment) is considered very important or important. European Commission, 'Summary Report. Public Consultation on the VAT in the Digital Age Initiative', https://ec.europa.eu/info/law/better-regulation/have-your-say/initiatives/13186-VAT-in-the-digital-age/F_en accessed 27 November 2022.
1062. It is generally accepted that VAT exemption plays a role in price differences, at least in the B2C market, and that VAT can have a direct impact on distorting the final market price of services competing in the same (or very close) relevant markets. European Commission, Directorate General for Taxation and Customs Union and others (n. 6) 143–147.

This seems particularly significant for entrepreneurs who benefit from the SME exemption due to operating below a specified threshold. It is worth noting that many countries imposing VAT adopt a registration threshold to exempt small businesses from the VAT system, as compliance burdens would be most severe for them, setting this threshold at a level that does not significantly impact VAT revenues. However, the distinction created by this threshold between businesses excluded from VAT and those fully integrated into the tax system leads to competitive distortions.[1063] These reduced tax burdens and compliance costs for unregistered enterprises incentivize businesses selling primarily to final consumers to remain below the threshold through real output changes or through avoidance or evasion activities. Empirical studies clearly show businesses bunching below a registration threshold in jurisdictions where this research has been conducted.[1064]

For this reason, the option to grant Member States the right to exclude SMEs from the scope of the deeming supplier rule seems highly detrimental, in terms of harmonizing the entire EU VAT tax system. Such a solution is likely to undermine the very purpose of introducing the deemed supplier regime for accommodation platforms, which is to level the playing field between traditional businesses and entities operating through platforms.[1065]

There are also other doubts as to whether the proposed solution will prevent distortions of competition in the STR market. First, it should be noted that VAT is not the only legal factor determining a competitive advantage for hosts operating through platforms. Such factors also include the different regulatory framework applicable to professional and private suppliers, as well as the higher risk of income tax evasion for the latter.[1066] Second, as indicated in the first chapter, the unambiguously negative impact of the platform economy on the traditional hotel industry is not a foregone conclusion. The results of some studies suggest that Airbnb renters do not treat hotels and other STR options as close substitutes, which means that taxing Airbnb is not an effective policy lever for those seeking to reduce Airbnb market activity in a given area.[1067] Evidence from some case studies also suggests that C2C accommodation offers do not have a negative impact on traditional operators. Thus, they do not deter travellers from booking hotels, indicating that the two offers are complementary.[1068] The competition for traditional accommodation suppliers seems to come from professional hosts using platforms,[1069] who include owners of several properties and investors who buy or rent flats or entire buildings, usually in the most tourism-oriented

1063. Zu (n. 333) 310.
1064. *Ibid.*, 345.
1065. Papis-Almansa and Sroka (n. 907).
1066. European Commission, Directorate General for Taxation and Customs Union and others (n. 6) 143–147.
1067. Bibler, Teltser and Tremblay (n. 441) 167.
1068. European Commission, Directorate General for Internal Market, Industry, Entrepreneurship and SMEs, VVA, and Spark Legal Network (n. 48) 41–43.
1069. Sigala (n. 179) 167.

areas of cities.[1070] It can be expected that such hosts are already required to register for and pay VAT, as are hotels, so that the business environment is level for them in this aspect. However, the deemed supplier regime will not apply to these entities. Therefore, if the activities of such operators are assumed to be in direct competition with the traditional accommodation industry, the introduction of the deemed supplier regime will not solve this problem. This regime will only affect small non-professional hosts (sub)renting their properties occasionally through platforms, who are probably not in direct competition with hotels.

Given these doubts, the introduction of this deemed supplier regime may prove controversial. Therefore, it seems worthwhile to observe countries implementing intermediary collection models to assess, among others: (i) how effective the collection is, (ii) whether it operates in a neutral manner, and (iii) whether the compliance costs justify the use of this mechanism.[1071] Additionally, it seems feasible to introduce the regime gradually. Initially, it could only apply to the largest platforms exceeding a certain revenue threshold and remain optional for smaller platforms.

3 COMPARISON OF THE EU MODELS OF THE DEEMED SUPPLIER REGIME

The deemed supplier regime models presented in the third chapter differ, but they also have some common features. Table 4.1 presents a summary of their key features and mechanisms.

Table 4.1 Comparison of EU Deemed Supplier Regimes for Platforms

	Digital Model	*E-commerce Model*	*Service Model*
General legal basis	Article 9a IR	Article 14a of the VAT Directive	Article 28a of the VAT Directive (project)
Specific provisions		Articles 31–33, 36b, 66a, 136a, 169, 205, 219a–221, 242, 242a of the VAT Directive and Articles 5b, 5c, 5d, 41a, 54b, 54c, 63c IR	Articles 46a, 135(3), 136b, 172a, 242a, 306 of the VAT Directive (project) and Article 9b–9g IR (project)
Status	Presumption (but practically impossible to challenge by the platform operator)	Provision imposing liability on platforms when certain conditions are met	Provision imposing liability on platforms when certain conditions are met

1070. Such investors represent over 70% of listings on major accommodation platforms in some of the most touristy cities, such as Barcelona and Lisbon. European Commission, Directorate General for Taxation and Customs Union and others (n. 6) 147–150.

1071. Millar (n. 384) 22.

	Digital Model	*E-commerce Model*	*Service Model*
Aims	Ensuring legal certainty to various entities involved in the transaction chain by clearly specifying who is the service provider		
	Ensuring effective and proper collection of VAT	Ensuring effective and proper collection of VAT	Ensuring effective and proper collection of VAT
		Limiting the administrative burden for underlying suppliers and tax administrations	Limiting the administrative burden for underlying suppliers and tax administrations
		Reducing the competitive advantage of suppliers from third countries over suppliers from the EU	Ensuring equal opportunities for traditional businesses competing with entities offering services through platforms
Legislative process	Controversies regarding the validity of Article 9a of the IR. Ultimately, it was determined that this provision is valid (judgment of the CJEU in the *Fenix* case)	Controversies regarding the adoption of Article 14a of the VAT Directive without an impact assessment concerning its subsidiarity and proportionality	
	The Subject Aspect		
Taxable persons	Operators of interface or a portal such as a marketplace for applications	Operators of electronic interface such as a marketplace, platform, portal or similar means	Operators of electronic interface such as a marketplace, platform, portal, or similar means
Type of activity	Taking part in a supply of services (in platform's own name but on behalf of the provider of those services)	Facilitating specific types of deliveries	Facilitating specific types of services

	Digital Model	*E-commerce Model*	*Service Model*
		'Facilitates' means the use of an electronic interface to allow a customer and a supplier offering goods for sale through the electronic interface to enter into contact, which results in a supply of goods through that electronic interface	'Facilitates' shall mean the use of an electronic interface to allow a customer and a supplier offering supplies of short-term accommodation rental or passenger transport through the electronic interface to enter into contact, which results in a supply of those services through that electronic interface
	Exception: provider is explicitly indicated as the supplier by that taxable person and that is reflected in the contractual arrangements between the parties. The following conditions shall be met: (a) the invoice issued or made available by each taxable person taking part in the supply of the electronically supplied services must identify such services and the supplier thereof; (b) the bill or receipt issued or made available to the customer must identify the electronically supplied services and the supplier thereof		

	Digital Model	*E-commerce Model*	*Service Model*
Excluded entities		Platform: (a) does not set, either directly or indirectly, any of the terms and conditions under which the supply of goods is made; (b) is not, either directly or indirectly, involved in authorizing the charge to the customer in respect of the payment made; (c) is not, either directly or indirectly, involved in the ordering or delivery of the goods	Platform: (a) does not set, either directly or indirectly, any of the terms and conditions under which the supply is made; (b) is not, either directly or indirectly, involved in authorizing the charge to the customer in respect of the payments made; (c) is not, either directly or indirectly, involved in the provision of those services
	Platform which only provides for processing of payments in respect of electronically supplied services or of telephone services provided through the internet, including VoIP	Platform which only provides the processing of payments in relation to the supply of goods	Platform which only provides the processing of payments in relation to the supply of short-term accommodation rental
	Platform which does not take part in the supply of electronically supplied services or telephone services	Platform which only provides the listing or advertising of goods	Platform which only provides the listing or advertising of short-term accommodation rental or passenger transport
		Platform which only provides the redirecting or transferring of customers to other electronic interfaces where goods are offered for sale, without any further intervention in the supply	Platform which only provides the redirecting or transferring of customers to other electronic interfaces where short-term accommodation rental is offered for sale, without any further intervention in the supply

	Digital Model	*E-commerce Model*	*Service Model*
Limitation of platform liability		Platform shall not be held liable for the payment of VAT in excess of the VAT which he declared and paid on these supplies where all of the following conditions are met:	Where, on the basis of information supplied by the person providing the underlying service, the platform does not act as the deemed supplier, that platform shall not be held liable for the payment of the VAT due should it be subsequently found that that platform should have been deemed to be the supplier, where all of the following conditions are met:
		(a) Platform is dependent on information provided by suppliers selling goods through platform or by other third parties in order to correctly declare and pay the VAT on those supplies	(a) Platform is dependent on information provided by the supplier of the services
		(b) The information is erroneous	(b) The information is erroneous
		(c) Platform can demonstrate that he did not and could not reasonably know that this information was incorrect	(c) Platform can prove that he or she did not and could not reasonably have known that that information was erroneous
		The Object Aspect	
Transactions covered by the regime	Electronically supplied services	Distance sales of goods imported from third territories or third countries in consignments of an intrinsic value not exceeding EUR 150	Supply of short-term accommodation rental

	Digital Model	*E-commerce Model*	*Service Model*
	Telephone services provided through the internet, including VoIP	The supply of goods within the Community by a taxable person not established within the Community to a non-taxable person	Supply passenger transport
		The transfer of own goods (project)	
Type of underlying transaction	No limitation	B2C	C2C, C2B
Determining the status of users	Unless he has information to the contrary, the supplier may regard a customer established within the Community as a non-taxable person when he can demonstrate that the customer has not communicated his individual VAT identification number to him	Unless he has information to the contrary, the platform shall regard: (a) the person selling goods through platform as a taxable person; (b) the person buying those goods as a non-taxable person.	Platform shall regard the person to whom those services were supplied as a non-taxable person where that person to whom those services were supplied does not provide a VAT identification number, unless that taxable person has information to the contrary
		Mode of Operation	
Main principles	Legal fiction of two identical services provided consecutively	Legal fiction of two consecutive supplies of goods	Legal fiction of two consecutive supplies of service
		Underlying transactions are currently subject to VAT; the deemed supplier regime means that the platform only 'replaces' the underlying supplier in the VAT settlement	Underlying transactions are currently outside the scope of VAT; the deemed supplier regime means that these transactions will be taxed and settled by platforms

	Digital Model	*E-commerce Model*	*Service Model*
Chargeable event	General principles of the VAT Directive (Articles 63–66)	Exception: the chargeable event of the supply of goods by platform and of the supply of goods to that platform shall occur, and VAT shall become chargeable at the time when the payment has been accepted	General principles of the VAT Directive (Articles 63–66)
Relation of underlying supply and platform fee	The service provided by the platform should be treated as integrated with the commissioned service – the platform will charge VAT on the total price of the service, not just on the agreed fee or commission for the intermediary service	Controversial issue: according to one perspective, the platform may still provide separate services. Another viewpoint suggests that the service provided by the platform should be treated as integrated with the commissioned service	Controversial issue: according to one perspective, the platform may still provide separate services. Another viewpoint suggests that the service provided by the platform should be treated as integrated with the commissioned service

Source: Own compilation.

While these models have considerable similarities in terms of the subject aspect and essentially the mechanisms, they differ quite substantially in terms of the object aspect. Of course, this difference is understandable, given the nature of the underlying transactions facilitated by the platforms. As the OECD points out, for the purpose of consumption taxes, the supply of digitized products should not be treated as a supply of goods.[1072] For example, the supply of electronic services is generally subject to a single VAT rate, but in the case of goods, there are many differences in VAT rates between categories of goods and between different Member States. The same is true for non-electronic services. Furthermore, in the case of the sale of goods and 'physical' services (such as STRs), certain aspects of the transaction or payment processing are carried out directly between buyer and seller, i.e., without the involvement of the platform (shipment of goods, handover of keys), which contrasts with the position of the intermediary in the supply of digital services which almost always appears to be involved in the delivery of the product. Paradoxically, although both the digital and service models refer to platforms that facilitate the supply of services, electronic and STR services respectively, there is a much greater similarity in terms of regulatory

1072. OECD, 'Electronic Commerce: Taxation Framework Conditions. A Report by the Committee on Fiscal Affairs, as Presented to Ministers at the OECD Ministerial Conference "A Borderless World: Realising the Potential of Electronic Commerce" on 8 October 1998'.

structure between the service model and the e-commerce model which includes platforms that facilitate the delivery of goods.

This difference also appears to be due to the fact that the digital model was introduced into the EU VAT system much earlier than the e-commerce and service models (in 2015, the e-commerce model appeared in 2021, and the service model is likely to come into force in 2027). Furthermore, the digital model, unlike the e-commerce and service models, is actually regulated by only one provision – Article 9a IR which provides further details of Article 28 of the VAT Directive. The e-commerce and service models are anchored directly in the VAT Directive (Article 14a of the VAT Directive and the proposed Article 28 of the VAT Directive) and are complemented by several clarifying regulations. The digital model seems to raise more questions of a legislative (the need for the CJEU to rule on whether Article 9a IR was valid at all) and practical (lack of definition of taking part in the supply of services, unclear relationship with Article 28 of the VAT Directive, the mechanism of operation derived more from its interpretation by the CJEU than from the direct wording of the provisions) nature than the other models.

In view of the above, in theoretical considerations of whether any of the other models would be more suitable for STR platforms than a dedicated service model, the digital model can be excluded. This model does not appear to be sufficiently advanced to encompass the complex sector of STR services supplied in the real world via platforms. The significant differences between the sale of digital services and the sale of physical services, such as STR services, seem to preclude the extension of the digital model framework for the platforms mediating this type of transaction.

The situation is different for the e-commerce model. It is so advanced that one can imagine extending it (after making the necessary modifications related to the nature of the underlying transactions, of course) to STR services supplied through platforms. In this case, the STR platform would be a deemed supplier for B2C services supplied through it. It seems that such a solution would have a positive impact on the efficiency of VAT collection (as has been the case with the e-commerce model) from professional hosts who appear to be more direct competition to traditional business models than non-professional suppliers. However, this type of extension seems problematic from a VAT enforcement point of view. For example, in a situation where the host is a VAT taxable person, resident in the country where the property is located and the platform through which the transaction is carried out is established in a third country, the tax authorities, instead of enforcing VAT against the host (the VAT due could be collected as a last resort through enforcement against the property), will be forced to enforce it against the foreign platform. As pointed out in the legal literature, tax enforcement has much higher success rates for resident taxable persons since they can be identified and located more easily, and information on their assets and enforcement procedures is readily available (bank account freeze, property seizure, lien on assets, judicial foreclosure), which contrasts with the bureaucratic procedures for exchange of information and with the burdensome processes for cross-border enforcement.[1073] It should

1073. Lucas-Mas and Junquera-Varela (n. 581) 81–83. The authors also note that usually, most jurisdictions tend to provide administrative and judicial cooperation to other countries in the

be noted that one of the reasons for the introduction of the e-commerce model was that many of the underlying suppliers are non-resident, and it is therefore more difficult to enforce VAT payment against them than against the platforms. No similar justification is available for the accommodation sector. In addition, as indicated in the legal literature, in this case, the information deficit of the underlying suppliers about EU tax obligations may be smaller than in the case of foreign suppliers of goods from third countries. In the case of property rental, hosts often must pay other taxes and fees related to these services in many Member States, so they should also be aware of the VAT rules.[1074] Therefore, although the potential extension of the e-commerce model to accommodation sector platforms is theoretically possible, it does not seem reasonable.

It should also be noted that if the service model comes into effect, platforms facilitating different types of transactions may soon be subject to three distinct models of the deemed supplier regime. This may result in additional administrative burdens and compliance difficulties for platforms. It is therefore rightly pointed out that the rules on the deemed supplier regime should be more aligned.[1075] It appears that greater consistency can increase compliance levels while reducing compliance costs and administrative burdens for platforms.

However, it does not seem possible to introduce a single deemed supplier model for all platforms. Although the business models of the platforms differ, the main reason why such a uniform form is not possible is because of differences in the VAT implications for the supplies of goods and services. The digital and service models are related to the supply of services and the e-commerce model to the delivery of goods. These transactions are already treated differently under the EU VAT system, which also requires differentiation under the deemed supplier regime. Furthermore, while all models serve to increase the efficiency of VAT collection, each has its own additional and distinct objectives. The digital model provides legal certainty for the different actors involved in the transaction chain by clarifying who is the supplier of the service. The e-commerce model levels the playing field between EU entrepreneurs and third-country vendors. And the service model levels the competitiveness of the traditional economy and platforms. Achieving each of these objectives requires separate regulations and appropriate modification of the operation of the deemed supplier regime.

Nevertheless, many elements of the deemed supplier regime models are common, especially in the area of their subject aspect. Therefore, regulations in this area could be partially unified. Introducing new but at the same time very similar presumptions for different platform economy sectors seems to add unnecessary complexity to

assessment and collection of taxes, ranging from exchanging information, including automatic exchanges, to recovering foreign tax claims. However, enforcing tax claims of market jurisdictions based on new nexus and profit attribution rules may not be well received, especially by residence countries where digital multinationals are domiciled.

1074. Pollak (n. 339) 294–295.

1075. Merkx (n. 573) 23–25.

the rules. This can bring legal uncertainty, risks and costs for businesses, tax authorities and courts.[1076]

For example, the EC could propose a uniform definition of 'electronic interface' for all models of the deemed supplier to increase legal certainty for those operating in the platform economy. As pointed out in the academic writings, as the role of intermediaries becomes fundamental, it would be appropriate to introduce a harmonized definition for these actors so that they can be sure whether the new regulatory provisions will apply to them.[1077] This position is shared by business representatives.[1078]

However, it is rightly discouraged to impose a strict definition of market facilitators (or electronic interfaces or platforms), as this is a concept that is likely to evolve over time,[1079] and therefore it seems more pertinent to refer to the way users interact with a system or program, with other terms (telecommunications network, portals, marketplaces, platforms, etc.) being merely procedures used by operators to achieve their objectives.[1080] Even though the types of platforms and their business models are continuously evolving, they generally build their activities on key functions. Thus, focusing on these indicators has the advantage to be more flexible to future changes.[1081]

In addition, assuming that the unified definition of 'electronic interface' will include the wording that the electronic interface operator 'facilitates' the provision of the underlying transaction, this concept can also be unified for the three deemed supplier models. The comments on the digital model point out that it is difficult to define the difference between the concept of 'taking part in the supply of services', as used in Article 9a IR, and the term 'facilitation' to which both Article 14a and the proposed Article 28a of the VAT Directive refer. The business model of platforms that mediate in the supply of digital services is not significantly different from the e-commerce or service models, so this terminological distinction seems unnecessary.[1082] It also seems that a uniform definition of 'facilitation' will help to assess whether the platform has sufficient and accurate information, as well as effective means, to meet its VAT obligations under the deemed supplier regime.

Given the differing interpretations as to whether a platform that is a deemed supplier is also providing an independent intermediation service at the same time or whether this service and the underlying supply are 'merged' and should be accounted

1076. As business representatives point out, a unified definition of intermediaries in the context of the platform economy, along with common presumptions ensuring legal and tax certainty, would be welcomed. BusinessEurope (n. 947).
1077. Brondolo (n. 584) 22–23; Pamela Floriani and Giulia Trabattoni, 'VAT Nella Digital Age: Il Ruolo Delle Piattaforme e Questioni Ancora Aperte' (2023) il fisco 2904; Matesanz, 'The Increasing Liability of Digital Platforms in the Collection of EU VAT' (n. 518).
1078. European Travel Agents' and Tour Operators' Association (n. 947).
1079. OECD, *The Role of Digital Platforms in the Collection of VAT/GST on Online Sales* (n. 551) 6; Thang and Shatalow (n. 422) 433.
1080. Brondolo (n. 584) 22–23; Matesanz, 'The Increasing Liability of Digital Platforms in the Collection of EU VAT' (n. 518).
1081. Scarcella (n. 391) 6–7.
1082. *See also*: Beretta (n. 344) 315–320.

for together, this issue should also be unambiguously regulated. All three models of the deemed supplier, in terms of their mechanism of operation, use very similar wording '[this taxable person] ... shall be deemed to have received and supplied those services himself' (Article 28 of the VAT Directive, the digital model), 'that taxable person shall be deemed to have received and supplied those goods himself' (Article 14a of the VAT Directive, the e-commerce model) and 'this taxable person ... shall be deemed to have received and supplied those services himself' (Article 28a of the VAT Directive, the service model). Therefore, the approach in this respect should be uniform and not raise any doubts over interpretation.

A concept also worth considering is the introduction of a threshold below which platforms would not be deemed suppliers or the regime would be optional for them.[1083] At present, such a solution is not envisaged by any of the deemed supplier models. Platforms are therefore deemed as a supplier regardless of their size, the business model adopted or the number of underlying transactions they facilitate and their value.

This solution undoubtedly has its good points. Introducing a threshold for the deemed supplier regime would add another level of complexity. There would be the problem of establishing a relationship between the thresholds for exempting SMEs and the thresholds for deemed suppliers, which would conflict with the businesses' proposal that the tax system should be simple to operate and understand.[1084] Legal literature highlights that the lack of simplicity invites tax avoidance.[1085] It is challenging to allow exemptions for smaller marketplaces as this could lead to challenges of VAT evasion – operators wishing to evade tax burdens may then migrate to smaller platforms to exploit tax differences.[1086] This would probably have a negative impact on the competitiveness of the market.

However, when introducing the deemed supplier regime into the tax system, the platform's ability to exert a certain level of influence and control over the underlying transaction should be taken into account – if it does not have access to the information or, moreover, the information cannot be readily obtained by the platform without radically changing its own business model, then the responsibility for VAT collection should not be shifted on it.[1087] In addition to access to information, the platform should also have the means and be able to collect VAT on such transactions. Indeed, with the deemed supplier regime, platform operators have become a kind of unpaid tax collectors.[1088] While helping governments collect large amounts of tax revenue, they incur significant costs, which also include indirect costs associated with the complexity

1083. *See also*: Sroka (n. 883).
1084. European Commission, 'Group on the Future of VAT No 122: VAT and the Platform Economy - Focus on Specific Issues - Follow up, Taxud.c.1(2022)3461477' (n. 887).
1085. Mirrlees (n. 388) 42.
1086. Asquith, 'Co-Opting Gig & Sharing Platforms as Tax Collectors' (n. 440). However, it seems that currently such risk does not appear to be too significant. This is due to the nature of the platform economy, where the largest platforms provide access to huge user bases, established reputation systems, often purchase guarantees, and other amenities that are challenging for smaller platforms to compete with.
1087. Beretta (n. 344) 298–301.
1088. Bal (n. 564).

of tax legislation.[1089] As indicated in the literature, increasing complexity favours larger entrepreneurs – small or new operators in the e-commerce market may in this situation choose not to start an online business, terminate it or operate in the grey zone.[1090]

As pointed out in the doctrine, assuming that all platforms would be able, without much difficulty, to fulfil a key role in collecting VAT reflects a lack of understanding of the platforms' business models in all their complexity.[1091] Differences in the functions and size of the platforms appear to have an impact on the platforms' ability to take on the role of the deemed supplier and comply with this regime. Some of the leading platforms already provide tax compliance services to their underlying suppliers. However, for many platforms, the deemed supplier regime would mean the need to develop and implement considerable system changes to ensure an appropriate level of efficiency of the new rules.[1092] The legal academics also emphasize that for smaller platforms, even determining the applicable VAT rate in different Member States entails a very heavy administrative burden.[1093] This difficulty may affect smaller platforms' decisions to enter new markets or to withdraw from markets in which they operated prior to the introduction of the deemed supplier regime, as well as their decision on who their underlying supplier is. Some platforms may restrict sales only to certain Member States or only by certain suppliers.[1094]

It should be noted that, as indicated in the first chapter, platforms have a natural tendency to create monopolies.[1095] Due to their rapid scalability, the first platforms in a given sector become strong market leaders, which is due to the fact that sellers and buyers prefer to use the platforms with the largest number of users, as this means more opportunities to transact. It is therefore difficult for smaller platforms to become a potential competitor to dominant platforms. This trend threatens to limit the ability of upcoming innovators to successfully enter the market and to narrow the choices for consumers.[1096]

There is no doubt that the deemed supplier role for platforms may create costs and burdens.[1097] As this cost is considered high, smaller platforms may struggle to meet their obligations.[1098] It is pointed out that this burden may even be unreasonable for smaller or purely domestic platforms.[1099] Such players may even prefer to forgo new

1089. *Ibid.*
1090. Barr and others (n. 652) 2.
1091. Lamensch and others (n. 104) 477–479.
1092. OECD, *The Role of Digital Platforms in the Collection of VAT/GST on Online Sales* (n. 551) 36–37.
1093. Pollak (n. 339) 296–297.
1094. *Ibid.*
1095. Sledziewska-Kołodziejska and Włoch (n. 74) 113–114.
1096. Council of the EU, 'Shaping Europe's Digital Future – Council Conclusions (9 June 2020), 8098/1/20' (n. 253).
1097. For example: European Commission, 'Summary Report. Public Consultation on the VAT in the Digital Age Initiative' (n. 1049); Scarcella (n. 391) 6–7.
1098. As indicated by the OECD, not all platforms that meet the deemed supplier criteria will be able to meet the requirements imposed by this regime, particularly start-up businesses and small platforms. OECD, *The Impact of the Growth of the Sharing and Gig Economy on VAT/GST Policy and Administration* (n. 47) 77–79.
1099. European Commission, 'Summary Report. Public Consultation on the VAT in the Digital Age Initiative' (n. 1049).

foreign markets rather than incur the costs of familiarizing themselves with local VAT taxation and the associated liability risks.[1100] The literature points out that, although the deemed supplier regime is generally a proportionate solution, there are doubts about this for smaller platforms and for platforms that are just starting out due to the particularly high increase in administrative burdens and costs for these players.[1101]

The deemed supplier regime rules could, therefore, be considered to provide a competitive advantage for bigger platforms, which have more means to deal with the implications of the new provisions.[1102] This is also due to the fact that bigger platforms can pass on additional costs to a larger number of users, meaning comparatively lower costs per user, compared to smaller platforms (economies of scale).[1103]

The measure therefore puts smaller platforms and new market entrants at a disadvantage, which may strengthen platform monopolies. Bigger platforms will cope with the complexity and regulatory burden, while smaller intermediaries may be driven out of the market. This is undesirable from a competition policy and antitrust law perspective[1104] and, in the long term, may limit innovation in the EU internal market.[1105] Already after the delivery of the judgment of the CJEU in the *Cali Apartments* case,[1106] which was unfavourable for the accommodation sector platforms, the literature stressed that European start-up STR platforms would not be able to compete with US and Chinese players because they would never grow up enough to compete on the global stage due to having to face an unfavourable regulatory framework and EU case law.[1107]

A solution that can be implemented to redress the balance is to adopt a provision that would reduce or eliminate the liability of certain platforms.[1108] To this end, a rule could be introduced whereby a platform whose annual turnover remains below a

1100. European Commission, Directorate General for Taxation and Customs Union and others (n. 6) 151–153.
1101. Pollak (n. 339) 317. While these remarks pertained to the e-commerce model, they appear to be equally relevant for all deemed supplier regime models.
1102. European Travel Agents' and Tour Operators' Association (n. 947); Merkx (n. 573) 25.
1103. Lamensch and others (n. 104) 477–479.
1104. Thang and Shatalow (n. 422) 438–439.
1105. European Commission, 'VAT Expert Group No 095: VAT Treatment of the Sharing Economy, Taxud.c.1(2020)5816454' (n. 338).
1106. In this judgment, the CJEU ruled, among other things, that the obligation to obtain a permit for STR activity to tourists is in line with EU law. *Cali Apartments SCI and HX v. Procureur général près la cour d'appel de Paris and Ville de Paris* (n. 296).
1107. Hatzopoulos (n. 297) 918–919.
1108. It is worth noting that in Japan, the Platform Taxation Regime applies only in cases where the National Tax Agency designates a platform as a specified digital platform operator. This happens if the total amount of consideration paid for electronic services supplied by foreign businesses to Japanese consumers through that digital platform and received through the operator in its taxable period exceeds JPY 5 billion (approximately EUR 32 million). If a platform operator reaches this threshold, they are required to notify the tax authorities. The National Tax Agency will publish the name of each specified digital platform operator on the National Tax Agency's website. Thus, in practice, suppliers do not need to consider whether the platform they use falls within the Platform Taxation Regime on a case-by-case basis. The Japanese system also provides two possibilities to lift the designation for platforms: when the specified digital platform operator goes below the JPY 5 billion threshold for three consecutive years, and when the National Tax Agency discretionarily lifts the designation, taking into account any circumstances where the specified digital platform operator is no longer capable

certain threshold would not be required to collect and remit VAT on the underlying transaction.[1109] It is worth noting that originally the EP, when introducing the e-commerce model, limited it to platforms that had an annual turnover exceeding EUR 1,000,000, in the current calendar year, to not impose an undue burden on SMEs or start-ups.[1110] Finally, the idea was abandoned. However, in setting a threshold for accommodation sector platforms, the EU legislator could follow either this solution or the solutions contained in the legislative proposal amending the Regulation of the European Parliament and of the Council on data collection and sharing relating to short-term accommodation rental services.[1111] According to this draft, when determining whether a platform in the accommodation sector qualifies as a small or micro enterprise, reference should be made to Commission Recommendation 2003/361/EC,[1112] as well as to the criterion of reaching, in the previous quarter, an average monthly number of at least 2,500 active landlords in the Union. As indicated in the doctrine, a sensible approach would also be to periodically review and adjust the threshold to balance changes in the real value of money and changes in administrative and compliance costs.[1113]

It is also reasonable to share the view that if the threshold in question were to be adopted for smaller platforms, they would be able to decide whether they wanted to act as deemed suppliers for facilitated underlying transactions.[1114] The deemed supplier regime should therefore be optional for them. Providing a choice to platforms to either use a deeming provision or not would create a more neutral and therefore fairer VAT collection model.[1115]

It seems that excluding small and medium-sized platform operators from the scope of the deemed supplier regime, or making the deemed supplier regime optional for them, is particularly relevant for STR platforms. It is pointed out that, unlike the e-commerce market, the service platform economy is not as dominated by big market players; therefore, the efficiency that can be achieved by taxing a few big platforms

of collecting and paying consumption tax. Masuda, (n. 656) 107. This solution seems very interesting, and it will be intriguing to see how it performs in practice (it will apply from 1 April 2025).

1109. Beretta (n. 344) 298–301.

1110. European Parliament, 'Report on the Proposal for a Council Directive Amending Directive 2006/112/EC and Directive 2009/132/EC as Regards Certain Value Added Tax Obligations for Supplies of Services and Distance Sales of Goods, A8-0307/2017'; Pollak (n. 339) 109–110.

1111. Proposal for a regulation of the European Parliament and of the Council on data collection and sharing relating to short-term accommodation rental services and amending Regulation (EU) 2018/1724 (n. 309).

1112. According to these recommendations, a small enterprise is defined as an enterprise which employs fewer than 50 persons and whose annual turnover and/or annual balance sheet total does not exceed EUR 10 million. A microenterprise is defined as an enterprise which employs fewer than 10 persons and whose annual turnover and/or annual balance sheet total does not exceed EUR 2 million. Commission Recommendation of 6 May 2003 concerning the definition of micro, small and medium-sized enterprises [OJ L 124, 20.5.2003, pp. 36–41].

1113. Zu (n. 333) 317.

1114. Merkx (n. 573) 26.

1115. *Ibid.*, 28.

instead of numerous small suppliers is achieved to a lesser extent.[1116] For this reason, it seems a good solution would be to exclude such platforms from the deemed supplier regime, at least temporarily, during the initial phase of the functioning of the new regulations.[1117]

Thus, while neutrality considerations require equal treatment of platforms in similar situations, it is equally important that the EU legislator give due consideration to the proportionality aspect for the deemed supplier regime. It therefore seems reasonable to exclude small and medium-sized platform operators from the scope of the deemed supplier regime or make the deemed supplier regime optional for them. Such a solution would likely have a positive impact on further innovations and development of smaller companies operating within the platform economy in the EU.

Improving the efficiency of VAT collection through the deemed supplier regime will also require closer international cooperation on taxation. There is now an issue as to how the tax authority of the jurisdiction of consumption is to ensure that the foreign platform has correctly remitted the VAT and how to enforce potential interest and penalties when it has no assets or physical presence in that jurisdiction. The existing mutual legal assistance treaties focus on direct taxation or are limited to the exchange of information about irregularities, with no further legal instruments to enforce compliance.[1118] In theory, therefore, shifting VAT liability to a non-resident platform may increase enforcement risk. However, as the OECD points out, in practice, platforms have significant incentives to comply with law, including reputational incentive (this is particularly true of listed platform operators).[1119] As is stressed in the legal literature, there has been an increased willingness worldwide on the part of digital and multinational corporations to collaborate, as it is essential to the brand and reputation of such businesses – successful operators should appreciate the value of being a tax-compliant business.[1120] However, this assertion deserves scrutiny – it is difficult to say whether consumers are truly concerned with the tax compliance reputation of suppliers and platforms.[1121] However, if enough larger companies register, tax revenues and issues of ensuring fair competition will be sufficiently safeguarded.[1122] Existing risks can therefore be considered acceptable when measured

1116. European Commission, 'VAT Expert Group No 095: VAT Treatment of the Sharing Economy, Taxud.c.1(2020)5816454' (n. 338).
1117. As indicated in the literature, enacting temporary regulations allows for gathering a greater quantity and better quality of data regarding the effects of controversial regulations, and also compels legislative bodies to periodically assess the impact of such regulations in order to extend their validity. For these reasons, temporary legislation becomes particularly attractive in contexts dominated by uncertainty, where the risk of excessive reaction is significant, as is the case with platform economies. Gabriel Doménech-Pascual, 'Sharing Economy and Regulatory Strategies towards Legal Change' (2016) 7 European Journal of Risk Regulation 717, 723–724 https://doi.org/10.1017/s1867299x0001014x.
1118. Thang and Shatalow (n. 422) 439–445.
1119. OECD, *The Impact of the Growth of the Sharing and Gig Economy on VAT/GST Policy and Administration* (n. 47) 77–79.
1120. Ina Kerschner, Maryte Somare and Wirtschaftsuniversität Wien (eds), *Taxation in a Global Digital Economy* (Linde 2017) 74–76.
1121. Thang and Shatalow (n. 422) 439–445.
1122. *Ibid.*

against the benefits of assumed general compliance.[1123] However, as experience accumulates, further changes may be necessary to strengthen international cooperation in this area.

4 SUMMARY

The deemed supplier regime has generated much controversy and differing opinions. The introduction of this arrangement could bring many benefits, providing both clarity about a platform's obligations regarding VAT on underlying supplies and increased efficiency in the collection of this tax. The costs and risks associated with VAT control may be reduced by shifting VAT obligations from smaller underlying suppliers to bigger market players such as platforms. At the same time, such a system also potentially reduces compliance costs for the underlying suppliers.

However, there are also concerns about the potential negative effects of placing responsibility for VAT collection on platforms instead of individual suppliers. These are related to possible distortions in the internal market and compliance with the principles of equality and neutrality. The introduction of the deemed supplier regime also increases the bureaucratic burden and costs for platforms, which could lead to the squeeze of smaller operators out of the market, damaging EU competitiveness. In addition, the challenge is how the tax authority of the jurisdiction of consumption can ensure that VAT is correctly accounted for by foreign platforms that have no assets or physical presence in that jurisdiction. In theory, shifting VAT liability to non-resident platforms could increase enforcement risk. Thus, the effectiveness of VAT collection through the deemed supplier regime may also require closer international tax cooperation. Therefore, it is important for tax authorities to strive for an appropriate balance between these challenges and opportunities.

Looking at the EU solutions, it is worth noting that the deemed supplier regime models have significant similarities in terms of the subject aspect and essentially the mechanism of operation, but they differ quite significantly in terms of the subject aspect. Because of these similarities, the deemed supplier regime rules could be aligned to a greater extent, but it nevertheless seems impossible to introduce a single deemed supplier model for all platforms. This is due to the fact that transactions of supply of goods and services are treated differently under the EU VAT system, which also requires differentiation in the deemed supplier regime.

In general, the deemed supplier regime in the digital model and the e-commerce model has proven successful. Therefore, the plan to introduce a similar solution for the STR sector should be welcomed. However, due to some doubts about the construction of the service model, its clarification seems crucial to ensure a better functioning of this solution.

The analysis of the EU deemed supplier regime models presented in the book allows the following *de lege ferenda* proposals to be formulated.

1123. *Ibid.*

First, the deemed supplier regime rules should be more harmonized, especially in the area of their subject aspect, where many elements are common. For example, the EC could propose a uniform definition of 'electronic interface' and the concept of 'facilitation' for all deemed supplier models, building on the concepts adopted for the e-commerce model. Introducing new yet very similar presumptions in this regard for different platform economy sectors adds unnecessary complexity to EU VAT rules. This may entail legal uncertainty. Greater consistency can increase compliance level while lowering compliance costs.

Second, because of the doubts about whether a platform being a deemed supplier is also providing at the same time an independent intermediation service or whether this service and the underlying supply are 'merged', and should be accounted for together, this issue should also be unambiguously regulated or clarified for all three deemed supplier models.

Third, also worth considering is the introduction of a threshold below which platforms would not be deemed suppliers, or the regime would be optional for them. This threshold could refer to EC Recommendation 2003/361/EC and EU Legislative Proposal 2018/1724 and apply to platforms employing fewer than 50 people, with an annual turnover or annual balance sheet total of less than EUR 10 million, and that have not reached a monthly average of at least 2,500 active landlords in the Union. The threshold would aim to reduce or eliminate the administrative burden and costs associated with the role of the deemed VAT supplier for small and medium-sized platform operators. In addition, the introduction of such a threshold would provide greater neutrality for different business models of platform which may have different capacities to cope with the requirements of the deemed VAT supplier regime. Finally, a threshold for platforms would indirectly promote innovation and competition in the platform economy sector, which can be threatened by established platform monopolies. The threshold could help create a more favourable environment for growth and innovation in the platform sector.

In summary, the growth of the STR platform economy has brought many challenges as EU VAT rules do not address the specifics of these transactions, leading to legal uncertainty. However, this growth also offers many potential benefits for EU VAT collection, as exemplified by the deemed supplier regime. The introduction of the service model dedicated to STR platforms can contribute not only to increasing the efficiency of VAT collection but also to levelling the playing field between traditional suppliers of accommodation services and hosts operating through platforms.

Bibliography

Acquier A, 'Uberization Meets Organizational Theory: Platform Capitalism and the Rebirth of the Putting-Out System' in Nestor M Davidson, Michèle Finck and John J Infranca (eds), *The Cambridge Handbook of the Law of the Sharing Economy* (Cambridge University Press 2018).

Acquier A and Carbone V, 'Sharing Economy and Social Innovation' in Nestor M Davidson, Michèle Finck and John J Infranca (eds), *The Cambridge Handbook of the Law of the Sharing Economy* (Cambridge University Press 2018).

Adamiak C, *Changes in the Global Airbnb Offer During the COVID-19 Pandemic* (Oikonomics 2021).

Airbnb, *Airbnb Report on Travel & Living* (2021).

Airbnb, 'Airbnb Welcomes EU Rules Proposals' (*Airbnb Newsroom*, 7 November 2022), https://news.airbnb.com/airbnb-welcomes-eu-rules-proposals/ accessed 20 July 2023.

'Airbnb, Booking, Expedia and Tripadvisor to Share Data with Eurostat', https://ec.europa.eu/eurostat/web/products-eurostat-news/-/cn-20200305-1 accessed 13 March 2024.

Airbnb Inc in Travel (World) (Euromonitor International 2018) https://www.euromonitor.com/airbnb-inc-in-travel/report accessed 12 February 2023.

Alaradi M and Moossdorff B, 'The Role of Digital Platforms in Collecting VAT in Selected Countries in the Middle East' (2024) 35 International VAT Monitor.

Aloisi A, 'The Role of European Institutions in Promoting Decent Work in the "Collaborative Economy"' in Maurizio Bruglieri (ed.), *Multidisciplinary Design of Sharing Services* (Springer International Publishing 2018).

Aloni E, 'Pluralism and Regulatory Responses' in Nestor M Davidson, Michèle Finck and John J Infranca (eds), *The Cambridge Handbook of the Law of the Sharing Economy* (Cambridge University Press 2018).

Amand C, 'Disclosed/Undisclosed Agent in EU VAT: When Is an Intermediary Acting in Its Own Name?' (2021) 32 International VAT Monitor.

Andrei AG and Zait A, 'The Sharing Economy in Post-Communist Societies: Insights from Romania' in Elena-Mădălina Vătămănescu and Florina Magdalena Pînzaru (eds), *Knowledge Management in the Sharing Economy*, vol 6 (Springer International Publishing 2018).

Annacondia F, 'Cross-Border B2C Digital Services: A New Way to Collect VAT?' (2018) 29 International VAT Monitor.

Annacondia F, 'VAT Registration Thresholds in Europe' (2023) 34 International VAT Monitor.

Arcidiacono D and Pais I, 'Individual Rewarding and Social Outcomes in the Collaborative Economy' in Maurizio Bruglieri (ed.), *Multidisciplinary Design of Sharing Services* (Springer International Publishing 2018).

Artinger K, *Taxing Consumption in the Digital Age: Challenges for European VAT* (1st edn, Nomos 2020).

Asquith R, 'Co-opting Gig & Sharing Platforms as Tax Collectors' (25 October 2021), https://www.vatcalc.com/global/co-opting-gig-sharing-platforms-as-tax-collectors/ accessed 28 November 2022.

Asquith R, 'EU Platform Economy Issues on Full Liability Model – VAT in the Digital Age' (11 May 2022), https://www.vatcalc.com/eu/eu-platform-economy-issues-on-fully-liability-model-vat-in-the-digital-age/ accessed 28 November 2022.

Asquith R, 'EU ViDA Agreement Delayed' (14 May 2024), https://www.vatcalc.com/eu/eu-vat-in-the-digital-age-vida-adopted-by-ec/ accessed 30 May 2024.

Asquith R, 'VAT in the Digital Age Won't Return to ECOFIN for Agreement Till October or November 2024' (9 July 2024), https://www.vatcalc.com/eu/eu-vat-in-the-digital-age-vida-adopted-by-ec/ accessed 23 July 2024.

Baker P, Pistone P and Perroun K, 'Third-Party Liability for the Payment of Taxes and Their Fundamental Rights' (2023) 15(1) World Tax Journal.

Bakker M, Hendrica E and Twining-Ward L, *Tourism and the Sharing Economy: Policy & Potential of Sustainable Peer-to-Peer Accommodation* (World Bank Group 2018).

Bal A, 'Managing EU VAT Risks for Platform Business Models' (2018) 72 Bulletin for International Taxation, ibfd.org accessed 4 February 2021.

Bal A, 'Platform Economy: Will The Real Tax Collector Please Stand Up?' (*Forbes*), https://www.forbes.com/sites/aleksandrabal/2023/03/15/platform-economy-will-the-real-tax-collector-please-stand-up/ accessed 4 April 2023.

Bal A, 'VAT and Platform Economy: Unanswered Questions and an Uncertain Future' (*Forbes*), https://www.forbes.com/sites/aleksandrabal/2024/06/23/vat-and-platform-economy-unanswered-questions-and-an-uncertain-future/ accessed 25 July 2024.

Bal A, 'VAT In The Digital Age: Impact Of Revised Proposals On EU Businesses' (*Forbes*), https://www.forbes.com/sites/aleksandrabal/2024/05/12/vat-in-the-digital-age-impact-of-revised-proposals-on-eu-businesses/?sh=f994c06188cb accessed 25 July 2024.

Barr R and others, *E-Commerce and EU VAT: Theory and Practice* (Wolters Kluwer 2021).

Belarmino A and Koh Y, 'A Critical Review of Research Regarding Peer-to-Peer Accommodations' (2020) 84 International Journal of Hospitality Management.

Belk R, 'Why Not Share Rather Than Own?' (2007) 611 The Annals of the American Academy of Political and Social Science.

Belk R, 'You Are What You Can Access: Sharing and Collaborative Consumption Online' (2014) 67 Journal of Business Research.

Beretta G, 'VAT and the Sharing Economy' (2018) 10 World Tax Journal.

Beretta G, *European VAT and the Sharing Economy* (Kluwer Law International, BV 2019).

Beretta G and van Hilten M, 'The New VAT Record Keeping and Reporting Obligations for Payment Service Providers' (2020) 31 International VAT Monitor.

Bibler AJ, Teltser KF and Tremblay MJ, 'Inferring Tax Compliance from Pass-Through: Evidence from Airbnb Tax Enforcement Agreements' (2021) 103(4) The Review of Economics and Statistics.

Bolt and others, 'Letter to the Swedish Presidency Dated May 31, 2023: Urgent Need to Review the EU's Proposed VAT Platform Rules'.

'Booking.Com Betaalt € 94 Miljoen Bij Schikking Belastingzaak Italië', https://www.taxlive.nl/nl/documenten/nieuws/bookingcom-betaalt-94-miljoen-bij-schikkin g-belastingzaak-itali%C3%AB/ accessed 4 March 2024.

Boswijk A, 'Transforming Business Value Through Digitalized Networks: A Case Study on the Value Drivers of Airbnb' (2017) 3 Journal of Creating Value 104.

Botsman R and Rogers R, *What's Mine Is Yours: How Collaborative Consumption Is Changing the Way We Live* (Rev and updated ed., Collins 2011).

Bradshaw T, 'Airbnb Moves "Aggressively" into Europe' (*Financial Times*, 31 May 2011), https://www.ft.com/ accessed 12 March 2024.

Bratianu C, 'The Crazy New World of the Sharing Economy' in Elena-Mădălina Vătămănescu and Florina Magdalena Pînzaru (eds), *Knowledge Management in the Sharing Economy*, vol 6 (Springer International Publishing 2018).

Brauckmann S, 'City Tourism and the Sharing Economy – Potential Effects of Online Peer-to-Peer Marketplaces on Urban Property Markets' (2017) 3 Journal of Tourism Futures.

Brescia R, 'Finding the Right "Fit": Matching Regulations to the Shape of the Sharing Economy' in Nestor M Davidson, Michèle Finck and John J Infranca (eds), *The Cambridge Handbook of the Law of the Sharing Economy* (Cambridge University Press 2018).

Brondolo J, *Administering the Value-Added Tax on Imported Digital Services and Low-Value Imported Goods* (International Monetary Fund 2021).

Busch C, 'Crowdsourcing Consumer Confidence. How to Regulate Online Rating and Review Systems in the Collaborative Economy' in Alberto De Franceschi (ed.), *European Contract Law and the Digital Single Market: The Implications of the Digital Revolution* (Intersentia 2016).

BusinessEurope, 'VAT in the Digital Age – BusinessEurope Reply to the Public Consultation', https://www.businesseurope.eu/publications/vat-digital-age-businesseurope-reply-public-consultation accessed 9 May 2023.

Cameron A, Khanal M and Tedds LM, 'Managing Airbnb: A Cross-Jurisdictional Review of Approaches for Regulating the Short-Term Rental Market' (2022) MPRA Paper.

Cameron A and Tedds LM, 'Managing the Short-Term Rental Market in Canada: A Comparative Analysis of Policy, Planning, and Regulatory Strategies in 25 Municipalities' (City of Calgary 2023).

Center for Responsible Travel, *The Case for Responsible Travel: Trends & Statistics 2020* (2020), www.responsibletravel.org.

CFE Tax Advisers Europe, 'Opinion Statement FC 6/2023 – Further CFE Comments on the EU Commission's VIDA Proposals of 8 December 2022'.

Čičin-Šain N, 'Newly Proposed VAT Rules for Sharing Economy Platforms – Some Fine-Tuning Needed?' (*Kluwer International Tax Blog*, 22 March 2023), https://kluwertaxblog.com/2023/03/22/newly-proposed-vat-rules-for-sharing-econom y-platforms-some-fine-tuning-needed/ accessed 4 April 2023.

Cohen JE, 'Law for the Platform Economy' (2017) 51 U.C. Davis Law Review.

Cohen JE, 'Law for the Platform Economy' (2017) 51 U.C. Davis Law Review 133.

Coles P and others, 'Airbnb Usage Across New York City Neighborhoods: Geographic Patterns and Regulatory Implications' in Nestor M Davidson, Michèle Finck and John J Infranca (eds), *The Cambridge Handbook of the Law of the Sharing Economy* (Cambridge University Press 2018).

Council of the EU, 'Shaping Europe's Digital Future – Council Conclusions (9 June 2020), 8098/1/20'.

Council of the EU, 'Council Conclusions on Fair and Effective Taxation in Times of Recovery, on Tax Challenges Linked to Digitalisation and on Tax Good Governance in the EU and beyond, FISC 226 ECOFIN 1097'.

Council of the EU, 'Statement by the Commission, Dated 8 May 2024, No 9680/24 ADD 1'.

Council of the EU, 'VAT in the Digital Age Package – Policy Debate, 9749/23'.

'COVID-19 and Online Platform Economy' (*Observatory on the Online Platform Economy*), https://platformobservatory.eu/news/covid-19-and-online-platform-economy/ accessed 13 August 2021.

Dalton J, 'Court of Appeal Ruling in Secret Hotels Confirms Economic over Contractual VAT Approach' (*ITR*, 13 December 2012), www.internationaltaxreview.com accessed 22 February 2023.

Davidson NM and Infranca JJ, 'The Place of the Sharing Economy' in Nestor M Davidson, Michèle Finck and John J Infranca (eds), *The Cambridge Handbook of the Law of the Sharing Economy* (Cambridge University Press 2018).

de la Feria R, 'Tax Fraud and Selective Law Enforcement' (2020) 47 Journal of Law and Society.

de la Feria R and Schoeman A, 'Addressing VAT Fraud in Developing Countries: The Tax Policy-Administration Symbiosis' (2019) 47 Intertax.

Delhomme V and Chapuis-Doppler A, 'Tax Legislation on Short-Term Rentals and Obligations of Intermediation Services Providers: Airbnb Ireland and Airbnb Payments UK' (2024) 61 Common Market Law Review.

Department of Finance Canada, 'Fall Economic Statement 2020. Supporting Canadians and Fighting COVID-19'.

'Digital Economy Report 2019. Value Creation and Capture: Implications for Developing Countries' (United Nations Conference on Trade and Development, UNCTAD 2019).

'Dlaczego Airbnb prosi o podanie informacji dotyczących Twojego kanadyjskiego GST – Centrum Pomocy Airbnb' (*Airbnb*), https://www.airbnb.pl/help/article/3198 accessed 4 December 2022.

Doesum A, 'Een Faciliterend Online Goederenplatform Is Nog Geen Commissionair' (2020) Weekblad Fiscaal Recht.

Doesum A and others, *Fundamentals of EU VAT Law* (2nd edn, Kluwer Law International BV 2020).

Doesum A, 'Revisiting the Commissionaire Fiction in EU VAT Law: Cause, Effect and the Role of Identical Supplies' (2024) 35 International VAT Monitor, ibfd.org accessed 25 July 2024.

Dogru T and others, 'Airbnb 2.0: Is It a Sharing Economy Platform or a Lodging Corporation?' (2020) 78 Tourism Management.

Doménech-Pascual G, 'Sharing Economy and Regulatory Strategies Towards Legal Change' (2016) 7 European Journal of Risk Regulation.

Doménech-Pascual G, 'Sharing Economy and Regulatory Strategies Towards Legal Change' (2016) 7 European Journal of Risk Regulation 717.

Dunne N, 'Competition Law (and Its Limits) in the Sharing Economy' in Nestor M Davidson, Michèle Finck and John J Infranca (eds), *The Cambridge Handbook of the Law of the Sharing Economy* (Cambridge University Press 2018).

Dyal-Chand R, 'Regulating Sharing: The Sharing Economy as an Alternative Capitalist System' (2015) 90 Tulane Law Review.

Easton C, 'European Union Information Law and the Sharing Economy' in Tatiana-Eleni Synodinou and others (eds), *EU Internet Law: Regulation and Enforcement* (Springer International Publishing 2017).

Ebril L, Keen M and Perry V, *The Modern VAT* (International Monetary Fund 2001).

Ecommerce Europe, 'Position Paper 3 April 2023. Ecommerce Europe's Feedback on the VAT in the Digital Age Proposal'.

'Economic Significance' (*Observatory on the Online Platform Economy*), https://platformobservatory.eu/state-of-play/economic-significance/ accessed 13 August 2021.

Elliot CB, 'Taxation of the Sharing Economy: Recurring Issues' (2018) 72 Bulletin for International Taxation, ibfd.org accessed 22 November 2022.

'EU: VAT Obligations of Digital Platforms Pre-2015 (CJEU Referral)' (*KPMG*, 12 March 2024), https://kpmg.com/us/en/home/insights/2024/03/tnf-eu-vat-obligations-digital-platforms-pre-2015-cjeu-referral.html accessed 17 March 2024.

European Commission, 'Communication from the Commission to the Council, the European Parliament and the Economic and Social Committee – Electronic Commerce and Indirect Taxation, COM(1998) 374 Final'.

European Commission, 'VAT Committee Guidelines Resulting from the 93rd Meeting of 1 July 2011: Electronic Services Supplied by Service Providers Using the Network of Telecommunications Provider, Taxud.c.1(2012)1410604 – 709'.

European Commission, *Explanatory Notes on the EU VAT Changes to the Place of Supply of Telecommunications, Broadcasting and Electronic Services That Enter into Force in 2015* (European Commission 2014).

European Commission, 'A Digital Single Market Strategy for Europe – Analysis and Evidence, SWD(2015) 100 Final'.

European Commission, 'A Digital Single Market Strategy for Europe, COM(2015) 192 Final'.

European Commission, 'VAT Committee Guidelines Resulting from the 105th Meeting of 26 October 2015: VAT Treatment of Sharing Economy, Taxud.c.1 (2016)1162824 – 889'.

European Commission, 'Upgrading the Single Market: More Opportunities for People and Business, COM(2015) 550 Final'.

European Commission, 'VAT Committee Working Paper No 895: Harmonised Application of the Presumption (Follow-up) from the 106th Meeting, Taxud.c.1 (2016)921938'.

European Commission, 'VAT Committee Guidelines Resulting from the 106th Meeting of 14 March 2016: VAT 2015 Harmonised Application of the Presumption, Taxud.c.1(2016)3604550 – 904'.

European Commission, 'Communication from the Commission to the European Parliament, the Council, and the European Economic and Social Committee on an Action Plan on VAT Towards a Single EU VAT Area – Time to Decide, COM(2016) 148 Final'.

European Commission, 'A European Agenda for the Collaborative Economy, COM(2016) 356 Final'.

European Commission, 'VAT Committee Guidelines Resulting from the 107th Meeting of 8 July 2016: Interaction Between Electronically Supplied Services and Intermediation Services and Initial Discussion on the Scope of the Concept of Intermediation Services When Taken in a Broader Context, Taxud.c.1(2017)1402399 – 914'.

European Commission, 'VAT Committee Guidelines Resulting from the 110th Meeting of 13 April 2018: The Significance of the VAT Identification Number, Taxud.c.1(2018)7386249 – 956'.

European Commission, 'VAT Committee Guidelines Resulting from the 111th Meeting of 30 November 2018: Services Provided by an Electronic Platform Connecting for Remuneration, by Means of a Smartphone Application, a Driver Using His Own Vehicle with Persons Who Wish to Make Urban Journeys, Taxud.c.1(2019)4045223 – 964'.

European Commission, 'Group on the Future of VAT No 086: VAT Treatment of the Sharing Economy, Taxud.c.1(2019)1950741'.

European Commission, *Explanatory Notes on VAT E-Commerce Rules. Council Directive (EU) 2017/2455. Council Directive (EU) 2019/1995. Council Implementing Regulation (EU) 2019/2026* (European Commission 2020).

European Commission, 'VAT Committee Working Paper No 990: Services Supplied by Digital Platforms Intervening in Short-Term Leasing or Renting of Immovable Property, Taxud.c.1(2020)1181920'.

European Commission, 'An Action Plan for Fair and Simple Taxation Supporting the Recovery Strategy, COM(2020) 312 Final'.

European Commission, 'VAT Expert Group No 095: VAT Treatment of the Sharing Economy, Taxud.c.1(2020)5816454'.

European Commission, 'Developing a Responsible, Fair and Trusted Single Market for Short-Term Rental Services. Workshop 1: Enhancing Transparency on Short-Term Accommodation Rentals in the EU. 22 October 2021 – Conclusions, GROW.G.3/CD'.

European Commission, 'Group on the Future of VAT No 116: VAT and the Platform Economy – Focus on Specific Issues – Follow up, Taxud.c.1(2022)669826'.

European Commission, 'Group on the Future of VAT No 122: VAT and the Platform Economy – Focus on Specific Issues – Follow up, Taxud.c.1(2022)3461477'.

European Commission, 'VAT Expert Group No 107: VAT and the Platform Economy – Focus on Specific Issues, Taxud.c.1(2020)4162479'.

European Commission, 'Impact Assessment Report, SWD(2022) 393 Final'.

European Commission, 'VAT Expert Group No 111: Summary Minutes 33rd Meeting 14 March 2023, Taxud.c.1(2023)3335919'.

European Commission, 'How Bringing VAT into the Digital Age Can Help Restore a Level Playing-Field in the Hospitality Sector', https://taxation-customs.ec.europa.eu/news/how-bringing-vat-digital-age-can-help-restore-level-playing-field-hospitality-sector-2023-03-31_en accessed 20 May 2023.

European Commission, 'How Bringing VAT into the Digital Age Can Help Restore a Level Playing-Field in the Hospitality Sector', https://taxation-customs.ec.europa.eu/news/how-bringing-vat-digital-age-can-help-restore-level-playing-field-hospitality-sector-2023-03-31_en accessed 20 May 2023.

European Commission, 'New EU VAT Rules for E-Commerce: Updated Revenue Figures Point to a Successful Implementation', https://taxation-customs.ec.europa.eu/news/new-eu-vat-rules-e-commerce-updated-revenue-figures-point-successful-implementation-2022-05-23_en accessed 9 May 2023.

European Commission, 'Priorities of the European Union 2019–2024', https://european-union.europa.eu/priorities-and-actions/eu-priorities/european-union-priorities-2019-2024_en accessed 12 May 2023.

European Commission, 'Summary Report. Public Consultation on the VAT in the Digital Age Initiative', https://ec.europa.eu/info/law/better-regulation/have-your-say/initiatives/13186-VAT-in-the-digital-age/F_en accessed 27 November 2022.

European Commission, 'VAT in the Digital Age', https://taxation-customs.ec.europa.eu/taxation-1/value-added-tax-vat/vat-digital-age_en accessed 1 May 2023.

European Commission and Joint Research Centre, *Who Owns the City? Exploratory Research Activity on the Financialisation of Housing in EU Cities* (Publications Office 2020).

European Commission, Joint Research Center and Institute for Prospective Technological Studies, *The Passions and the Interests: Unpacking the 'Sharing Economy'* (Publications Office 2016).

European Commission, Directorate General for Communications Networks, Content and Technology and others, *Study on 'Support to the Observatory for the Online Platform Economy': Final Report* (Publications Office 2021).

European Commission, Directorate General for Internal Market, Industry, Entrepreneurship and SMEs and others, *Study to Monitor the Economic Development of the Collaborative Economy at Sector Level in the 28 EU Member States: Final Report* (Publications Office 2018).

European Commission, Directorate General for Internal Market, Industry, Entrepreneurship and SMEs and others, *Study to Monitor the Economic Development of the Collaborative Economy at Sector Level in the 28 EU Member States: Final Report* (Publications Office 2018), https://data.europa.eu/doi/10.2873/83555 accessed 26 August 2021.

European Commission, Directorate General for Internal Market, Industry, Entrepreneurship and SMEs and TNS Political & Social, *The Use of the Collaborative Economy* (Publications Office 2018).

European Commission, Directorate General for Internal Market, Industry, Entrepreneurship and SMEs, VVA, and Spark Legal Network, *Study on the Assessment of the Regulatory Aspects Affecting the Collaborative Economy in the Tourism Accommodation Sector in the 28 Member States (580/PP/GRO/IMA/15/15111J): Final Report* (Publications Office 2018).

European Commission, Directorate General for Taxation and Customs Union and others, *VAT in the Digital Age: Final Report. Volume 2, The VAT Treatment of the Platform Economy* (Publications Office 2022).

European Commission, Directorate General for Taxation and Customs Union and others, *VAT in the Digital Age: Final Report. Volume 3, Single Place of VAT Registration and Import One Stop Shop* (Publications Office 2022).

European Commission, Directorate General for Taxation and Customs Union and Deloitte, *VAT Aspects of Cross-Border e-Commerce: Options for Modernisation: Final Report. Lot 3, Assessment of the Implementation of the 2015 Place of Supply Rules and the Mini-One Stop Shop* (Publications Office 2016).

European Parliament, 'Resolution on a European Agenda for the Collaborative Economy, P8_TA (2017) 0271'.

European Parliament, 'Amendments to Directive 2006/112/EC as Regards VAT Rules for the Digital Age, 2022/0407(CNS)'.

European Parliament, 'Report on the Proposal for a Council Directive Amending Directive 2006/112/EC and Directive 2009/132/EC as Regards Certain Value Added Tax Obligations for Supplies of Services and Distance Sales of Goods, A8-0307/2017'.

European Parliament, 'European Parliament Legislative Resolution of 30 November 2017 on the Proposal for a Council Directive Amending Directive 2006/112/EC and Directive 2009/132/EC as Regards Certain Value Added Tax Obligations for Supplies of Services and Distance Sales of Goods, P8_TA(2017)0471'.

European Travel Agents' and Tour Operators' Association, 'Feedback on the ViDA Regulation Proposal 4.04.2023'.

Evans C and Krever R, 'Counting the Costs of VAT Compliance' in Robert F van Brederode, *Virtues and Fallacies of VAT* (Wolters Kluwer Law International 2021).

Evans P and Gawer A, *The Rise of the Platform Enterprise: A Global Survey* (The Center for Global Enterprise 2016).

Fernando L and Acuna R, 'Privatization of Tax Administration' in Richard M Bird, Milka Casanegra de Jantscher and International Monetary Fund (eds), *Improving Tax Administration in Developing Countries* (International Monetary Fund 1992).

Fetzer T and Dinger B, 'The Digital Platform Economy and Its Challenges to Taxation' (2019) 12 Tsinghua China Law Review.

Finck M, 'The Sharing Economy and the EU' in Nestor M Davidson, Michèle Finck and John J Infranca (eds), *The Cambridge Handbook of the Law of the Sharing Economy* (Cambridge University Press 2018).

Floriani P and Trabattoni G, 'VAT Nella Digital Age: Il Ruolo Delle Piattaforme e Questioni Ancora Aperte' (2023) il fisco.

Foramitti J, Varvarousis A and Kallis G, 'Transition within a Transition: How Cooperative Platforms Want to Change the Sharing Economy' (2020) 15 Sustainability Science.

Frenken K and others, 'Safeguarding Public Interests in the Platform Economy' (2020) 12 Policy & Internet.

Frenken K and Schor J, 'Putting the Sharing Economy into Perspective' (2017) 23 Environmental Innovation and Societal Transitions.

Gallardo JS and Echevarría G, 'The Platform Economy Will Have Its Own VAT Regime in 2025' (2023) 34 International VAT Monitor, ibfd.org accessed 7 August 2023.

Galluzzo L and Gerosa G, 'Shared Hospitality Platforms: Possible Design Repercussions, Introverted and Extroverted' in Maurizio Bruglieri (ed.), *Multidisciplinary Design of Sharing Services* (Springer International Publishing 2018).

Gazzola P, 'Behind the Sharing Economy: Innovation and Dynamic Capability' in Elena-Mădălina Vătămănescu and Florina Magdalena Pînzaru (eds), *Knowledge Management in the Sharing Economy*, vol 6 (Springer International Publishing 2018).

Gepp I, 'Chile Taking Baby Steps: VAT on Digital Services' (2020) 31 International VAT Monitor, ibfd.org accessed 5 February 2021.

Gerwe O and Silva R, 'Clarifying the Sharing Economy: Conceptualization, Typology, Antecedents, and Effects' 34 Academy of Management Perspectives 65.

Goring J, 'VAT: Agent vs Principal', https://www.crowe.com/uk/insights/avp-vat accessed 25 November 2022.

Goudin P, *The Cost of Non-Europe in the Sharing Economy Economic, Social and Legal Challenges and Opportunities* (European Parliament 2016).

Grambeck H-M, 'Online Intermediation Services – The Italian Case of Booking.Com' (2022) 33 International VAT Monitor.

Grlica I, 'How the Sharing Economy Is Challenging the EU VAT System' (2017) 28 International VAT Monitor.

Guglyuvatyy E and Milogolov N, 'GST Treatment of Electronic Commerce: Comparing the Singaporean and Australian Approaches' (2021) 19 eJournal of Tax Research.

Gyódi K, 'Airbnb and Booking.Com: Sharing Economy. Competing Against Traditional Firms?' (2017) Working Paper DELab UW.

Hallward-Driemeier M and others, *Europe 4.0. Addressing the Digital Dilemma* (World Bank Group 2020).

Halsema F, 'New EU Rules to Stop Illegal Short-Term Rentals Are a Welcome Change' (*euronews*, 1 March 2024), https://www.euronews.com/my-europe/2024/03/01/new-eu-rules-to-stop-illegal-short-term-rentals-are-a-welcome-change accessed 2 March 2024.

Han X, Martinez V and Neely A, 'Service in the Platform Context: A Review of the State of the Art and Future Research' in Anssi Smedlund, Arto Lindblom and Lasse Mitronen (eds), *Collaborative Value Co-creation in the Platform Economy*, vol 11 (Springer Singapore 2018).

Hatzopoulos V, 'Disarming Airbnb – Dismantling the Services Directive? Cali Apartments' (2021) 58 Common Market Law Review.

Hauben H, Lenaerts K and Waeyaert W, *The Platform Economy and Precarious Work* (Publication for the Committee on Employment and Social Affairs, Policy Department for Economic, Scientific and Quality of Life Policies, European Parliament 2020).

Hautamäki A and Oksanen K, 'Digital Platforms for Restructuring the Public Sector' in Anssi Smedlund, Arto Lindblom and Lasse Mitronen (eds), *Collaborative Value Co-creation in the Platform Economy*, vol 11 (Springer Singapore 2018).

Havich M, 'Are Short-Term Rental Hosts Ready for a Technologically Powered Compliance Crackdown in 2023?' (*American City and County*, 13 February 2023), www.americancityandcounty.com accessed 1 March 2023.

Henkow O, 'Acting in One's Own Name on Someone Else's Behalf: A Changing Concept?' in Karina Kim Egholm Elgaard (ed.), *Momsloven 50 år* (Første udgave, første oplag, Ex Tuto Publishing 2017).

'HomeExchange – #1 Home Exchange Community' (*HomeExchange*), https://www.homeexchange.com/ accessed 6 September 2021.

Hossain M, 'Sharing Economy: A Comprehensive Literature Review' (2020) 87 International Journal of Hospitality Management.

Hossain M, 'Sharing Economy: A Comprehensive Literature Review' (2020) 87 International Journal of Hospitality Management 102470.

'Host a Sister – Connecting Sisters Around The Globe' (*Host A Sister*), https://hostasister.global/ accessed 4 March 2024.

Inara S and Brown E, 'Redefining and Regulating the New Sharing Economy' (2017) 19 University of Pennsylvania Journal of Business Law 6553.

Inglese M, *Regulating the Collaborative Economy in the European Union Digital Single Market* (Springer International Publishing 2019).

Interian J, 'Up in the Air: Harmonizing the Sharing Economy Through Airbnb Regulations' (2016) 39 Boston College International and Comparative Law Review.

Janssen A, 'The Problematic Combination of EU Harmonized and Domestic Legislation Regarding VAT Platform Liability' (2021) 32 International VAT Monitor.

Jetten DNL, *The VAT Liability of Digital Platforms: The EU Rules in the Light of the OECD Guidelines* (Lund University 2021).

Katz V, 'Regulating the Sharing Economy' (2015) 30 (Annual Review 2015) Berkeley Technology Law Journal.

Kerschner I, Somare M and Wirtschaftsuniversität Wien (eds), *Taxation in a Global Digital Economy* (Linde 2017).

Kollmann J, *Taxable Supplies and Their Consideration in European VAT: With Selected Examples of the Digital Economy* (IBFD 2019).

Kuijper B, Cameron T and Szatmari Z, 'Technology-Enabled Tax Compliance' (2020) 74 Bulletin for International Taxation.

Lamensch M, 'Is There Any Future for the Vendor Collection Model in the 21st Century Economy?' (2016) 27 International VAT Monitor.

Lamensch M, 'Rendering Platforms Liable to Collect and Pay VAT on B2C Imports: A Silver Bullet?' (2018) 29 International VAT Monitor.

Lamensch M, 'New EU VAT-Related Obligations for E-Commerce Platforms Worldwide: A Qualitative Impact Assessment' (2021) 13 World Tax Journal.

Lamensch M, 'Qualitative Assessment of Two Recent EU Commission Proposals to Impose (More) VAT Obligations on Platforms' (2024) 16 World Tax Journal, ibfd.org accessed 29 April 2024.

Lederman L, 'Statutory Speed Bumps: The Roles Third Parties Play in Tax Compliance' (2007) 60 Stanford Law Review.

Lesman U, 'Gigantyczna strata Airbnb. Firma wciąż wierzy w odbicie' *Rzeczpospolita e-wydanie* (26 February 2021), https://www.rp.pl/Biznes/302269921-Gigantyczna-strata-Airbnb-Firma-wciaz-wierzy-w-odbicie.html accessed 8 March 2021.

Lewis N, 'Latest Trends: Covid Boosts Demand for Medium-Term Renting' (27 April 2021), https://www.landlordzone.co.uk/ accessed 17 September 2021.

Li J, Moreno A and Zhang DJ, 'Agent Pricing in the Sharing Economy: Evidence from Airbnb' in Ming Hu (ed.), *Sharing Economy: Making Supply Meet Demand* (Springer International Publishing 2019).

Lobel O, 'Coase and the Platform Economy' in Nestor M Davidson, Michèle Finck and John J Infranca (eds), *The Cambridge Handbook of the Law of the Sharing Economy* (Cambridge University Press 2018).

Lone S and Weltevreden JWJ, '2022 European E-Commerce Report' (Amsterdam University of Applied Sciences & Ecommerce Europe 2022).

Lopez-Cordova E, *Digital Platforms and the Demand for International Tourism Services* (World Bank Group 2020).

Loquet E and Karoutis D, 'European Union – VAT Considerations on ECJ's Ruling That Airbnb Is Not a Real Estate Agent' (2020) 31 International VAT Monitor.

Lucas-Mas CO and Junquera-Varela RF, *Tax Theory Applied to the Digital Economy: A Proposal for a Digital Data Tax and a Global Internet Tax Agency* (The World Bank 2021).

Mair J and Reischauer G, 'Capturing the Dynamics of the Sharing Economy: Institutional Research on the Plural Forms and Practices of Sharing Economy Organizations' (2017) 125 Technological Forecasting and Social Change.

Majdowski F, 'Obowiązki Sprawozdawcze Operatorów Platform Cyfrowych w Unii Europejskiej – Kolejny Przykład "Wielkiego Brata" w Podatkach?' (2022) Przegląd Podatkowy.

Masuda T, 'Japan Introduced Full VAT Liability Regime to Digital Platforms' (2024) 35 International VAT Monitor.

Matesanz F, 'VAT Treatment of the Sharing Economy' (2021) 32 International VAT Monitor.

Matesanz F, 'The Increasing Liability of Digital Platforms in the Collection of EU VAT' (2023) 34 International VAT Monitor (online).

Matesanz F, 'What Does the Fenix Case Mean for VAT Management?' (*ITR*, 14 March 2023), www.internationaltaxreview.com accessed 23 March 2023.

Matesanz F, 'Present and Future Challenges of the Special VAT Scheme for Travel Agents' (2024) 35 International VAT Monitor.

Matesanz F, 'IVA La Vida. Primera Parte. IVA y Economía Colaborativa', https://www.legaltoday.com/opinion/blogs/fiscal-y-legal/blog-sobre-tributacion-indirecta/iva-la-vida-primera-parte-iva-y-economia-colaborativa-2023-01-02/ accessed 23 March 2023.

Merkx M, 'Platform Liability: An Efficient and Fair Collection Model for VAT?' in Christian Amand and others, *VAT Challenges and Opportunities in the New Digital Economy* (Madrid VAT Forum Foundation 2022).

Merkx M, 'VAT in the Digital Age Package: Singling Out the Single VAT Registration' (2023) 32(4) EC Tax Review.

Merkx M, 'VAT in the Digital Age Package: Viva La ViDA or Livin' La ViDA Loca?' (2023) 32(3) EC Tax Review.

Merkx M, Janssen A and Leenders M, 'Platforms, a Convenient Source of Information Under DAC7 and the VAT Directive: A Proposal for More Alignment and Efficiency' (2022) 31 EC Tax Review.

Messina S, 'EU "Distance Sales of Goods Imported" and Customs Duties: Mind the Link' (2024) 35 International VAT Monitor.

Messina S, 'VAT E-Commerce Package: Customs Bugs in the System?' (2021) 13 World Tax Journal.

Michalczak R and Pach M, 'Lex Specialis Derogat Legi Generali' in Monika Florczak-Wątor (ed.), Andrzej Grabowski, *Argumenty i rozumowania prawnicze w konstytucyjnym państwie prawa: Komentarz* (Ksiegarnia Akademicka Publishing 2021).

Migai CO, de Long J and Owens JP, 'The Sharing Economy: Turning Challenges into Compliance Opportunities for Tax Administrations' (2019) 16 Journal of Tax Research.

Millar R, 'VAT/GST in a Global Digital Economy – Looking Ahead: Potential Solutions and the Framework to Make Them Work' (2016) Sydney Law School Research Paper.

Miller SR, 'First Principles for Regulating the Sharing Economy' (2016) 53 Harvard Journal on Legislation.

Mirrlees JA, 'The Economic Approach to Tax Design' in James A Mirrlees, Stuart Adam and Institute for Fiscal Studies (Great Britain) (eds), *Tax by Design: The Mirrlees Review* (Oxford University Press 2011).

Möhlmann M and Geissinger A, 'Trust in the Sharing Economy: Platform-Mediated Peer Trust' in Nestor M Davidson, Michèle Finck and John J Infranca (eds), *The Cambridge Handbook of the Law of the Sharing Economy* (Cambridge University Press 2018).

Nguyen HN, Rintamäki T and Saarijärvi H, 'Customer Value in the Sharing Economy Platform: The Airbnb Case' in Anssi Smedlund, Arto Lindblom and Lasse Mitronen (eds), *Collaborative Value Co-creation in the Platform Economy*, vol 11 (Springer Singapore 2018).

Nieuwland S and van Melik R, 'Regulating Airbnb: How Cities Deal with Perceived Negative Externalities of Short-Term Rentals' (2020) 23 Current Issues in Tourism.

OECD, 'Electronic Commerce: Taxation Framework Conditions. A Report by the Committee on Fiscal Affairs, as Presented to Ministers at the OECD Ministerial Conference "A Borderless World: Realising the Potential of Electronic Commerce" on 8 October 1998'.

OECD (ed.), *Addressing the Tax Challenges of the Digital Economy: Action 1: 2015 Final Report* (OECD 2015).

OECD (ed.), *Mechanisms for the Effective Collection of VAT/GST* (OECD 2017).

OECD, *Tax Challenges Arising from Digitalisation – Interim Report 2018: Inclusive Framework on BEPS* (OECD 2018).

OECD, *An Introduction to Online Platforms and Their Role in the Digital Transformation* (OECD 2019).

OECD, *The Role of Digital Platforms in the Collection of VAT/GST on Online Sales* (OECD 2019).

OECD, 'Code of Conduct: Co-Operation Between Tax Administrations and Sharing and Gig Economy Platforms', www.oecd.org accessed 5 April 2021.

OECD, *OECD Digital Economy Outlook 2020* (OECD 2020).

OECD, *The Impact of the Growth of the Sharing and Gig Economy on VAT/GST Policy and Administration* (OECD 2021).

Oladipo D, 'House Swaps and Dog Walks: Travelers Find Cheaper Alternatives to Lodging' (*Reuters*, 30 May 2023), https://www.reuters.com/business/retail-consumer/house-swaps-dog-walks-travelers-find-cheaper-alternatives-lodging-2023-05-22/ accessed 7 January 2024.

'Opinion of Advocate General Kokott Delivered on 16 November 2023 in Case C-606/22 Dyrektor Izby Administracji Skarbowej w Bydgoszczy v B. Sp. z o.o.'.

'Opinion of Advocate General Kokott Delivered on 24 February 2005 in Case C-305/03 Commission of the European Communities v United Kingdom of Great Britain and Northern Ireland'.

'Opinion of Advocate General Rantos Delivered on 15 September 2022 in Case C-695/20 Fenix International Limited v Commissioners for Her Majesty's Revenue and Customs'.

'Opinion of Advocate General Richard de La Tour Delivered on 1 October 2020 in Case C-501/19 UCMR – ADA Asociaţia Pentru Drepturi de Autor a Compozitorilor v Pro Management Insolv IPURL, Acting as Liquidator of Asociaţia Culturală "Suflet de Român"'.

Oskam J and Boswijk A, 'Airbnb: The Future of Networked Hospitality Businesses' (2016) 2 Journal of Tourism Futures.

Oskam JA, *The Future of Airbnb and the 'Sharing Economy': The Collaborative Consumption of Our Cities* (Channel View Publications 2019).

Pantazatou K, 'Taxation of the Sharing Economy in the European Union' in Nestor M Davidson, Michèle Finck and John J Infranca (eds), *The Cambridge Handbook of the Law of the Sharing Economy* (1st edn, Cambridge University Press 2018).

Papis-Almansa M, *Insurance in the European VAT: On the Current and Preferred Treatment in the Light of the New Zealand and Australian GST Systems* (Lund University 2016).

Papis-Almansa M, 'VAT and Electronic Commerce: The New Rules as a Means for Simplification, Combatting Fraud and Creating a More Level Playing Field?' (2019) 20 ERA Forum.

Papis-Almansa M and Sroka ET, 'Questioning the Proportionality of the ViDA Rules on the Platform Economy: Are We Veering Off Course?' (2024) 35 International VAT Monitor.

Parodi E, 'Booking.Com Settles Italian Tax Dispute with 94-Million Euro Payment' (*Reuters*, 10 November 2023), https://www.reuters.com/business/retail-consumer/bookingcom-pay-94-million-euros-settle-italian-tax-dispute-2023-11-10/ accessed 4 March 2024.

Pawlicz A, *Ekonomia współdzielenia na rynku usług hotelarskich: niedoskonałości, pośrednicy, regulacje* (Wydawnictwo Naukowe Uniwersytetu Szczecińskiego 2019).

Petruzzi M, Marques C and Sheppard V, 'To Share or to Exchange: An Analysis of the Sharing Economy Characteristics of Airbnb and Fairbnb.Coop' (2021) 92 International Journal of Hospitality Management.

Pînzaru FM, Mitan A and Mihalcea AD, 'Reshaping Competition in the Age of Platforms: The Winners of the Sharing Economy' in Elena-Mădălina Vătămănescu and Florina Magdalena Pînzaru (eds), *Knowledge Management in the Sharing Economy: Cross-Sectoral Insights into the Future of Competitive Advantage* (Springer International Publishing 2018).

'Platform Economy: Developments in the COVID-19 Crisis' (*Eurofound*, 7 August 2021), https://www.eurofound.europa.eu/data/platform-economy/dossiers/developments-in-the-covid-19-crisis accessed 7 August 2021.

'Platform Workers: Council Confirms Agreement on New Rules to Improve Their Working Conditions', https://www.consilium.europa.eu/en/press/press-releases/2024/03/11/platform-workers-council-confirms-agreement-on-new-rules-to-improve-their-working-conditions/ accessed 13 March 2024.

Pollak C, *Platforms in EU VAT Law: A Legal Analysis of the Supply of Goods* (Kluwer Law International, BV 2022).

Pollak CM, *How Should Peer-to-Peer Housing and Transportation Services Provided via Sharing Economy Platforms Be Treated under the VAT Directive?* (Lund University 2018).

Poutanen S and Kovalainen A, 'New Economy, Platform Economy and Gender' in Seppo Poutanen and Anne Kovalainen (eds), *Gender and Innovation in the New Economy: Women, Identity, and Creative Work* (Palgrave Macmillan US 2017).

'Power over Users' (*Observatory on the Online Platform Economy*), https://platformobservatory.eu/state-of-play/power-over-users/ accessed 13 August 2021.

Pozvek M, 'VAT in Digital Electronic Commerce' (2017) 4 Journal for the International and European Law, Economics and Market Integrations.

Prete BD, 'Airbnb: A New Way of Housing Between Individual Experience and Collective Narration' in Maurizio Bruglieri (ed.), *Multidisciplinary Design of Sharing Services* (Springer International Publishing 2018).

Ranchordás S, Gedeon Z and Zurek K, *Home-Sharing in the Digital Economy: The Cases of Brussels, Stockholm, and Budapest* (European Commission 2016).

Scarcella L, 'E-Commerce and Effective VAT/GST Enforcement: Can Online Platforms Play a Valuable Role?' (2020) 36 Computer Law & Security Review.

Schippers ML, 'Proposals to Reform the EU Customs Union' (2023) 32 EC Tax Review 253.

Scott M, 'AccorHotels of France Buys Onefinestay for $169 Million' (*The New York Times,* 5 April 2016), https://www.nytimes.com/2016/04/05/business/dealbook/accorhotels-of-france-buys-onefinestay-for-169-million.html#:~:text=AccorHotels%2C%20one%20of%20Europe%E2%80%99s%20largest%20hotel%20groups%2C%20announced,company%2C%20for%20148%20million%20euros%2C%20or%20%24169%20million accessed 3 August 2021.

Scullica F and Elgani E, 'Reinventing the Hospitality: Sharing Economy and New Hospitality Formats' in Maurizio Bruglieri (ed.), *Multidisciplinary Design of Sharing Services* (Springer International Publishing 2018).

Sdino L and Magoni S, 'The Sharing Economy and Real Estate Market: The Phenomenon of Shared Houses' in Adriano Bisello and others (eds), *Smart and Sustainable Planning for Cities and Regions* (Springer International Publishing 2018).

Selloni D, 'New Forms of Economies: Sharing Economy, Collaborative Consumption, Peer-to-Peer Economy' in Daniela Selloni, *CoDesign for Public-Interest Services* (Springer International Publishing 2017).

'Short-Stay Accommodation Booked via Collaborative Economy Platforms: First Data', https://ec.europa.eu/eurostat/web/products-eurostat-news/-/ddn-20210629-2 accessed 6 November 2021.

Sigala M, 'Market Formation in the Sharing Economy: Findings and Implications from the Sub-Economies of Airbnb' in Sergio Barile, Marco Pellicano and Francesco Polese (eds), *Social Dynamics in a Systems Perspective* (Springer International Publishing 2018).

Sledziewska-Kołodziejska K and Włoch R, *Gospodarka cyfrowa: jak nowe technologie zmieniają świat* (Wydawnictwo Uniwersytetu Warszawskiego 2020).

Smedlund A and others, 'Platform Ecosystem Orchestration for Efficiency, Development, and Innovation' in Anssi Smedlund, Arto Lindblom and Lasse Mitronen (eds), *Collaborative Value Co-creation in the Platform Economy*, vol 11 (Springer Singapore 2018).

Smith AMC, 'New Zealand. Extending the Tax Net to the Gig Economy' (2023) 29 Asia-Pacific Tax Bulletin.

Smorto G, 'Regulating (and Self-Regulating) the Sharing Economy in Europe: An Overview' in Maurizio Bruglieri (ed.), *Multidisciplinary Design of Sharing Services* (Springer International Publishing 2018).

Sroka ET, 'Comparing Deemed Supplier Regimes: E-Commerce and Short-Term Rental/Passenger Transport Platforms in the EU VAT System' (2024) CIDEEFF – Centre for Research in European, Economic, Fiscal and Tax Law, https://www.cideeff.pt/pt/publicacoes/working-papers/comparing-deemed-supplier-regimes-e-commerce-and-short-term-rentalpassenger-transport-platforms-in/6264/ accessed 3 April 2024.

Suso MÁ, 'E-Platforms Providing Services in the Short-Term Rental Accommodation Market: The Challenges for Taxation of These Services under the EU VAT' (2020) 31 International VAT Monitor.

Suso MÁ, 'European Union – E-Platforms Providing Services in the Short-Term Rental Accommodation Market: The Challenges for Taxation of These Services under the EU VAT' (2020) 31 International VAT Monitor.

Teigland R, Holmberg H and Felländer A, 'The Importance of Trust in a Digital Europe: Reflections on the Sharing Economy and Blockchains' in Antonina Bakardjieva Engelbrekt and others (eds), *Trust in the European Union in Challenging Times: Interdisciplinary European Studies* (Springer International Publishing 2019).

'Terms of Use – Home Exchange' (6 September 2021), https://www.homeexchange.com/p/general-terms-of-use accessed 6 September 2021.

Terra BJM and Kajus J, 'Chapter 10 – Taxable Transactions', *Introduction to European VAT* (IBFD online 2022).

Terra BJM, Kajus J and Szatmari Z, 'Chapter 4 – Taxable Transactions', *Commentary on European VAT* (IBFD online 2022).

Thang S and Shatalow N, 'Digital Cross-Border Supplies' in Robert F van Brederode, *Virtues and Fallacies of VAT* (Wolters Kluwer Law International 2021).

'The Battle Is for the Customer Interface' (*TechCrunch*), https://techcrunch.com/2015/03/03/in-the-age-of-disintermediation-the-battle-is-all-for-the-customer-interface/ accessed 13 August 2021.

'The Belgian Presidency Programme', https://belgian-presidency.consilium.europa.eu/en/programme/the-belgian-presidency-programme/ accessed 12 January 2024.

The Committee of the Regions, 'The Local and Regional Dimension of the Sharing Economy, 2016/C 051/06'.

The Committee of the Regions, 'Platform Work – Local and Regional Regulatory Challenges, 2020/C 79/07'.

The Committee of the Regions, 'A European Framework for Regulatory Responses to the Collaborative Economy, 2020/C 79/08'.

Theurl T and Meyer E, 'Cooperatives in the Age of Sharing' in Kai Riemer, Stefan Schellhammer and Michaela Meinert (eds), *Collaboration in the Digital Age: How Technology Enables Individuals, Teams and Businesses* (Springer International Publishing 2019).

'Tourist Services - Short-Term Rental Initiative' (*Tourist Services – Short-Term Rental Initiative*, 14 October 2021), https://ec.europa.eu/info/law/better-regulation/have-your-say/initiatives/13108-Tourist-services-short-term-rental-initiative_en accessed 13 March 2024.

Treapăt L-M, Gheorghiu A and Ochkovskaya M, 'A Synthesis of the Sharing Economy in Romania and Russia' in Elena-Mădălina Vătămănescu and Florina Magdalena Pînzaru (eds), *Knowledge Management in the Sharing Economy*, vol 6 (Springer International Publishing 2018).

Trenta C, 'European VAT and the Digital Economy: Recent Developments' (2019) 17 eJournal of Tax Research.

'Uber and AirBnB Call on EU to Support "Collaborative Economy"' (*the Guardian*, 11 February 2016), http://www.theguardian.com/technology/2016/feb/11/uber-airbnb-eu-support-collaborative-economy accessed 31 August 2021.

van Brederode RF, 'Introduction: VAT Does Well, but Does It Do Well Enough?', *Virtues and Fallacies of VAT* (Wolters Kluwer Law International 2021).

'VAT Committee - European Commission', https://taxation-customs.ec.europa.eu/vat-committee_en accessed 15 March 2024.

Vaughan R and Daverio R, *Assessing the Size and Presence of the Collaborative Economy in Europe* (European Commission 2016).

Vázquez JM, 'Airbnb (C-83/21). Compatibility of the Italian Tax Regime for Short-Term Property Rentals with EU Law' (*Kluwer International Tax Blog*, 3 May 2023), www.kluwertaxblog.com accessed 7 August 2023.

Vienken C, Abdelkafi N and Tangour C, 'Multi-Sided Platforms in the Sharing Economy - A Case Study Analysis for the Development of a Generic Platform' in Rim Jallouli and others (eds), *Digital Economy. Emerging Technologies and Business Innovation* (Springer International Publishing 2019).

Villari B, 'A Service Design Approach to Analyse, Map and Design Sharing Services' in Maurizio Bruglieri (ed.), *Multidisciplinary Design of Sharing Services* (Springer International Publishing 2018).

Ville P, 'New VAT Rules on E-Commerce' (2021) 32 International VAT Monitor.

Viswanathan M, 'Tax Compliance and the Sharing Economy' in Nestor M Davidson and Michèle Finck, John J Infranca (eds), *The Cambridge Handbook of the Law of the Sharing Economy* (1st edn, Cambridge University Press 2018).

Walpole M, 'The Australian GST Cross-Border Rules in a Global Context' (2020) 18 eJournal of Tax Research.

'Warunki Swiadczenia Usług - Centrum Pomocy Airbnb' (*Airbnb*), https://www.airbnb.pl/help/article/2908 accessed 16 September 2021.

Wirtz J and others, 'Platforms in the Peer-to-Peer Sharing Economy' (2019) 30 Journal of Service Management.

Xie KL and Kwok L, 'The Effects of Airbnb's Price Positioning on Hotel Performance' (2017) 67 International Journal of Hospitality Management.

Yakimowa J, 'New Rules for a Responsible and Transparent Short-Term Rental Sector | Aktuelles | Europäisches Parlament' (29 February 2024), https://www.europarl.europa.eu/news/de/press-room/20240223IPR18094/new-rules-for-a-responsible-and-transparent-short-term-rental-sector accessed 4 March 2024.

Yoo C, 'Network Effect – Concurrences', https://www.concurrences.com/en/dictionary/Network-effect accessed 12 March 2024.

Zale K, 'When Everything Is Small: The Regulatory Challenge of Scale in the Sharing Economy' (2016) 53 San Diego Law Review.

Zale K, 'Scale and the Sharing Economy' in Nestor M Davidson, Michèle Finck and John J Infranca (eds), *The Cambridge Handbook of the Law of the Sharing Economy* (Cambridge University Press 2018).

Zechner L, 'Understanding VAT in Three-Party, Platform-Based Business Models: Which Party Is Supplying Which Service?' (2022) 31 EC Tax Review.

Zervas G, Proserpio D and Byers JW, 'The Rise of the Sharing Economy: Estimating the Impact of Airbnb on the Hotel Industry' (2017) 54 Journal of Marketing Research.

Zieba M and Durst S, 'Knowledge Risks in the Sharing Economy' in Elena-Mădălina Vătămănescu and Florina Magdalena Pînzaru (eds), *Knowledge Management in the Sharing Economy*, vol 6 (Springer International Publishing 2018).

Zu Y, 'VAT/GST Thresholds and Small Businesses: Where To Draw the Line?' (2018) 66 Canadian Tax Journal.

Table of Court Rulings

Airbnb Ireland and Airbnb Payments UK [2022] CJEU C-83/21

Airbnb Ireland UC v. Région de Bruxelles-Capitale [2022] CJEU C-674/20

Alpenchalets Resorts GmbH v. Finanzamt München Abteilung Körperschaften [2018] CJEU C-552/17

Amărăşti Land Investment SRL v. Direcţia Generală Regională a Finanţelor Publice Timişoara and Administraţia Judeţeană a Finanţelor Publice Timiş [2019] CJEU C-707/18

Asociación Profesional Elite Taxi v. Uber Systems Spain, SL [2017] CJEU C-434/15

Avon Cosmetics Ltd v. The Commissioners for Her Majesty's Revenue and Customs [2017] CJEU C-305/16

Belgian State v. Pierre Henfling and Others [2011] CJEU C-464/10

Cali Apartments SCI and HX v. Procureur général près la cour d'appel de Paris and Ville de Paris [2020] CJEU C-724/18

Criminal proceedings against Uber France [2018] CJEU C-320/16

Criminal proceedings against X, interveners: YA, Airbnb Ireland UC, Hôtelière Turenne SAS, Association pour un hébergement et un tourisme professionnels (AHTOP), Valhotel [2019] CJEU C-390/18

Direktor na Direktsia 'Obzhalvane i upravlenie na izpalnenieto' – grad Burgas pri Tsentralno upravlenie na Natsionalnata agentsia za prihodite v. Orfey Balgaria EOOD [2012] CJEU C-549/11

Dyrektor Krajowej Informacji Skarbowej (TVA – Agrégateur de services hôteliers) [2023] CJEU C-108/22

Elisabeth Blasi v. Finanzamt München I [1998] CJEU C-346/95

European Commission v. Grand Duchy of Luxembourg [2017] CJEU C-274/15

Fenix International [2023] CJEU C-695/20

Finanzamt Hamburg-Altona CJEU C-101/24

Gábor Tóth v. Nemzeti Adó- és Vámhivatal Észak-magyarországi Regionális Adó Főigazgatósága [2012] CJEU C-324/11

ITH Comercial Timişoara SRL v. Agenţia Naţională de Administrare Fiscală – Direcţia Generală Regională a Finanţelor Publice Bucureşti and Agenţia Naţională de

Administrare Fiscală – Direcţia Generală Regională a Finanţelor [2020] CJEU C-734/19

Jarosław Słaby v. Minister Finansów and Emilian Kuć and Halina Jeziorska-Kuć v. Dyrektor Izby Skarbowej w Warszawie [2011] CJEU C-180/10 and C-181/10

LVK – 56 EOOD v. Direktor na Direktsia 'Obzhalvane i upravlenie na izpalnenieto' – Varna pri Tsentralno upravlenie na Natsionalnata agentsia za prihodite [2013] CJEU C-643/11

Mahagében Kft v. Nemzeti Adó- és Vámhivatal Dél-dunántúli Regionális Adó Főigazgatósága and Péter Dávid v. Nemzeti Adó- és Vámhivatal Észak-alföldi Regionális Adó Főigazgatósága [2012] CJEU C-80/11 and C-142/11

Mecsek-Gabona Kft v. Nemzeti Adó- és Vámhivatal Dél-dunántúli Regionális Adó Főigazgatósága [2012] CJEU C-273/11

Netto Supermarkt GmbH & Co OHG v. Finanzamt Malchin [2008] CJEU C-271/06

Santogal M-Comércio e Reparação de Automóveis Lda v. Autoridade Tributária e Aduaneira [2017] CJEU C-26/16

Serebryannay vek EOOD v. Direktor na Direktsia 'Obzhalvane i upravlenie na izpalnenieto' – Varna pri Tsentralno upravlenie na Natsionalna agentsia za prihodite [2013] CJEU C-283/12

Société Arcelor Atlantique et Lorraine and Others v. Premier ministre, Ministre de l'Écologie et du Développement durable and Ministre de l'Économie, des Finances et de l'Industrie [2008] CJEU C-127/07

South Dakota v. Wayfair, Inc, et al [2018] Supreme Court of the United States Nos 17–494

Staatssecretaris van Financiën v. Schoenimport 'Italmoda' Mariano Previti vof and Turbu.com BV and Turbu.com Mobile Phone's BV v. Staatssecretaris van Financiën [2014] CJEU C-131/13

The Commissioners for Her Majesty's Revenue and Customs v. Secret Hotels2 Limited (formerly Med Hotels Limited) [2014] British Supreme Court [2014] UKSC 16

Uber BV and others v. Aslam and others [2021] British Supreme Court UKSC 2019/0029

UCMR – ADA Asociaţia pentru Drepturi de Autor a Compozitorilor v. Asociatia culturala 'Suflet de Român' [2021] CJEU C-501/19

Vlaamse Oliemaatschappij NV v. FOD Financiën [2011] CJEU Case C-499/10

Table of Legislation

Commission Delegated Regulation (EU) 2015/2446 of 28 July 2015 supplementing Regulation (EU) No 952/2013 of the European Parliament and of the Council as regards detailed rules concerning certain provisions of the Union Customs Code [OJ L 343, 29.12.2015, pp. 1–557]

Commission Implementing Decision (EU) 2021/942 of 10 June 2021 laying down rules for the application of Council Directive 2006/112/EC as regards the establishment of the list of third countries with which the Union has concluded an agreement on mutual assistance similar in scope to Council Directive 2010/24/EU and Council Regulation (EU) No 904/2010 [OJ L 205, 11.6.2021, pp. 80–81]

Commission Implementing Regulation (EU) 2020/194 of 12 February 2020 laying down detailed rules for the application of Council Regulation (EU) No 904/2010 as regards the special schemes for taxable persons supplying services to non-taxable persons, making distance sales of goods and certain domestic supplies of goods [OJ L 40, 13.2.2020, pp. 114–124]

Commission Implementing Regulation (EU) 2020/1318 of 22 September 2020 amending Implementing Regulations (EU) 2020/21 and (EU) No 2020/194 as regards the dates of application in response to the COVID-19 pandemic [OJ L 309, 23.9.2020, pp. 4–6]

Commission Implementing Regulation (EU) 2021/965 of 9 June 2021 amending Implementing Regulation (EU) 2020/194 as regards the exchange of records held by taxable persons or their intermediaries and the designation of competent authorities responsible for coordinating administrative enquiries [OJ L 214, 17.6.2021, pp. 1–33]

Commission Implementing Regulation (EU) 2021/1218 of 26 July 2021 amending Implementing Regulation (EU) No 79/2012 as regards the storage of and automated access to the information on the VAT exempted importations under the 'import scheme' [OJ L 267, 27.7.2021, pp. 12–13]

Commission Recommendation of 6 May 2003 concerning the definition of micro, small and medium-sized enterprises [OJ L 124, 20.5.2003, pp. 36–41]

Consolidated version of the Treaty on the Functioning of the European Union [OJ C 326, 26.10.2012, pp. 47–390]

Council Decision (EU) 2020/1109 of 20 July 2020 amending Directives (EU) 2017/2455 and (EU) 2019/1995 as regards the dates of transposition and application in response to the COVID-19 pandemic [OJ L 244, 29.7.2020, pp. 3–5]

Council Directive 2006/112/EC of 28 November 2006 on the common system of value added tax [OJ L 347, 11.12.2006, pp. 1–118]

Council Directive 2011/16/EU of 15 February 2011 on administrative cooperation in the field of taxation and repealing Directive 77/799/EEC [OJ L 64, 11.3.2011, pp. 1–12]

Council Directive (EU) 2017/2455 of 5 December 2017 amending Directive 2006/112/EC and Directive 2009/132/EC as regards certain value added tax obligations for supplies of services and distance sales of goods [OJ L 348, 29.12.2017, pp. 7–22]

Council Directive (EU) 2019/1995 of 21 November 2019 amending Directive 2006/112/EC as regards provisions relating to distance sales of goods and certain domestic supplies of goods [OJ L 310, 2.12.2019, pp. 1–5]

Council Directive (EU) 2020/284 of 18 February 2020 amending Directive 2006/112/EC as regards introducing certain requirements for payment service providers [OJ L 62, 2.3.2020, pp. 7–12]

Council Directive (EU) 2021/514 of 22 March 2021 amending Directive 2011/16/EU on administrative cooperation in the field of taxation [OJ L 104, 25.3.2021, pp. 1–26]

Council Implementing Regulation (EU) 2017/2459 of 5 December 2017 amending Implementing Regulation (EU) No 282/2011 laying down implementing measures for Directive 2006/112/EC on the common system of value added tax [OJ L 348, 29.12.2017, pp. 32–33]

Council Implementing Regulation (EU) 2019/2026 of 21 November 2019 amending Implementing Regulation (EU) No 282/2011 as regards supplies of goods or services facilitated by electronic interfaces and the special schemes for taxable persons supplying services to non-taxable persons, making distance sales of goods and certain domestic supplies of goods [OJ L 313, 4.12.2019, pp. 14–27]

Council Implementing Regulation (EU) 2020/1112 of 20 July 2020 amending Implementing Regulation (EU) 2019/2026 as regards the dates of application in response to the COVID-19 pandemic [OJ L 244, 29.7.2020, pp. 9–10]

Council Implementing Regulation (EU) No 282/2011 of 15 March 2011 laying down implementing measures for Directive 2006/112/EC on the common system of value added tax [OJ L 77, 23.3.2011, pp. 1–22]

Council Implementing Regulation (EU) No 1042/2013 of 7 October 2013 amending Implementing Regulation (EU) No 282/2011 as regards the place of supply of services [OJ L 284, 26.10.2013, pp. 1–9]

Council Regulation (EU) 2017/2454 of 5 December 2017 amending Regulation (EU) No 904/2010 on administrative cooperation and combating fraud in the field of value added tax [OJ L 348, 29.12.2017, pp. 1–6]

Council Regulation (EU) 2020/1108 of 20 July 2020 amending Regulation (EU) 2017/2454 as regards the dates of application in response to the COVID-19 pandemic [OJ L 244, 29.7.2020, pp. 1-2]

Directive (EU) 2015/1535 of the European Parliament and of the Council of 9 September 2015 laying down a procedure for the provision of information in the field of technical regulations and of rules on Information Society services [OJ L 241, 17.9.2015, pp. 1–15]

Directive (EU) 2016/1148 of the European Parliament and of the Council of 6 July 2016 concerning measures for a high common level of security of network and information systems across the Union [OJ L 194, 19.7.2016, pp. 1–30]

Directive (EU) 2019/2161 of the European Parliament and of the Council of 27 November 2019 amending Council Directive 93/13/EEC and Directives 98/6/EC, 2005/29/EC and 2011/83/EU of the European Parliament and of the Council as regards the better enforcement and modernisation of Union consumer protection rules [OJ L 328, 18.12.2019, pp. 7–28]

Draft Council Directive amending Directive 2006/112/EC as regards VAT rules for the digital age - compromise text 8 May 2024 [2022/0407(CNS)]

Draft Council Implementing Regulation amending Implementing Regulation (EU) No 282/2011 as regards information requirements for certain VAT schemes - compromise text 8 May 2024 [2022/0410 (NLE)]

First Council Directive 67/227/EEC of 11 April 1967 on the harmonisation of legislation of Member States concerning turnover taxes [OJ 71, 14.4.1967, pp. 1301–1303]

Proposal for a Council Directive amending Directive 2006/112/EC and Directive 2009/132/EC as regards certain value added tax obligations for supplies of services and distance sales of goods [COM/2016/0757 final]

Proposal for a Council Directive amending Directive 2006/112/EC as regards VAT rules for the digital age [COM/2022/701 final]

Proposal for a Council Directive amending Directive 2006/112/EC as regards VAT rules relating to taxable persons who facilitate distance sales of imported goods and the application of the special scheme for distance sales of goods imported from third territories or third countries and special arrangements for declaration and payment of import VAT 2023 [COM(2023) 262]

Proposal for a Council directive laying down rules relating to the corporate taxation of a significant digital presence [COM/2018/0147 final]

Proposal for a Council directive on the common system of a digital services tax on revenues resulting from the provision of certain digital services [COM/2018/0148 final]

Proposal for a Council Implementing Regulation amending Implementing Regulation (EU) No 282/2011 as regards information requirements for certain VAT schemes [COM/2022/704 final]

Proposal for a Council Regulation amending Regulation (EU) No 904/2010 as regards the VAT administrative cooperation arrangements needed for the digital age [COM/2022/703 final]

Proposal for a directive of the European Parliament and of the Council on improving working conditions in platform work [COM/2021/762 final]

Proposal for a regulation of the European Parliament and of the Council on data collection and sharing relating to short-term accommodation rental services and amending Regulation (EU) 2018/1724 [COM(2022) 571 final]

Protocol (No 2) on the application of the principles of subsidiarity and proportionality [OJ C 115, 9.5.2008, pp. 206–209]

Regulation (EU) 2017/2394 of the European Parliament and of the Council of 12 December 2017 on cooperation between national authorities responsible for the enforcement of consumer protection laws and repealing Regulation (EC) No 2006/2004 [OJ L 345, 27.12.2017, pp. 1–26]

Regulation (EU) 2019/1150 of the European Parliament and of the Council of 20 June 2019 on promoting fairness and transparency for business users of online intermediation services [OJ L 186, 11.7.2019, pp. 57–79]

Second Council Directive 67/228/EEC of 11 April 1967 on the harmonisation of legislation of Member States concerning turnover taxes – Structure and procedures for application of the common system of value added tax [OJ 71, 14.4.1967, pp. 1303–1312]

Sixth Council Directive 77/388/EEC of 17 May 1977 on the harmonization of the laws of the Member States relating to turnover taxes – Common system of value added tax: uniform basis of assessment [OJ L 145, 13.6.1977, pp. 1–40]

Index

E

F

G

H

EUCOTAX Series on European Taxation

(1) Peter HJ Essers, Guido JME de Bont & Eric CCM Kemmeren (eds), *The Compatibility of Anti-Abuse Provisions in Tax Treaties with EC Law*, 1998 (ISBN 90-411-9678-1).
(2) Gerard TK Meussen (ed.), *The Principle of Equality in European Taxation*, 1999 (ISBN 90-411-9693-5).
(3) Michael Lang (ed.), *Tax Treaty Interpretation*, 2001 (ISBN 90-411-9857-1).
(4) Pasquale Pistone, *The Impact of Community Law on Tax Treaties: Issues and Solutions*, 2002 (ISBN 90-411-9860-1).
(5) René Offermanns, *The Entrepreneurship Concept in a European Comparative Tax Law Perspective*, 2002 (ISBN 90-411-9887-3).
(6) Michael Lang & Mario Züger, *Settlement of Disputes in Tax Treaty Law*, 2002 (ISBN 90-411-9904-7).
(7) Carlo Pinto, *Tax Competition and EU Law*, 2003 (ISBN 90-411-9913-6).
(8) Michael Lang, Hans-Jörgen Aigner, Ulrich Scheuerle & Markus Stefaner, *CFC Legislation, Tax Treaties and EC Law*, 2004 (ISBN 90-411-2284-2).
(9) Mattias Dahlberg, *Direct Taxation in Relation to the Freedom of Establishment and the Free Movement of Capital*, 2005 (ISBN 90-411-2363-6).
(10) Michael Lang, Judith Herdin & Ines Hofbauer, *WTO and Direct Taxation*, 2005 (ISBN 90-411-2371-7).
(11) Dennis Weber, *Tax Avoidance and the EC Tray Freedoms: A Study of the Limitations under European Law for the Prevention of Tax Avoidance*, 2005 (ISBN 90-411-2402-0).
(12) Félix Alberto Vega Borrego, *Limitations on Benefits Clauses on Double Taxation Conventions*, 2005 (ISBN 90-411-2370-9).
(13) Michael Lang, Josef Schuch & Claus Staringer, *ECJ-Recent Developments in Direct Taxation*, 2006 (ISBN 90-411-2509-4).
(14) Reuven S. Avi-Yonah, James R. Hines Jr. & Michael Lang, *Comparative Fiscal Federalism. Comparing the European Court of Justice and the US Supreme Court's Tax Jurisprudence*, 2007 (ISBN 978-90-411-2552-1).
(15) Christiana HJI Panayi, *Double Taxation, Tax Treaties, Treaty-Shopping and the European Community*, 2007 (ISBN 978-90-411-2658-0).
(16) Dennis Weber, *The Influence of European Law on Direct Taxation: Recent and Future Developments*, 2007 (ISBN 978-90-411-2667-2).
(17) Michael Lang & Pasquale Pistone, *The EU and Third Countries: Direct Taxation*, 2007 (ISBN 978-90-411-2665-8).
(18) Oskar Henkow, *Financial Activities in European VAT: A Theoretical and Legal Research of the European VAT System and Preferred Treatment of Financial Activities*, 2007 (ISBN 978-90-411-2703-7).
(19) Michael Lang (ed.), *Tax Compliance Costs for Companies in an Enlarged European Community*, 2008 (ISBN 978-90-411-2666-5).

(20) Michael Lang (ed.), *Source versus Residence. Problems Arising from the Allocation of Taxing Rights in Tax Treaty Law and Possible Alternatives*, 2008 (ISBN 978-90-411-2763-1).
(21) Ioanna Mitroyanni, *Integration Approaches to Group Taxation in the European Internal Market*, 2008 (ISBN 978-90-411-2779-2).
(22) Rolf Eicke, *Tax Planning with Holding Companies. Repatriation of US Profits from Europe: Concepts, Strategies, Structures*, 2008 (ISBN978-90-411-2794-5).
(23) Peter Essers et al. (ed.), *The Influence of IAS/IFRS on the CCCTB, Tax Accounting, Disclosure and Corporate Law Accounting Concepts: 'A Clash of Cultures'*, 2008 (ISBN 978-90-411-2819-5).
(24) Tonny Schenk-Geers, *International Exchange of Information and the Protection of Taxpayers*, 2009 (ISBN 978-90-411-3142-3).
(25) Raymond Adema, *UCITS and Taxation: Towards Harmonization of the Taxation of UCITS*, 2009 (ISBN 978-90-411-2839-3).
(26) Michael Lang, Jianwen Liu & Gongliang Tang (eds), *Europe–China Tax Treaties*, 2010 (ISBN 978-90-411-3216-1).
(27) Michael Lang, Pasquale Pistone, Josef Schuch & Claus Staringer (eds), *Procedural Rules in Tax Law in the Context of European Union and Domestic Law*, 2010 (ISBN 978-90-411-3376-2).
(28) Sjaak J.J.M. Jansen, *Fiscal Sovereignty of the Member States in an Internal Market: Past and Future*, 2011 (ISBN 978-90-411-3403-5).
(29) Dennis Weber & Bruno da Silva, *From Marks & Spencer to X Holding: The Future of Cross-Border Group Taxation*, 2011 (ISBN 978-90-411-3399-1).
(30) Claus Bohn Jespersen, *Intermediation of Insurance and Financial Services in European VAT*, 2011 (ISBN 978-90-411-3732-6).
(31) Sabine Heidenbauer, *Charity Crossing Borders: The Fundamental Freedoms' Influence on Charity and Donor Taxation in Europe*, 2011 (ISBN 978-90-411-3813-2).
(32) Michael Lang, et al., *The Future of Indirect Taxation: Recent Trends in VAT and GST Systems around the World*, 2012 (ISBN 978-90-411-3797-5).
(33) Harm van den Broek, *Cross-Border Mergers within the EU: Proposals to Remove the Remaining Tax Obstacles*, 2012 (ISBN 978-90-411-3824-8).
(34) Michael Lang, et al. (eds), *Tax Treaty Case Law around the Globe – 2011*, 2012 (ISBN 978-90-411-3876-7).
(35) Dennis Weber (ed.), *CCCTB: Selected Issues*, 2012 (ISBN 978-90-411-3872-9).
(36) Daniël Smit, *EU Freedoms, Non-EU Countries and Company Taxation*, 2012 (ISBN 978-90-411-4041-8).
(37) Rita de la Feria, *VAT Exemptions: Consequences and Design Alternatives*, 2013 (ISBN 978-90-411-3276-5).
(38) Karin Simader, *Withholding Taxes and the Fundamental Freedoms*, 2013 (ISBN 978-90-411-4842-1).
(39) Madeleine Merkx, *Establishments in European VAT*, 2013 (ISBN 978-90-411-4554-3).
(40) Carla De Pietro, *Tax Treaty Override*, 2014 (ISBN 978-90-411-5406-4).

(41) G.K. Fibbe & A.J.A. Stevens (eds), *Hybrid Entities and the EU Direct Tax Directives*, 2015 (ISBN 978-90-411-5942-7).
(42) Gerard Staats, *Personal Pensions in the EU*, 2015 (ISBN 978-90-411-5953-3).
(43) Michael Lang & Ine Lejeune (eds), *VAT/GST in a Global Digital Economy*, 2015 (ISBN 978-90-411-5952-6).
(44) Massimo Basilavecchia, Lorenzo del Federico & Pietro Mastellone (eds), *Tax Implications of Environmental Disasters and Pollution*, 2015 (ISBN 978-90-411-5611-2).
(45) Cristina Trenta, *Rethinking EU VAT for P2P Distribution*, 2015 (ISBN 978-90-411-6137-6).
(46) Marie Lamensch, Edoardo Traversa & Servaas van Thiel (eds), *Value Added Tax and the Digital Economy: The 2015 EU Rules and Broader Issues*, 2016 (ISBN 978-90-411-6612-8).
(47) Raffaele Petruzzi, *Transfer Pricing Aspects of Intra-Group Financing*, 2016 (ISBN 978-90-411-6732-3).
(48) Mario Grandinetti (ed.), *Corporate Tax Base in the Light of the IAS/IFRS and EU Directive 2013/34: A Comparative Approach*, 2016 (ISBN 978-90-411-6745-3).
(49) Bruno da Silva, *The Impact of Tax Treaties and EU Law on Group Taxation Regimes*, 2016 (ISBN 978-90-411-6905-1).
(50) Michael Lang, Alfred Storck & Raffaele Petruzzi (eds), *Transfer Pricing in a Post-BEPS World*, 2016 (ISBN 978-90-411-6710-1).
(51) Marta Papis-Almansa, *Insurance in European VAT: Current and Preferred Treatment in the Light of the New Zealand and Australian GST Systems*, 2017 (ISBN 978-90-411-8360-6).
(52) Wolfgang Speckhahn, *Real Estate Investment Trusts In Europe: Europeanising Tax Regimes*, 2017 (ISBN 978-90-411-8360-6).
(53) Frank J.G. Nellen, *Information Asymmetries in EU VAT*, 2017 (ISBN 978-90-411-8837-3).
(54) Erik Ros, *EU Citizenship and Direct Taxation*, 2017 (ISBN 978-90-411-8584-6).
(55) Werner Haslehner, Georg Kofler & Alexander Rust (eds), *EU Tax Law and Policy in the 21st Century*, 2017 (ISBN 978-90-411-8815-1).
(56) Claudia Sanò, *National Legal Presumptions and European Tax Law*, 2018 (ISBN 978-90-411-6613-5).
(57) Christoph Marchgraber, *Double (Non-)Taxation and EU Law*, 2018 (ISBN 978-90-411-9410-7).
(58) Dennis Weber & Jan van de Streek (eds), *The EU Common Consolidated Corporate Tax Base: Critical Analysis*, 2018 (ISBN 978-90-411-9233-2).
(59) Werner Haslehner (ed.), *Investment Fund Taxation: Domestic Law, EU Law, and Double Taxation Treaties*, 2018 (ISBN 978-90-411-9669-9).
(60) Jérôme Monsenego, *Selectivity in State Aid Law and the Methods for the Allocation of the Corporate Tax Base*, 2018 (ISBN 978-90-411-9413-8).
(61) José Manuel Almudí Cid, Jorge A. Ferreras Gutiérrez & Pablo A. Hernández González-Barreda (eds), *Combating Tax Avoidance in the EU: Harmonization and Cooperation in Direct Taxation*, 2019 (ISBN 978-94-035-0154-3).

(62) Werner Haslehner, Georg Kofler & Alexander Rust (eds), *Time and Tax: Issues in International, EU, and Constitutional Law*, 2019 (ISBN 978-94-035-0354-7).
(63) Nathalie Wittock, *Sales Promotion Techniques and VAT in the EU*, 2019 (ISBN 978-94-035-0861-0).
(64) Carla De Pietro (ed.), *New Perspectives on Fiscal State Aid: Legitimacy and Effectiveness of Fiscal State Aid Control*, 2019 (ISBN 978-94-035-1415-4).
(65) Giorgio Beretta, *European VAT and the Sharing Economy*, 2019 (ISBN 978-94-035-1435-2).
(66) Claudio Cipollini, *Special Tax Zones and EU Law: Theory, Implementations, and Future Challenges*, 2020 (ISBN 978-94-035-1885-5).
(67) Gianluigi Bizioli, Mario Grandinetti, Leopoldo Parada, Giuseppe Vanz & Alessandro Vicini Ronchetti (eds), *Corporate Taxation, Group Debt Funding and Base Erosion: New Perspectives on the EU Anti-Tax Avoidance Directive*, 2020 (ISBN 978-94-035-1170-2).
(68) Ronald Hein & Ronald Russo (eds), *Co-operative Compliance and the OECD's International Compliance Assurance Programme*, 2020 (ISBN 978-94-035-1951-7).
(69) Jeffrey Owens & Jonathan Leigh Pemberton, *Cooperative Compliance: A Multi-stakeholder and Sustainable Approach to Taxation*, 2021 (ISBN 978-94-035-3193-9).
(70) Christina Pollak, *Platforms in EU VAT Law: A Legal Analysis of the Supply of Goods*, 2022 (ISBN 978-94-035-1026-2).
(71) Shu-Chien Chen, *Towards a Neutral Formulary Apportionment System in Regional Integration*, 2023 (ISBN 978-94-035-3276-9).
(72) Maria Júlia Ildefonso Mendonça, *International Juridical Double Taxation from an Ability-to-Pay Perspective under EU Law*, 2024 (ISBN 978-94-035-0298-4).
(73) Carla De Pietro, Cees Peters & Eric Kemmeren, *A Journey Through European and International Taxation: Liber Amicorum in Honour of Peter Essers*, 2024 (ISBN 978-94-035-3197-7).
(74) Emilia Teresa Sroka, *Short-Term Rental Platforms as Deemed Suppliers in the EU VAT System*, 2024 (ISBN 978-94-035-4308-6).

www.ingramcontent.com/pod-product-compliance
Lightning Source LLC
Chambersburg PA
CBHW071243230926
51849CB00001B/208
9789403543086